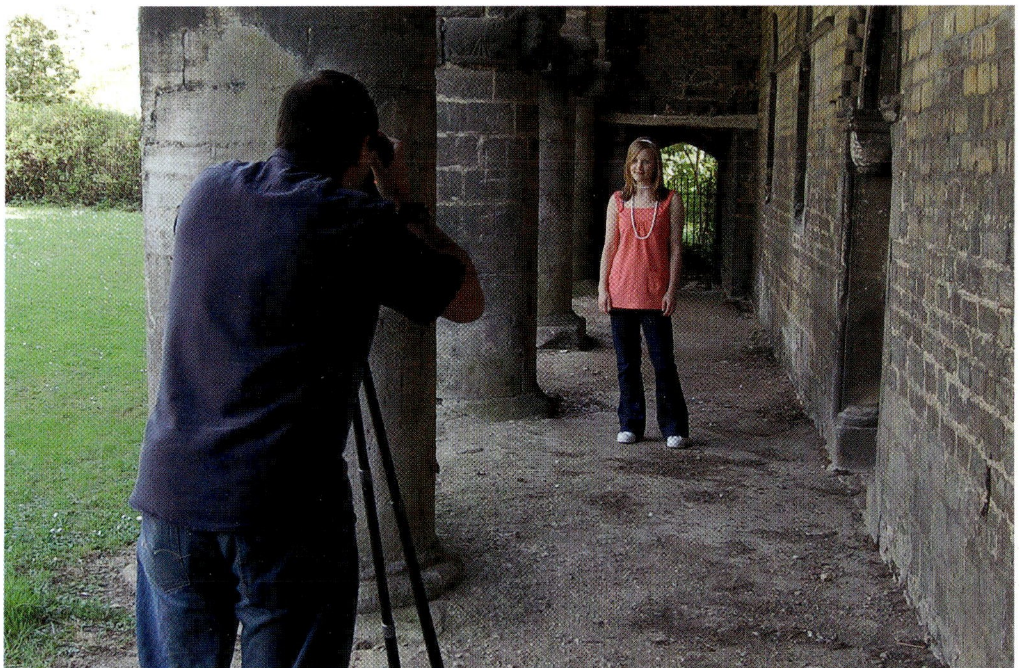

Welcome...

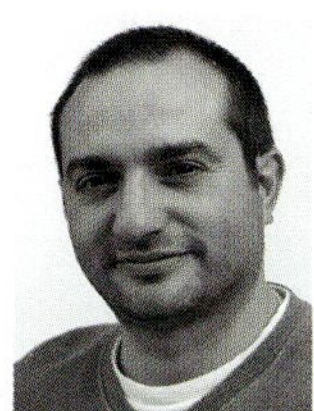

"Along with countless other photographers, nothing in photography comes close to inspiring or exciting me as much as great portraiture. Shot the right way, a portrait can retain my attention and capture my imagination better than any other type of imagery. Often it's the best portraits that appear deceptively simple in terms of composition and technique, yet that is the skill of the photographer: combining all their talents to deliver a perfect portrait with ease. This special edition guide was produced to provide all aspiring portrait photographers with the expert advice, techniques and inspiration that they need to take great pictures. From how to pose a subject and light them perfectly – whether you're working with ambient light or studioflash – to choosing and using the right equipment, this guide offers essential advice, creative ideas and inspiration to help you develop your own portraiture style. Whether you want to take your best family photos indoors or on location, or develop your skills using studioflash, this guide covers everything you need to know to improve your photography skills. Remember that portraiture requires patience and a friendly rapport between you and your subjects, so above all, have fun while you're taking pictures and your subjects will too. All the best!"

DANIEL LEZANO, EDITOR

Meet our panel of portrait experts

All our portrait experts are regular contributors to *Digital SLR Photography* magazine. For further advice and inspiration to help you improve your photo skills, pick up the latest issue, available on the second Tuesday of every month. For more information, visit: www.digitalslrphoto.com

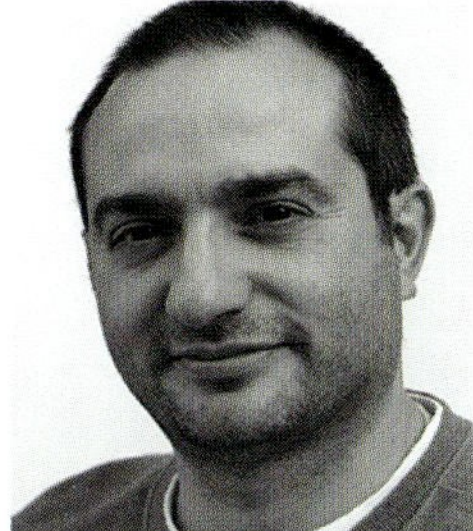

DANIEL LEZANO
An enthusiast photographer for over 25 years, Daniel specialises in portraiture and is author of several books, including *100 Ways to Take Better Portrait Photographs*.

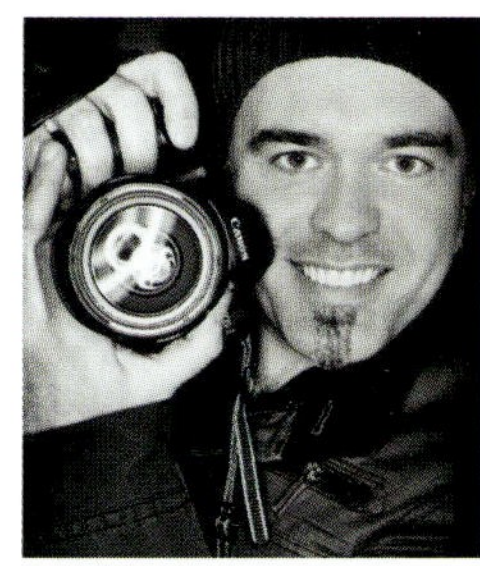

BRETT HARKNESS
Brett is one of the UK's leading portrait and social photographers and runs regular photo workshops. For further details, visit: www.brettharkness.com

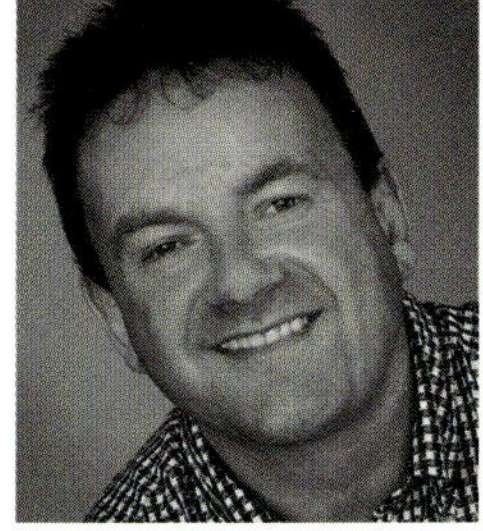

BJORN THOMASSEN
Bjorn is a successful portrait photographer, a master of lighting and leading speaker at seminars and courses. For more information, visit: www.bjornatinspire.com

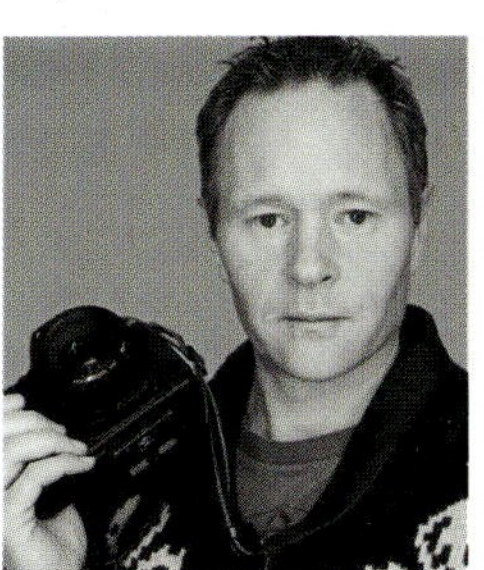

PAUL WARD
Paul is a professional portrait and fashion photographer who specialises in location and studio shoots. For more details, visit: www.paulwardphotography.com

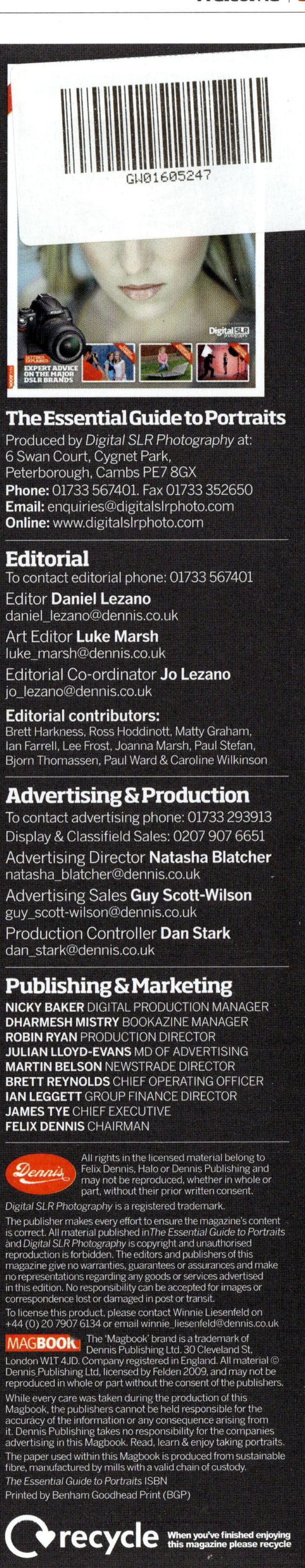

GW01605247

The Essential Guide to Portraits

Produced by *Digital SLR Photography* at:
6 Swan Court, Cygnet Park,
Peterborough, Cambs PE7 8GX
Phone: 01733 567401. Fax 01733 352650
Email: enquiries@digitalslrphoto.com
Online: www.digitalslrphoto.com

Editorial

To contact editorial phone: 01733 567401
Editor **Daniel Lezano**
daniel_lezano@dennis.co.uk
Art Editor **Luke Marsh**
luke_marsh@dennis.co.uk
Editorial Co-ordinator **Jo Lezano**
jo_lezano@dennis.co.uk

Editorial contributors:
Brett Harkness, Ross Hoddinott, Matty Graham, Ian Farrell, Lee Frost, Joanna Marsh, Paul Stefan, Bjorn Thomassen, Paul Ward & Caroline Wilkinson

Advertising & Production

To contact advertising phone: 01733 293913
Display & Classifield Sales: 0207 907 6651
Advertising Director **Natasha Blatcher**
natasha_blatcher@dennis.co.uk
Advertising Sales **Guy Scott-Wilson**
guy_scott-wilson@dennis.co.uk
Production Controller **Dan Stark**
dan_stark@dennis.co.uk

Publishing & Marketing

NICKY BAKER DIGITAL PRODUCTION MANAGER
DHARMESH MISTRY BOOKAZINE MANAGER
ROBIN RYAN PRODUCTION DIRECTOR
JULIAN LLOYD-EVANS MD OF ADVERTISING
MARTIN BELSON NEWSTRADE DIRECTOR
BRETT REYNOLDS CHIEF OPERATING OFFICER
IAN LEGGETT GROUP FINANCE DIRECTOR
JAMES TYE CHIEF EXECUTIVE
FELIX DENNIS CHAIRMAN

The Essential Guide to Portraits ISBN
Printed by Benham Goodhead Print (BGP)

CONTENTS

THE ESSENTIAL GUIDE TO PORTRAITS

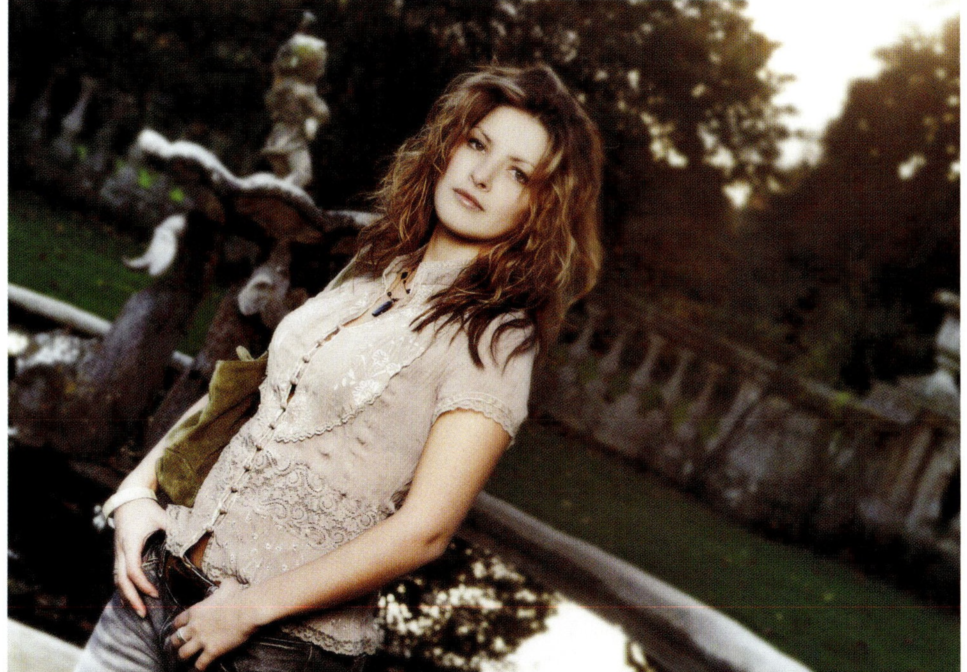

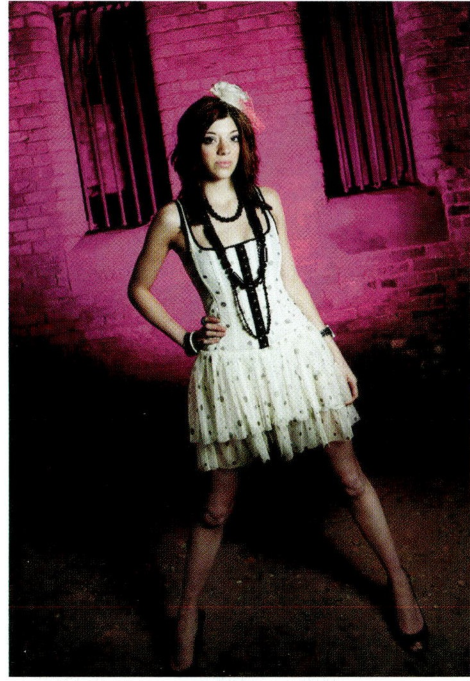

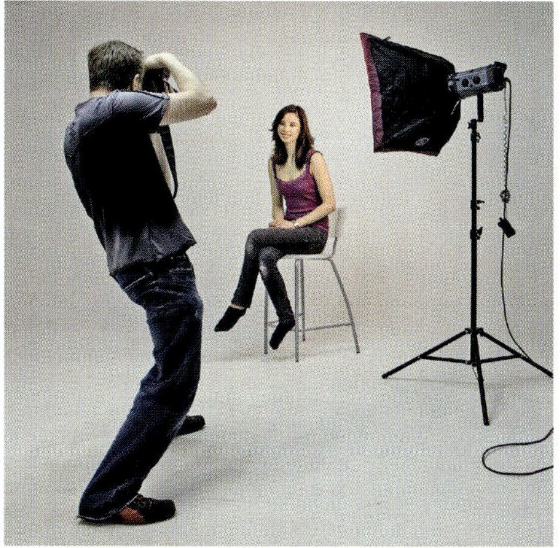

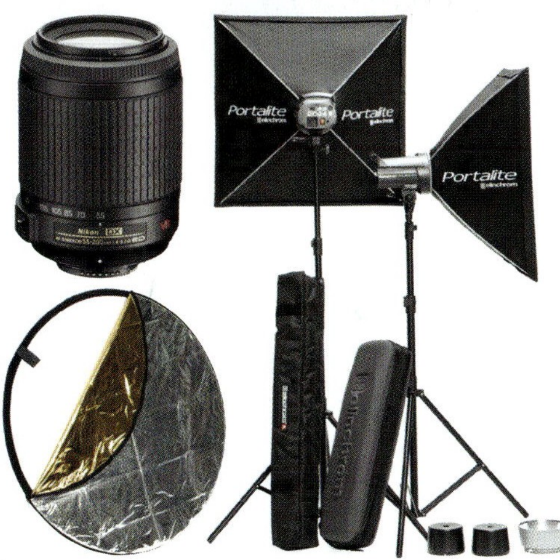

TURN TO PAGE 129 TO FIND OUT ABOUT OUR FANTASTIC SUBSCRIPTION OFFERS

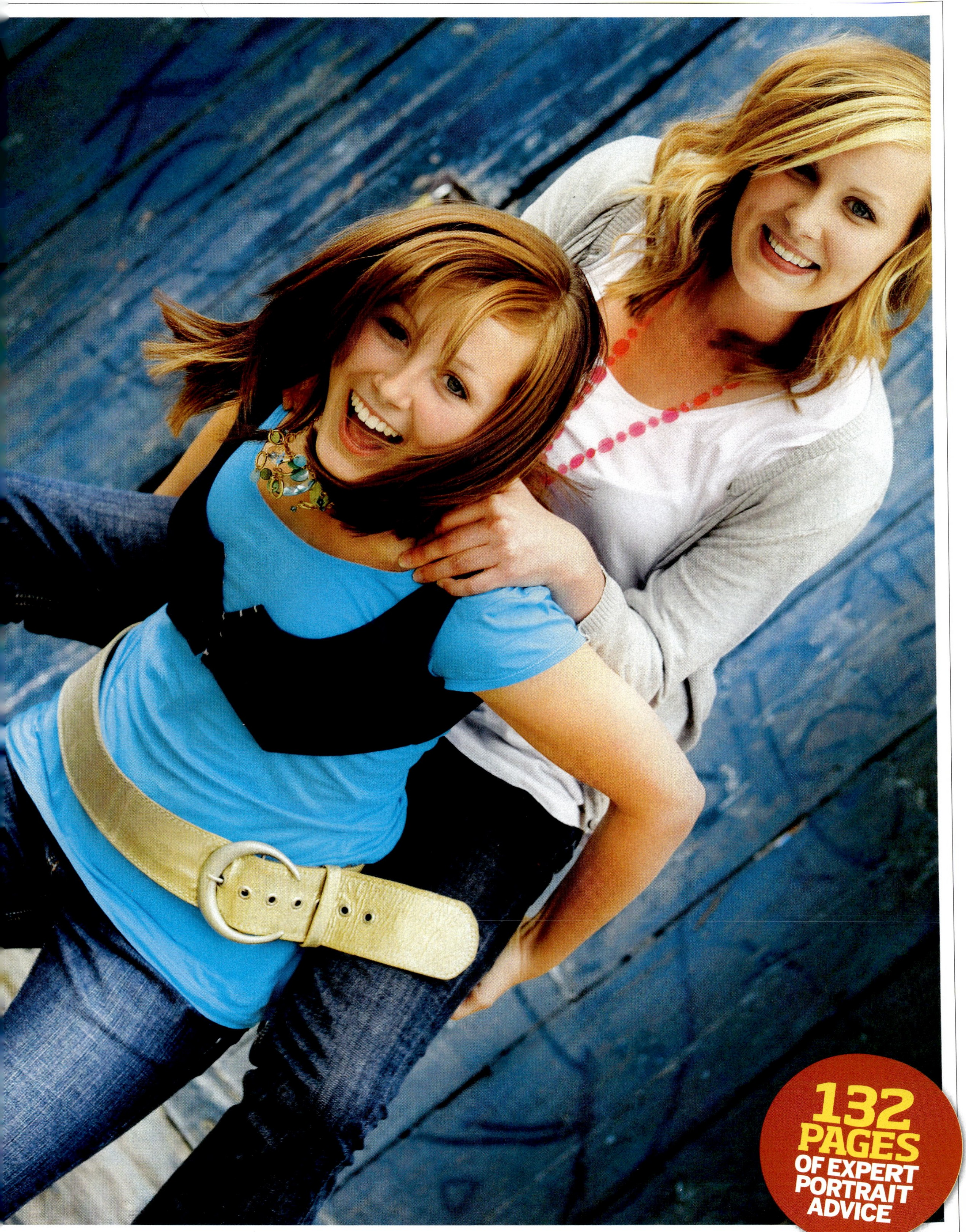
132
PAGES
OF EXPERT
PORTRAIT
ADVICE

Setting up your DSLR

Your digital SLR has a bewildering array of features and while this is great in some respects, the choice can lead to confusion about which settings to select to suit a particular shooting scenario. Here we explain the key tools of your DSLR you need to know when trying to shoot portraits

EXPOSURE MODE Don't think about using the Portrait program mode – you're more than a happy snapper if you're reading this guide. Instead, select aperture-priority AE mode (A or Av), which lets you choose the aperture, while automatically setting the appropriate shutter speed. For most types of portraiture, you'll want to use a wide aperture to throw the background out of focus. To start off, use f/5.6, as this blurs the background but gives enough depth-of-field to keep the entire face (eyes, nose and ears) in focus. By selecting aperture-priority, you'll be using ambient light only. While flash has its uses, using (and controlling) daylight will give you more natural results and help you learn to manipulate available light.

ISO RATING & THE RECIPROCAL RULE In terms of quality, the lower the ISO the better, so we would recommend you set ISO 100 or 200 to begin with. Hand-holding your DSLR will allow you more freedom to move around and shoot candids, but watch out for camera shake. The simplest way to do this is to use the reciprocal rule. All this means is you shouldn't let your shutter speed drop below the reciprocal of the lens you're using. Sounds complicated but it isn't. If you're using the lens at 100mm then ensure the shutter speed is above 1/100sec to reduce the risk of shake. If you're using the lens at 200mm then make sure the shutter speed is above 1/200sec, etc. Easy, eh!

Increasing the ISO rating is an easy way to achieve a faster shutter speed to avoid shake. Try to avoid going above ISO 800 as otherwise you'll notice increased noise in the image. In low light, whenever possible, we'd recommend you use a tripod. It allows you to use a lower ISO rating as shutter speeds aren't such a concern, while also helping with composition.

WHITE BALANCE You should set the White Balance to the lighting conditions you're shooting in. If you're working in mixed light and are a little unsure, then Auto (AWB) is the best compromise. Of course, if you're shooting Raw, you can always change the White Balance when you open the image on your computer. Something to bear in mind is that setting the wrong WB preset can be used to purposely shift the colour balance. For instance, setting Cloudy in daylight will add warmth to the tones, while selecting Tungsten will result in a very cool, blue cast. Be creative.

IMAGE QUALITY We would recommend you shoot Raw, as it will allow you to play with settings, particularly White Balance later. If your camera has a facility to shoot Raw + JPEG, use it with JPEG set to 'Small/Basic'. Then when you're reviewing images, you can go through the small JPEGs quickly, choose your favourites and work on the appropriate Raw files. If you're confident in your ability, and don't expect to need to make tweaks to the exposure or White Balance in post-production, opt for the best quality JPEG for optimum results and to save room on your memory card.

AUTOFOCUS With the vast majority of portraits, it's important that the eyes of your subject are sharply in focus because, more often than not, they're the main focal point. Your camera most likely has multi-point AF, which allows you to choose between leaving all the AF points active or to select individual AF points. You could leave all the AF points active to ensure you don't miss a great shot, but you run the risk that you'll not focus on the eyes and instead catch the nose as it's the nearest object to the camera.

A better option is to select a single AF point and use this to focus on the eye. The central AF sensor is usually the most sensitive, so you can use this to lock the AF by placing the central AF point over one of the subject's eyes, then pressing the shutter button halfway down. Once the AF is locked, recompose and fire. It sounds tricky, but with practice it will become second nature. Another option is to select the AF point that sits over the subject's eye in the frame. Doing this means that you don't have to recompose so much, allowing you to work quicker. This is a better option if you intend to rattle off a sequence of shots with a very similar composition. If you do intend to lock the focus, remember to ensure that your camera is set to single-shot AF as otherwise you won't be able to lock on your subject's eye.

METERING Your digital SLR's multi-zone meter should be capable of exposing portraits perfectly in most situations. Take a test shot, check the screen and use the exposure compensation facility to add/subtract a little exposure if you feel the shot is too dark or light. Where your camera's multi-zone meter may falter is if your subject has very light or dark skin tones, is wearing light or dark clothing or is strongly backlit. In these situations, either use exposure compensation, or select the spot meter and use the AE-L (Auto-Exposure Lock) button to take a reading from a mid-tone in the scene, or from an 18% grey card that you place near the subject.

Setting up your DSLR for portraits

A little unsure how to select the exposure, White Balance or AF systems on your digital SLR? Let us show you the way via five popular DSLRs

CANON EOS 450D/500D

(1) Set the top-plate dial to Av to select aperture-priority. In front of the dial is the ISO button. Press and set the ISO. The next few steps are via the four-way control and SET button on the rear.

(2) Press the Up button on the four-way controller and select the White Balance. Follow this up by pushing the right button to set AF to One-Shot AF. Press the Set button, move to the metering icon and set a pattern (we recommend Evaluative).

(3) To set image quality (we recommend Raw + JPEG), press MENU, and you'll find the quality setting under the first menu tab.

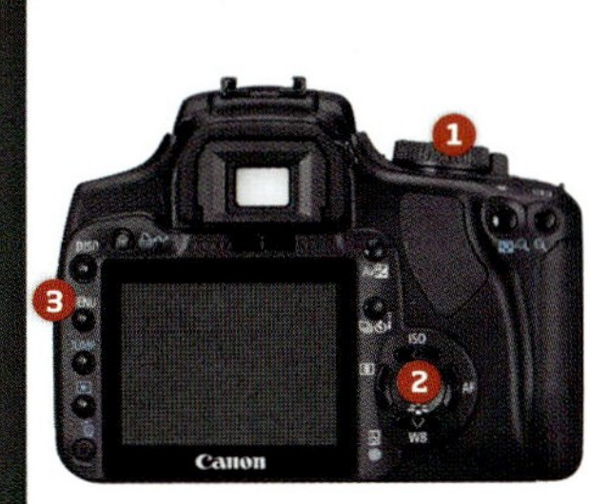

NIKON D80

(1) Set the top-plate dial to A to select aperture-priority.

(2) Press the metering mode button on the top-plate and select a pattern (we recommend Matrix). Now press AF and set the autofocus to AF-S.

(3) To set the White Balance, press WB and use the top-plate LCD and input dial to choose a WB setting. Press ISO and follow the same procedure to set the ISO rating. Press QUAL and set the image quality (we recommend Raw + JPEG) in the same manner.

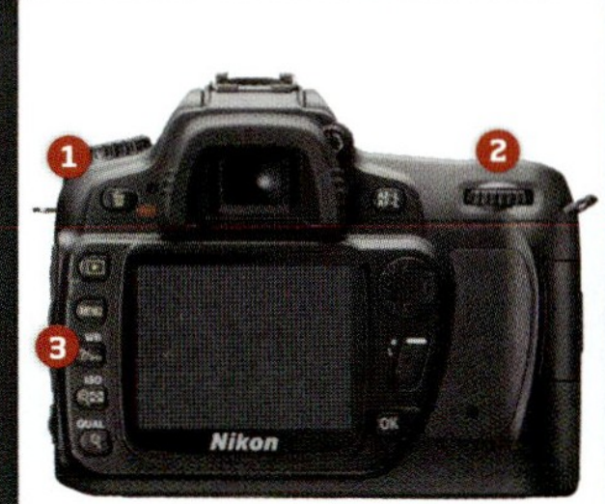

OLYMPUS E-400/410/420

(1) Set the top-plate dial to A to select aperture-priority. The other settings are made using the Fn button, four-way controller and the OK button.

(2) To set the autofocus, press OK, select AF, and set S-AF.For metering, press OK, go to the metering icon, select multi-zone and press OK. Set the ISO rating, White Balance and image quality using the same procedure.

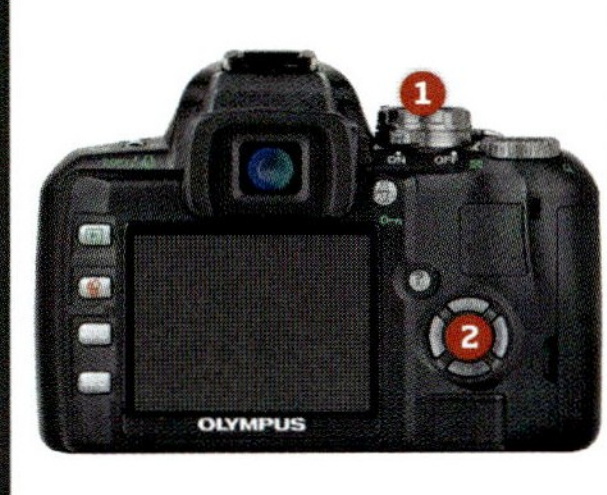

PENTAX K100/K200D

(1) Set the top-plate dial to Av to select aperture-priority.

(2) Press the Fn button and press right on the four-way control to select an ISO rating, followed by OK to set.

(3) Press left to set the White Balance in the same way.

(4) To choose the AF mode, press MENU and the Rec. Mode tab, go down to AF mode, then right to set (we recommend AF-S). Set the metering mode in the same way (we recommend multi-zone). Image quality is also set this way.

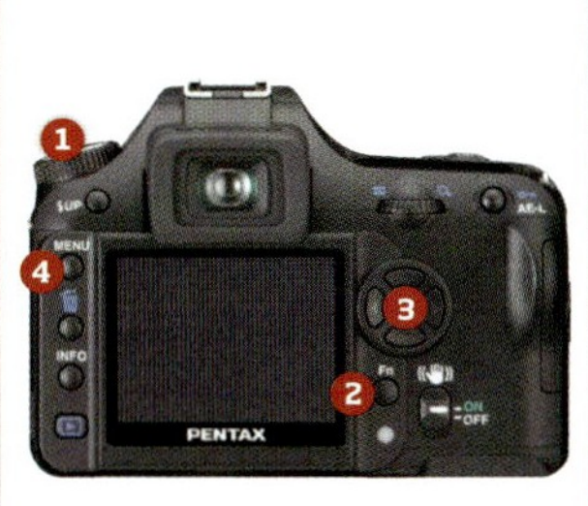

SONY ALPHA 350

(1) Set the exposure dial on the left of the top-plate to A for aperture-priority.

(2) Press MENU and on the first tab select the image quality (preferably Raw & JPEG). The following settings are selected using the Fn button and the four-way control on the rear.

(3) Press Fn, go to Metering mode and select Multi segment. Press Fn, go to AF mode and set AF-S. Press Fn, go to White Balance and choose a setting.

(3) Press the ISO button and set the ISO rating you wish to use.

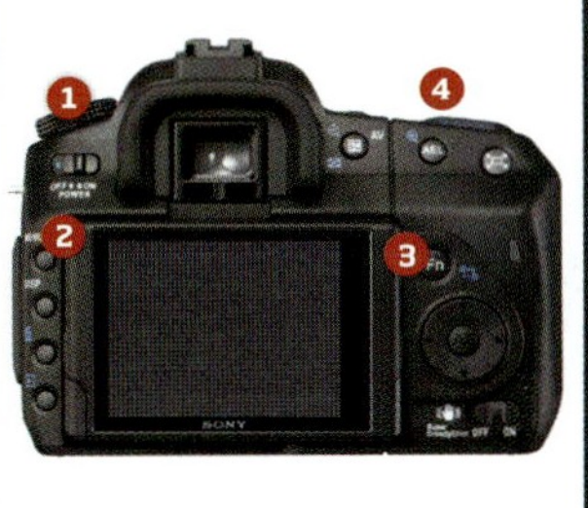

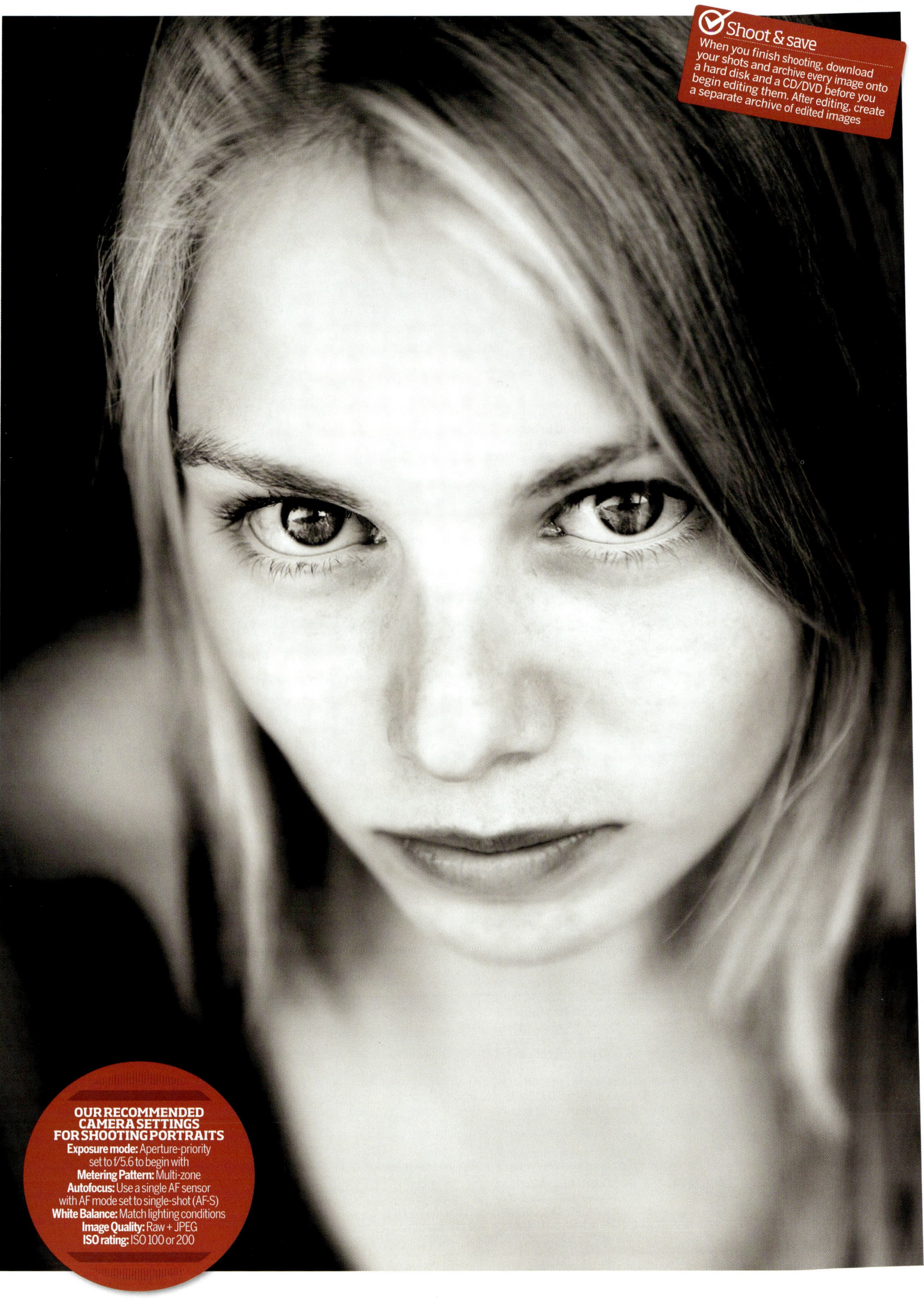

Shoot & save

When you finish shooting, download your shots and archive every image onto a hard disk and a CD/DVD before you begin editing them. After editing, create a separate archive of edited images

OUR RECOMMENDED CAMERA SETTINGS FOR SHOOTING PORTRAITS

Exposure mode: Aperture-priority set to f/5.6 to begin with
Metering Pattern: Multi-zone
Autofocus: Use a single AF sensor with AF mode set to single-shot (AF-S)
White Balance: Match lighting conditions
Image Quality: Raw + JPEG
ISO rating: ISO 100 or 200

The basics of exposure

Our jargon-free guide to the fundamentals of exposure provides everything you need to know to get to grips with apertures and shutter speeds

If you're new to digital SLR photography, it's essential that you understand the fundamentals of exposure. Every exposure you take is made up of a combination of an aperture and shutter speed that determines how much light will reach the sensor. The aperture is the iris in the lens, much like the pupil of the eye, which can widen to allow more light through or contract to restrict the amount of light that enters the lens. Use a wide aperture and more light is able to pass through during a set time span than if you had selected a small aperture setting.

The shutter is a barrier in front of the sensor that moves out of the light's path when you press the shutter release, allowing light to reach the sensor and expose an image. The duration of the exposure is determined by the shutter speed. There is an obvious relationship between the aperture and the shutter speed in determining the correct exposure and this is selected by the exposure mode. While a Full Auto mode provides point-and-shoot simplicity by automatically selecting a combination of aperture and shutter speed, and allows beginners to take great pictures with the minimum of fuss, the beauty and enjoyment of digital SLR photography is to take control and directly determine how the picture will look.

The first major step to doing this is to take your camera off Full Auto and select one of the exposure modes that allow for far more creative photography. Follow our guide and experiment with apertures and shutter speeds – after all, it's not like you'll be wasting any film! Before you know it, you'll soon be creating imaginative images rather than just shooting snaps.

Exposure controls

Many beginners believe it's difficult to use aperture- or shutter-priority mode but in fact it's very easy to do. Once you've selected the exposure mode (1), it's simply a case of rotating the input dial (2) until the aperture or shutter speed you'd like to use appears on the top-plate (or rear) LCD panel (3). Depress the shutter button halfway and the camera works out the rest. It's as easy as that!

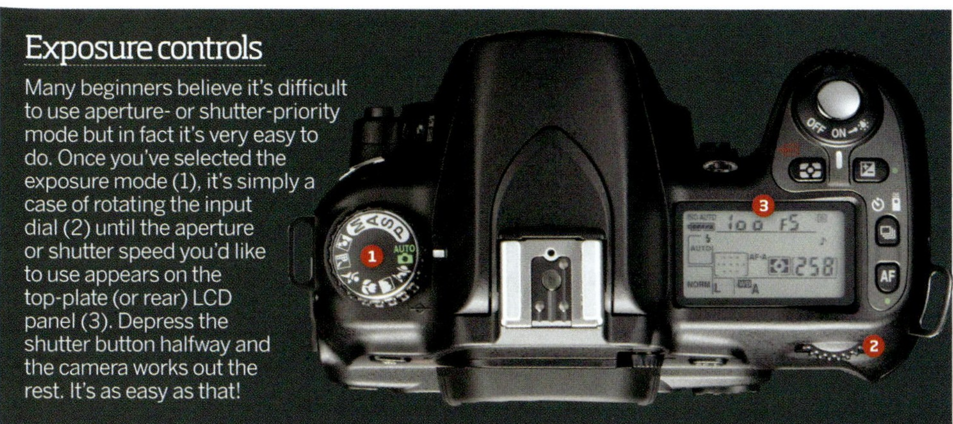

UNDERSTANDING SHUTTER SPEEDS

Exposure settings are made by changing either the aperture or the shutter speed. The increments at which you change these settings are normally referred to as 'stops'. When you change a setting by a 'stop', you are either doubling or halving the exposure. So for instance, changing from 1/500sec to 1/250sec doubles the duration of the exposure. As well as full stops, you can also vary exposure in 1/2 or 1/3 stops depending on the camera model you use. The diagram below shows shutter speeds from one second to 1/4000sec.

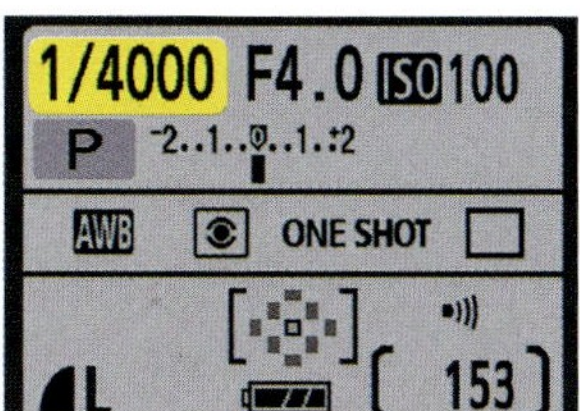

Full stops	1sec	1/2sec	1/4sec	1/8sec	1/16sec	1/30sec	1/60sec	1/125sec	1/250sec	1/500sec	1/1000sec	1/2000sec	1/4000sec
Half stops	0.7sec	1/3sec	1/6sec	1/10sec	1/20sec	1/45sec	1/90sec	1/180sec	1/350sec	1/750sec	1/1500sec	1/3000sec	

UNDERSTANDING APERTURE SETTINGS

The illustration below shows the iris at one-stop increments, i.e. each step from left to right halves the amount of light passing through the lens. The maximum aperture setting refers to the iris wide open (in this instance f/2.8) and the minimum aperture is the iris at its smallest setting (f/32 in this case). An explanation of where the f/number derives from would require an extensive scientific explanation, but the key to you understanding apertures is to learn how f/numbers correlate with the size of the aperture.

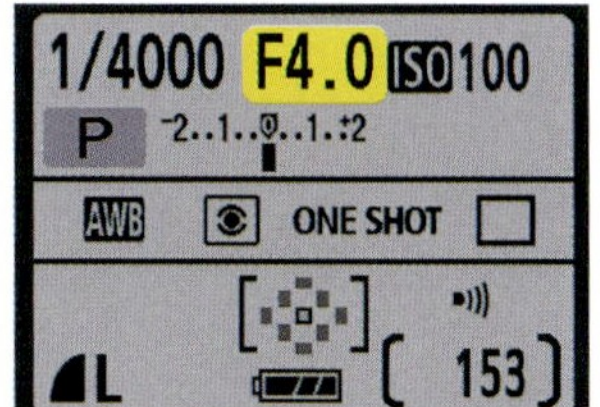

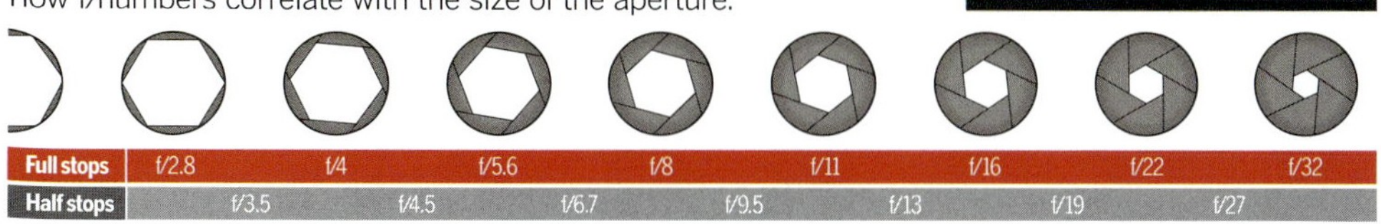

Full stops	f/2.8	f/4	f/5.6	f/8	f/11	f/16	f/22	f/32
Half stops	f/3.5	f/4.5	f/6.7	f/9.5	f/13	f/19	f/27	

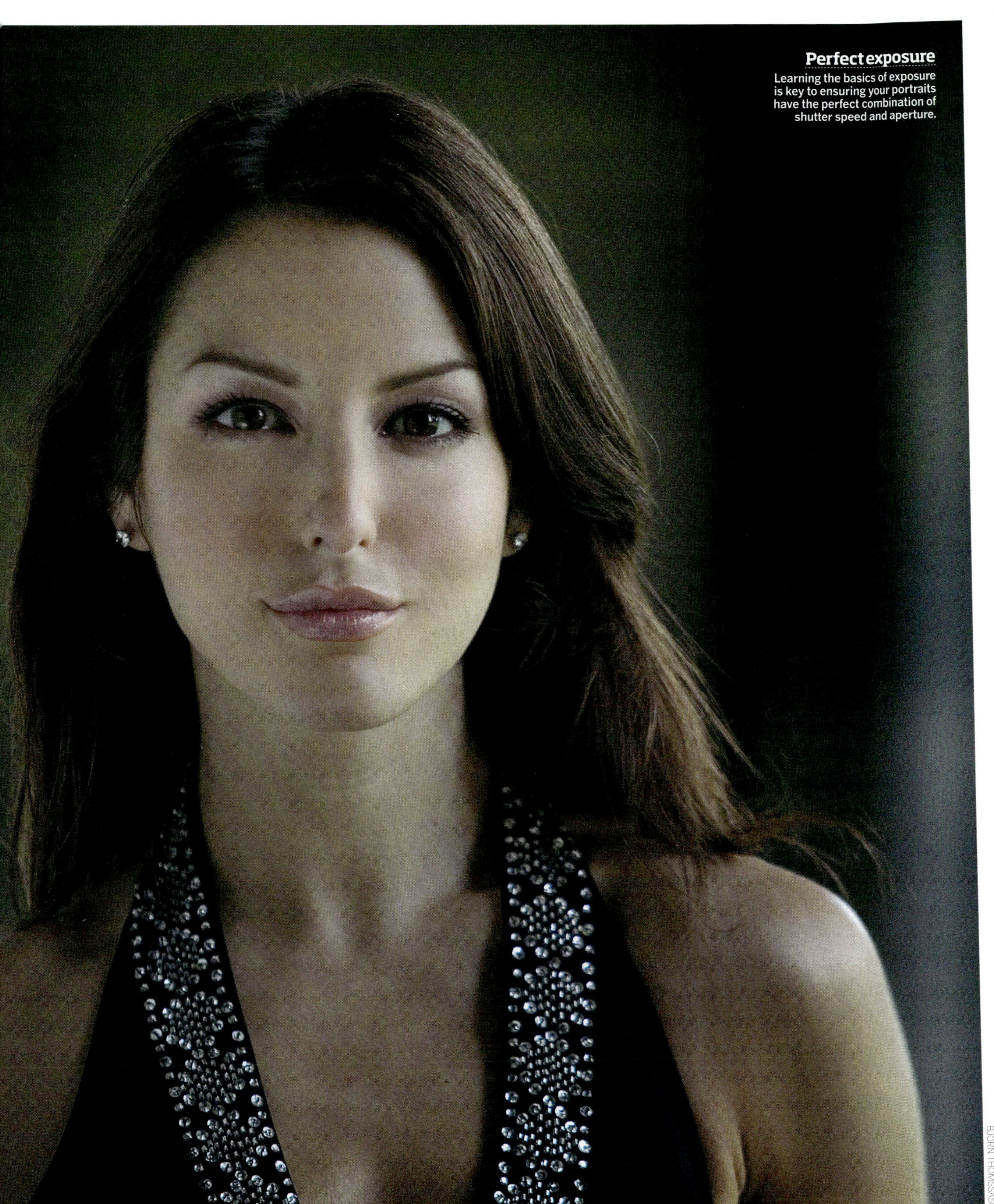

Perfect exposure

Learning the basics of exposure is key to ensuring your portraits have the perfect combination of shutter speed and aperture.

BJORN THOMASSEN

Understanding your DSLR's metering system

Before looking at how you can influence the exposure, it's best to understand how your camera's metering works. Here we've covered the essentials that you need to know in order to pick the best metering mode for different shooting conditions

DIGITAL SLRS BOAST complex exposure systems and offer a choice of metering patterns, each working out the exposure in a different way to suit varying lighting conditions. A camera's exposure system works on the assumption that the area of the scene that is being metered is a mid-tone, or 18% grey to be exact; the average if all dark, lights and mid-tones were mixed together. It's a tried and tested method and the basis of all metering patterns. It's important to be aware of this when you're taking pictures (even if you don't fully understand it) as it helps you to know when you may have problems with exposure.

While this system is fine in the majority of shooting situations, it can lead to incorrect exposures when the scene or subject is considerably lighter or darker in tone than 18% grey. For example, very dark subjects or scenes can fool the metering system into thinking that the general scene is much darker than it really is and, as a result, will overexposed the image. Similarly, very light subjects or scenes can fool the camera into underexposing them – making them appear darker than they are – as the light meter will take a reading designed to render them as a mid-tone. It's in these trickier lighting situations, where the popular multi-zone pattern that provides the correct exposure for around 90 percent of shots struggles as it tries to meter the entire scene. It's in cases like this where using the other patterns such as partial and spot are useful as they offer more control.

As a camera is trying to render an image grey, it's your job to ensure you compensate to keep the tones true to life. To do this you have to either overexpose the camera's reading to give a lighter result than the camera wants, or underexpose to give a darker result than the camera wants. So with a portrait in a dark scene, the camera's exposure reading will lead to overexposure, resulting in bleached faces, so you need to reduce the exposure to keep it black. With the light scene it's giving less exposure than is necessary, producing a darker than required subject, so you need to add exposure to make it record correctly. If you're still a little unsure, don't worry, when you start shooting light or dark scenes and then try to override the camera's readings, you'll soon get to grips with it. By following our expert advice you should also increase the chances of keeping any exposure errors to a minimum.

Multi-zone metering

In theory, you could take every picture using multi-zone metering and never have a bad exposure. Well almost... The multi-zone pattern is the newest and most sophisticated type of metering pattern and the one most photographers stick to for the majority of their shots. While every manufacturer has their own types of multi-zone meter, each with varying numbers and shapes of zones, all work in much the same way. Basically, the entire image area is divided into a number of zones and when activated, individual meter readings are taken from each one of them. The camera's micro-processor then evaluates all these individual readings and uses complex algorithms to calculate the final exposure. To improve accuracy, many cameras also boast a library of tens of thousands of images taken in various lighting conditions, which are compared in a micro-second with the new scene to produce the exposure value. This system has proven highly reliable and gets the exposure correct more than 90 percent of the time. Its weak spots however, are unusually light or very dark scenes or subjects. Multi-zone meters can also have trouble with very high-contrast scenes, in particular backlit subjects. This is why there are other metering patterns available, as well as a choice of exposure overrides, to help you ensure the perfect exposure.

Recognising the multi-zone pattern icon

Every camera brand has their own set of icons for metering patterns and below we show you what to look for on four popular brands

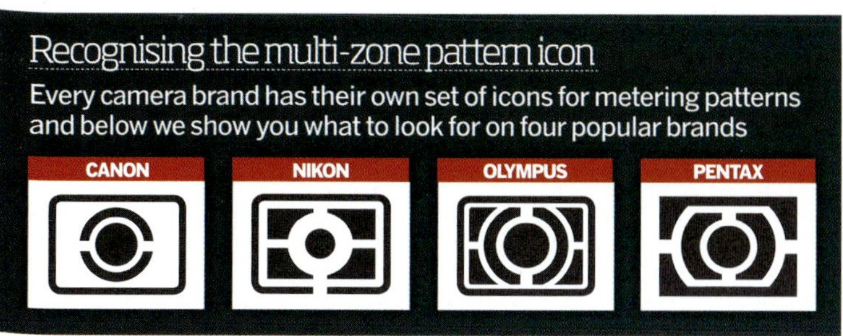

How to choose metering patterns

Selecting a metering pattern is a straightforward procedure, but we've provided a guide on how to do it for a number of leading digital SLRs from the six most popular brands

CANON EOS 400D/450D

The metering pattern icon appears at the centre of the display. To change metering patterns, press the button on the four-way controller to show the metering modes, use the left/right controller button to select and press SET.

CANON EOS 30D/40D/50D

Some EOS models, such as the EOS 20D and 30D, have push button controls. With these models, (1) press the metering mode button and (2) rotate the input dial until the top-plate LCD illustrates the relevant metering pattern icon.

SONY ALPHA 230

Press the Fn button (1) and select the Metering mode icon by pressing the AF button (2). Choose the pattern you'd like to use and press AF again to set.

NIKON D80

With the D80, and other Nikon models aimed at enthusiasts, to choose the metering pattern: (1) press the metering mode button on the top-plate and rotate the rear input dial (2) until the relevant icon appears on the top-plate LCD.

OLYMPUS E-400/E-410/E-420

You can go through the MENU system but a quicker way is to press OK, highlight the metering icon using the four-way controller, press OK, select the pattern with the dial or four-way controller and press OK to confirm.

PENTAX K100D/K200D

Most Pentax DSLRs select the metering mode in the same way as the K100D. Press MENU to get to the Rec Mode display and use the four-way controller dial to go down to AE Metering, select the required pattern and press OK.

BJORN THOMASSEN

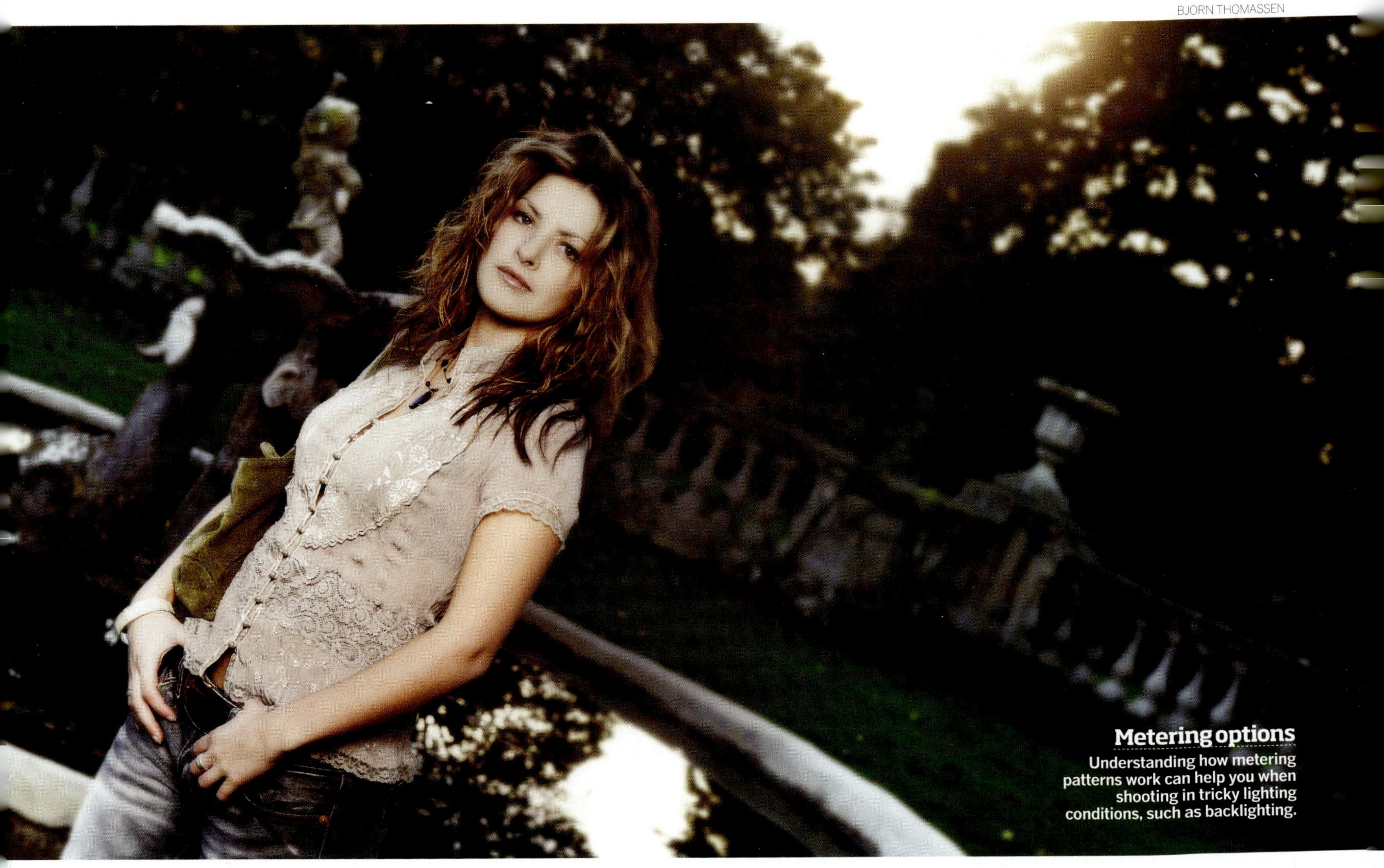

Metering options

Understanding how metering patterns work can help you when shooting in tricky lighting conditions, such as backlighting.

Centre-weighted average

Despite the arrival of newer patterns, this veteran still has its place on digital SLRs. This is the oldest metering pattern and was the number one choice until the multi-zone pattern was introduced. As its name suggests, it takes an average reading from the entire frame, with a slight emphasis given to the central area. While less sophisticated compared to newer patterns, its past popularity means it is still featured in all cameras, as many experienced photographers feel more comfortable using this pattern. It is also a good choice when used in combination with the AE-Lock exposure override, which is covered in more detail shortly.

Recognising the centre-weighted icon

You will find the centre-weighted pattern available on your DSLR but you will rarely need to have to use it in preference to multi-zone metering

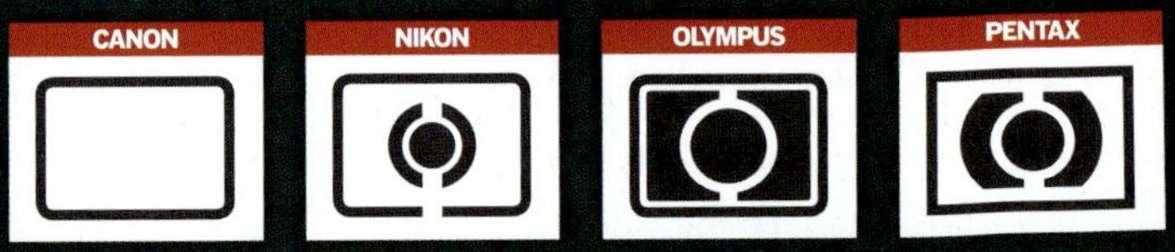

CANON

NIKON

OLYMPUS

PENTAX

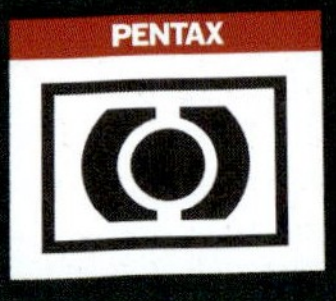

Spot and partial metering

This is a great pattern when you want to take a reading from a specific area of the frame – but it must be used with care. While multi-zone metering takes measurements from the entire image area, spot and partial metering concentrates on the central area of the frame (you can see the measuring circle at the centre of the viewfinder screen). This allows you to precisely control where the exposure reading for the shot is taken from, as only the area of the frame within the measuring circle is used to determine the exposure. Spot and partial metering is a great way to ensure you get the proper exposure when you're shooting in difficult lighting conditions. Spot and partial are very similar in how they work. The main difference is spot offers a very precise measuring circle (usually around 3% of the image area), while partial usually measures the central 9% of the frame. The more precise spot meter is found on most DSLRs, while partial is less common, and a handful of cameras boast both. You must take great care when using spot or partial metering: always take a reading from a mid-tone and not a light or dark subject, otherwise you will produce an incorrect exposure.

Recognising the spot/partial icon

You need to select spot or partial by pressing the metering selector button and picking the respective icon on the LCD monitor. The spot icon is normally shown as a single dot at the centre of the rectangle, while partial is represented as two small curved lines that form the outline of a near-circle close to the centre of the frame. Some DSLRs offer both metering options.

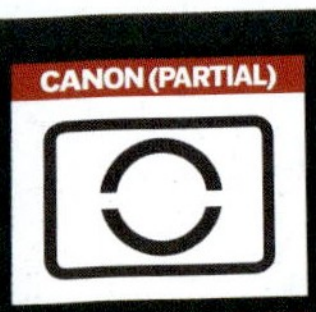

REMEMBER: It's vital that you position the spot/partial meter over a mid-tone to get the correct exposure. Spot-meter off a dark subject and you'll overexpose it and vice-versa. Try some practice shots to get used to how it works.

CANON (PARTIAL)

NIKON

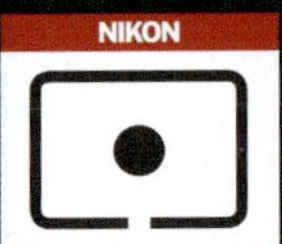

CANON (SPOT)

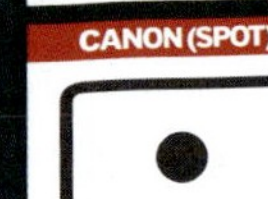

OLYMPUS

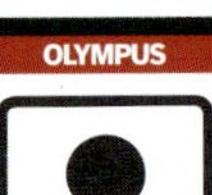

PENTAX

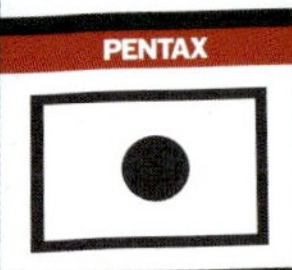

Exposure compensation

This is the most commonly used override and allows you to make adjustments to increase or decrease the exposure

ONCE YOU ARE aware of how metering systems work, and have gained a little experience using your DSLR, the times when the exposure system is likely to make mistakes become easier to predict and compensate for. The simplest way to override your camera's metered exposure is to use exposure compensation, which allows you to dial in a set exposure increment to increase (+) or decrease (–) the exposure. For instance, a subject that is significantly lighter than a mid-tone, like a bride's white wedding dress, is likely to be underexposed by your camera, so you need to select positive (+) compensation. If the subject is much darker than a mid-tone, for instance the subject is wearing very dark clothing, then it is likely to be rendered overexposed. Therefore, apply negative (–) compensation. Applying exposure compensation is quite straightforward and with experience you'll be able to judge how much is needed. All digital SLRs have a dedicated exposure compensation button to make it a quick and easy process in either automatic or semi-automatic exposure modes. The compensation you set is often shown as + or – E.V (Exposure Value). If you add a half-stop of exposure it will display as +1/2EV, while a 1/3-stop reduction is shown as -1/3EV.

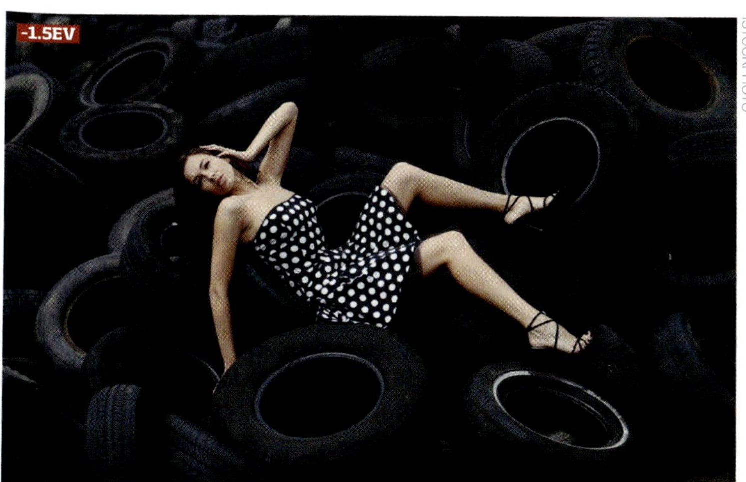
-1.5EV
ISTOCKPHOTO

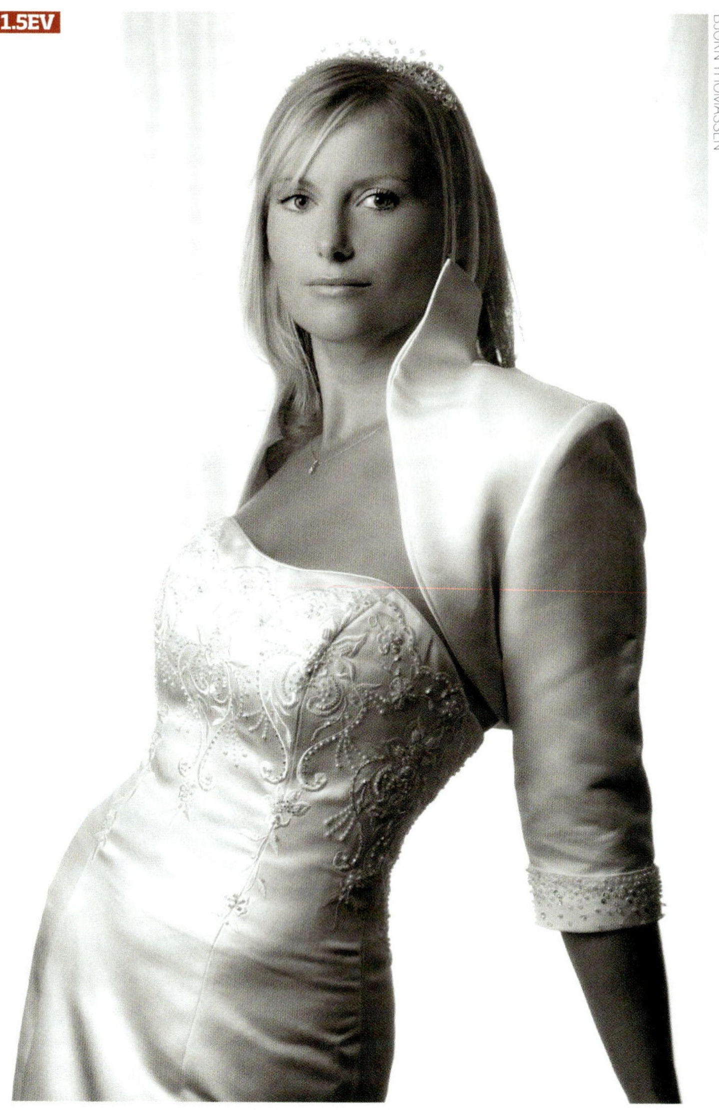
+1.5EV
BJORN THOMASSEN

How does exposure compensation work?

Exposure compensation functions differently depending on the exposure mode that you are using. In aperture-priority, the compensation is applied by changing the shutter speed, but when using shutter-priority, it's the aperture that's adjusted. In program mode, the camera automatically decides between the aperture and/or shutter speed depending on the light levels so to minimise camera shake.

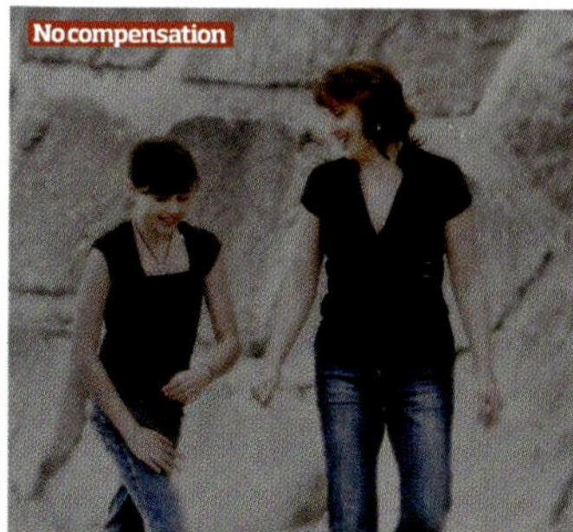
No compensation

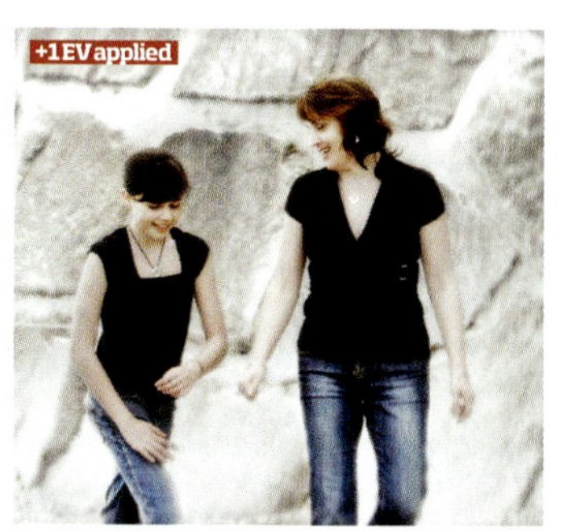
+1EV applied

EXPOSURE COMPENSATION
This is a typical example of when a subject deceives a metering system. When photographing this scene, the camera attempted to record it as a mid-tone and the first result was underexposed. Positive compensation of +1EV was applied, rendering the subjects in the subsequent image to be correctly exposed.

SUMMARY: EXPOSURE COMPENSATION

Set a + value to add exposure to an underexposed scene, for example when shooting a light-toned subject. ***Set a - value*** to reduce the exposure, for example when shooting a darker than average scene.

Using exposure compensation

Your DSLR's exposure compensation facility is useful in any situation when you wish to make a picture brighter/lighter or darker than the exposure set by the camera. While exposure compensation is designed for corrective purposes, the effect can be used creatively. It's extremely easy to use: try applying '+' and '–' settings on subjects with different tones and see the effect it has. Here's how to do it:

1) Press and hold in your camera's exposure compensation button (normally indicated by a +/- icon).
2) Rotate the input dial to select the level of compensation you want. A negative value means you're decreasing the exposure, a positive value means you are increasing it.
3)The exposure compensation scale is displayed in the camera's viewfinder and/or control panel.
4) The compensation you apply will affect all subsequent shots unless you reset it to +/- 0 EV.

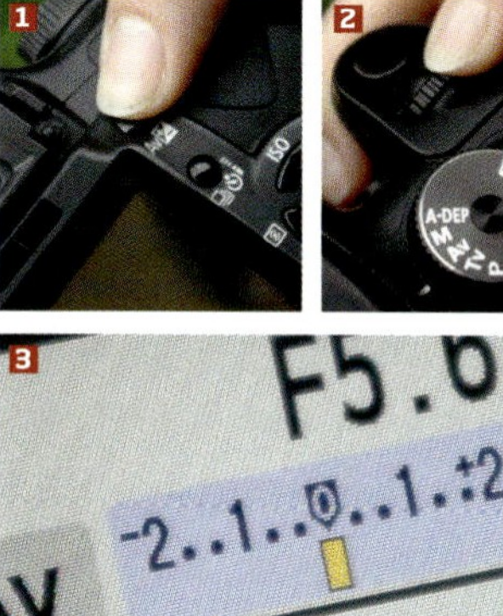

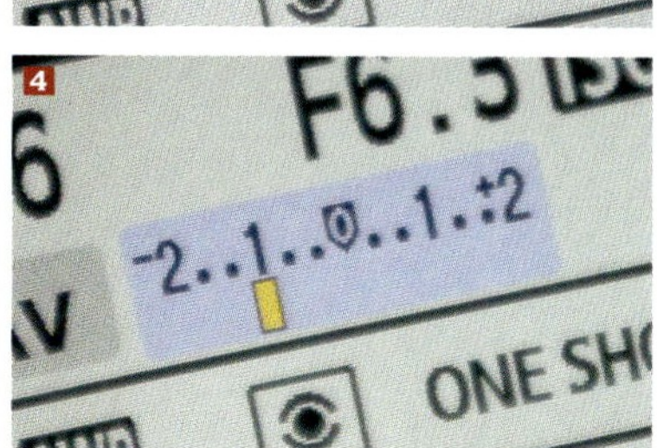

Auto Exposure Lock (AE-L)

This function allows you to 'lock' an exposure from a subject independently of the focusing system and is useful to avoid exposure error with very dark or light subjects or scenes

AE-L

PRACTICALLY EVERY DSLR has an AE-L button, which is normally found on the top right of the camera's rear, or near the LCD monitor. AE-L is an abbreviation for Auto Exposure Lock. It is designed to secure the current exposure setting so that it doesn't change when you recompose your image, even if the incoming light levels change. AE-L can be used in any exposure mode, although it is pointless if you are shooting in manual mode.

When you press the shutter button down halfway, you engage the autofocus and the metering system to take a reading. This is ideal most of the time, but what about when you want to focus and meter from different subjects or parts of the scene? This is where AE-Lock comes in. This useful feature allows you to take an exposure reading independently of where you focus, which is ideal if your subject is very dark or light or positioned in a bright or dim area of the scene. AE-L is most commonly used with the spot or centre-weighted metering pattern in order to 'lock' the reading taken from a specific area of the frame. This is particularly useful in tricky lighting conditions that can fool your metering system, such as backlit objects or subjects with very dark or light backgrounds. For instance, if you are shooting a scene containing a bright light source in part of the frame, your camera's multi-zone meter could be fooled by into reading the scene as brighter than it actually is and will underexpose as a result. To achieve the correct exposure, you want to take a meter reading that excludes the light region. This is possible by taking a spot/partial meter reading from the subject itself or an area of the scene that is a mid-tone and locking the result with the AE-Lock button, before recomposing the shot and taking the picture. Using the same principle, AE-L is useful when shooting subjects that are positioned off-centre. AE-Lock is also useful when you want to shoot a series of images using exactly the same exposure settings. For example, if you wish to stitch together several shots to create a panorama, it is important that the shooting parameters employed for each frame are consistent – using the AE-Lock button ensure contant exposures for each shot.

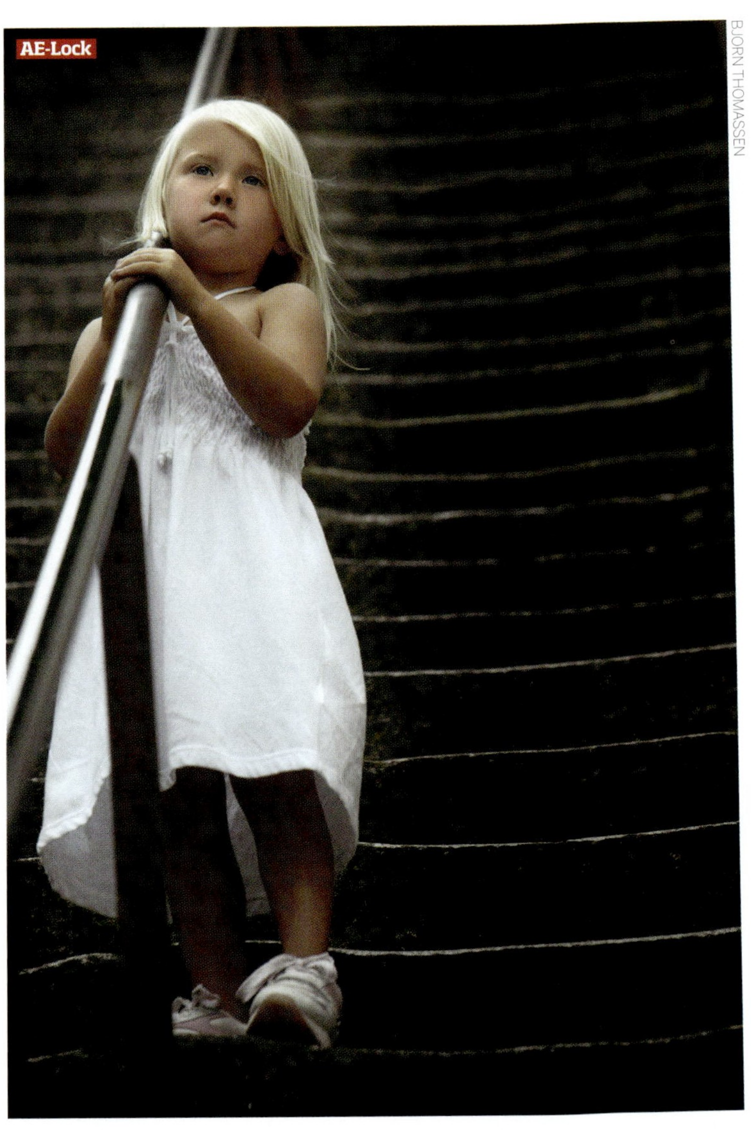

AE-Lock

BJORN THOMASSEN

The AE-Lock button is an essential exposure aid when shooting subjects with very dark or light backgrounds that can easily fool your camera's multi-zone metering into over or underexposure. In this instance, the very dark backdrop fooled the camera into thinking the scene was darker than it actually was. As a result, it has set a shutter speed longer than was required and so the subject is overexposed. In order to achieve the correct exposure, a spot-meter reading was taken from a wall to the side of the stairs. This reading was then locked using the AE-Lock button. The image was recomposed and the image taken. The result is perfectly exposed.

Using AE-Lock

The AE-L button, combined with spot or centre-weighted metering, is one of the most accurate forms of achieving the correct exposure settings for any given subject.

1) Select your camera's spot (or partial) meter.

2) Direct the camera so that the metering circle is positioned over the area or subject that you wish to meter from.

3) Activate AE-Lock by pressing the button. Note: on some models you have to keep it depressed, so consult your user's manual. The letters 'AE-L' may display in the viewfinder to indicate the lock is activated.

4) Move the camera and recompose the image as you want. Your exposure settings will not change, even if the incoming light levels alter as a result of changing composition.

6) Fully depress the shutter release button to take the shot.

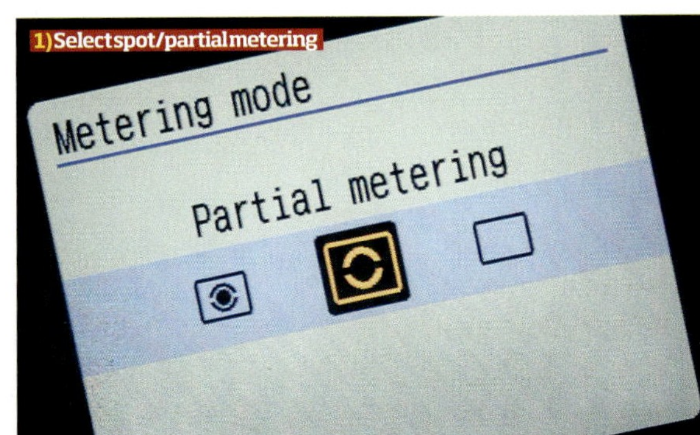

1) Select spot/partial metering

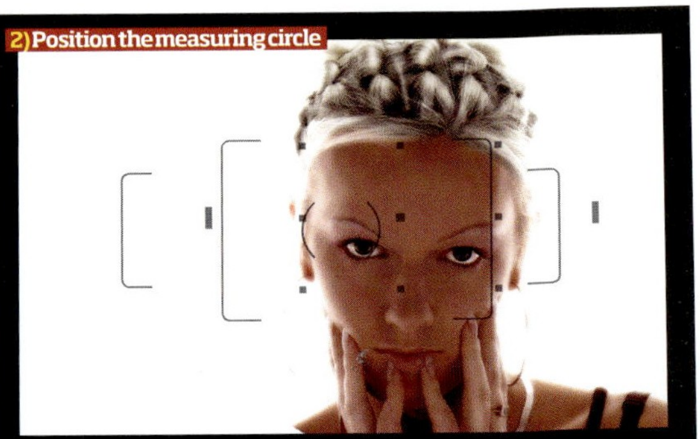

2) Position the measuring circle

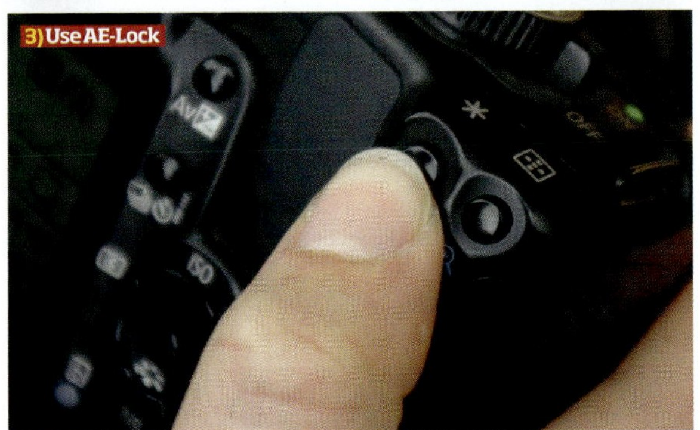

3) Use AE-Lock

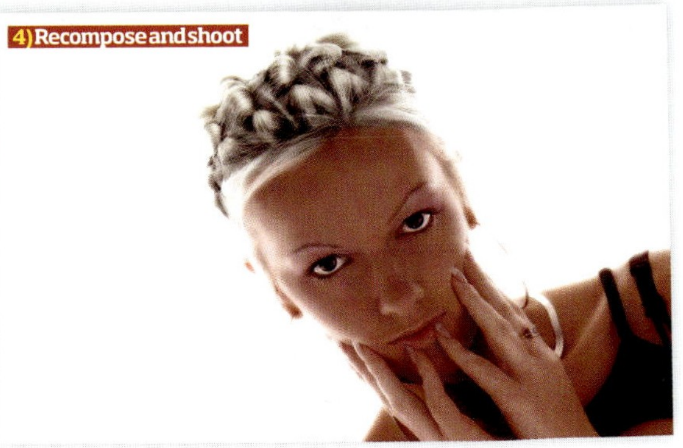

4) Recompose and shoot

BJORN THOMASSEN

Exposing backlit subjects

Paul Stefan shows you to how to perfectly exposure a backlit portrait using the spot meter, a reflector and a bit of fill-in flash

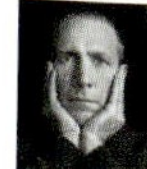

SHOOTING A BACKLIT subject (i.e. with the sun behind them) is not something I do too often, as it certainly comes with its challenges. If you're not prepared for it, your results can often be quite unpredictable and, more often than not, your subject will be underexposed and look rather flat. This tutorial will help you to understand the relatively straightforward technique to achieving great results.

Let's begin with why letting the camera make the decisions for you is not the best option. It's often so easy to stick your camera on Full Auto mode and let it decide the exposure. For portraits that have the light shining on the subject's face, or off slightly to the side, using auto mode sometimes works fine, as the exposure levels may not be too extreme. However, if you position your subject so that the light source is behind them (so you're shooting towards them and the sun or light source), your camera is likely to get confused and the exposure terribly wrong. What usually happens is your subject gets underexposed, sometimes silhouetted, often resulting in an awful picture. The reason for this is that the camera's multi-zone exposure system will evaluate the overall scene. Given that you are pointing the camera towards the light source, it will always look to expose the shot for a bright scene, causing the darker areas – in this case the person – to be underexposed.

Taking more control over your camera will greatly improve the image and enable you to get the exposure you really want. One of the easiest ways to do this is to set your DSLR to aperture-priority mode and to use the spot meter along with AE-Lock to fix the light reading. With this method, you take a spot meter reading from the person's face, regardless of the lighting conditions around the subject, which should result in a perfectly-exposed person nearly every time. The exception, when it might be slightly trickier, is when your subject is very dark-skinned. If that's the case, use the same technique but take a spot meter reading off a mid-tone in the same lighting conditions, this could be a piece of clothing, grass or ideally an 18% grey card.

While spot metering is quick and easy, it may cause your subject's surrounding scene to be overexposed if it's lighter than your subject. If you want to include the environment in the shot, one way around this is to take a meter reading from an in-between subject and then use your camera's flash to fill in the foreground with light, balancing the overall scene's exposure. Equally, a reflector will also help this, as it will bounce natural light back towards your subject and have a similar fill-in effect. If you're feeling really adventurous, why not try a mixture, using both flash and a reflector.

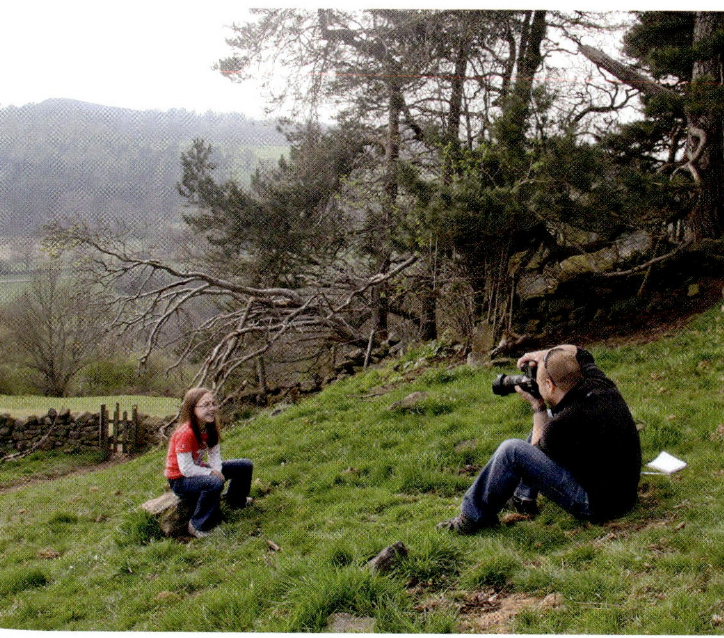

1) Take a shot with your DSLR set to Full Auto
I was keen for my portrait to have a picturesque backdrop, so I chose a south-facing hillside near my home, with a view looking out to Robin Hood's Stride and Cratcliffe in the Peak District. My first shot was to see how the camera's Auto mode handled the exposure of my subject with the sun directly behind and above her. With this set up, I was shooting towards the sun, which would certainly challenge the camera's multi-zone metering system.

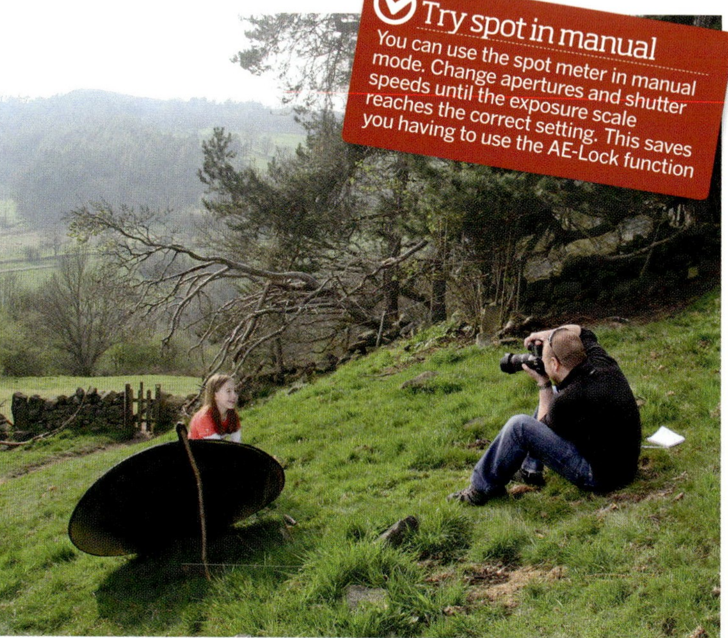

Try spot in manual
You can use the spot meter in manual mode. Change apertures and shutter speeds until the exposure scale reaches the correct setting. This saves you having to use the AE-Lock function

2) Using spot metering and a reflector
The shot taken in Full Auto wasn't a disaster, but it could certainly be improved with the use of spot metering. By switching my DSLR to aperture-priority and setting the metering mode to spot, I was able to meter from Emily's face and lock the reading using AE-Lock. I did this by looking through the viewfinder and placing the central circle over the her face and pressing the AE-Lock button to ensure a perfect exposure. I then focused on her face, recomposed and took the shot.

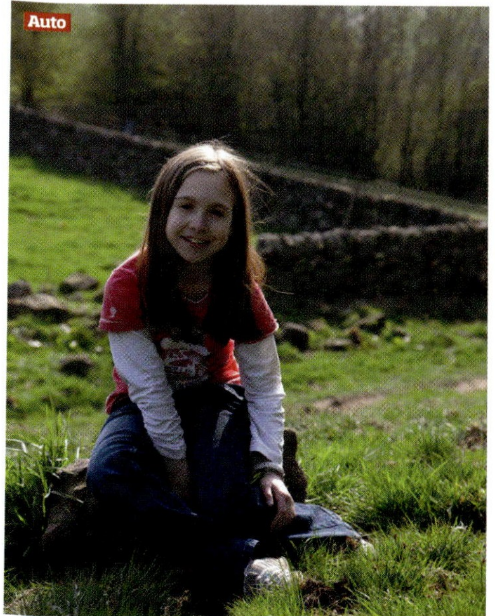

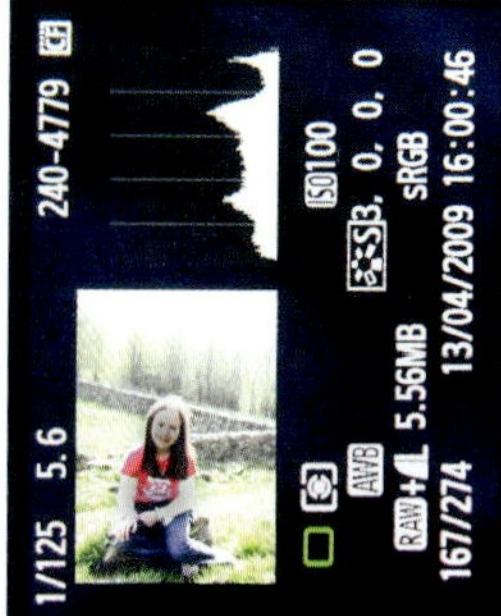

The result from my DSLR wasn't actually too bad as the face of my subject, my eldest daughter Emily, wasn't completely underexposed, but it could definitely be improved. This would have been much worse if the sun was lower and in direct view of the shot. Other DSLRs may not have coped as well as my Canon EOS 5D MkII either.

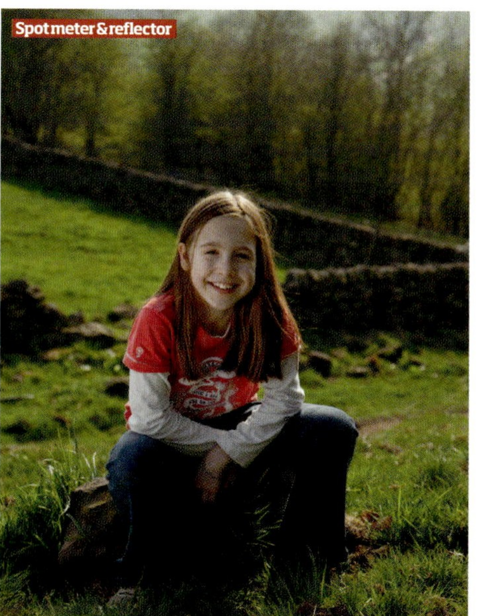

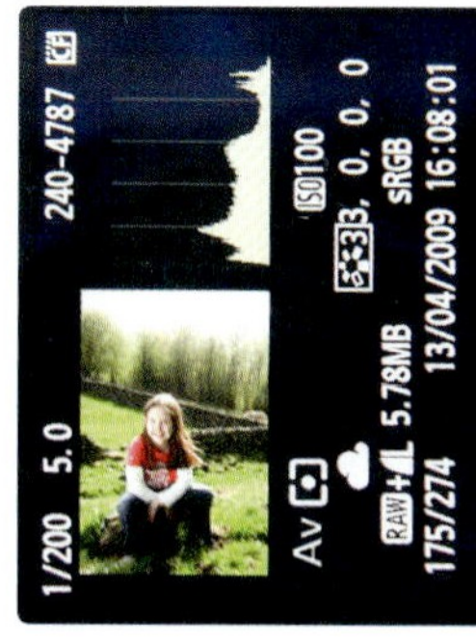

Spot metering has improved the scene greatly, but to make it even better, I placed a portable reflector just out of shot, perched on a stick, to throw some of that lovely warm sunlight back onto Emily's face, giving the shot added depth. This really made a difference, revealing so much more detail and depth, both in her face and in her clothes.

3) Use fill-in flash

I like the natural look of the spot-metered and reflector shot, but for this example I wanted to show a further change to the set-up, to create a more dramatic portrait. Therefore, I hooked up my flashgun to my camera with a stretchy sync lead, to allow me to hold the flash unit away from the camera and over to one side. This is a useful technique that causes your flash to give a more flattering look to the subject, rather than blasting them directly in the face. With this set-up, I also left the reflector in place, used the same exposure settings from the previous shot and pointed the flashgun toward Emily's body, rather than her face.

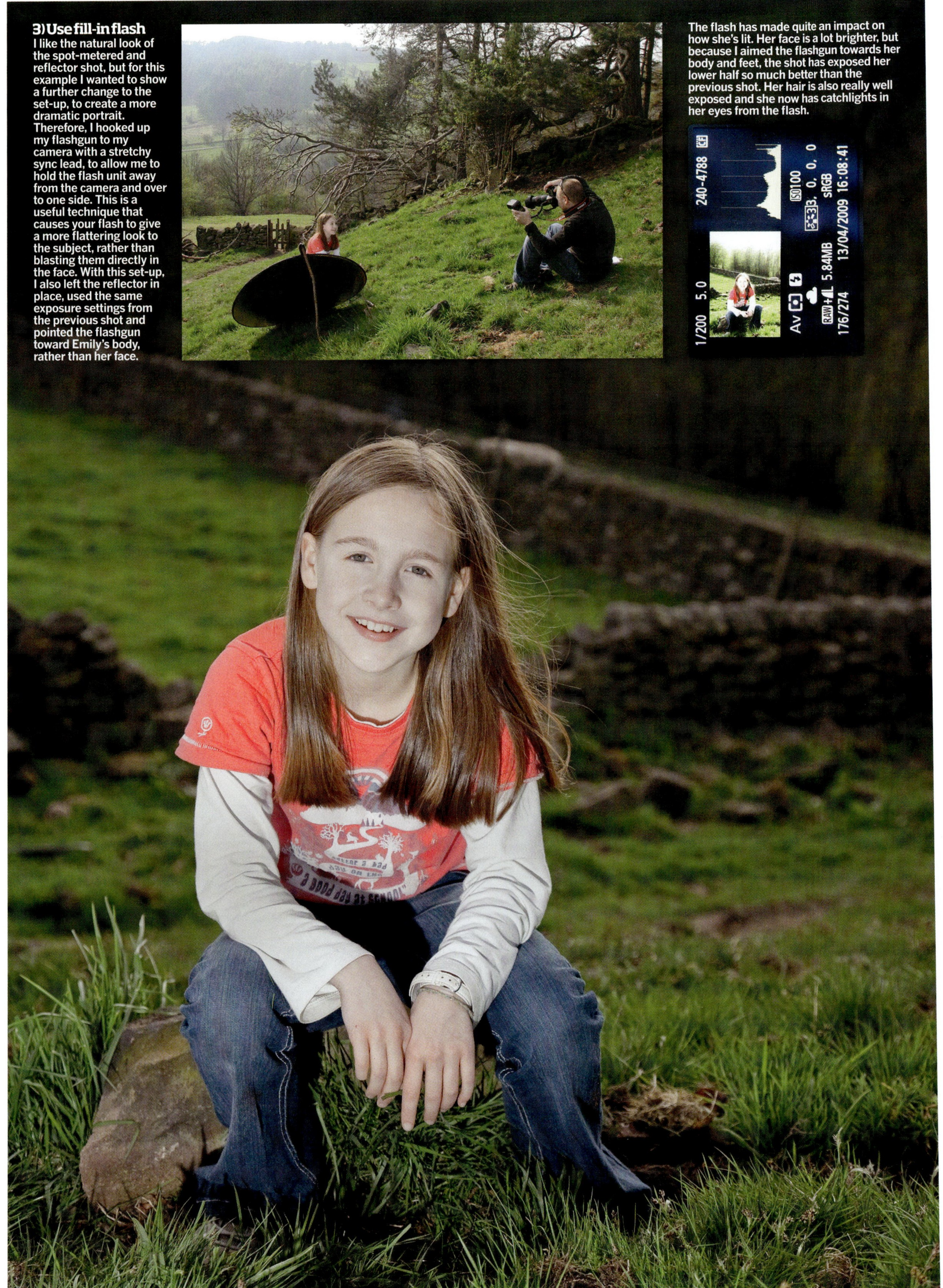

The flash has made quite an impact on how she's lit. Her face is a lot brighter, but because I aimed the flashgun towards her body and feet, the shot has exposed her lower half so much better than the previous shot. Her hair is also really well exposed and she now has catchlights in her eyes from the flash.

Exposing for a subject that is small in the frame

Paul Stefan explains how you can use spot metering to get good results from difficult, high-contrast scenes

"I'M LOOKING FOR SOMETHING like a black cat in a snow scene, or a white lamb in a coal pit" was my brief for showing you how to handle high-contrast scenes. I do enjoy a challenge, but even that one seemed a little beyond me, as there wasn't a snowflake in sight and the chances of me getting a lamb into a coal pit were about as remote as, well, finding a black cat in a snow scene! The examples did however make it very clear the sort of familiar scenario that leave most beginner photographers scratching their heads at one point or another. When you are trying to photograph a scene that is high in contrast, allowing the camera to decide the exposure will always give you less than perfect results. The answer, therefore, is to take control yourself! Using the suggestion of a black cat in a snow scene as an example, there is clearly a huge tonal variation between each of the elements. Expose the overall shot for the black cat and all the snow will be completely blown out. Expose the scene for the snow and the black cat becomes a black blob with no detail.

Clearly, taking this photograph on any camera's auto mode is likely to result in an incorrect exposure, as the majority of the shot will be snow, therefore causing the camera's multi-zone metering system to lean towards the most prominent subject in the scene, and expose for that. Unfortunately, this will leave you with a very sad looking black cat.

The ideal solution to getting an accurate exposure for a high-contrast scene like this would be to find a middle-ground in the huge variation between the snow and the cat, and expose for that. Easy! This can only really be done using AE-lock or spot metering, as both will allow you to take control of the exposure and then set the scene how you want. I used spot metering for the photographs you'll see on this spread, simply because it's my personal preference and it enables me to take more control over the exposure.

The critical thing here is to find a mid-toned subject that falls between the extremes of contrast, such as a grey rock, from which you can take a spot reading. Set the camera up to expose for the neutral rock, employ the AE-lock function, and then compose the shot without changing the exposure settings. In my step-by-step guide, I tried to get as close to my brief as I could by dressing one of my daughters up in a lamb-like jacket and putting her in a dark scene that was as close to coal as I could find – some recently burnt heather on Stanton Moor in the Peak District.

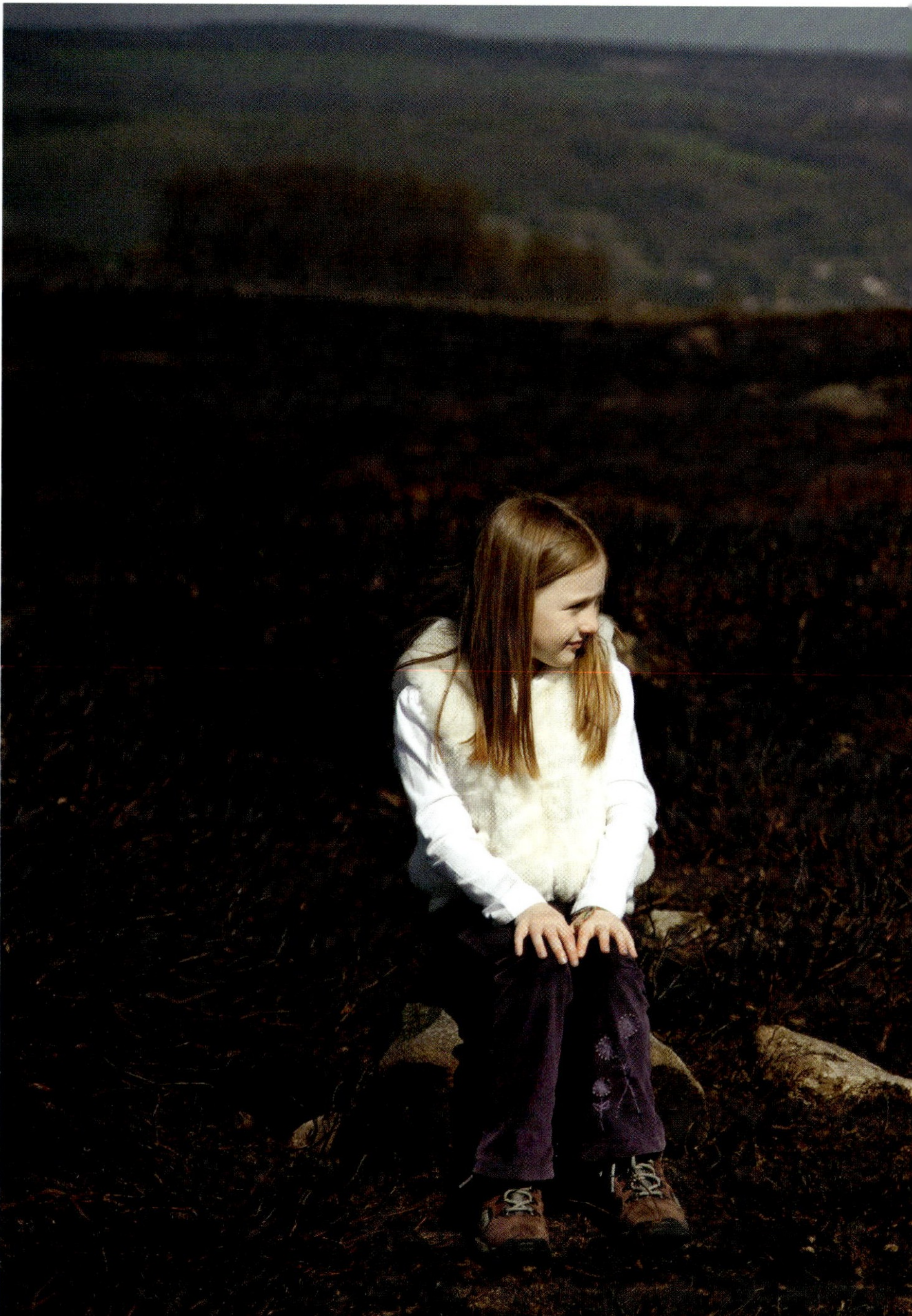

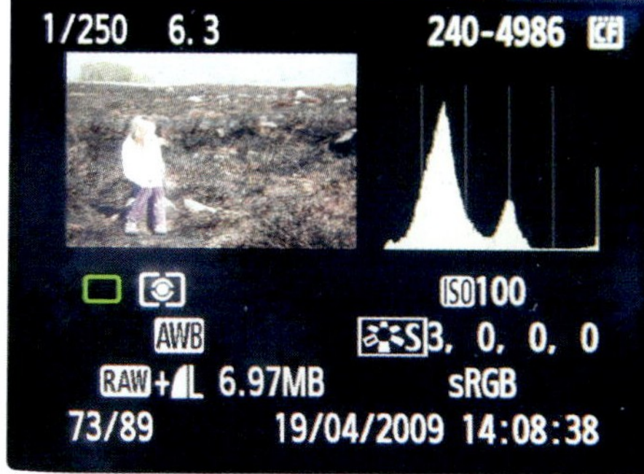

1) Taking a shot set to Auto

Once I'd found my location and composed the image, I put the camera into Full Auto mode to take the shot. This uses the multi-zone metering to set the exposure for the scene. As you can see, it's not a terrible shot, but you will notice that it appears to have weighted more on the side of the dark, burnt heather, which has caused the white, lamb-like jacket, as well as the subject's face, to be grossly overexposed. This is because the dark heather covers the majority of the scene and this is what the multi-zone metering will take into account more than the small area of white. Above are the settings that the camera used in Full Auto mode.

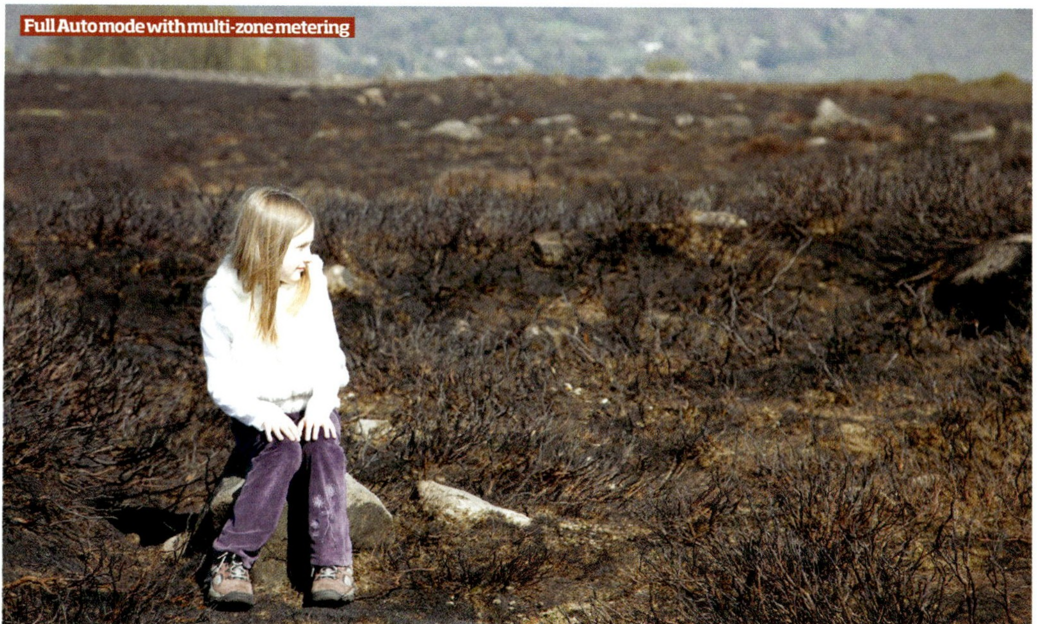

Full Auto mode with multi-zone metering

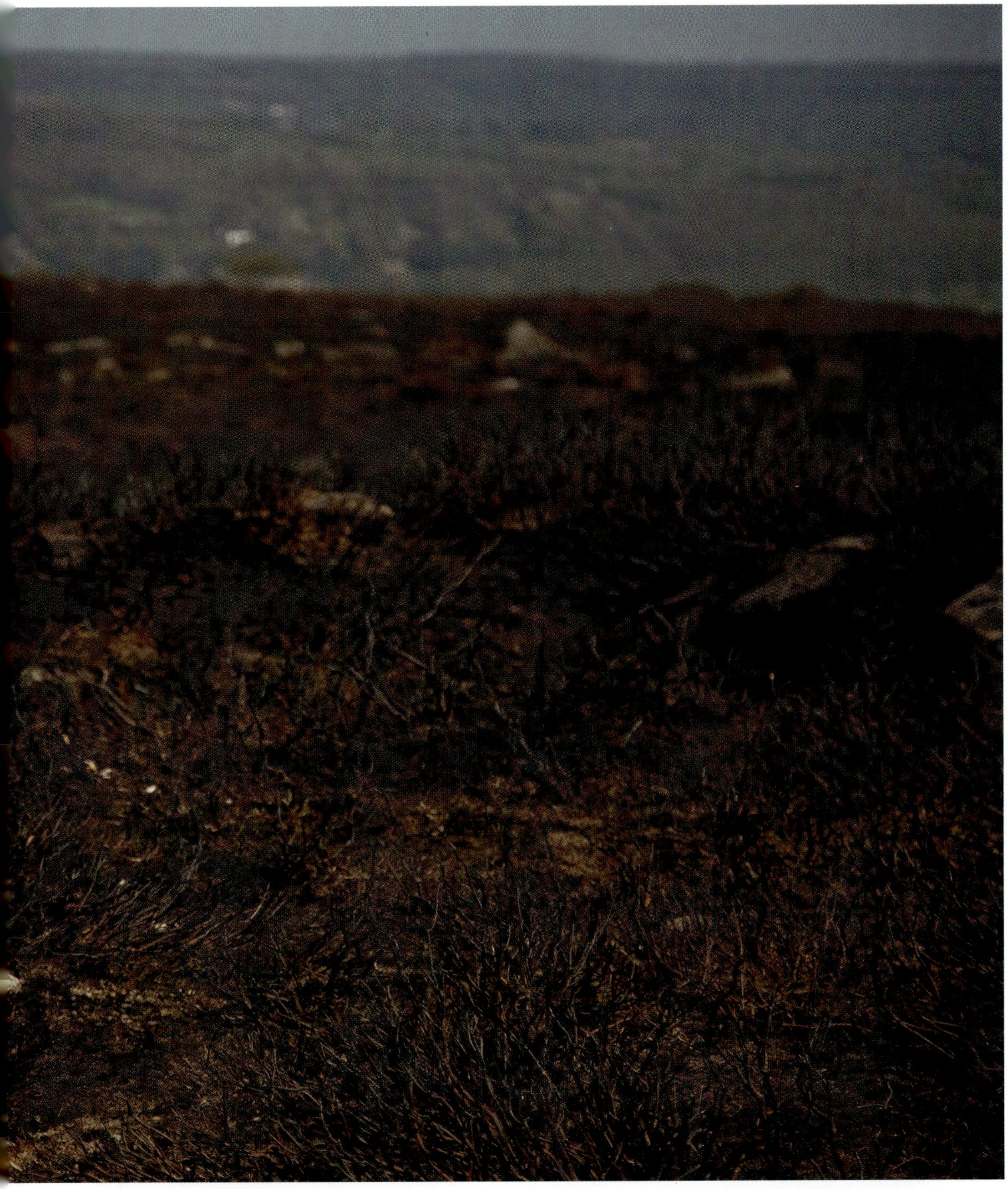

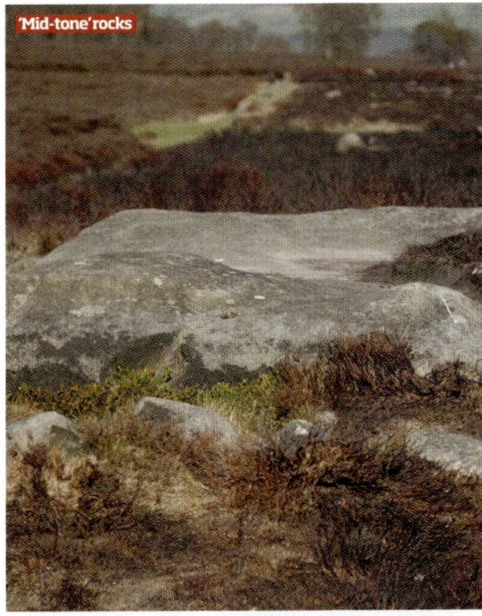
'Mid-tone' rocks

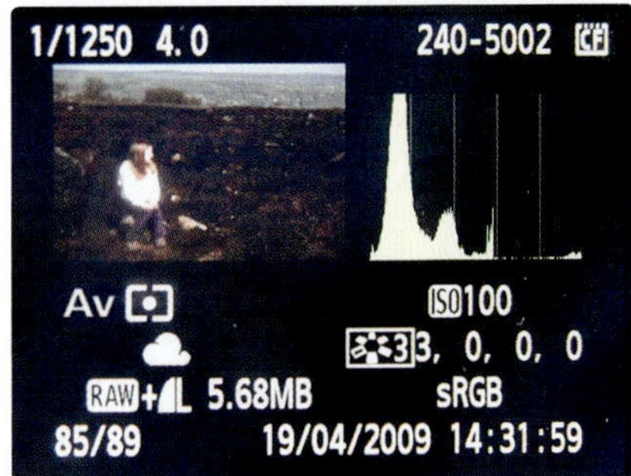

3) Now take full control

I didn't want an underexposed scene surrounding my subject, or an overexposed white jacket. I also didn't like the result that my camera's Full Auto mode had given me, which was weighted towards the dark heather. The solution was for me to take control and look for a mid-tone, allowing me to set the best average exposure I could. Luckily, there was a number of large lumps of Peak District grit stone lying around. These provided an excellent mid-point between the dark heather and the bright white of the jacket – perfect for a spot meter reading. If you face a scene without such a convenience, simply introduce a grey card to spot from.

By selecting aperture-priority mode, choosing an aperture, making sure I had spot metering set and then pointing the camera's spot metering circle in the viewfinder towards the grit stone, I could then lock my exposure, focus on my subject and capture this result.

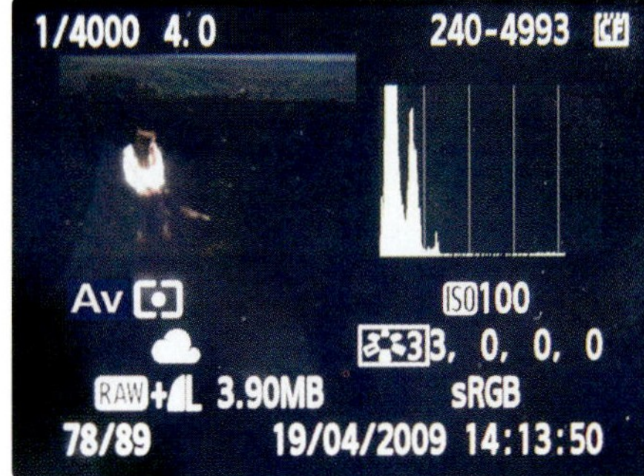

2) Results of spot Metering

Spot metering allows you to meter from a specific subject in a scene. This works well if the exposure doesn't vary hugely across the shot, but in our example, taking a spot meter reading from the white subject or the dark scene would still not give the desired results. For this shot, I locked a spot reading from the white jacket, which is beautifully exposed, but at the expense of the rest of the scene. The next shot shows what happened when I metered from the heather and exposed for that. The heather is perfectly exposed but the jacket is now completely overexposed, which doesn't look great and obviously shows no detail.

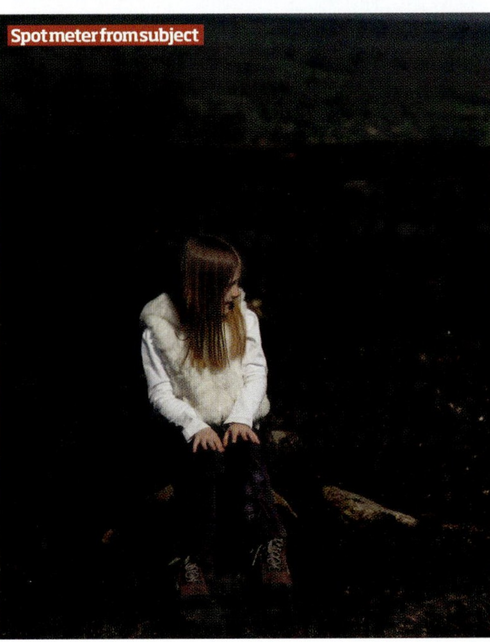
Spot meter from subject

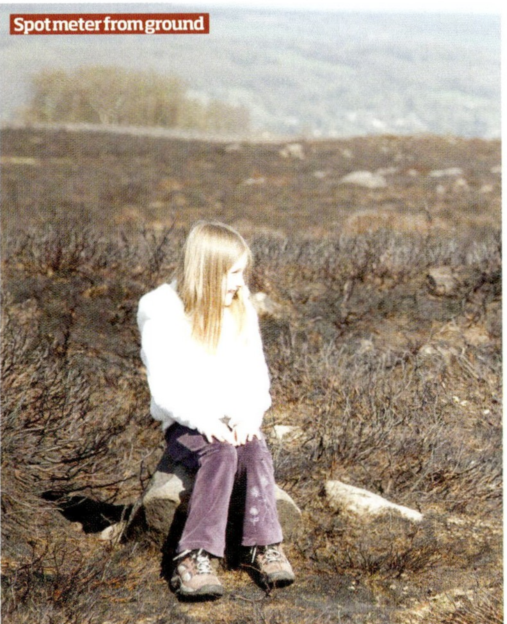
Spot meter from ground

Portrait composition

There are no rules, only guidelines when it comes to composition but, like lighting, it has the potential to make or break a portrait. Developing your style will take time and practice but here are a few of the main considerations to take into account and to help you along your way

1) Landscape or upright orientation?

It's natural to tilt the camera upright when you're shooting a portrait as it allows you to fill the frame with the subject's head and shoulders or entire body. It's a good format to adopt when you're trying to exclude as much of the background as possible to concentrate attention on the subject. Because this format is used so often when shooting people, the upright format is often termed the portrait format. Photographing portraits with the camera held normally to produce a landscape-orientated image often allows you to employ more creative compositions. For one, it means you can place the subject off-centre to include some of the backdrop in the frame. It also allows you to crop tightly into the face, which can add drama and impact to the image. Both options are worth trying while looking through the viewfinder to see which works best and, if in doubt, take a shot using both formats!

We have cropped the same image (see right) into a landscape and portrait format. Which do you prefer? The orientation you opt for plays a crucial role in the strength of your portrait and it's a choice you need to make each time you compose a shot.

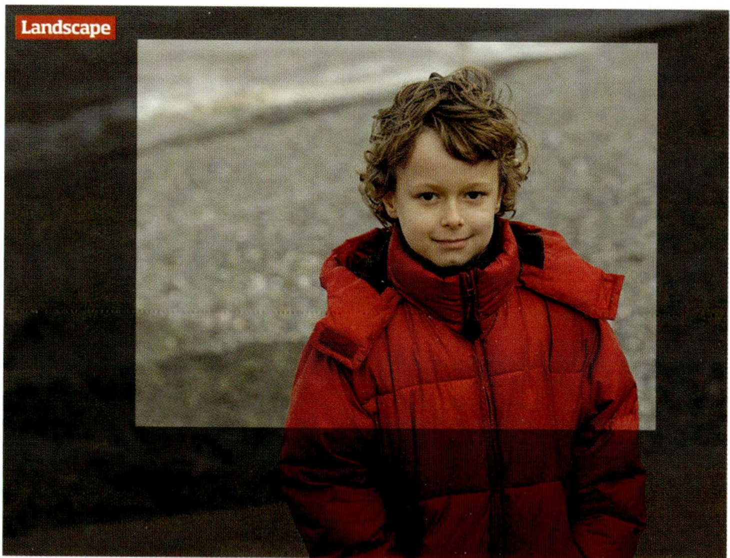

Landscape

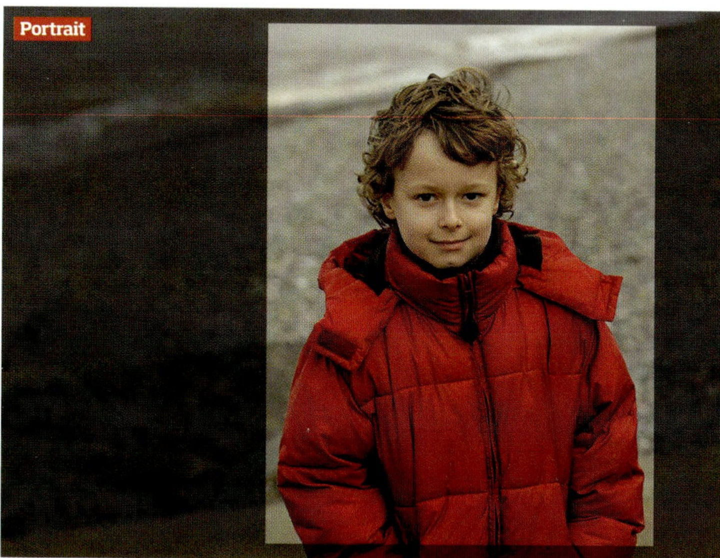

Portrait

2) Viewpoint

It's natural when taking a picture to stand and shoot from your normal eye-level. However, while there is nothing wrong with this, shooting from your standard viewpoint is a little unimaginative. Also, it's not always the most flattering angle for your subject – you'll find that by shooting from slightly above and down on your subject, you'll capture a better picture. Experiment by shooting from a much higher or lower viewpoint to your subject and see how the results turn out.

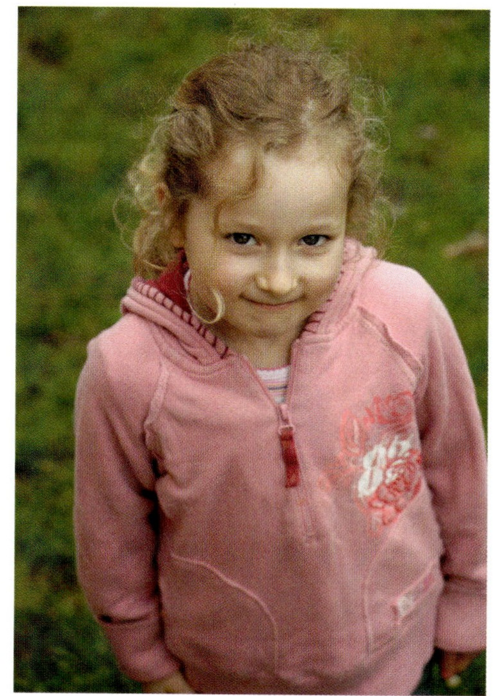

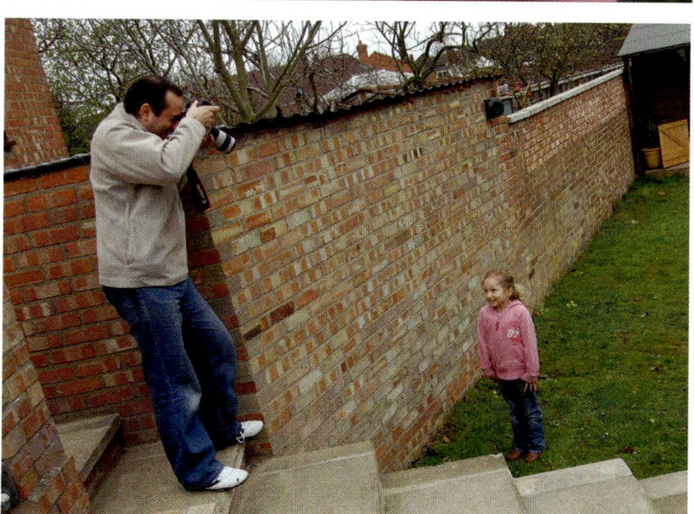

Shooting a subject from halfway up some steps provides a very high viewpoint and produces an unusual and quirky result. Give it a try!

3) Breaking the rules: New angles to try

USE A WIDE-ANGLE LENS

Set your standard zoom to wide-angle (or use an ultra wide-angle zoom) and shoot portraits with a difference. Because they completely distort perspective, it's possible to shoot very unusual portrait images, where the part of the subject closest to the lens appears much larger than the parts of the body that are further away.

EYE CONTACT

Yep, we harp on about making sure you get both eyes sharply in focus with the subject looking at the camera, yet there are many stunning examples where the subject's looking away or their eyes are obscured. A lack of eye contact can add intrigue to your portrait or give it a candid feel, so don't be afraid of having your subject looking away from the camera.

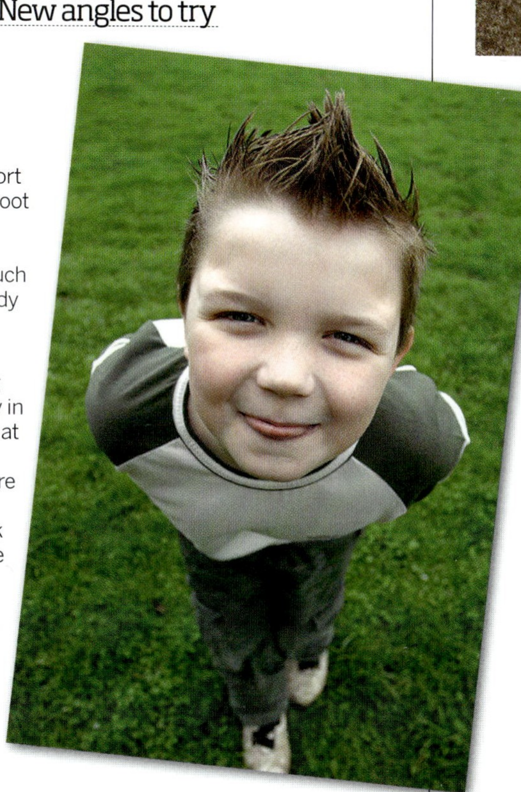

Look how the wide-angle lens used on this shot has distorted perspective. You can get some quirky portraits from using unconventional techniques.

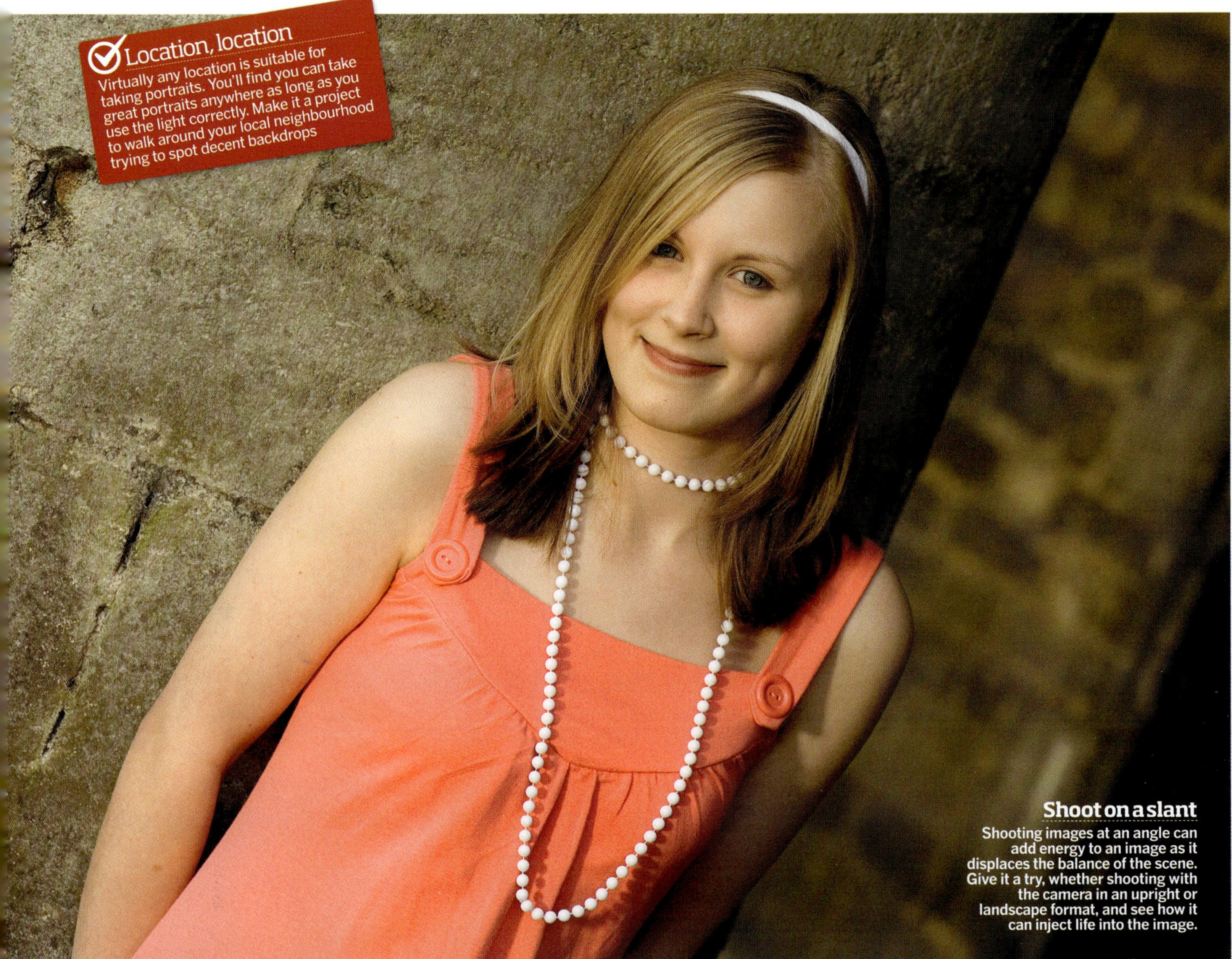

Location, location
Virtually any location is suitable for taking portraits. You'll find you can take great portraits anywhere as long as you use the light correctly. Make it a project to walk around your local neighbourhood trying to spot decent backdrops

Shoot on a slant
Shooting images at an angle can add energy to an image as it displaces the balance of the scene. Give it a try, whether shooting with the camera in an upright or landscape format, and see how it can inject life into the image.

Frequently asked questions

My camera has scene modes, why should I not use Portrait mode?
While it takes the fuss out of taking a picture, Portrait mode removes any chance of being creative. As with all scene modes, the Portrait program automatically activates certain picture-taking options. Depending on which camera you use, you'll find that setting Portrait mode results in the following: *White Balance: Auto; Autofocus: Multi-point AF/One-shot mode; ISO Rating: Automatically selected; Metering pattern: Multi-zone; Built-in flash: Auto.*

While these settings are suitable for those looking for point-and-shoot simplicity, for those of you wanting to develop your photographic skills, it's quite prohibitive and the fact that you can't control aspects such as the flash and White Balance can really affect the result you're trying to achieve. Instead, learn how to get the best from semi-automatic modes such as aperture-priority.

What should subjects wear?
The most important thing is that your subject feels comfortable. So don't get them to overdress or wear items that they don't like.

Ideally, ask to see a selection of clothing and talk through what they like the most. You don't want colours to dominate the image, so a plain neutral top is usually a good starting point, along with casual trousers or a pair of jeans.

How should I get them to pose?
It's vital that they appear natural and comfortable, whether they're sitting, standing or lying down. You'll find that subjects are normally unsure of what to do with their hands, resulting in them looking clumsy or awkward in the frame. A good starting point is to have them keep their hands in their trouser pockets if standing, hanging over their knees or between their legs if sat down. Buy fashion and lifestyle magazines and tear out pages where a model has a pose you like, then show it to your subject and ask them to recreate it.

Have you got any make-up tips?
We asked professional make-up artist Fay Bacon for expert advice:
1) Always thoroughly cleanse, tone and moisturise the skin before applying any make-up. It will help the products to sit better on the skin.
2) Apply an illuminator over the top of a moisturiser. This helps lift the skin and increase its radiance underneath the foundation, so skin appears more youthful.
3) Always apply foundation with a foundation brush as it reduces the amount of foundation used on the skin and prevents patchiness or lines on the face, making the skin appear extra-flawless and natural.
4) Use a translucent, loose powder and dust it lightly over the 'T-Zone' area. This reduces the appearance of shiny, oily skin.
5) Always use concealer for disguising dark circles and unwanted blemishes. There is an enormous difference between foundation and concealer; foundation evens out the skin tone while concealer covers. You need to use both to achieve flawless-looking skin.
6) In terms of colour such as eye shadows, blushers and lipsticks etc, always consider the colour contrasts of skin tone, eyes and lips. Dependent upon the style and theme of the photography shoot certain make-up rules do not apply. However, most make-up artists would advise using lighter and more intense shades such as purples, blues and greens on darker skin and eyes, as this helps echo the beauty and vibrancy of the skin tone.

Pastel, neutral and darker shades are better suited for paler skin as they help intensify the eye area and the skin tone by allowing both to stand out more.

Put the 'rules' into practice

Taking photographs of people is something that nearly everyone with a camera does. Whether it be a friend, a family member or a professional model, it's often easy to snap away at a person and end up with, well... a snapshot. A little bit of consideration for composition, however, will go a long way to improving your portraits and hopefully capture your subject's personality better too.

The standard rules of composition remain the same for portraits as they do for most photographs. The rule-of-thirds, filling the frame and thinking about your setting/background are all factors that will drastically improve a portrait and ultimately determine its success. If used correctly and creatively, these guidelines will help convert your photographs from snapshots to pictures to be proud of. In the next few steps, we'll show what the difference applying these rules can have on your photographs.

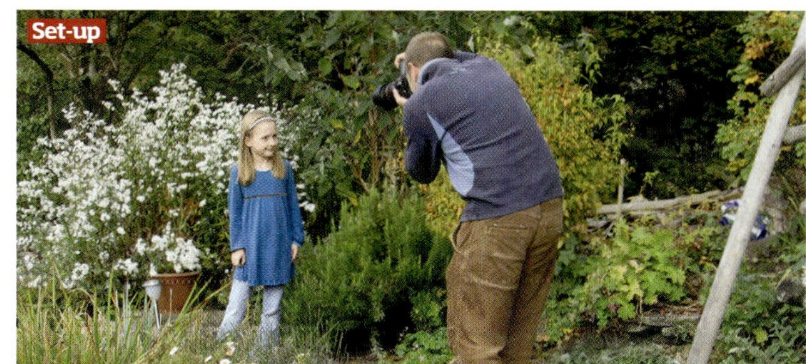

Set-up

Step 1 This first shot is an example of what not to do. Without considering the rules of composition, you may end up with a nice enough snapshot, but the main focal point (the eyes) aren't in a third, making the composition look awkward. In addition, the building work in the background is distracting for the viewer and the green trees sticking out of the subject's head don't look good. As a beginner, thinking about the background is definitely one of the easiest ways to improve the composition of your portraits quickly.

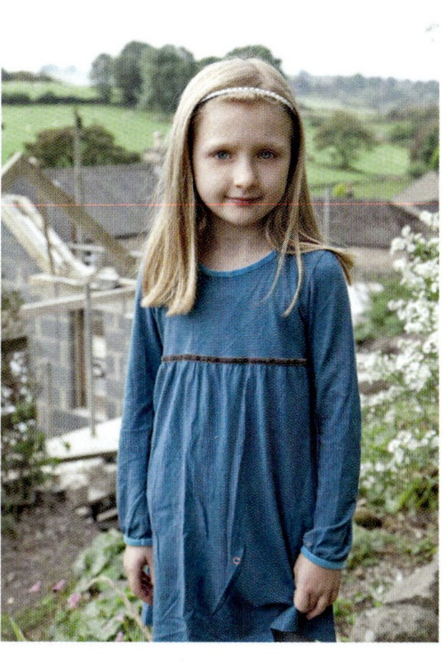

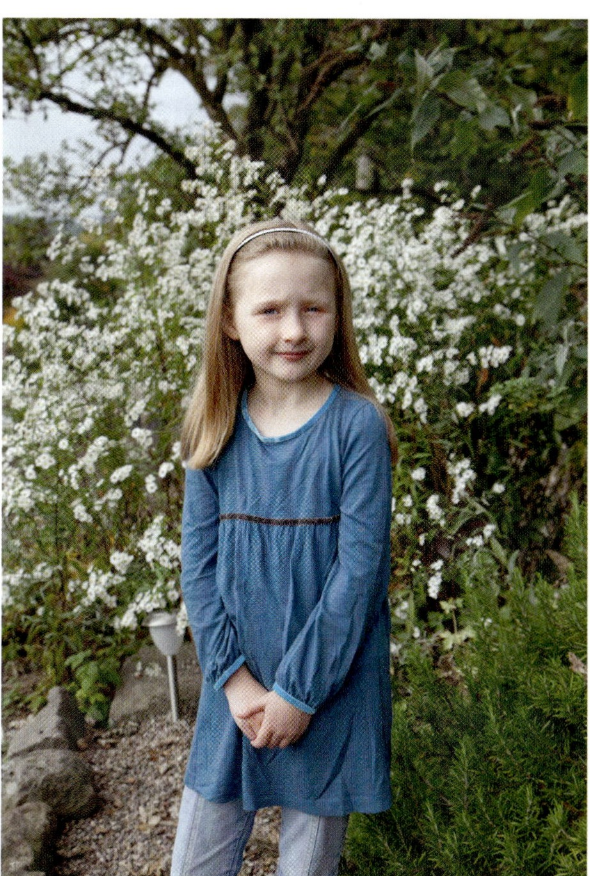

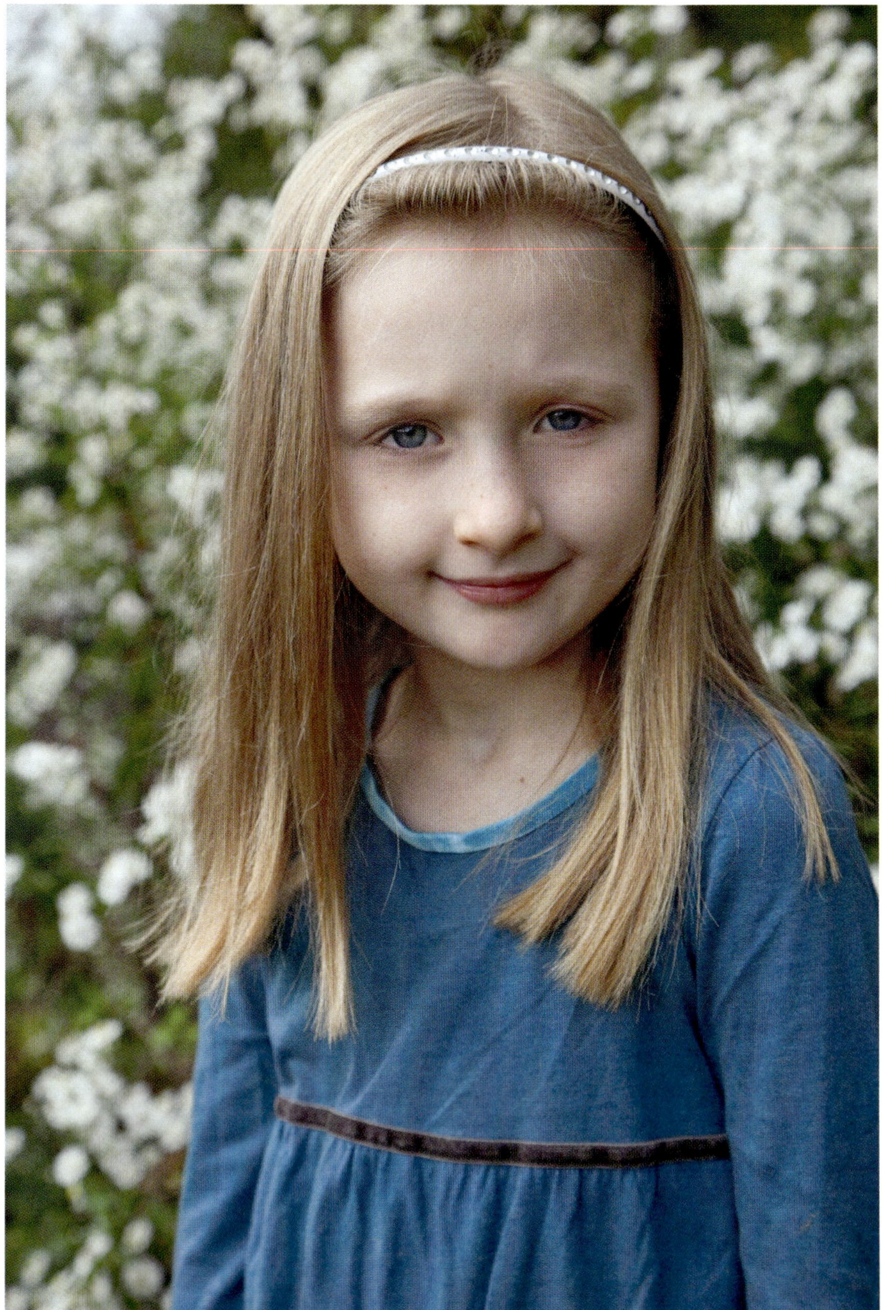

Left: Step 2 As all Rocky Horror fans will say: "It's just a jump to the left!" In the next shot, the subject was asked to take one step to her left, this immediately improved composition by incorporating a much simpler backdrop. Compared to the first image, you can immediately see the improvement it's made to the overall impact of the picture. The texture and tone is much simpler, keeping the viewer's eye focused on the model's face.

Above: Step 3 The placement of the eyes within the frame is paramount to improving composition. Generally, a portrait works best if the eyes are in the top third of the shot, as it guides the viewer from top to bottom. Getting a bit closer and using a 70mm focal length, as opposed to the 50mm used in the previous two shots, has meant the subject now fills the frame with more of the her face. Getting closer also helps blur the background more.

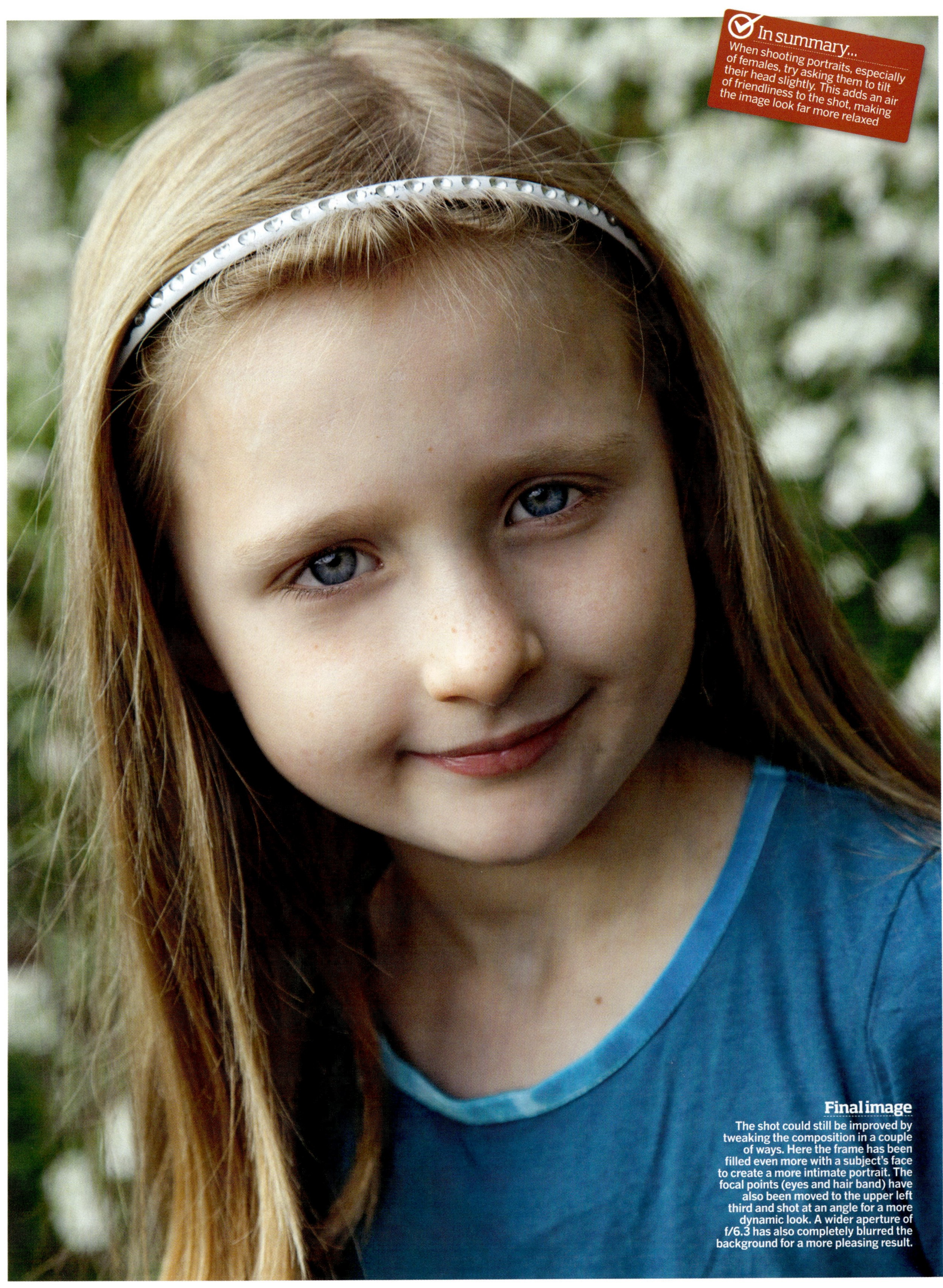

Final image

The shot could still be improved by tweaking the composition in a couple of ways. Here the frame has been filled even more with a subject's face to create a more intimate portrait. The focal points (eyes and hair band) have also been moved to the upper left third and shot at an angle for a more dynamic look. A wider aperture of f/6.3 has also completely blurred the background for a more pleasing result.

Breaking rules is child's play!

APPLYING THE RULES of composition to portraits, such as the placement of the eyes in the upper third and using diagonals and lead-in lines, are great ways of improving your portrait photographs. But as you'll no doubt have discovered, sometimes rules are there to be broken, and when it comes to the composition of portraits, breaking these rules can lead to some quirky results.

This step-by-step guide aims to show you how to shoot portraits with a difference. Instead of using a typical portrait lens like a 50mm, we've opted to use a 17-40mm wide-angle zoom at its widest focal length. This type of lens can often be very unflattering for a portrait, as your model can end up with distorted features, so composition becomes even more important! You should still pay particular attention to elements such as the rule-of-thirds, your subject's background and so on, but don't be afraid to consider these more as guidelines than rules. You should look for unconventional ways of approaching a portrait, bending the rules a little to get a more unusual and creative portrait.

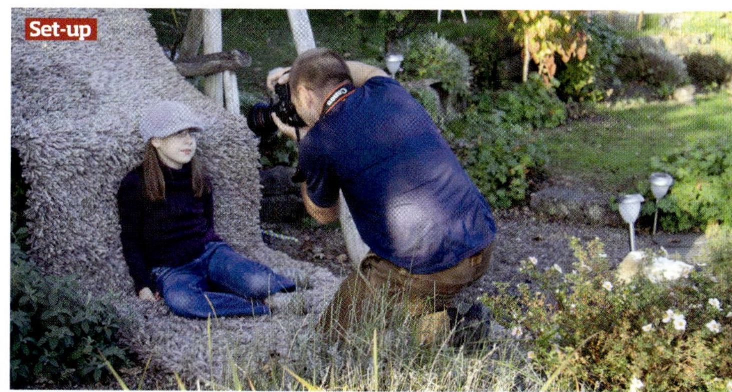
Set-up

Step 1 This first shot, using the zoom set at 17mm, gives a very distorted view of the subject and is a good example of how not to bend the rules. Little thought has been given to the positioning of the eyes, which is usually the focal point, so they have ended up in the centre of the frame. Nor has much attention been paid to what's going on with the background and surroundings. The slightly quirky angle has also made the composition a little too awkward, although the lead-in lines of the legs work well. Breaking the compositional rules in this shot hasn't worked out as well as it should have and can certainly be improved.

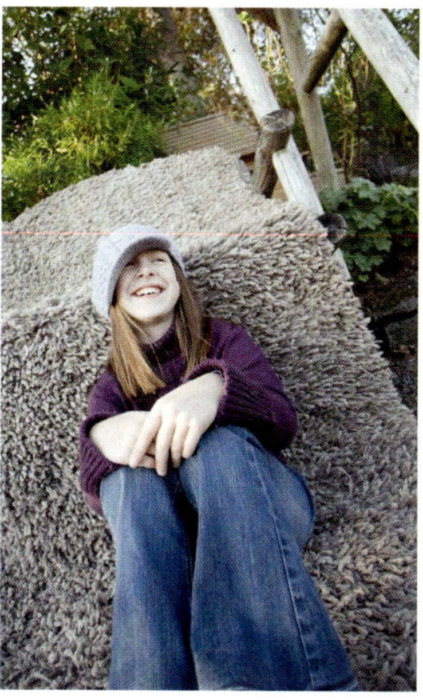

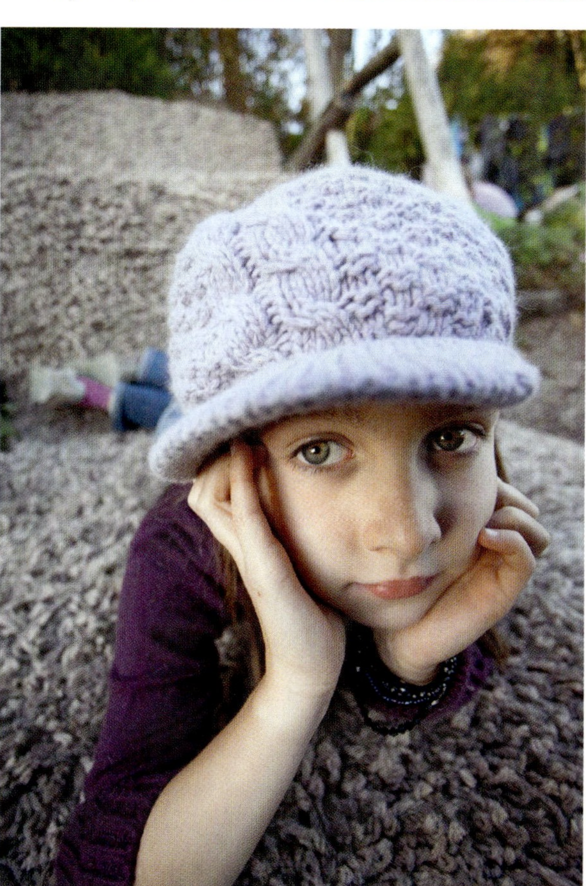

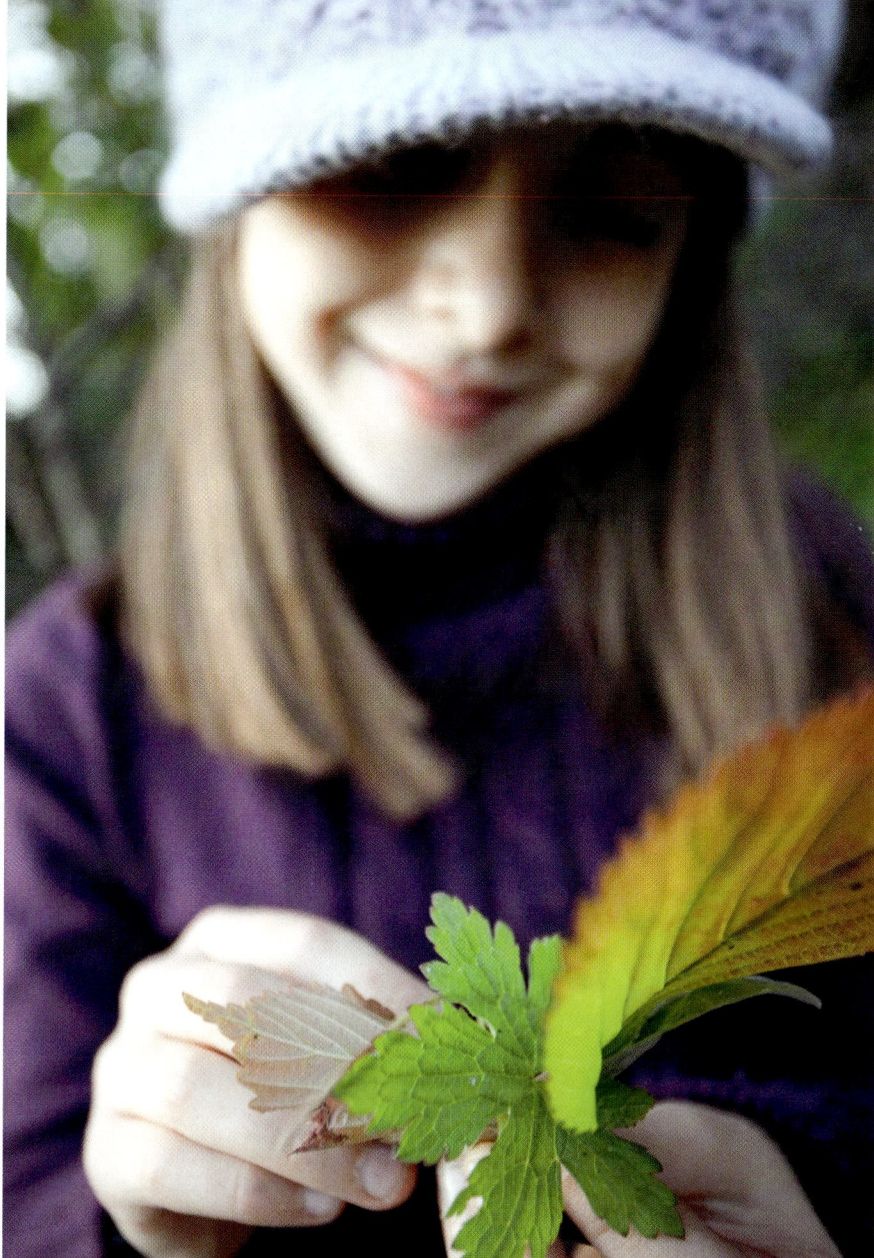

Left: Step 2 For the second shot, the focal length was kept at 17mm and the model has turned around for a more frame-filling shot. Although the model's eyes aren't on a third, which could improve the image, having the lead-in line created by the elbow from the bottom left does work better than the previous shot. Typically in a portrait you wouldn't want your model to have tiny feet but breaking this rule gives the shot an interesting perspective.

Above: Step 3 This shot has challenged the rules of focusing, and it works well. Instead of concentrating on the subject's eyes, the focus is on the leaves in her hand. Using an aperture of f/4 has meant her face is blurred, which is not something you would usually want to do with a portrait. This has made the image more intriguing and with a wider angle, I've been able to place the two main subjects of the shot at the top and the bottom of the image.

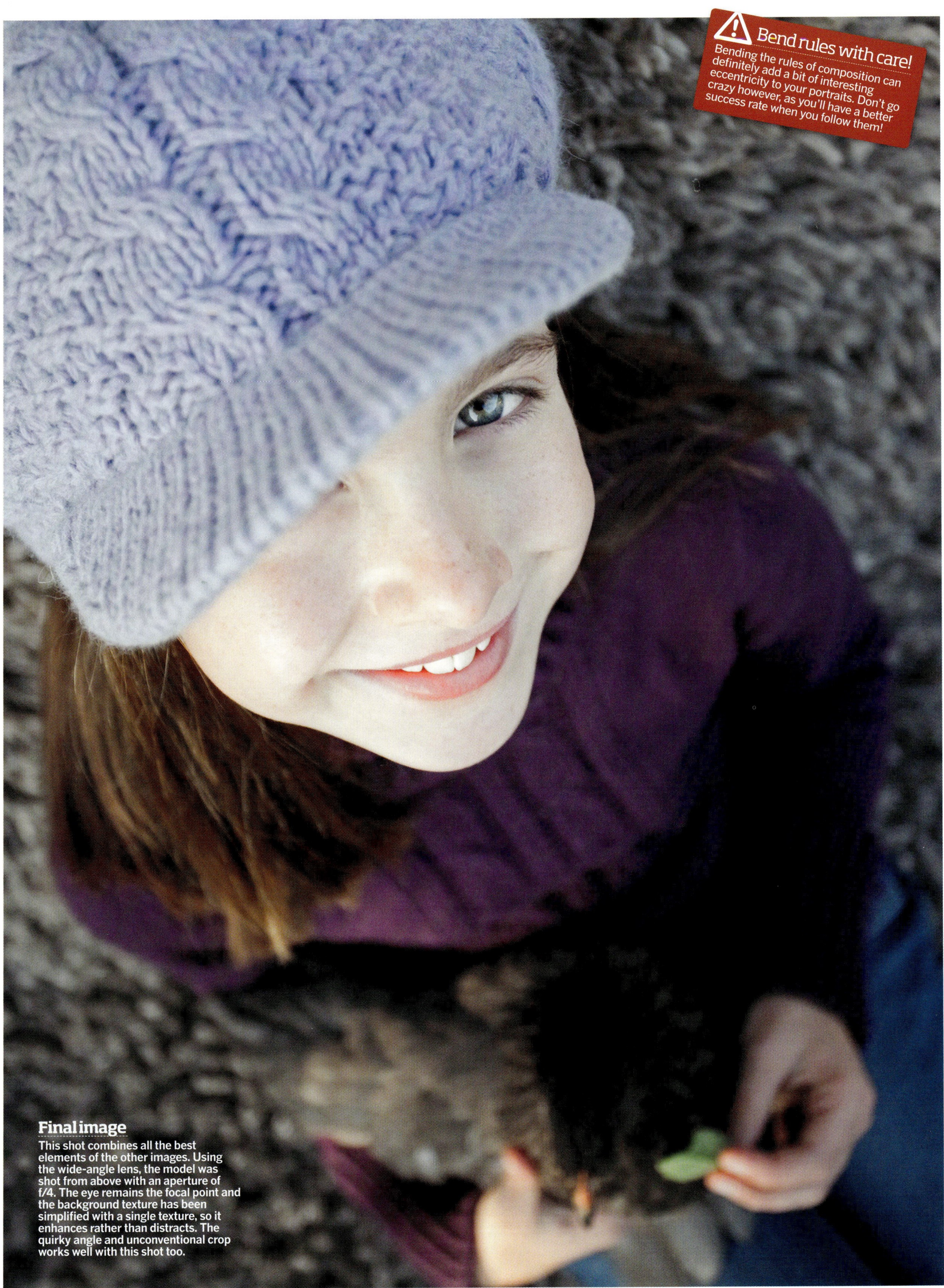

Final image

This shot combines all the best elements of the other images. Using the wide-angle lens, the model was shot from above with an aperture of f/4. The eye remains the focal point and the background texture has been simplified with a single texture, so it enhances rather than distracts. The quirky angle and unconventional crop works well with this shot too.

Focusing fundamentals

While the autofocus systems of digital SLRs are highly responsive, we can help to improve their accuracy

AUTOFOCUS IS ONE OF THOSE THINGS that all photographers take for granted at one time or another. Half-press the shutter release and it does its job quickly and quietly. While everything is working well, you don't really need to think about what's happening and why, but taking control of the autofocus (AF) can help you improve, especially when your DSLR struggles to interpret what you are trying to do. Understanding how this highly advanced technology works will ultimately help you to use it more effectively in your photography.

HOW AUTOFOCUS SYSTEMS WORK

There are two main kinds of autofocus system used in modern cameras: contrast detection AF and phase detection AF. In DSLRs, the latter of these is used most of the time. Phase detection AF works by taking some of the light entering the camera through the lens, splitting it into two and directing it onto a pair of sensors. The point where it hits the sensors tells the camera if the image is in focus or not, and if not by how much it's out and in what direction. This means that the camera can find the correct focus very quickly. The downside of phase detection AF is that it needs contrast in order to work. Point your camera at a blank wall and the system simply won't function.

Phase detection AF also requires a DSLR's mirror to be down, meaning it doesn't work so well in Live View mode. This is when we need contrast detection AF – the same system that is used in compact cameras. It works by continuously monitoring the overall contrast in a scene while focusing, the idea being that an image has the most contrast when it's at its sharpest. It's a slower method, suited to tripod-mounted work where speed isn't so important.

AUTOFOCUS MODES

DSLRs have two popular AF modes. The first, and perhaps the most useful, is Single-Shot AF (know as One-Shot on Canon EOS DSLRs). In this mode, you typically press halfway down on your camera's shutter release to engage AF. Once this has happened, focus is locked at this distance until you release the button and half-press it again. Single-Shot AF mode also prevents the shutter firing unless the subject is in focus. Continuous autofocus mode, on the other hand, will let the shutter fire at any point regardless of whether the scene is in focus or not, and will carry on focusing even when your finger is half-pressing the shutter button. It's the mode best suited to photographing moving subjects, as we'll see shortly. While we are on the subject of focus modes, it's worth mentioning good-old manual mode too. There are times when autofocus is simply not the best option, and focusing manually produces better results, such as with night photography, where low light confuses AF, and macro, where focusing is so critical that it is often best to focus manually.

MULTI-POINT AUTOFOCUS

Early AF systems used a single sensor at the centre of the frame. DSLRs now have multiple AF points grouped centrally and occupying up to half the frame. The advantage of this is that you're not limited to focusing on whatever is in the middle of a scene, allowing the AF system to comfortably handle off-centre subjects or objects that are moving around in the frame.

The most focusing points in a DSLR is currently 51 (Nikon) but the average is around 11. Shoot with all points activated and the camera will focus on what is closest to you – handy in most situations, but with portraits, can result in the lens focusing on the tip of the nose rather than the eyes. You usually have the option of reducing the number of active focus points, which increases focus speed precision and allows you to focus on a precise point.

Not all focus points are the same either, in fact there are two distinct types. Line-type sensors are the most common, but least sensitive. They are oriented in one direction only (usually top-to-bottom) and need to be looking at detail that crosses them perpendicularly (left-to-right) to focus accurately. Cross-type sensors look for detail in both directions, and are faster and more sensitive. The central focus point will usually be a cross-type sensor, though more advanced DSLRs often have a number of them clustered together.

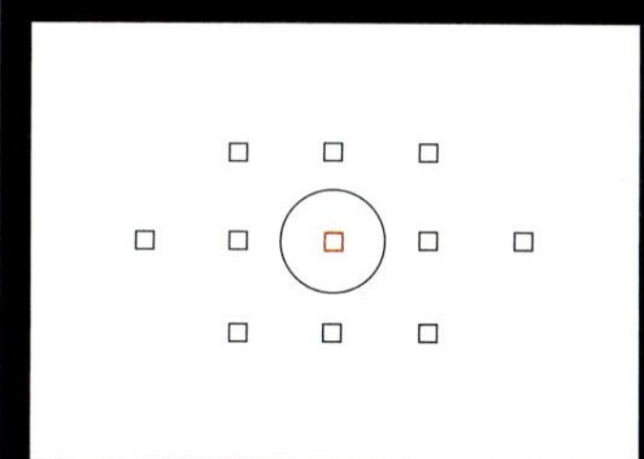

Single-point AF

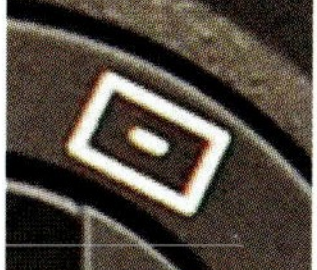

Select single-point AF and focus precisely on your chosen subject. Choosing the central point is usually best.

Multi-point AF

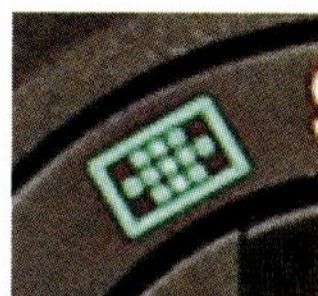

Multi-point AF activates all the sensors and usually focuses on whatever is closest to you. It's ideal for tracking subjects such as a child running.

Setting autofocus modes on your DSLR

Selecting the autofocus mode and the number of active AF points differs from camera to camera. Here's we show how it works on five popular models from the leading brands – you'll find your DSLR works in a similar way

CANON EOS 500D

AF MODE: Press the AF button (located on the right side of the four-way control) and choose from One Shot, AI Focus or AI Servo mode.

AF POINTS: Press the AF point selection button on the top right of the rear of the camera and use the input dial by the shutter release button to choose the AF point.

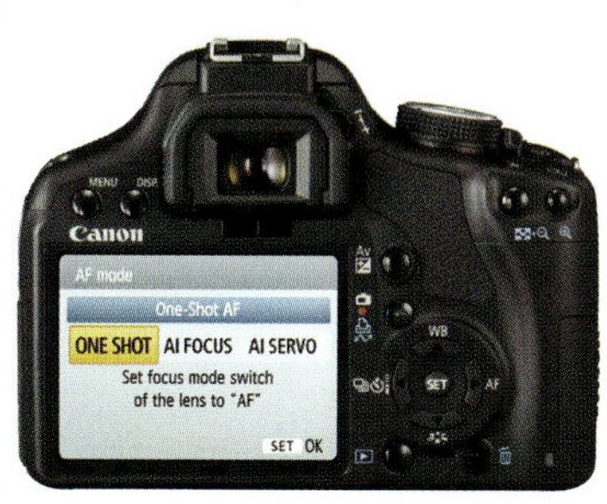

NIKON D60

AF MODE: Press the info button (bottom left of LCD) and scroll to Focus mode. Use the four-way control and OK button to select AF-A, AF-S, AF-C or manual focus.

AF POINTS: Press the info button and scroll down to the AF-area mode option. Choose between Closest Subject, Dynamic Area where you can select a focus point for tracking, or Single Point.

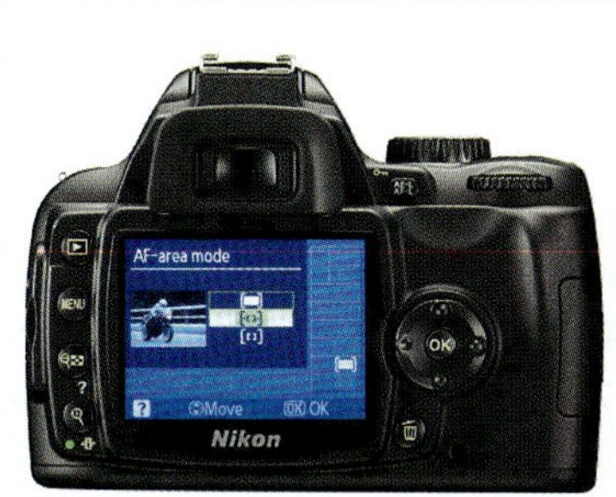

OLYMPUS E-420

AF MODE: Press OK and scroll to the AF mode option. Press OK again and choose between S-AF (single-shot AF), C-AF (continuous AF) and MF (manual focus).

AF POINTS: Press OK and scroll to the AF Area option. You can then use the command dial to select all the AF points or select an individual point.

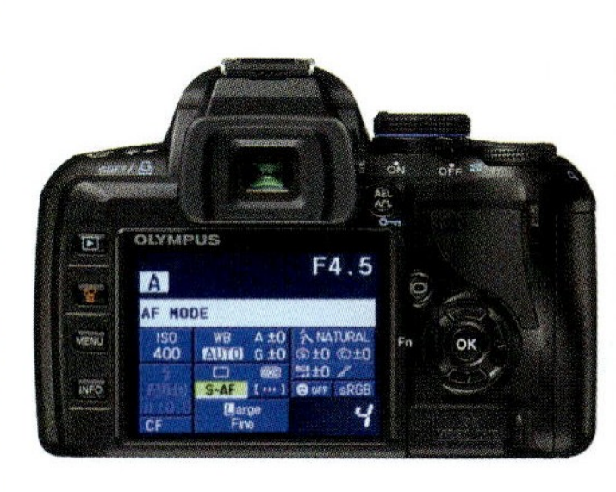

PENTAX K200D

AF MODE: Press the MENU button and use the four way control to select AF Mode. AF.S is the single-shot AF mode, while AF.C is continuous AF mode.

AF POINTS: Press the MENU button and use the four-way control to go down to Select AF point. Choose from Auto, multi-point or spot AF (the camera uses the central AF point only.

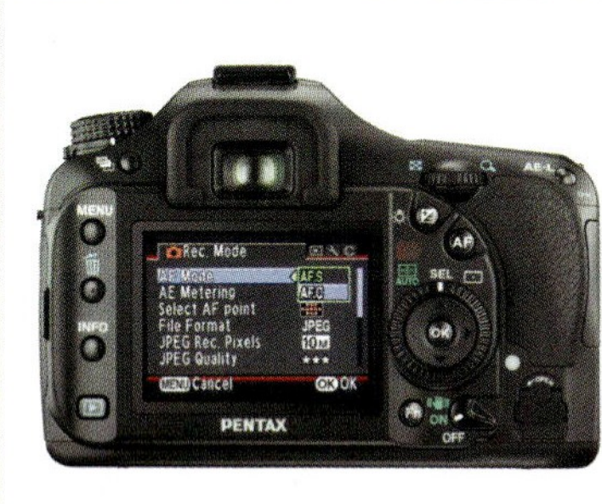

SONY ALPHA 350

AF MODE: Press Fn and choose the Autofocus mode option using the four way control. Choose between AF-S AF-A or AF-C mode.

AF POINTS: Press the Fn button and then choose the AF area option using the four-way control. Choose between Wide (all points), Spot (centre point) and Local (manual selection of any AF point).

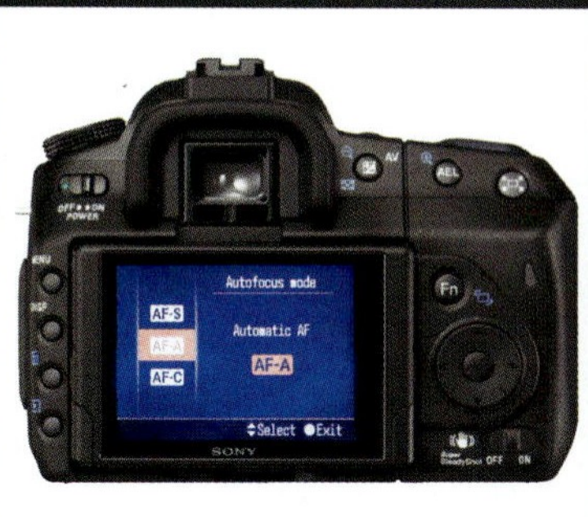

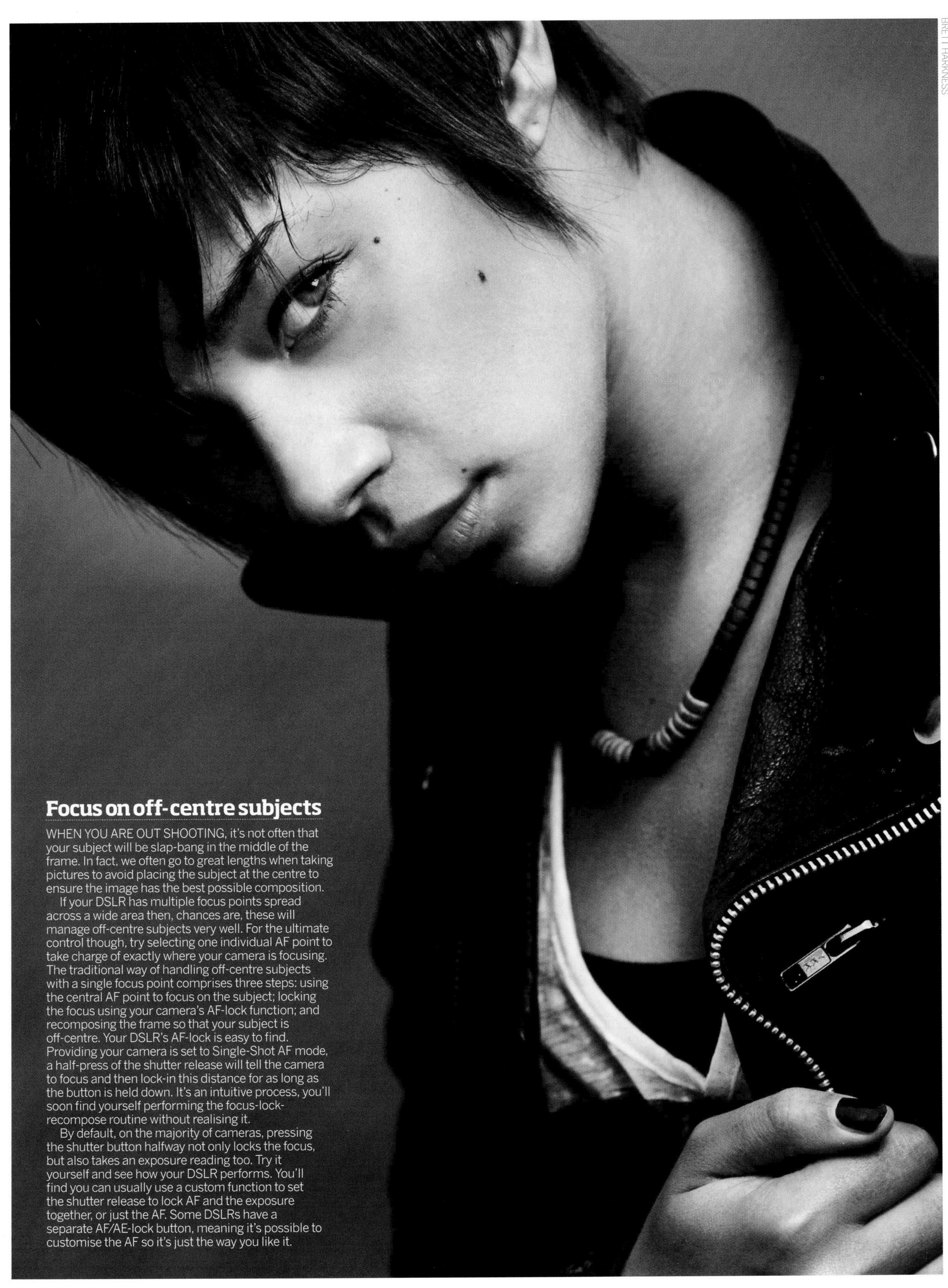

BRETT HARKNESS

Focus on off-centre subjects

WHEN YOU ARE OUT SHOOTING, it's not often that your subject will be slap-bang in the middle of the frame. In fact, we often go to great lengths when taking pictures to avoid placing the subject at the centre to ensure the image has the best possible composition.

If your DSLR has multiple focus points spread across a wide area then, chances are, these will manage off-centre subjects very well. For the ultimate control though, try selecting one individual AF point to take charge of exactly where your camera is focusing. The traditional way of handling off-centre subjects with a single focus point comprises three steps: using the central AF point to focus on the subject; locking the focus using your camera's AF-lock function; and recomposing the frame so that your subject is off-centre. Your DSLR's AF-lock is easy to find. Providing your camera is set to Single-Shot AF mode, a half-press of the shutter release will tell the camera to focus and then lock-in this distance for as long as the button is held down. It's an intuitive process, you'll soon find yourself performing the focus-lock-recompose routine without realising it.

By default, on the majority of cameras, pressing the shutter button halfway not only locks the focus, but also takes an exposure reading too. Try it yourself and see how your DSLR performs. You'll find you can usually use a custom function to set the shutter release to lock AF and the exposure together, or just the AF. Some DSLRs have a separate AF/AE-lock button, meaning it's possible to customise the AF so it's just the way you like it.

Use depth-of-field to give your portraits much more impact

By altering your shooting distance, being creative with your focusing and thinking about your choice of aperture, you stand a great chance of make your portraits outstanding

THERE ARE FEW, IF ANY, MORE rewarding feelings in photography than capturing a portrait that not only pleases you, but has the subject over the moon with how they look in the shot. Most people have had their picture taken, but few get the chance to have their portrait shot. There is a subtle difference to the two: one is a quick snap, with little attention given to anything but basic composition and the other is far more creative and carefully considered.

It's often said that a good portrait captures a little bit of the person's personality and it's true. But what it also does is record the sitter in a different way to other pictures taken of them. By using a couple of simple techniques based around depth-of-field and focusing, you can produce distinctive results, as you will discover shortly.

The general rule for portraits is that you should focus on the eyes and set a wide aperture (usually at least f/5.6) to throw the background out of focus, while keeping the face sharp. The 'f/5.6 rule' is one that is used frequently and successfully by many professional lifestyle photographers, who like to work fast and prefer to concentrate on their interaction with the subject rather than changing settings. If you want to include more of the environment, however, in the frame, a smaller aperture (usually coupled with a wider lens) is required to keep the background, as well as the subject, in sharp focus.

While ambient light is quite often sufficient – and sometimes ideal – you should also consider using studioflash. As well as allowing you to control the direction of the light, you can adjust the intensity to provide the exact amount of light you need for any given aperture. Once you learn how to use it correctly, a one or two-light set-up can also open up scope for creative opportunities.

Portraits can look exceptionally flattering when the zone of sharpness is extremely shallow. The easiest way to do this is to follow all the 'tricks' that are required to give an image the shallowest depth-of-field, namely using a telezoom set to the maximum aperture with a relatively short shooting distance. The result is a tight crop of the face where, bar a small focused area, much of the frame is thrown out of focus. The result is a very 'soft' image that, with some thought given to lighting, can look romantic if lit by diffused light, or more arty and striking if used with strong directional light. When using this technique, be sure to focus on the appropriate part of the face, usually an eye but sometimes the mouth, depending on where you want the viewer's gaze drawn to. It's certainly worth giving it a go with a friend or family member and seeing how you get on.

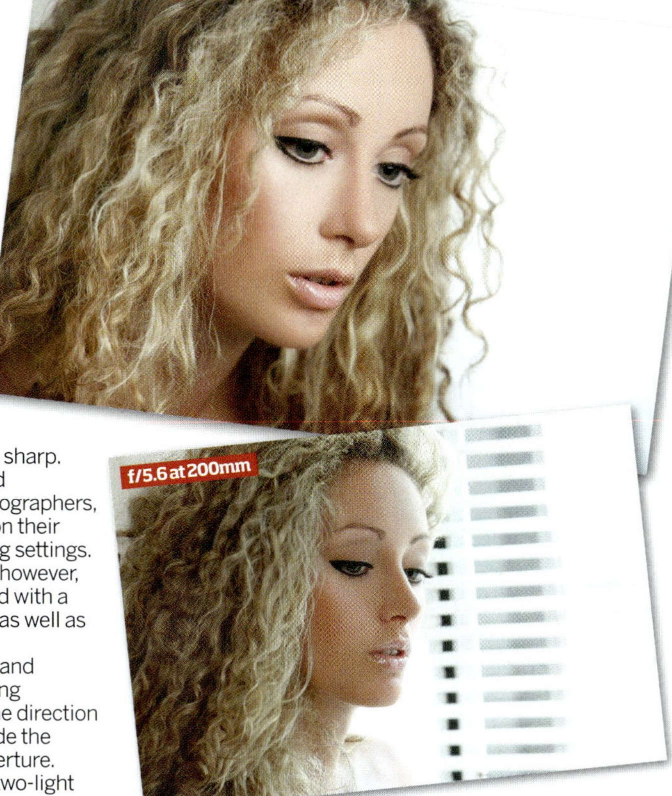

f/5.6 at 200mm

f/5.6 at 200mm

SHOOTING DISTANCE
Both shots were taken using the same lens and aperture, but depth-of-field was altered by changing the shooting distance. The shorter distance gives less depth-of-field, which blurs the window blinds.

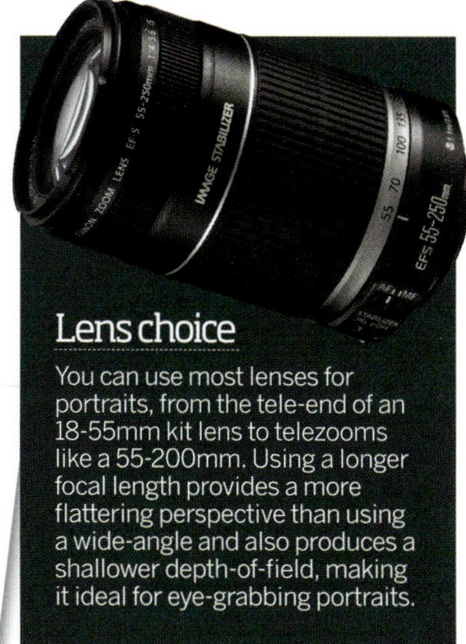

Lens choice

You can use most lenses for portraits, from the tele-end of an 18-55mm kit lens to telezooms like a 55-200mm. Using a longer focal length provides a more flattering perspective than using a wide-angle and also produces a shallower depth-of-field, making it ideal for eye-grabbing portraits.

Portrait top tips

1) SHOOT HANDHELD It will enable you to move more freely and frame quicker. Better still, use a monopod. Using the maximum aperture provides the fastest possible shutter speed, but if it's still low, use the image stabiliser if your DSLR or lens has it and/or raise the ISO rating.

2) CHECK YOUR DISTANCE At very wide apertures, you have to be careful not to move forward or backward after focusing as this will lead to an unsharp shot.

3) EYE CONTACT Ensure that the subject's eyes are clean and make-up has been carefully applied. Try some shots with the subject looking into the lens and others with them looking away.

4) USE THE SHADOWS Pay attention to the lighting and to where the shadows fall, as they can add drama to an image.

5) CONSIDER MONO It's always worth converting portraits to black & white and seeing how they compare to colour images.

Differential focusing

Another popular technique when using shallow depth-of-field is differential focusing. It's a simple one to master but the secret is knowing when to use it. The basic principle is to use a very wide aperture to emphasise a particular subject within the frame by having it in focus while the rest of the scene (background or foreground) is out of focus. It's particularly effective when there is a lot of depth in the scene and you're using a wide aperture that blurs elements in the frame to the point that it's still recognisable. Use it to pick out a particular person in a crowd or to produce a creative portrait with a story to tell.

HIDE AND SEEK: These images illustrate the effect differential focusing has on an image. The same exposure was used in both shots but the focus was changed to reveal different elements in the scene.

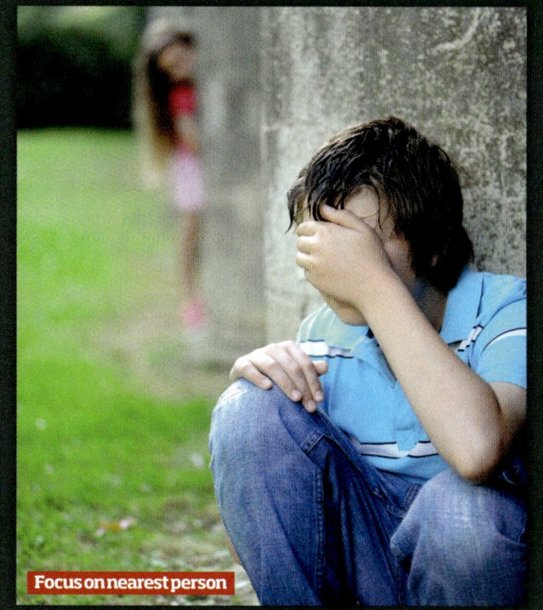

Focus on nearest person

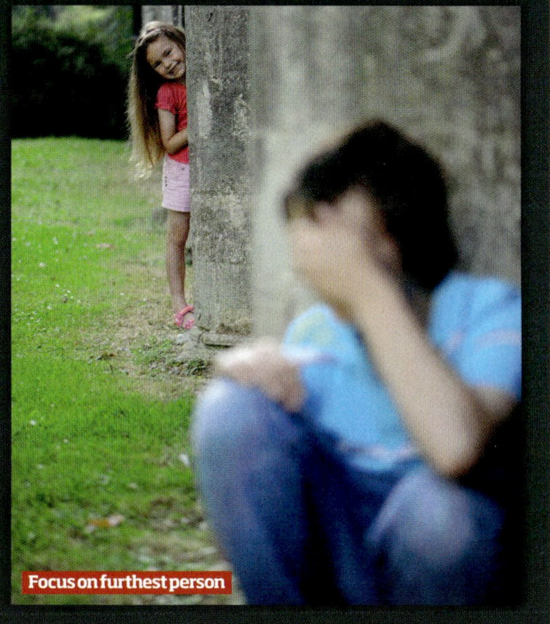

Focus on furthest person

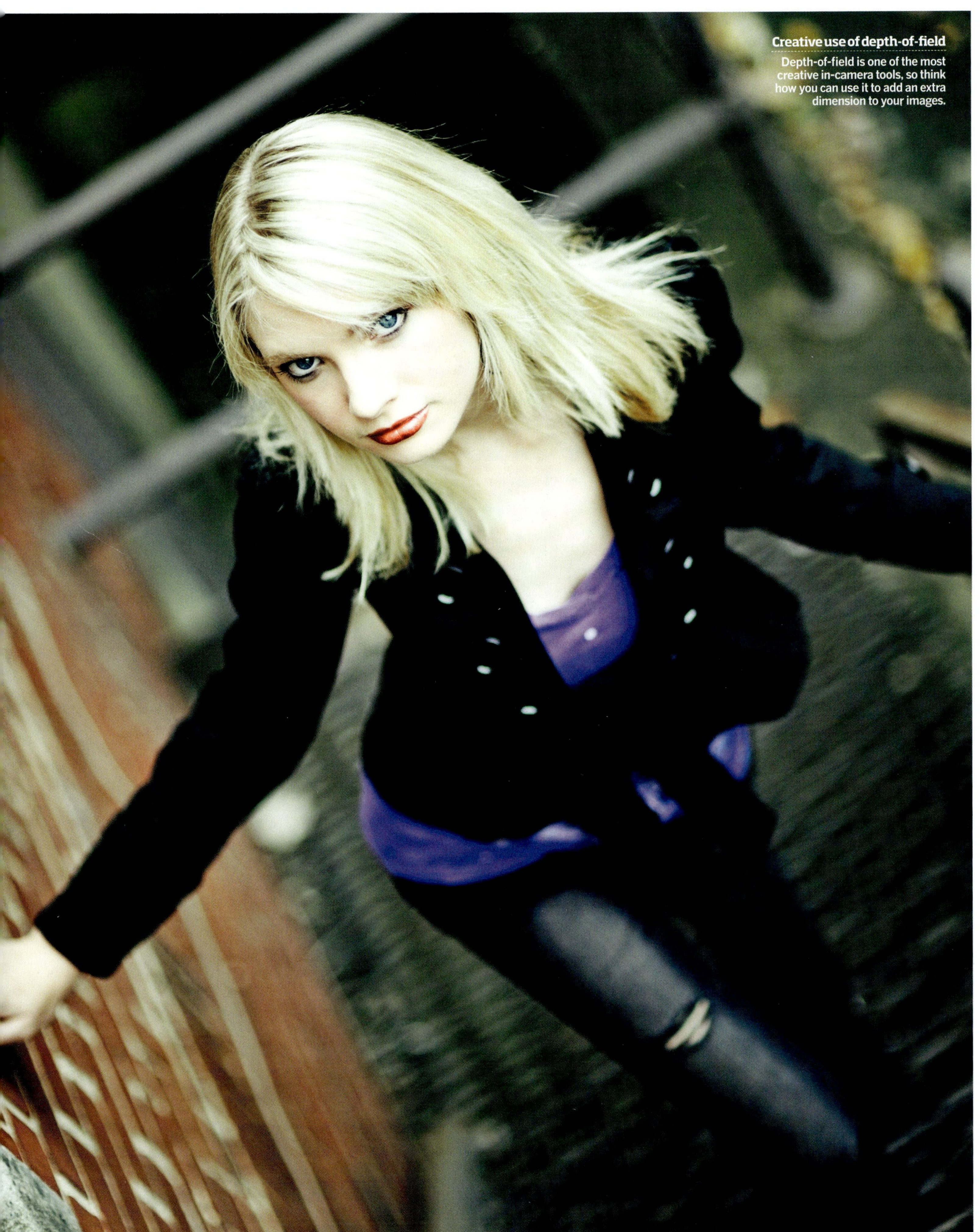

Creative use of depth-of-field

Depth-of-field is one of the most creative in-camera tools, so think how you can use it to add an extra dimension to your images.

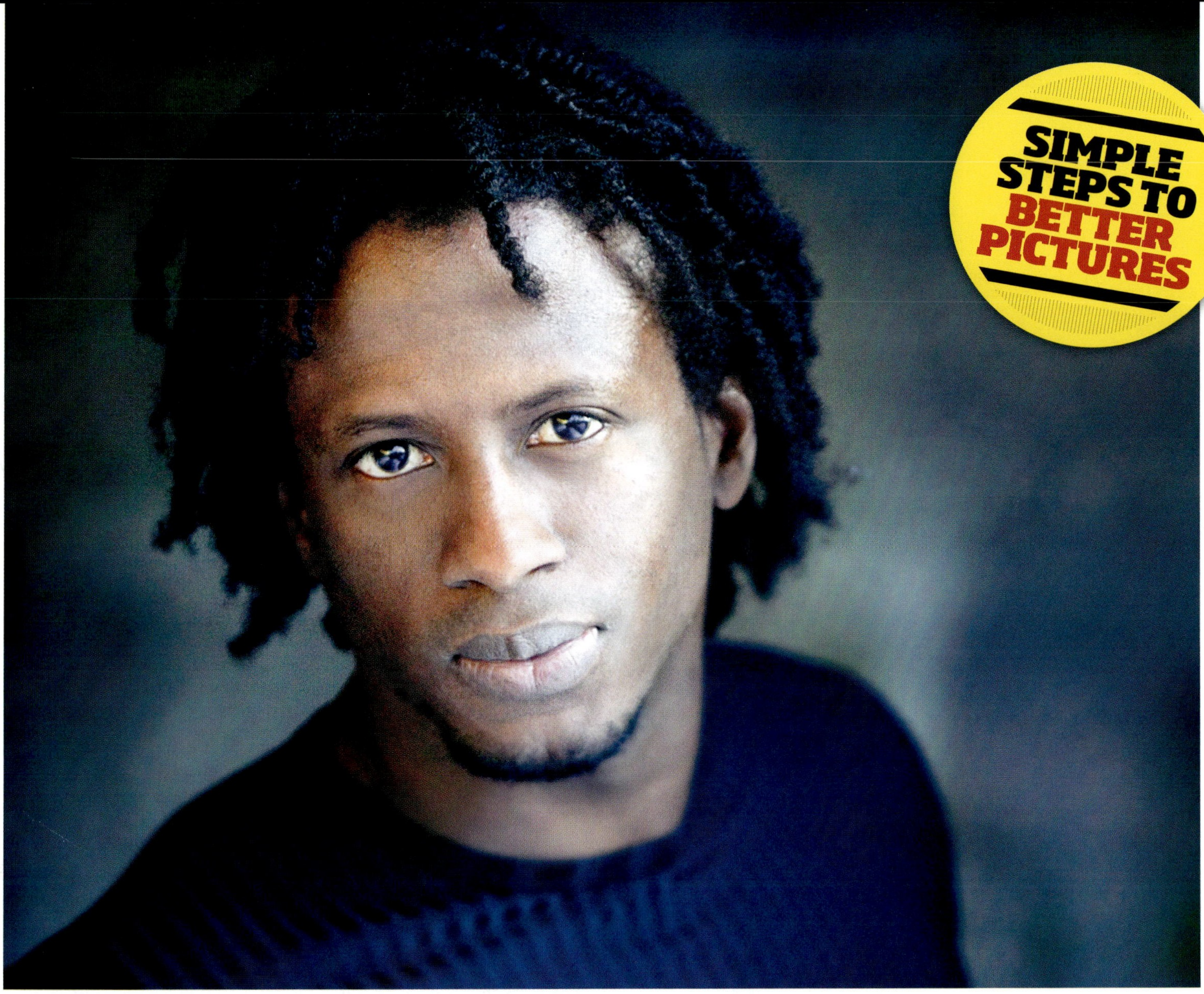

SIMPLE STEPS TO BETTER PICTURES

PORTRAIT LIGHTING

ESSENTIAL ADVICE & TECHNIQUES THAT WILL HELP YOU TO CONTROL LIGHT LIKE A PRO

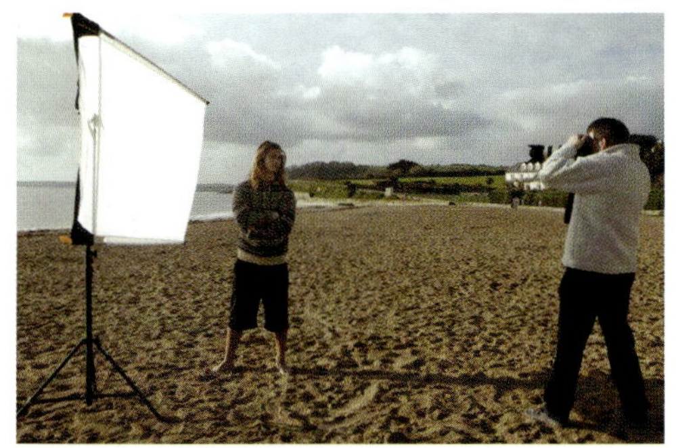

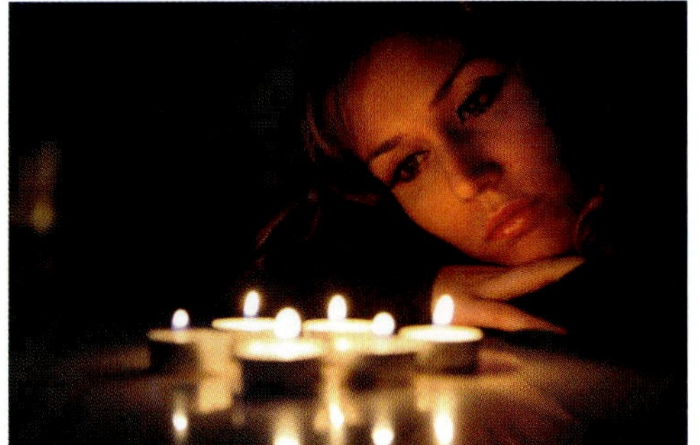

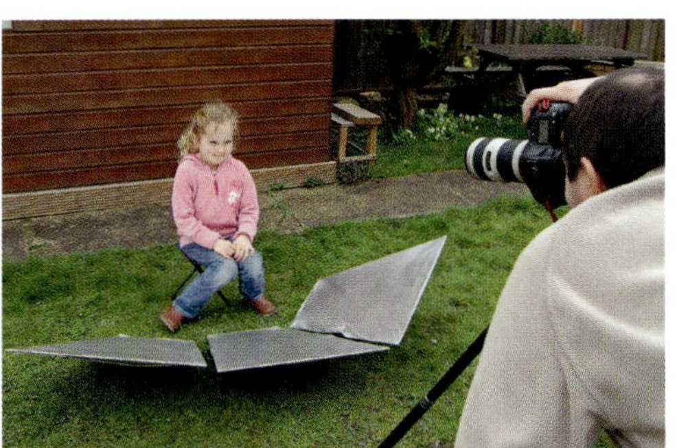

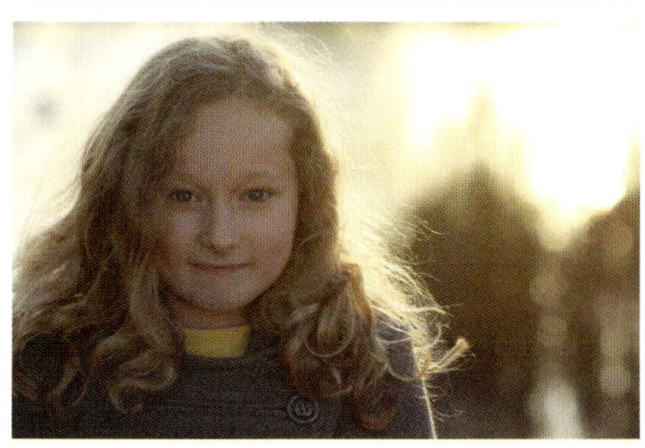

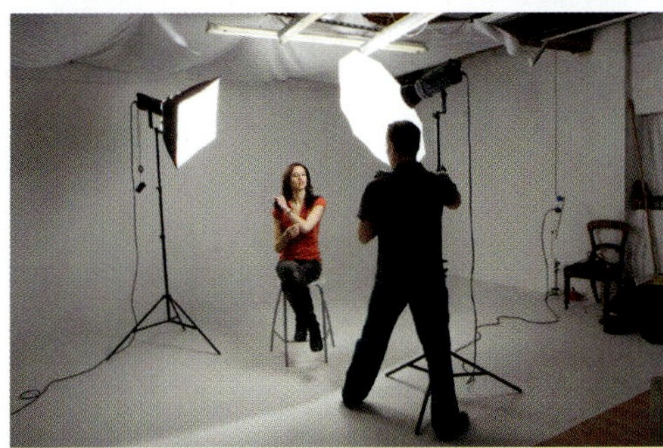

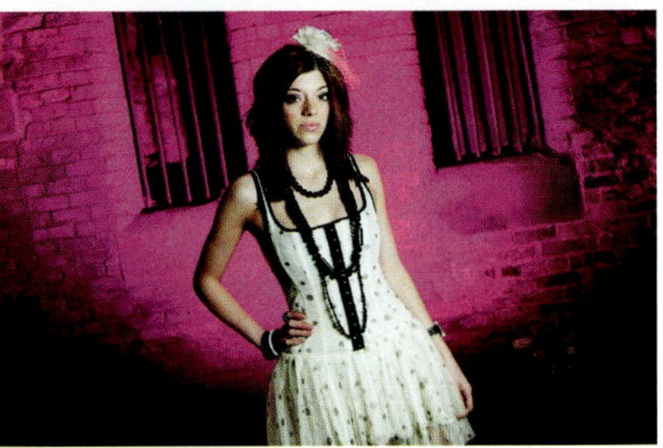

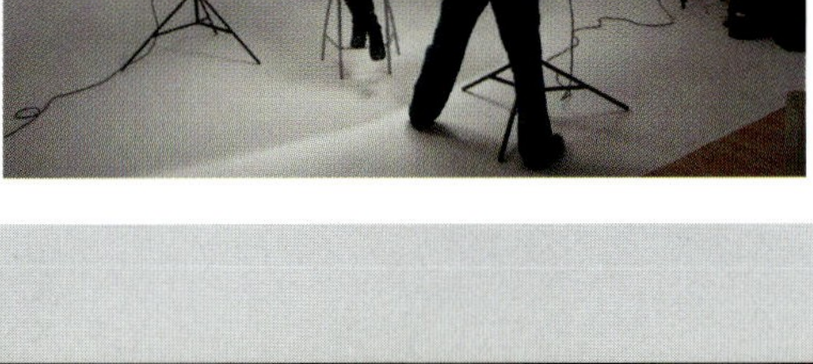

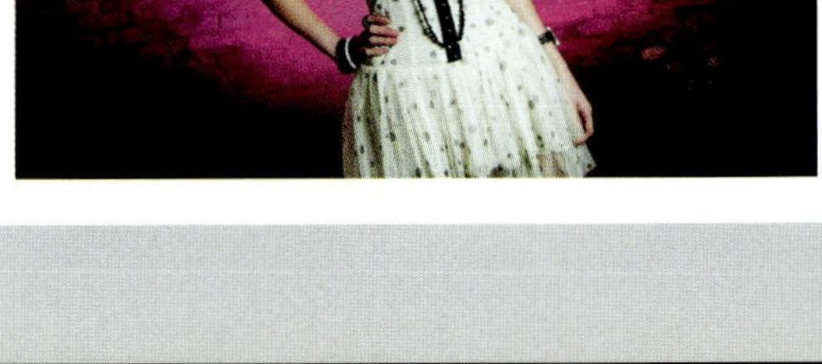

How to control daylight

Understanding how to manipulate available light is an essential skill for the portrait photographer to master

WORKING WITH DAYLIGHT has several advantages and disadvantages for the portrait photographer compared to artificial light sources such as studioflash and flashguns. Daylight is incredibly versatile: the range of images that are possible, depending on the weather and the time of day, and the wide variety of lighting effects are tremendous. And, lets not forget it's free! However, unfortunately, available light – as it's often termed – has the problem of also being unavailable – both at night or on days of particularly poor weather when light levels are too low to justify the effort. One of the most wonderful things about working with daylight is that it allows you the chance to shoot outdoors in literally any location. Whether it's in the local park, a scrapyard or down by the coast, the options for great daylight portraits are limited only by your imagination and the ability you have to control daylight. And in the respect of the latter, despite the light source being millions of miles away, you still have plenty of control over how daylight falls on the subject, simply through the use of basic lighting aids such as reflectors and diffusers. Over the course of the following pages we'll show you how using the most basic of lighting accessories and techniques can transform your daylight portraits. As you'll discover, compared to shooting a straightforward snap, the extra effort required to place your subject correctly and use a lighting aid is minimal, but the difference it makes to the final images will be evident. So invest in a reflector or two and, should you be really keen on shooting outdoor portraits, buy a diffuser too, they'll really help to improve your portrait pictures.

Setting up your DSLR for daylight portraits

EXPOSURE Before you head outdoors, take a minute to prepare your DSLR so once you're on location, you can begin shooting without delay. Firstly, you should set your camera to aperture-priority mode, as you'll want to ensure that the depth-of-field is limited. We'd recommend you start by shooting at f/5.6. If shutter speeds are low enough to risk shake, raise the ISO rating to 400 and switch on image stabilisation if you have it.

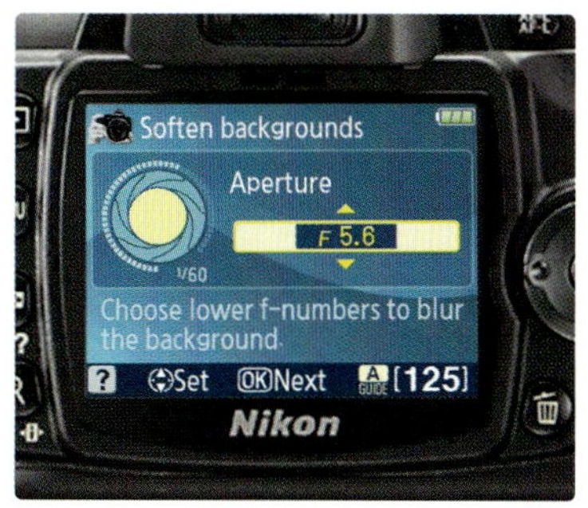

METERING In terms of metering, you should find the multi-zone pattern to be perfectly adequate, but if you're shooting a dark-skinned person close-up, be prepared to add one to two stops exposure compensation.

FOCUSING We'd suggest you switch from multi-point AF to central-point focus as otherwise you risk focusing on the subject's brows or nose, rather than the eyes. Point the central AF point over the eye and half-depress the shutter button to lock focus, then recompose and shoot.

ALSO CONSIDER... While you can shoot with the White Balance set to Auto (AWB), you're better off setting it once you've arrived at the scene to the most suitable preset, especially if you're shooting in JPEG only. We'd strongly recommend you shoot in Raw + JPEG, though; this way you can review the smaller JPEG images on your computer. Then open and process your Raw files for ultimate quality, including any adjustments to White Balance or exposure that you need to make.

Which lens is best?

Using a telephoto focal length, which flattens perspective, is the best choice as it gives the most flattering portraits. You can get away with using the tele-end of your standard zoom, but you'll find a telephoto zoom, such as a 55-200mm, is a far better choice. Alternatively, you could go 'old-school' and shoot with a prime lens such as a 50mm f/1.8 (effectively an 80mm with APS-C sensors), which has the advantage of a wider maximum aperture than zooms.

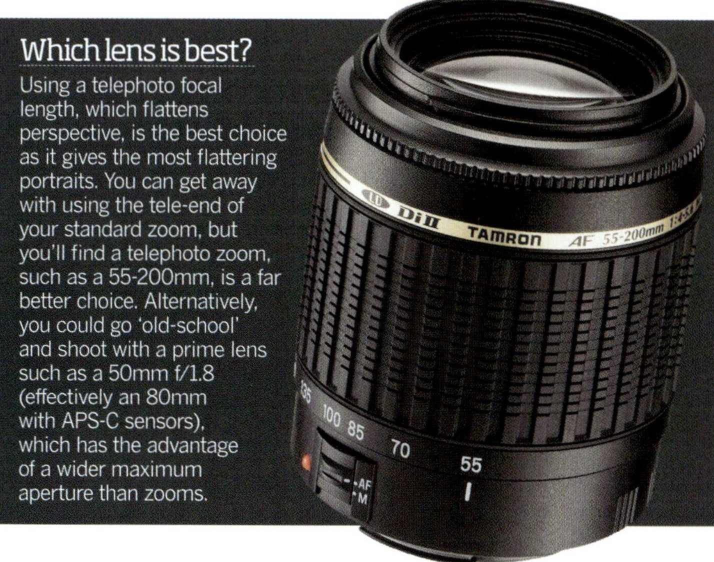

Setting your DSLR for daylight portraits

Select aperture priority, set the White Balance for the shooting conditions and centre-point AF. You're now ready to shoot!

CANON EOS 500D

1) Set the mode dial on the right of the top-plate to Av to select aperture-priority mode.

2) Press the WB button and use the four-way control to select White Balance. Select the WB preset you want to use and then press the OK button.

3) Press the AF points button and select central-point AF.

4) Press the AF button and set the AF mode to One Shot.

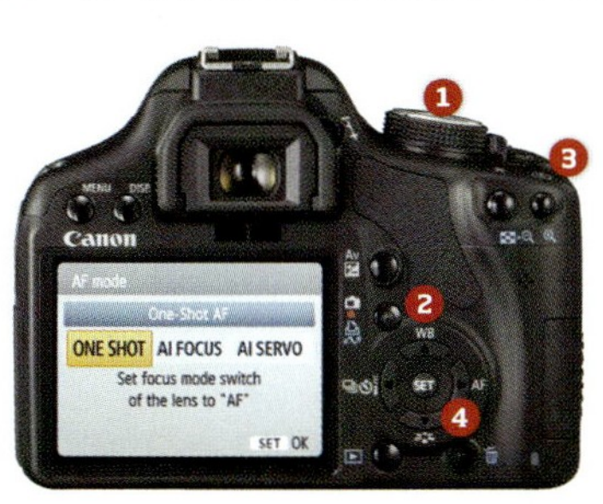

NIKON D60

1) Set the mode dial on the right of the top-plate to A to select aperture-priority mode.

2) Press the i button and use the four-way control to select White Balance. Select the WB preset you want to use and then press the OK button.

Press i again and set the AF mode to AF-S and the AF-area mode to central-point only.

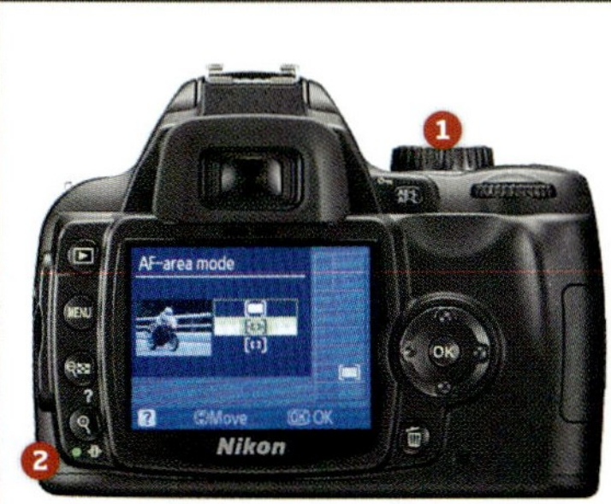

OLYMPUS E-420

1) Set the mode dial on the right of the top-plate to A to select aperture-priority mode.

2) Press the OK button and use the four-way control to select White Balance. Select the WB preset you want to use and then press the OK button.

Press OK again and set the AF mode to S-AF and the AF points to central-point only.

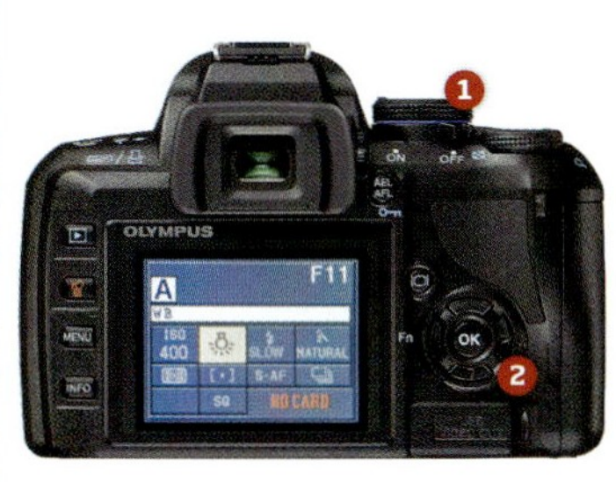

PENTAX K200D

1) Set the mode dial on the left of the top-plate to Av to select aperture-priority mode.

2) Press the OK button and use the four-way control to select White Balance. Select the WB preset you want to use and then press the OK button.

3) Press MENU, then select the Rec. Mode tab and set the AF mode to AF.S and then select the central AF point.

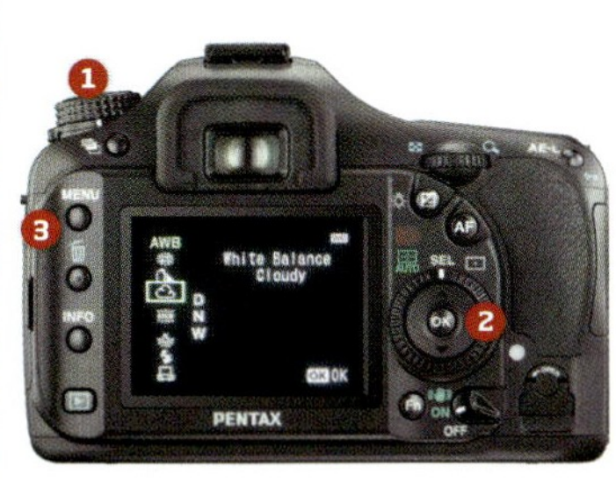

SONY ALPHA 200

1) Set the mode dial on the left of the top-plate to A to select aperture-priority mode.

2) Press the Fn button and use the four-way control to select White balance. Press the AF button and select the WB preset you want to use.

Now press the Fn button again, select Autofocus mode and select Spot in AF area and AF-S in Autofocus mode.

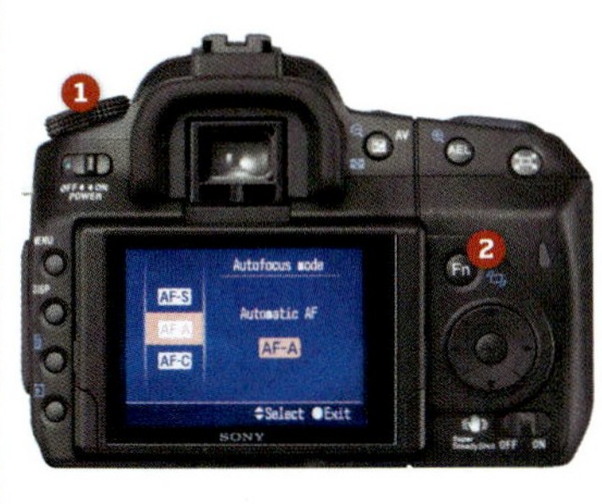

BRETT HARKNESS

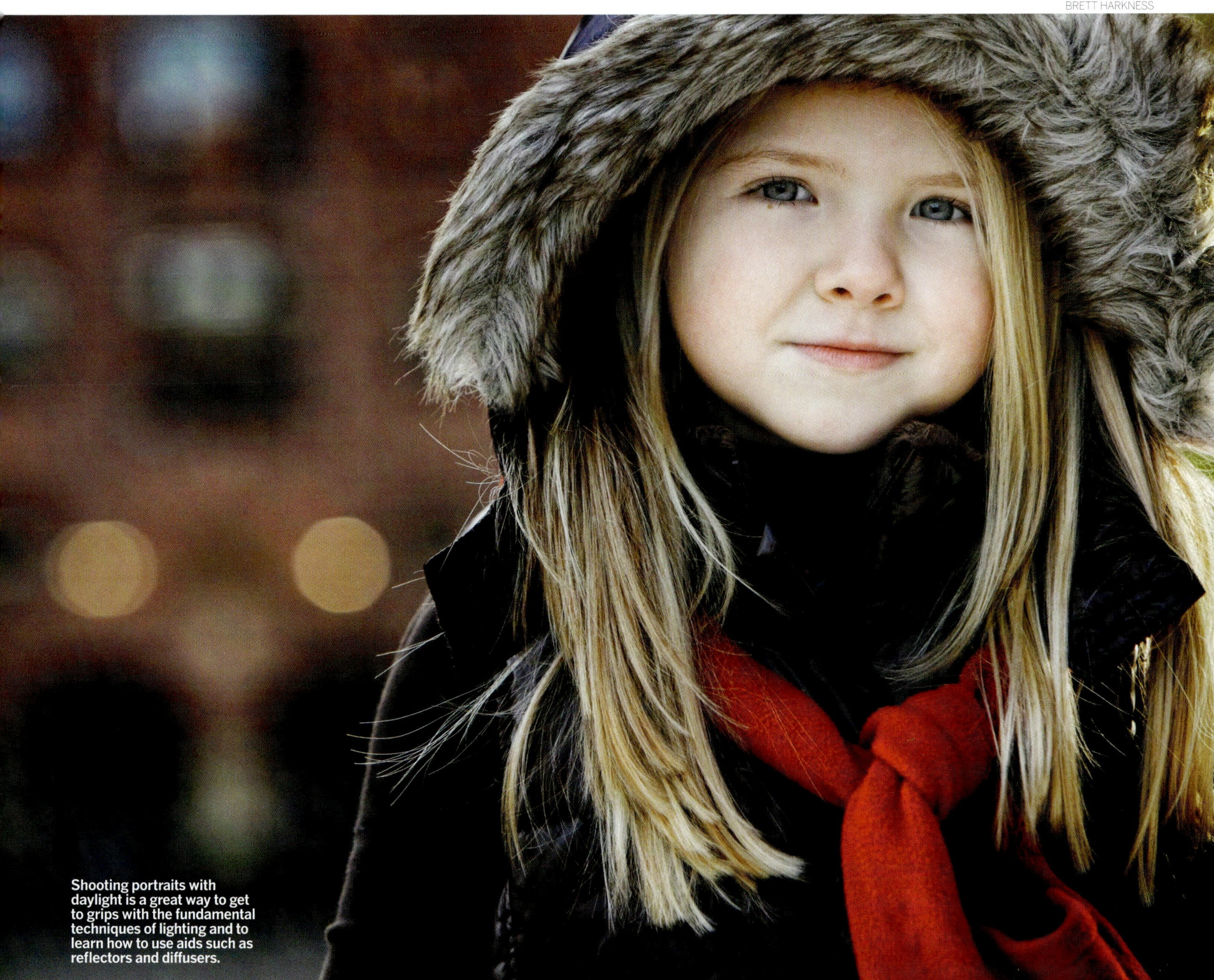

Shooting portraits with daylight is a great way to get to grips with the fundamental techniques of lighting and to learn how to use aids such as reflectors and diffusers.

Main lighting accessories for daylight portraits

When working with daylight, you don't have the level of control that studioflash allows with lighting direction and intensity. But while you can't control the sun itself, by using reflectors, diffusers or a combination of the two, you can control the amount of daylight reaching your subject. Reflectors and diffusers come in various forms, with the most common covered here.

REFLECTORS This simple accessory is incredibly effective at filling in shadows and can make a major improvement to your portraits. The standard type – and the one you should begin with – has a white side and a silver side (1). The white side reflects a clean, neutral light and is ideal when you can place it relatively close to the subject, as it reflects an even spread of light. The silver is far more efficient, producing a stronger result, so can be overpowering in bright sunlight or if placed too close to the subject, but is ideal in very overcast conditions or when shooting in shade. Gold reflectors are also available and like silver, are very efficient, but add a warm golden glow to the light. You should look for collapsible reflectors as they're light and easy to store away. The larger the reflector, the wider the area they cover – look for a minimum diameter of 80cm and don't go too big as they can be cumbersome to use. Those with grips, such as Lastolite's Tri-Grip, are great when you have no assistance, as you can hold it with one hand. Other reflectors to check out are those that come with a silver and gold slip-on sleeve (2) or those with a lightweight frame, such as the California Sunbounce (3).

Learning to control sunlight

Bjorn Thomassen explains how to control and manipulate daylight in sunny conditions to produce professional-looking portraits

IN MY OPINION, DAYLIGHT is the most exquisitely beautiful of all light sources. Unfortunately, it seldom provides us with exactly the type and quality of light we need at any one specific time. However, with a little knowledge of meteorology and by monitoring local forecasts, we can to a certain extent anticipate what time of the day will yield the best lighting conditions for an outdoor shoot. But, as we all know, the weather doesn't always conform to the forecaster's predictions, and even the best laid plans can sometimes give way to Mother Nature enforcing her stubborn will. I had to wait nearly a month to get a clear sunny day to shoot these portraits.

However, once the sun arrives, there are a number of techniques that allow us to control and manipulate the natural light that falls upon our subject. Diffusers and reflectors are our allies when it comes to taking control of strong sunlight, and I feel it is vital that you are well versed in the use of both, as this will enable you to tackle even the most challenging of lighting conditions.

A reflector does what it says on the tin – it reflects light and is ideal when you need to fill in shadows or maximise limited light. Reflectors also come in a wide range of shapes and sizes, and are made from a variety of materials of varying colours and reflectance values, so you have several options to suit your different lighting conditions.

Diffusers, on the other hand, soften and spread the light as it passes through, and again there is a wide range of diffusers of varying materials, and some have quite sophisticated applications. I hope this step by step will make it easier for you to manage direct sunlight and inspires you with some new ideas to further your portraiture. Outdoor lighting provides us with such exciting challenges and the diversity and range of lighting conditions ensures thousands of permutations and endless hours of exploration. Good luck!

Diffusers and reflectors

There are a number of essential lighting accessories that you should consider investing in if you're serious about shooting daylight portraits.

A diffuser should without a doubt be placed at the top of your list. Direct sunlight on your subject will result in very unflattering images due to the harshness of the light and the strong shadows it produces. Diffusers soften and control the amount of light on your subjects and make all the difference in strong sunlight. You can buy handheld diffusers but if you have no assistance, choose one that has its own stand – just be aware that they easily topple over in windy conditions.

You should also think about getting a couple of reflectors in different sizes to redirect light back on to the subject, or better still a 3-in-1 or a 5-in-1 reflector. Introducing a reflector will help fill in any shadows and enhance skin tones, as well as help shape the contours of the face. Reflectors also help to balance the foreground and background light levels. As with diffusers, you'll find reflectors available in a range of sizes and colours – white is my favourite, followed by silver (for stronger reflectance) and gold for a warmer tone. I'd recommend you check out Lastolite and California Sunbounce products. Always scout your location for in-situ reflectors and diffusers that can be used, such as white walls or trees that offer shade.

Shot 1

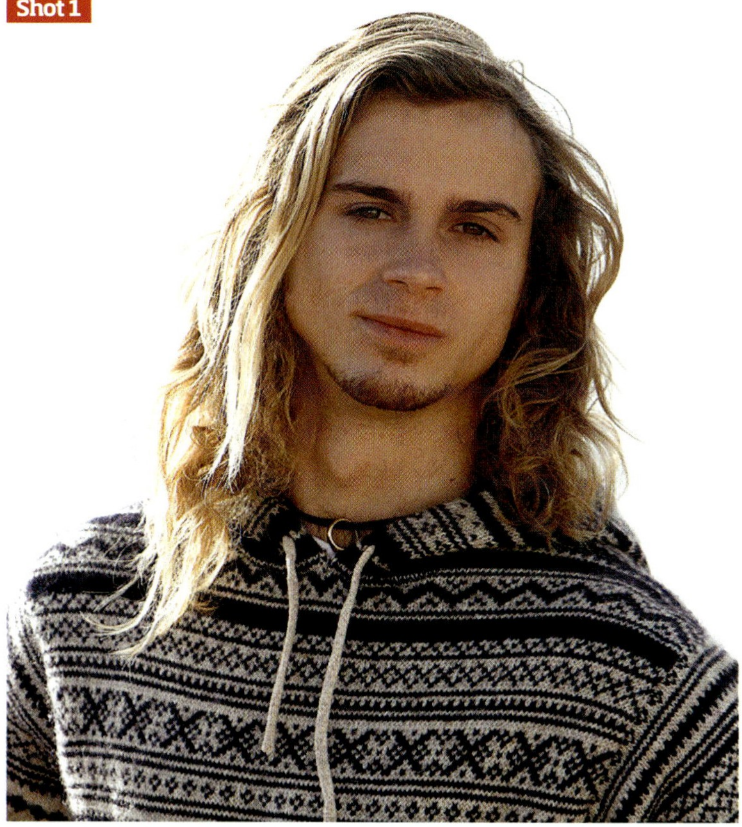

Set-up

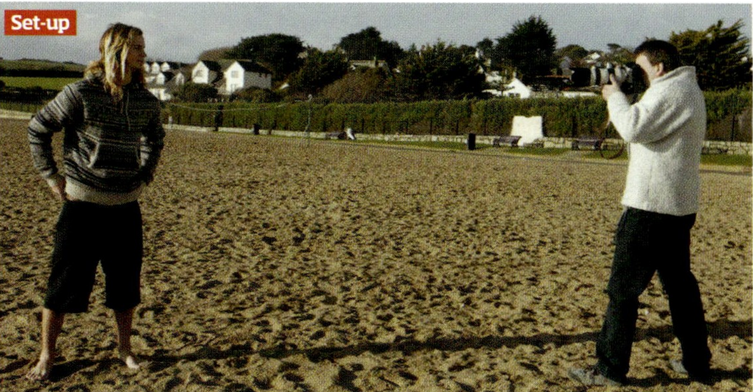

Shot 1 This shot was taken with very strongly backlighting and the lighting ratio, with Olly's face being in shade, contrasts heavily with the sunlight behind him. The camera struggled to get an accurate exposure, causing a loss in background detail and Olly's hair. The resulting bleached highlights are quite unappealing.

Shot 2

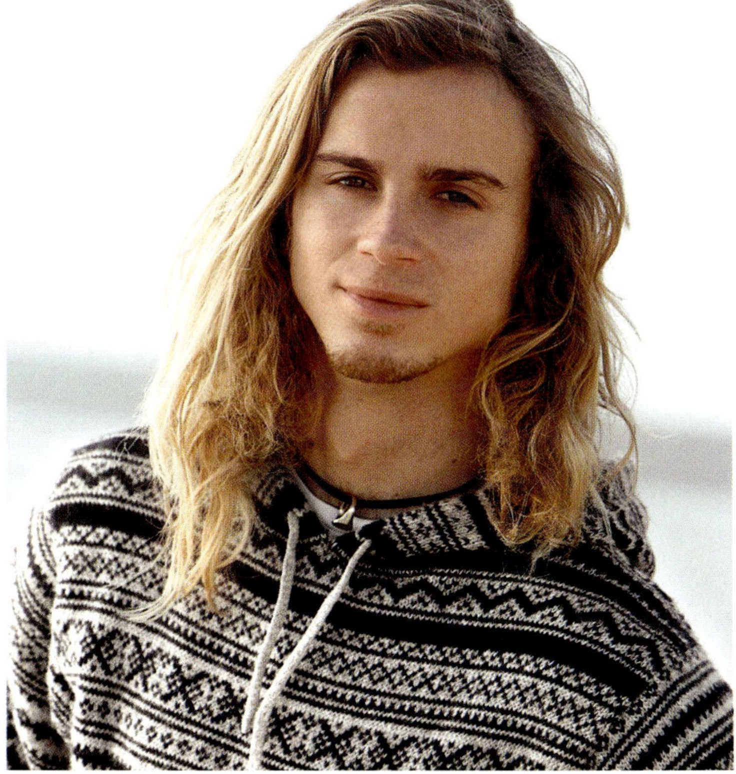

Set-up

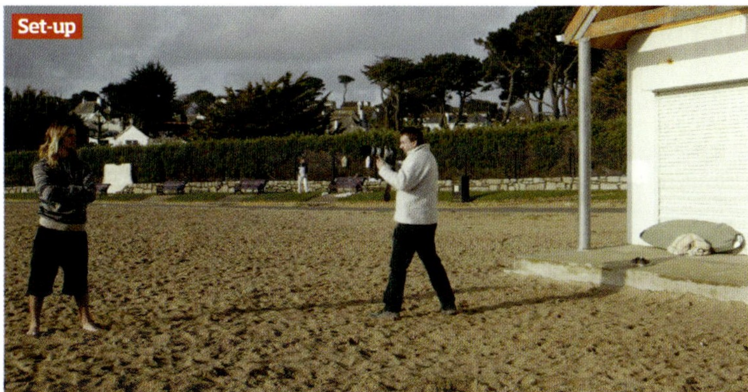

Shot 2 Shot within minutes of the first image, I asked Olly to move towards a large white building. The white wall acted as a very efficient reflector, bouncing light back onto his face and torso, filling in shadow and reducing the contrast to a more agreeable level, while holding detail in his hair.

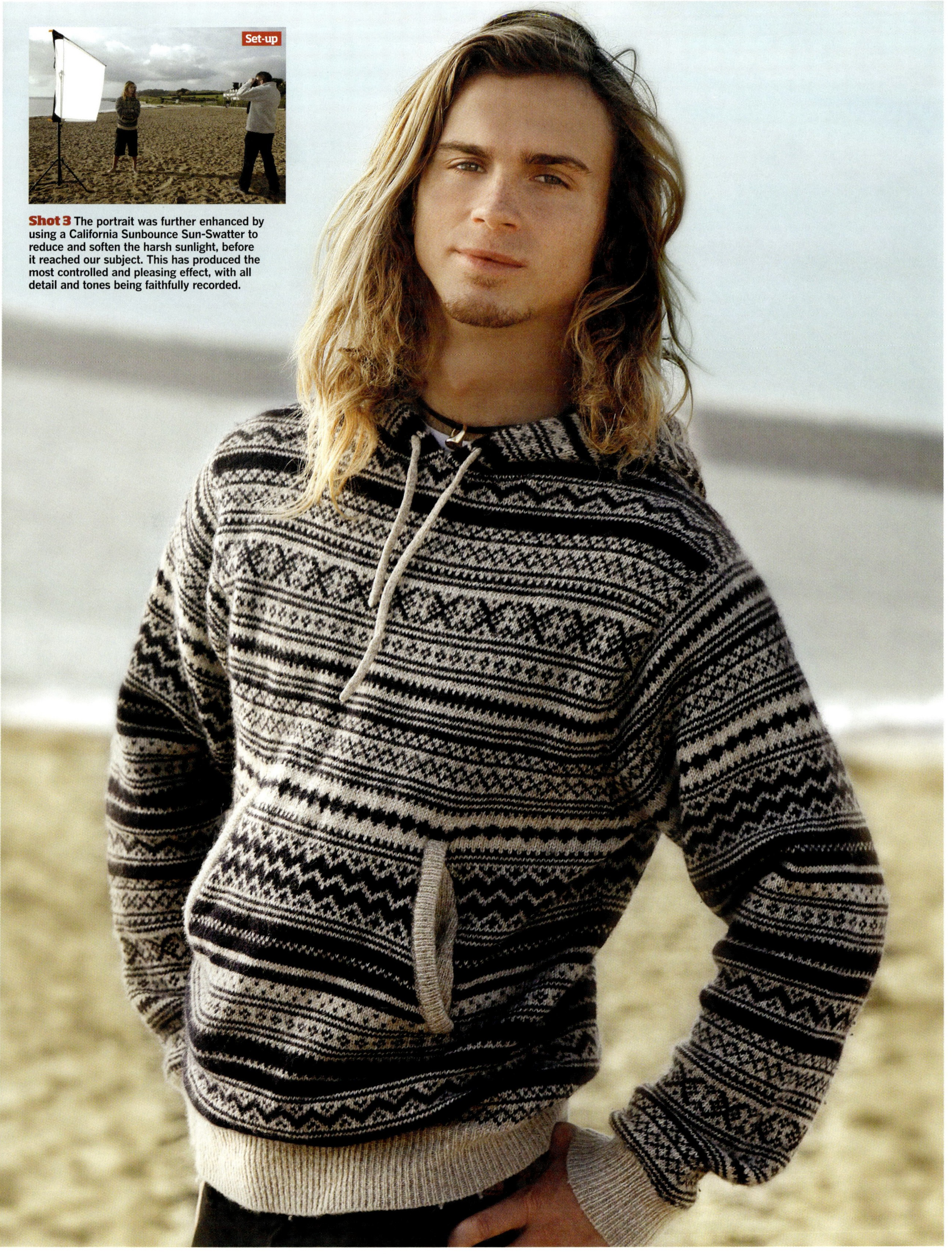

Shot 3 The portrait was further enhanced by using a California Sunbounce Sun-Swatter to reduce and soften the harsh sunlight, before it reached our subject. This has produced the most controlled and pleasing effect, with all detail and tones being faithfully recorded.

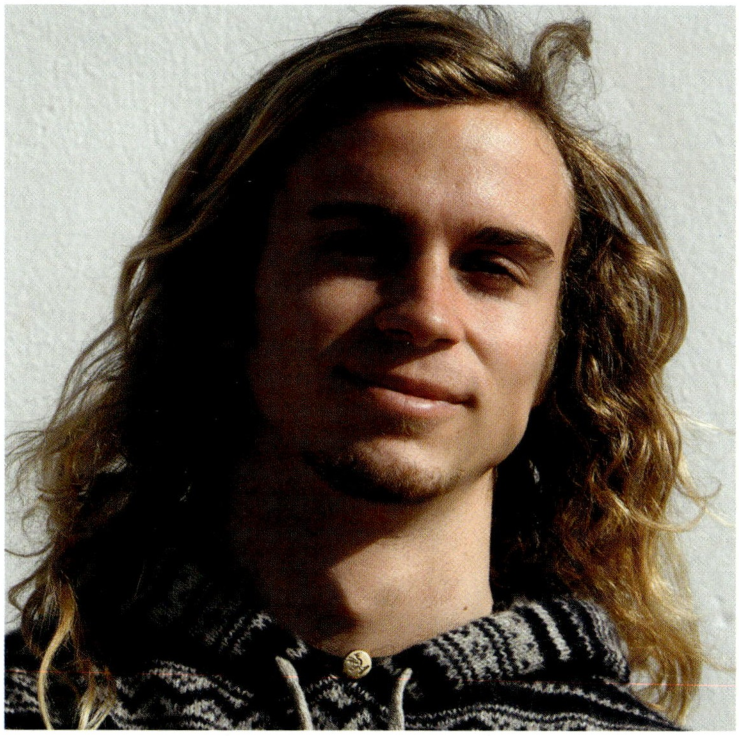

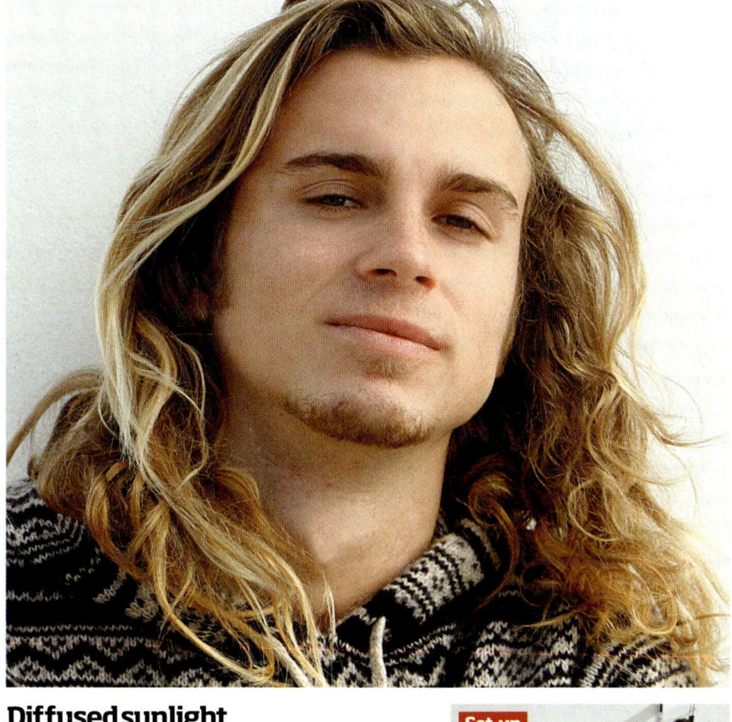

Strong direct sunlight

While most of us yearn for a warm and sunny day, sunshine can produce the most unflattering light for portraiture. Eye sockets are black holes, cheeks can be raised, and the blinding light forces the subject to squint. The contrast is generally harsh and unacceptable.

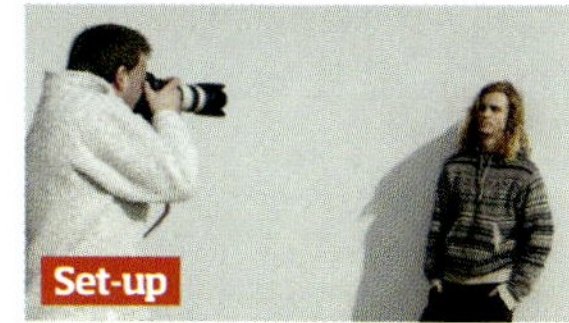

Diffused sunlight

With our subject in the same location, we softened and diffused the light using a California Sunbounce Sun-Swatter. Some light was also redirected back towards Olly using a Lastolite Triflector. This simple technique has produced a far more flattering light.

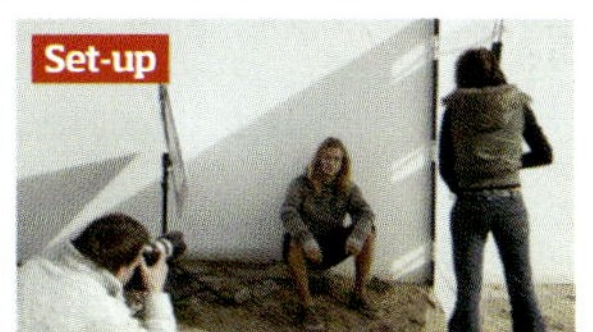

Set-up

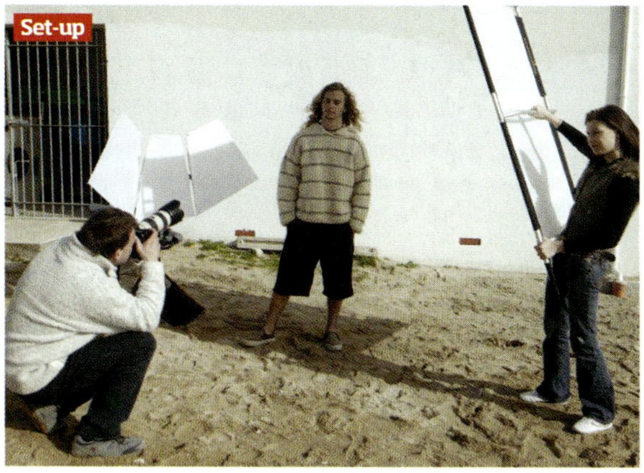

Triflector & California Sunbounce

Using the same diffuser and reflector as before, we asked Olly to take a few steps forward to move him a couple of metres away from the wall. By doing this, we have now created a beautiful high-key backdrop by allowing the bright sunlight to strike and overexpose the background wall, while the light on our subject is diffused and softened.

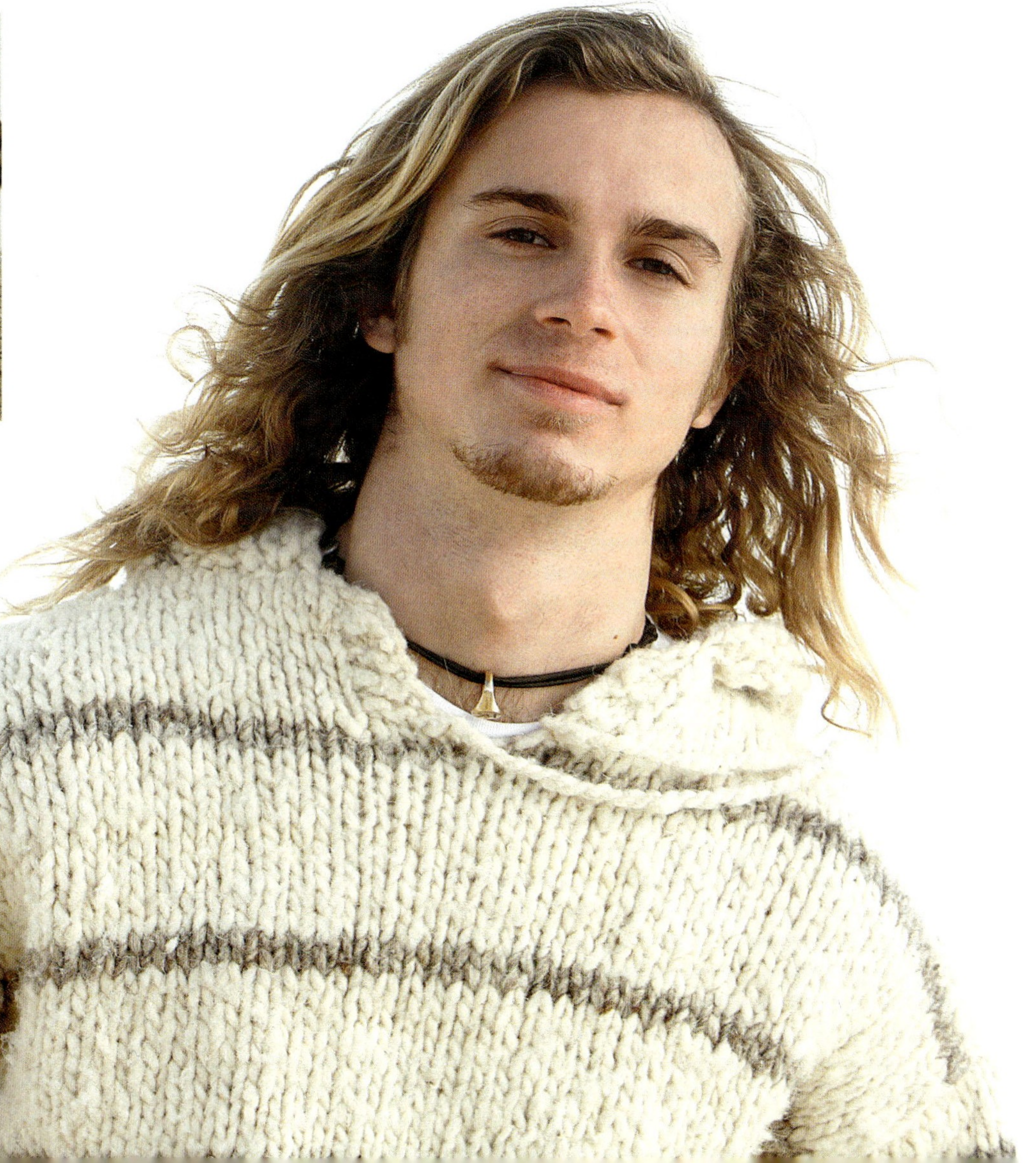

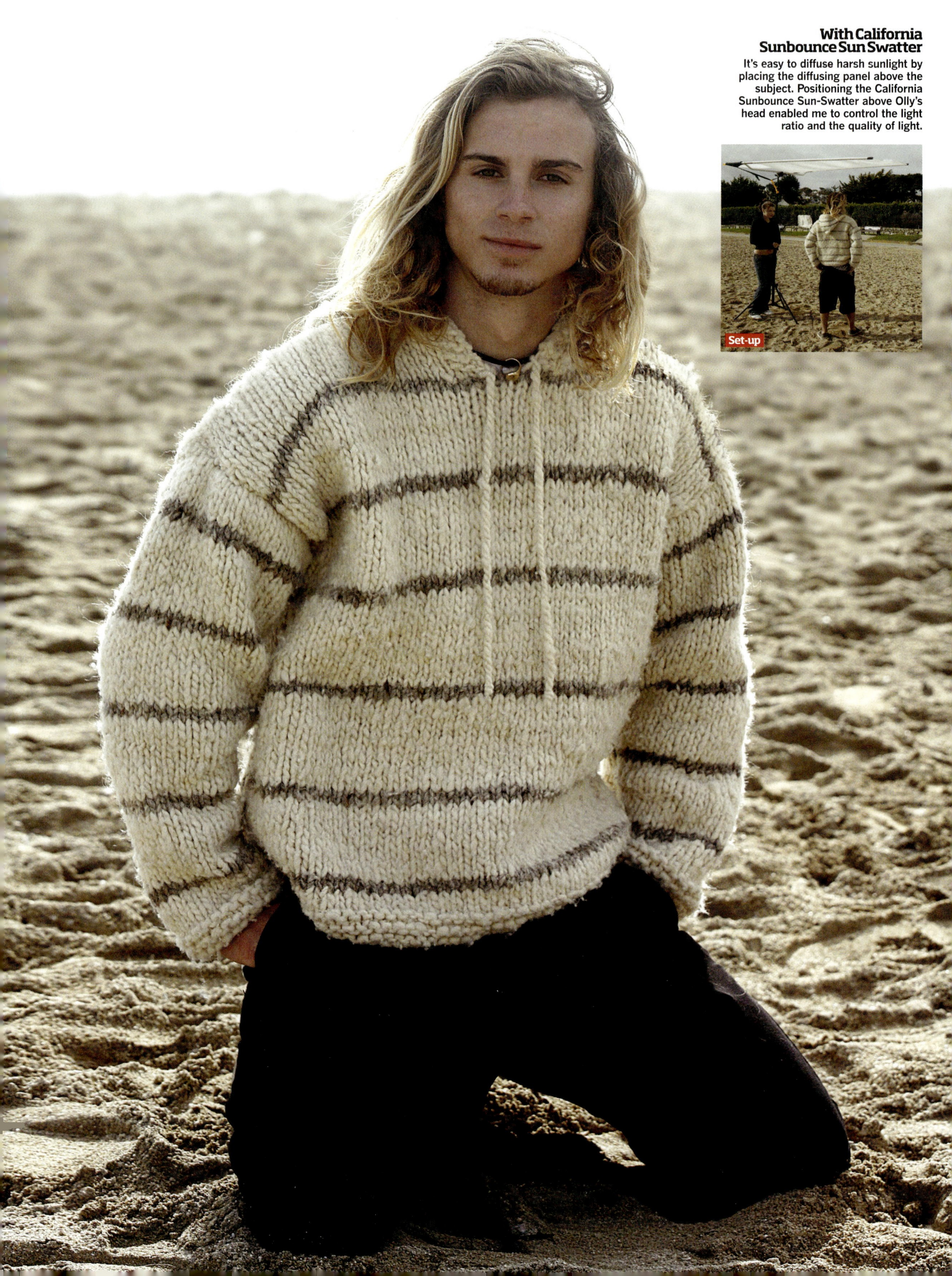

With California Sunbounce Sun Swatter

It's easy to diffuse harsh sunlight by placing the diffusing panel above the subject. Positioning the California Sunbounce Sun-Swatter above Olly's head enabled me to control the light ratio and the quality of light.

Taking great portraits in shade

Bjorn Thomassen explains the wonderful virtues of shade and reveals how careful control of this diffused form of light can create powerful portraits

SHADED LIGHTING IS SIMPLY PERFECT for portraits; its soft and diffused nature creates supple skin tones and a wide, smooth tonal range. The lack of contrast works particularly well if your subject's skin or clothing is near black or white in tone. However, it's important to know how to control this diffused light to maximise its benefits as light levels will be low. A reflector is essential in order to direct the light where you need it, but pick a type that best suits the scenario: a white reflector provides a soft light, while silver is more powerful and gold adds a warm tone. Because shade is non-directional, it can be difficult to judge the effect of the reflector but with practice you will be able to see even subtle changes and learn how to position it to shape the light on the subject. Considering the colour of the scene will help with controlling light, as pale tones will reflect light while dark tones will absorb it. Strong colours reflect coloured light, so take care not to place your subject too close otherwise they may well adopt a colour cast. While many photographers would not consider shooting in shade as light levels are relatively low, if you can learn to control and harness the soft, diffused nature of light in the shadows, you'll produce exceptional portraits.

Our first attempt at capturing Dwight was to shoot him beside some yellow doors so as to add some colour into the frame as well as bouncing some light towards the subject. However, the wide open space meant that even with a large white reflector, I wasn't happy with the lighting ratio. Some major changes were necessary...

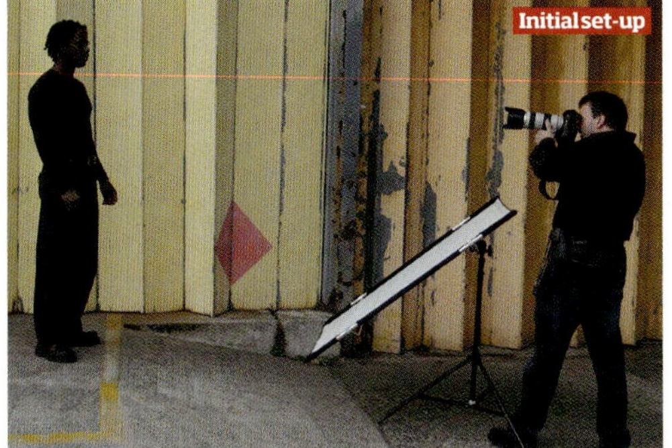
Initial set-up

Bjorn's outfit for shooting in shade

I believe that you should keep your lighting set-ups as simple as possible, especially if you're new to lighting control. Here's my kit for the shoot:

DIGITAL SLR I used a Canon EOS-1DS MkII, although any model is suitable.

LENS Canon 70-200mm f/2.8 as this type of zoom is perfect for portraiture. I generally shoot with the zoom between 100mm and 150mm for the most flattering effect.

REFLECTOR The white reflector wasn't suitable for this shoot as light levels were too low, but the Lastolite Triflector fitted with the silver reflectors really delivered in terms of the intensity of light that it bounced back on the subject. It also enabled me to control the direction of light to shape it on Dwight's face.

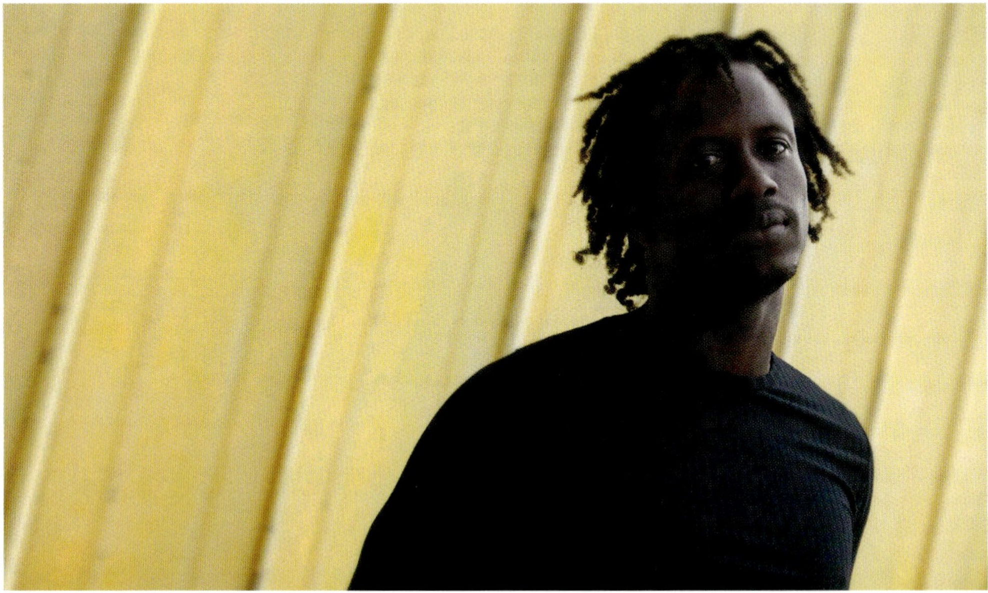

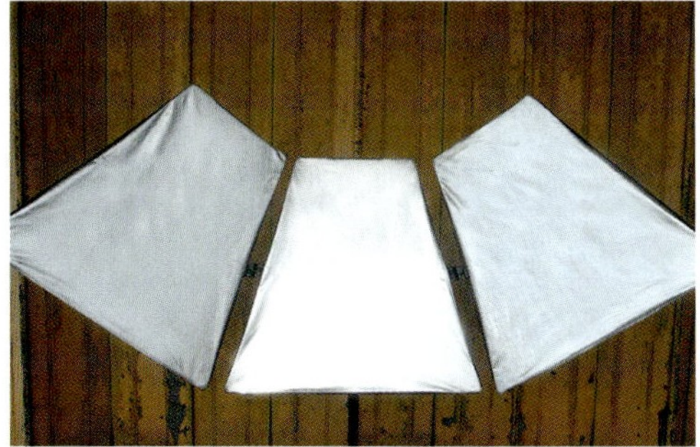
Step 1 The first thing that I did was to replace my standard white reflector with a Lastolite Triflector, which has three adjustable panels for better control over shaping the light on Dwight's face.

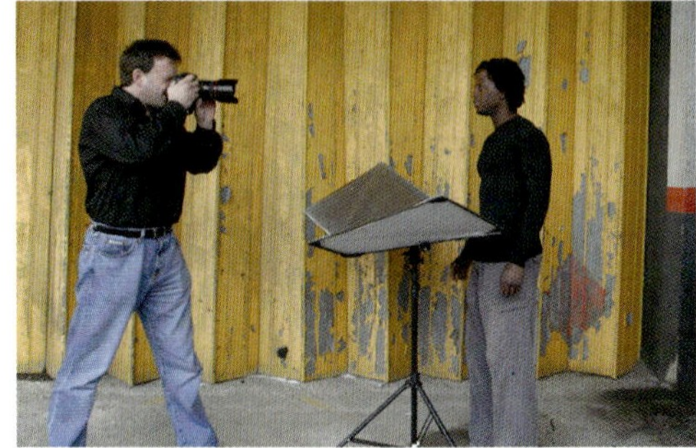
Step 2 The reflective panels of the Triflector can be removed from their frame and replaced with either silver, white or gold panels. I stuck with the silver side to maximise the intensity of the light.

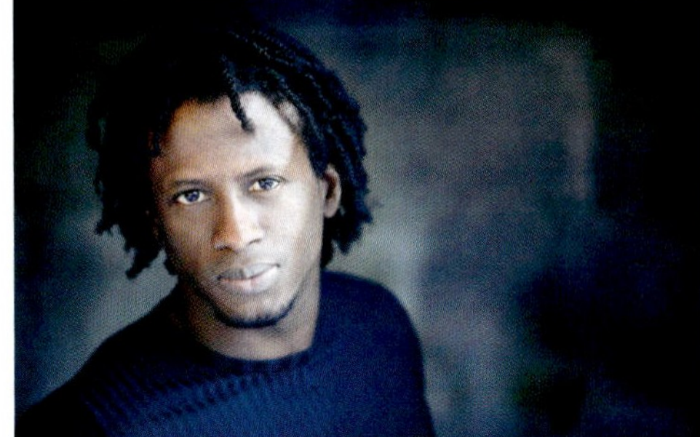
Step 3 The highly reflective silver panels efficiently bounce available light, even in shade, which has really highlighted Dwight's face and lifted it from the general gloom of the backdrop.

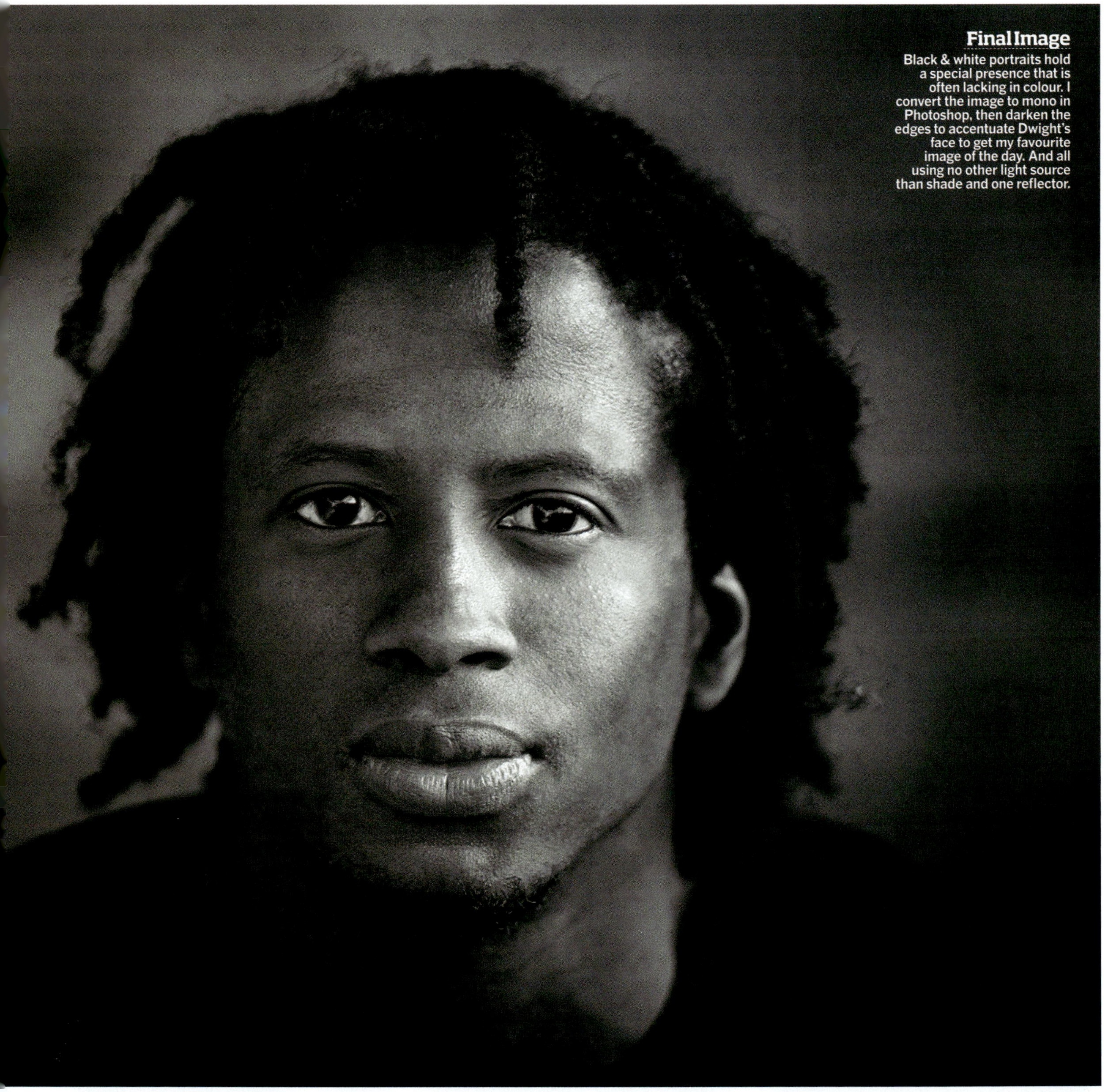

Final Image
Black & white portraits hold a special presence that is often lacking in colour. I convert the image to mono in Photoshop, then darken the edges to accentuate Dwight's face to get my favourite image of the day. And all using no other light source than shade and one reflector.

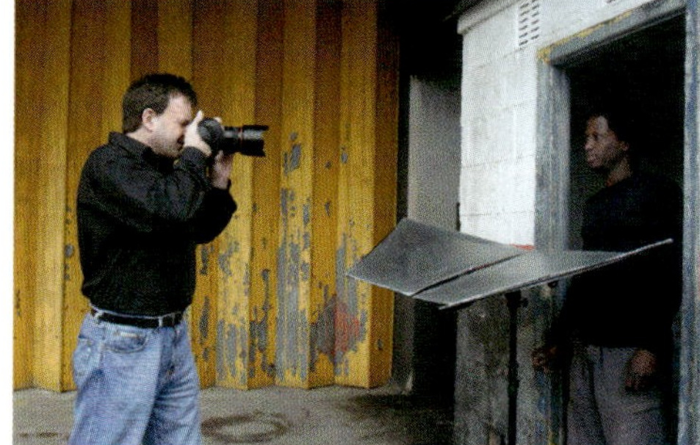

Step 4 As much as I liked the portrait, I wanted to bounce light around his head to reveal more detail in his hair. Therefore, I positioned Dwight beneath a light-coloured door to also use as a reflector.

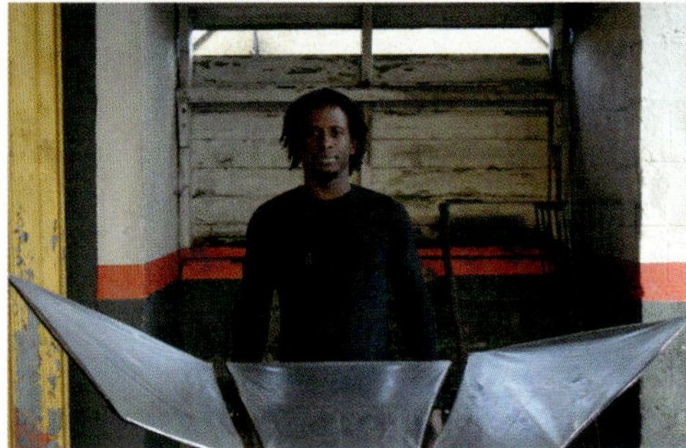

Step 5 As you can see, Dwight is now surrounded by a much lighter backdrop. I positioned the panels carefully, angled towards his face, so they spread the available light around his head.

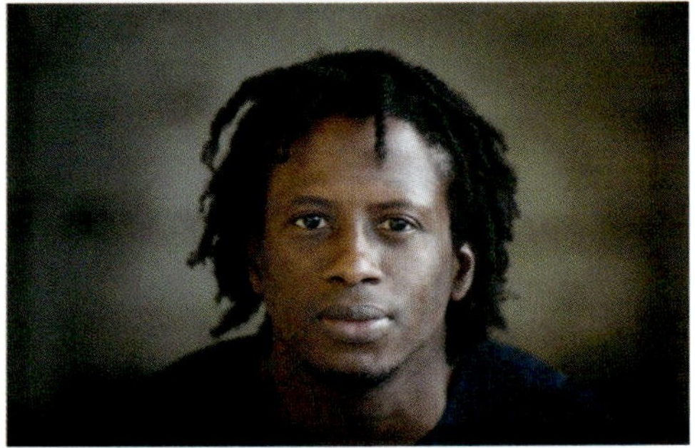

Step 6 The result is a portrait where the light is more controlled, less directional and harsh. However, I feel it lacks the mood of the earlier shot, but making it black & white should sort this out.

Cloudy-day portraits

Overcast conditions are perfect for photographing portraits outdoors, find out why and how to make the most of them

IF YOU WERE PLANNING to shoot landscapes and looked out the window to find the sky filled with grey clouds, you would not be happy. However, for the portrait photographer, a blanket of cloud is viewed as Mother Nature's own diffuser. Overcast conditions take away much of the pain of shooting outdoors, as there is no need to worry about strong sunlight. However, that's not to say because there's no direct light there is no way for you to manipulate light. Even on the dullest of days, using a white or metallic reflector can bounce light back on to the subject. And because you have no directional light to contend with, you have almost total freedom to position your subject where you want as there's no sun to contend with. Bear in mind that because the light source is diffused from above, you'll find it better to keep the reflector below the subject and angled to point upwards. Move the reflector towards and away from the subject to achieve the intensity of reflectance you need. Also, change its position and angle to help 'shape' the light that bathes your subject's face.

The following step-by-step was taken on a day when the sky was completely overcast. We photographed Ruby in her garden, sat in front of a brown playhouse, which provided a dark, neutral backdrop with the minimum of distractions. She wore a light pink top that injected some colour into the scene without being too over-powering.

Environmental reflectors

Keep your eye out for objects in the location that can act as a reflector. White walls are ideal not only as a backdrop but also to provide reflected light. You'll also find that the light that bounces from standard house-bricks works well too. Bear in mind that colour walls will reflect coloured light so avoid strong colour walls like red, blue or green.

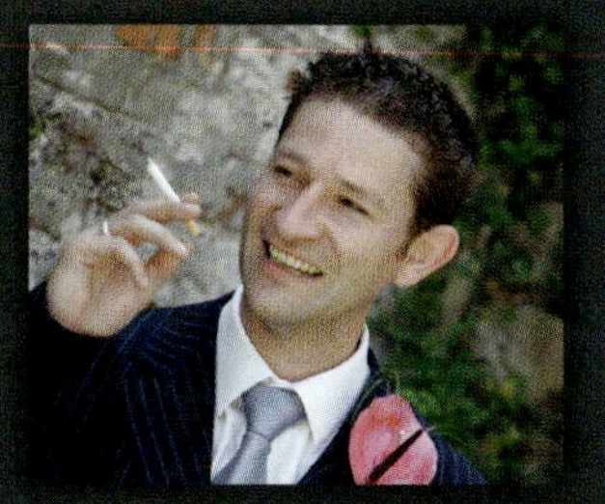

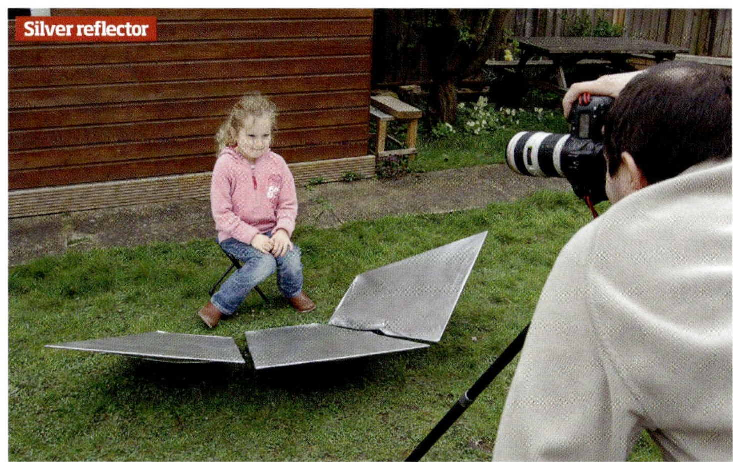

Silver reflector

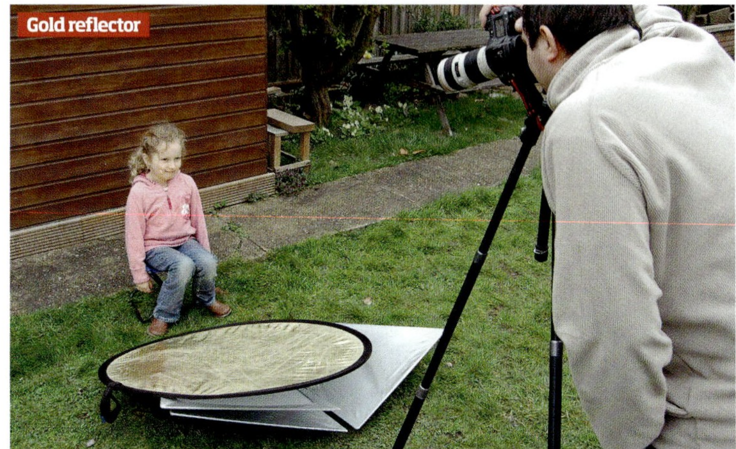

Gold reflector

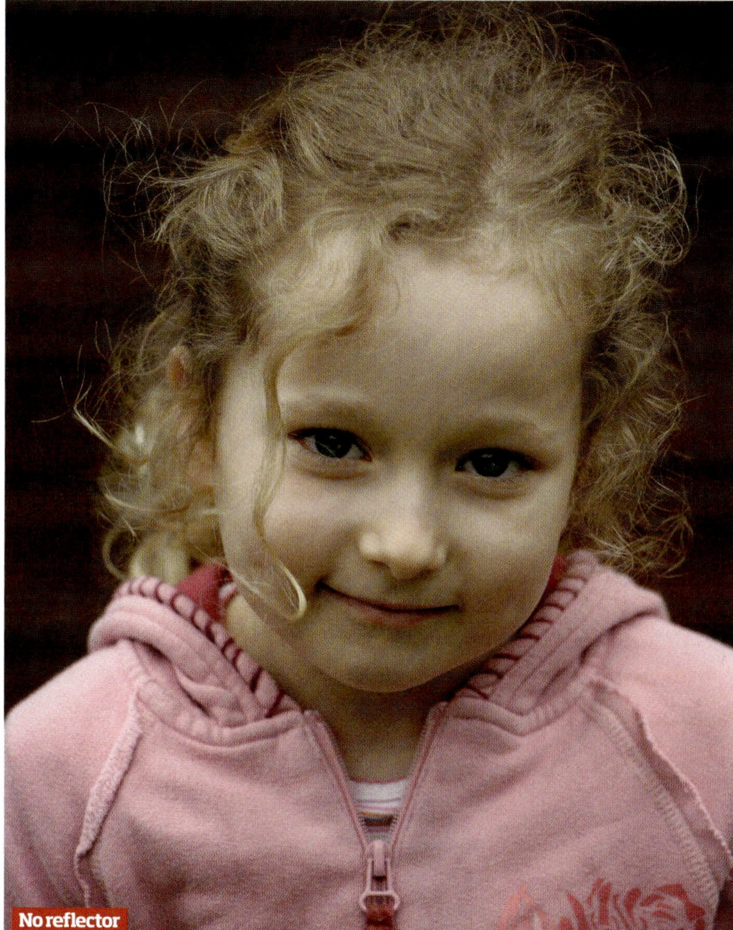

No reflector

1 This is Ruby photographed without any form of lighting control. The shot's OK, but the shadows under her eyes and on the lower parts of her cheeks and chin aren't very attractive. Tilting her head up would remove many of them but then the pose would look awkward. To get around the problem, I try using a white reflector but the dull light means it has minimal effect.

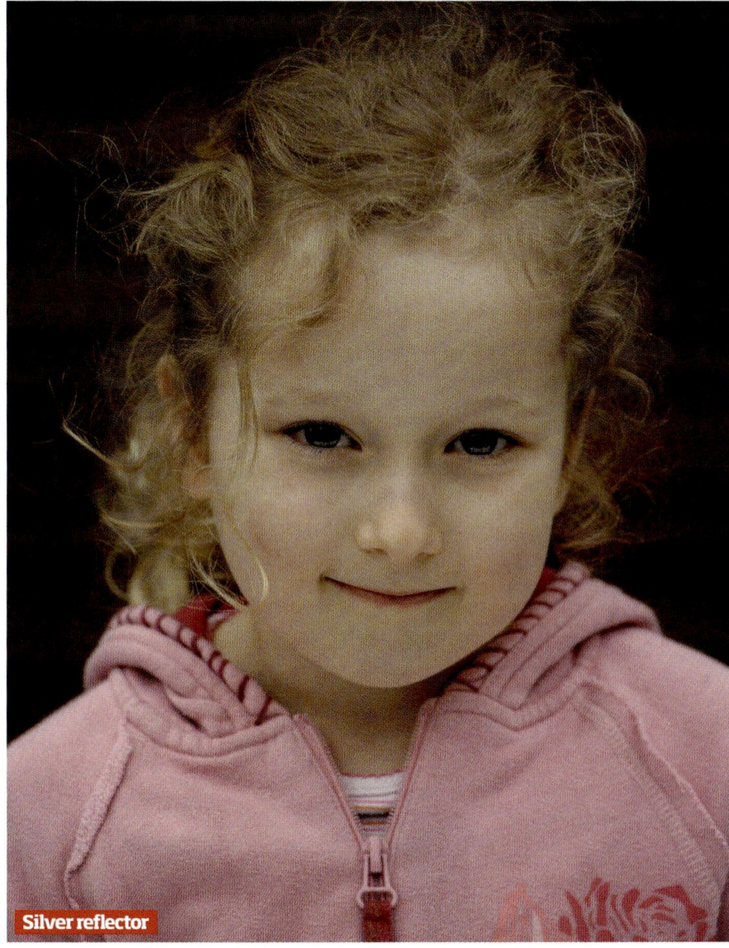

Silver reflector

2 Next, we opt for a silver reflector. The Lastolite Triflector is a versatile accessory that uses three separate panels so that you can control the angle of reflectance. It's placed on the ground quite close to Ruby and below my eye level, so that I'm shooting over the top of it. As you can see, its effect is obvious – shadows are removed and the effect is more flattering than before.

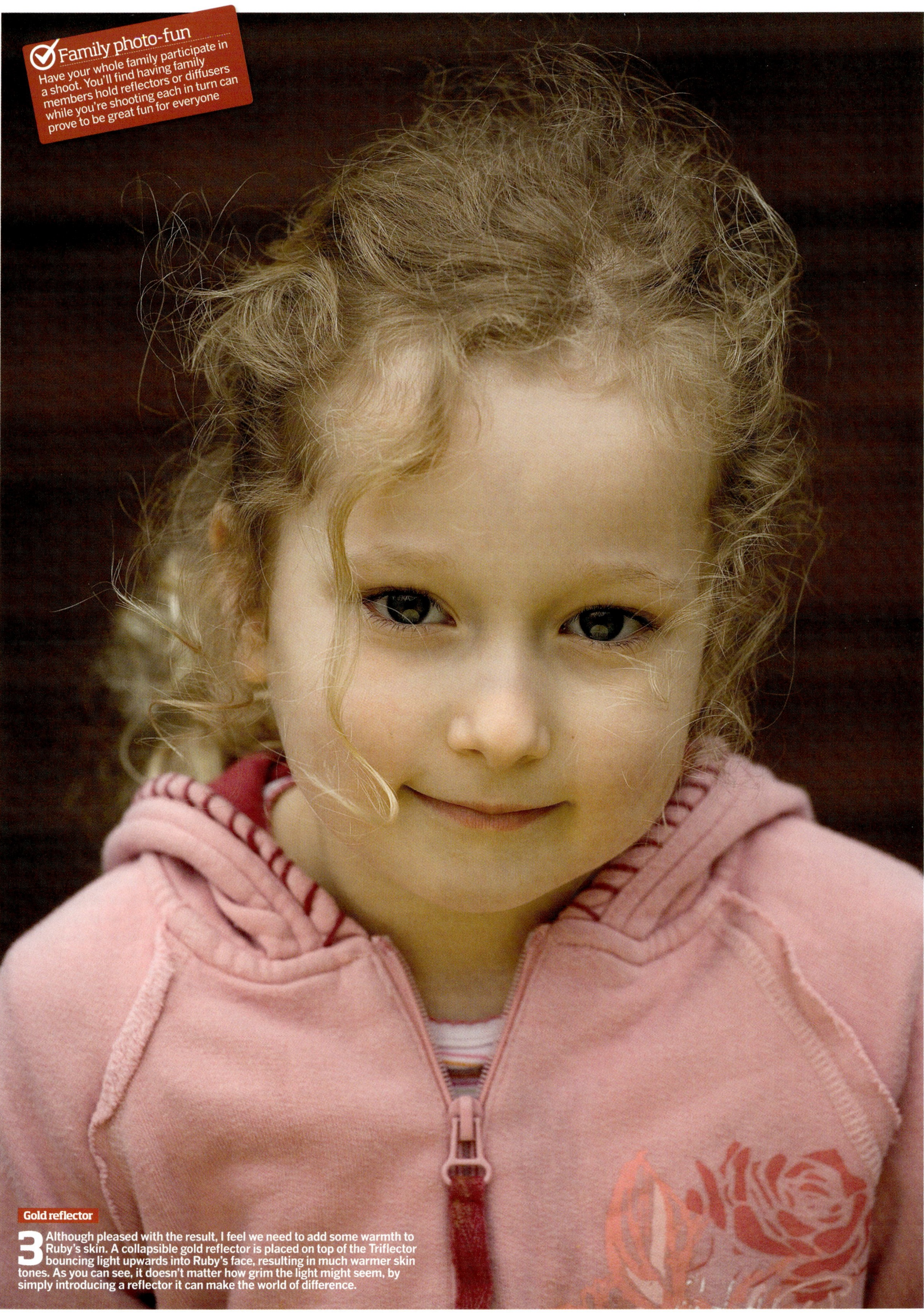

Family photo-fun

Have your whole family participate in a shoot. You'll find having family members hold reflectors or diffusers while you're shooting each in turn can prove to be great fun for everyone

Gold reflector

3 Although pleased with the result, I feel we need to add some warmth to Ruby's skin. A collapsible gold reflector is placed on top of the Triflector bouncing light upwards into Ruby's face, resulting in much warmer skin tones. As you can see, it doesn't matter how grim the light might seem, by simply introducing a reflector it can make the world of difference.

Shooting late in the day

Daniel Lezano reveals the challenges and rewards of shooting in the final minutes of the day's light

THE 'MAGIC HOUR' IS A PHRASE that's commonly used by landscape photographers to describe the period of time early in the morning or late in the day, when the sun is so low in the sky that the light it casts has a strong golden hue. For landscape images, this type of light can give scenes a three-dimensional feel as the low light creates shadows that reveal the depth and contours of the scenery. For portrait photography, this time of day provides a golden light that will add warmth to a subject's skin tone and backdrop.

Picking this time of day for your shoot has its benefits but also means you have to work fast, because you literally have minutes to take advantage of the setting sun before it disappears. You also need to be aware that you're at the mercy of the weather, as if it's cloudy, you will have little or no golden light to play with. However, if you are lucky enough to have this wonderful light appear, as well as shooting with the subject facing the light, it's also worth using the sunset as a colourful backdrop.

What is also ideal about this time of day is you're guaranteed soft light once the sun has dropped low in the sky, as the entire scene will be in shade. This means that you can work without any lighting aids if you want, although even with low-light levels, you'll find reflectors still produce some illumination, seemingly out of nothing! The extra reflectance will come in useful when trying to avoid camera shake, as the very low light results in a longer shutter speed.

To provide an example of the sort of daylight portrait you could shoot in these conditions, I headed to a local park to capture a couple of shots of a friend's daughter. Ruby has blonde curly hair, which I felt would be good for the late afternoon shoot, backlit by the sunlight. Rather than go for colourful clothing that would contrast with the browns and greens of the park, I arranged for Ruby to wear neutral tones to complement the colour of the scenery more.

With such a short time period to work in, it's best to arrive at your chosen location ten minutes ahead of when you plan to shoot, so you can spot potential viewpoints and backgrounds. I decided to shoot close to the bank of a pond, as it meant the horizon was unobstructed and I would have the light for longer than if I was to shoot within the park where trees would block the falling sun.

I took with me a white, silver and gold reflector, which Ruby's mum was happy to hold in position when required. The white reflector, while a number one choice in most daylight shoots, might prove to be too inefficient to bounce enough daylight when light levels fell very low. In this instance the silver or gold reflector could prove more useful, although care would need to be taken with the gold reflector when combined with the already golden light from the low sun, that it didn't create too warm a cast.

As with the majority of my portrait shoots, I used my DSLR (with 50mm f/1.8 lens) set to aperture-priority, with the initial aperture setting at f/5.6. The White Balance was set to AWB, due to the changing lighting conditions, and I shot in Raw + JPEG, to allow me to tweak WB if necessary in post-production.

Avoiding camera shake

Due to the relatively slow shutter speeds that occur when shooting at this time of day, avoiding camera shake should be at the forefront of your mind. The easiest way to do this is use image stabilisation if your camera or lens has it, stick to a wide aperture of around f/4-5.6 and set the ISO rating to at least 400. You should also use a moderate telephoto lens of between 50mm to 100mm, rather than a longer telephoto, which increase the risk of shake. Using the reciprocal rule can help you determine when you run the risk of shake. To do this, ensure your shutter speed is at least equal or faster than the reciprocal of the lens in use. For instance, if you are using a focal length of 100mm, ensure the shutter speed is at least 1/100sec, at 200mm use 1/200sec or faster, and so on.

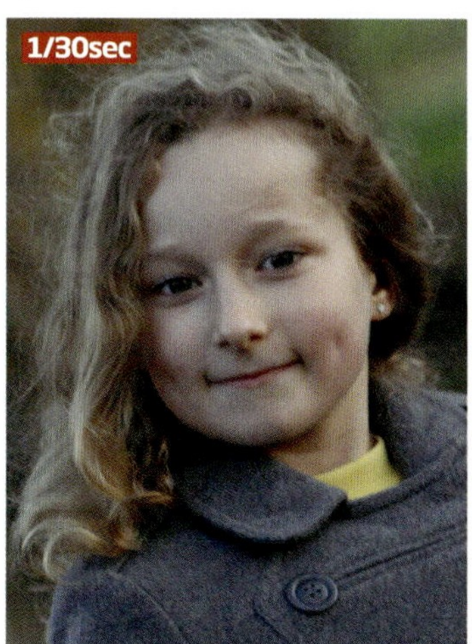

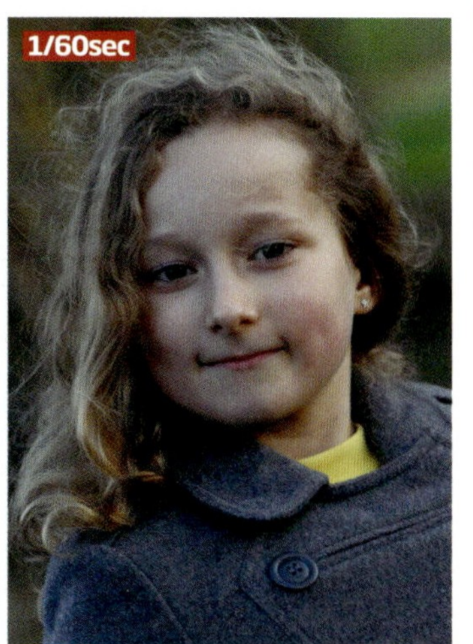

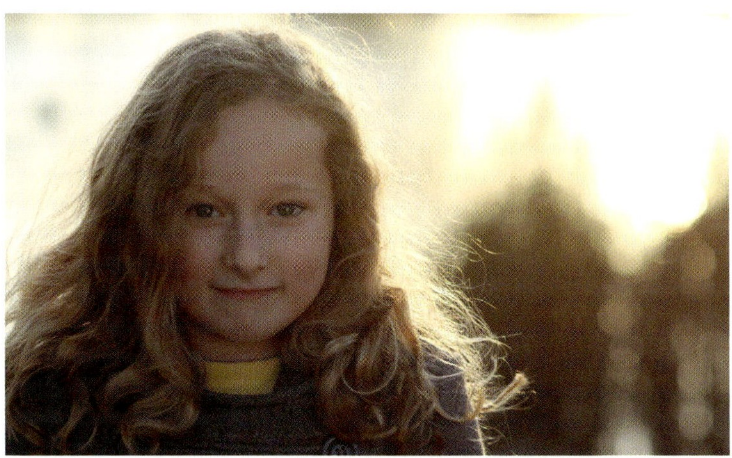

With the sun's orb still visible in the sky, I position Ruby in front of a lake, with her back to the sun to make the most of the golden colours of the backdrop. While the low sun creates a glow in her hair, the glare effect is too strong, reducing contrast and adversely affecting the image.

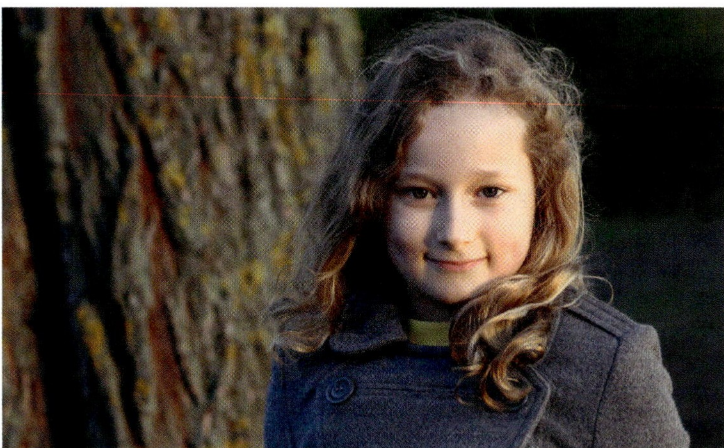

I move Ruby to stand in front of a tree and try shooting from a variety of viewpoints, remembering to alternate the format by taking portrait and landscape images. The texture of the tree adds interest and the golden light from the sun, to Ruby's left, adds a lovely warmth to her skin.

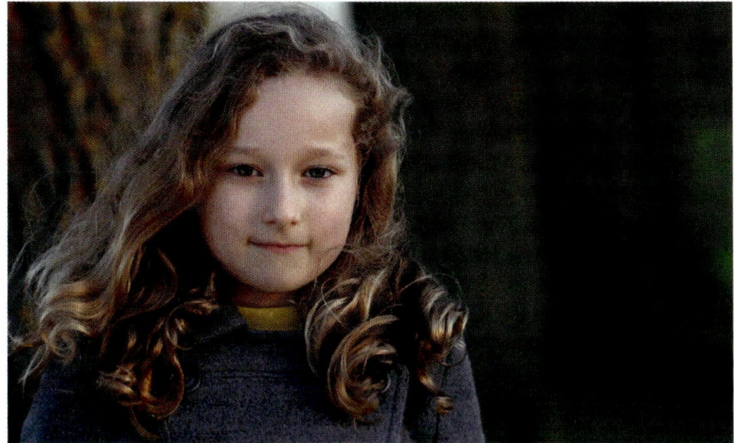

Before the sun has completely set, and the scene becomes totally shaded, the light still has a very slight touch of gold to it, adding colour to her hair. Positioning a white reflector to Ruby's left side allows me to bounce a little extra light in to fill any shadows, yet retain the skin's natural tones.

Going too gold!

Take care with the gold reflector: using it with a setting sun can overdo the warm effect, especially if the reflector is positioned too close to the subject. Save the gold for when the subject is in deep shade and try a silver or white reflector instead.

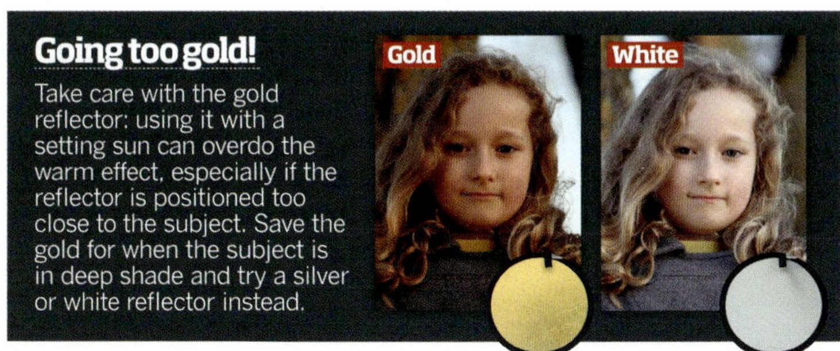

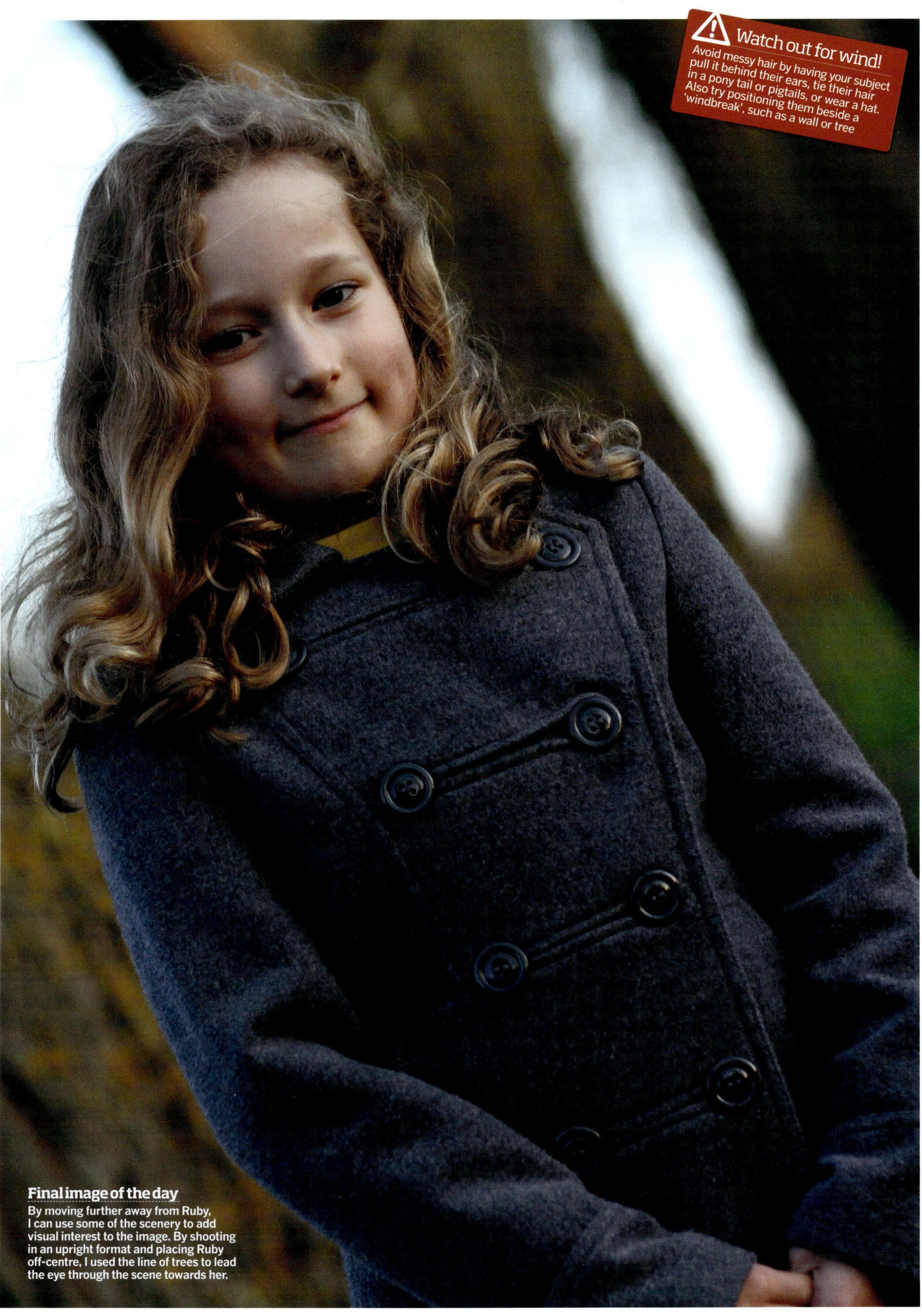

Final image of the day

By moving further away from Ruby, I can use some of the scenery to add visual interest to the image. By shooting in an upright format and placing Ruby off-centre, I used the line of trees to lead the eye through the scene towards her.

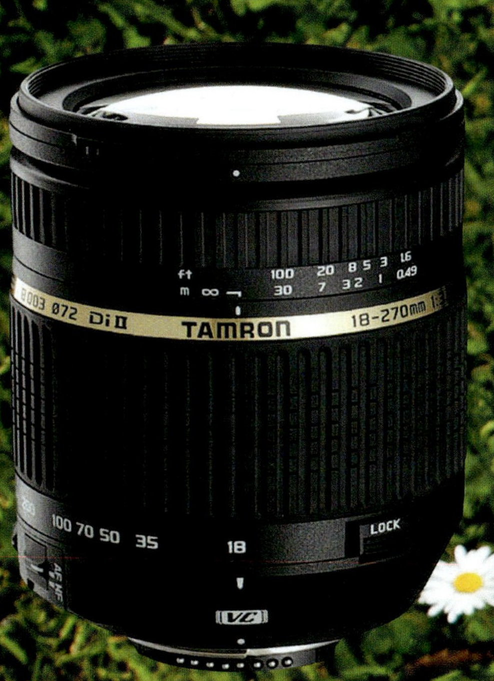

TAMRON 18-270mm f/3.5-6.3 Di II VC LD Aspherical (IF) Macro

Portraits

Few subjects are as popular or as challenging to photograph as people. Most people feel self-conscious and awkward as soon as a lens is pointed in their direction, so achieving natural-looking portraits is far from easy.

Good communication is vital for a portrait photographer, to help your subject feel comfortable and at ease. Lens focal length is another key factor, and the lens you use will dictate the feel of the image. A wide-angle lens can create an impression of space, solitude or scale, while a telephoto lens will isolate your subject from their surroundings and allow you to work from a distance. By taking pictures from further away, your subject will be less aware of the camera and therefore will act and behave more naturally.

Different focal lengths can create very different perspectives. However, when shooting portraits, you don't want to waste valuable time by constantly switching lenses. With Tamron's 18-270mm zoom, you don't have to.

Few optics can rival the versatility of Tamron's AF 18-270mm f/3.5-6.3 Di II VC LD Aspherical (IF). The world's first lens to deliver a zoom ratio of 15x, it covers wide-angle to telephoto and has a range equivalent in 35mm terms to around 28-419mm when attached to a DSLR with an APS-C sensor. It is a 'one lens does all' zoom, allowing you to quickly adapt to any shooting situation.

This can make the difference between success and failure when photographing people, particularly children. Kids have a tendency to do anything apart from what you want them to do when you try to take their photo. However, using the telephoto end of the 18-270mm, you can shoot from a distance and capture those magical and genuine expressions, and shoot frame-filling portraits, bursting with mood and energy.

Of course, some children love having their photo taken. If you know a child that's happy to pose, try using a shorter focal length. The widest setting of the 18-270mm allows you to capture dynamic-looking portraits, full of depth, life and fun.

When photographing people, lens selection really is important. In order to react to your subject's movements, you will often want to shoot handheld when photographing people, which makes image stabilisation technology vital.

The Tamron 18-270mm is equipped with a highly effective Vibration Compensation (VC) mechanism. This tri-axial anti-shake system helps ensure sharp handheld images, even at the zoom's longest telephoto setting.

Despite its impressive focal range and technology, this lens is compact and lightweight, and its handling is intuitive. It zips quickly and quietly into focus when using AF, and with a maximum magnification of 1:3.5, it's also useful for isolating detail and interest.

With its impressive zoom ratio, this is a lens suited to practically any subject, including landscape, action or wildlife photography. However, photographers wishing to take images of people – either commercially, or to capture professional-looking images of friends or family – are sure to be impressed with the quality and versatility of the Tamron 18-270mm.

SPECIFICATIONS

Construction: 18 elements in 13 groups
Maximum aperture: f/3.5-6.3
Minimum aperture: f/22
Minimum focus: 49cm
Maximum magnification: 1:3.5
Filter thread: 72mm
Angle of view: 75° 33' to 5° 55'
Diameter x length: 79.6x101mm
Weight: 550g
AF fittings: Canon EF and Nikon F
Supplied accessory: Petal-shaped lens hood

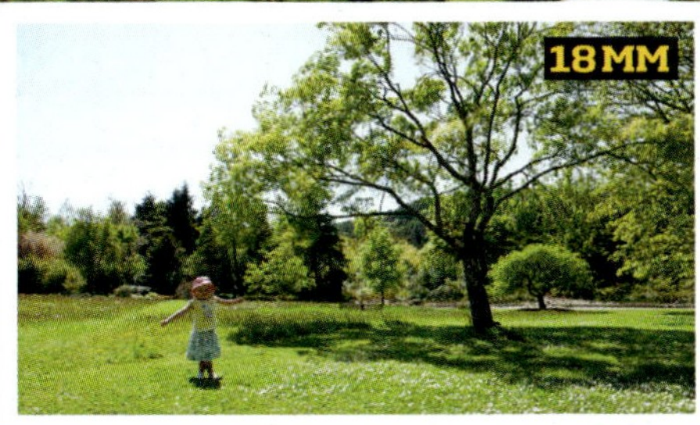
18MM

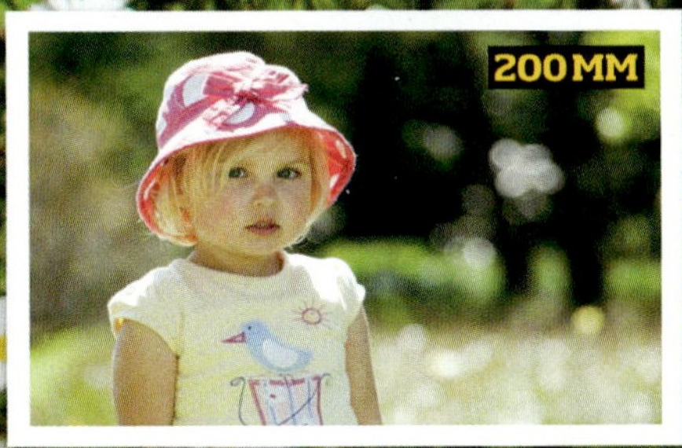
200MM

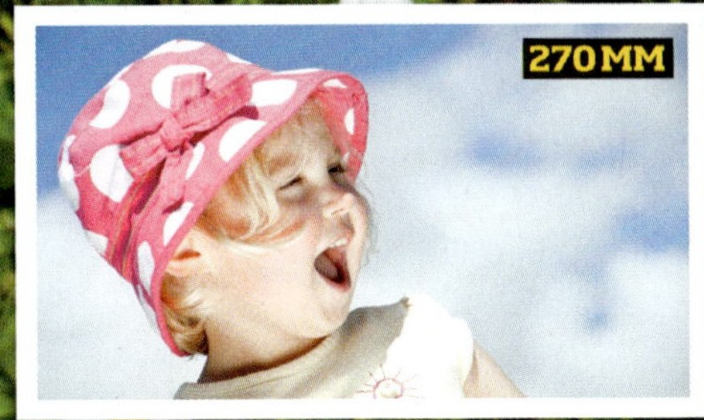
270MM

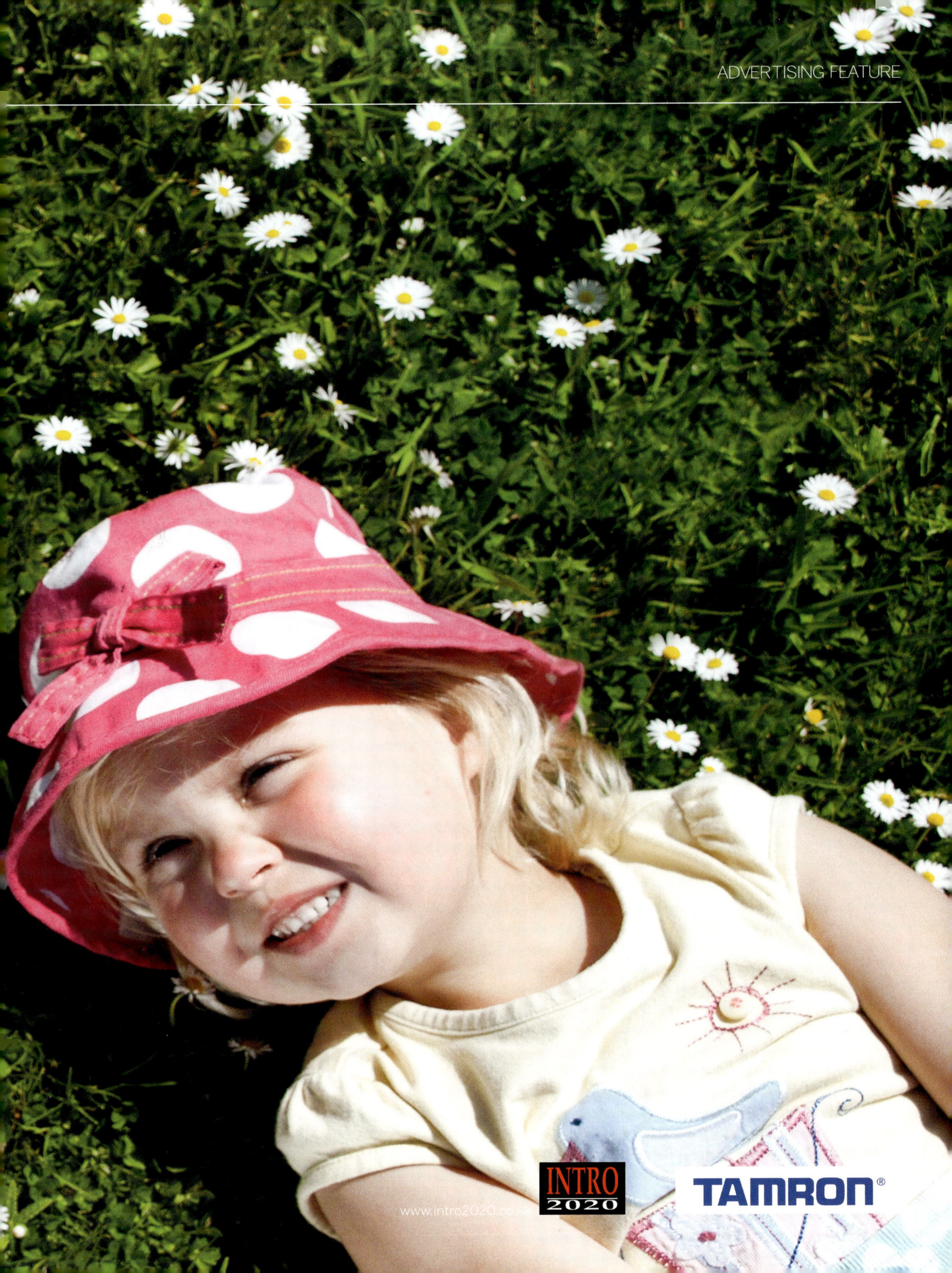
INTRO
2020
www.intro2020.co.uk
TAMRON®

FEW OF US HAVE THE LUXURY of a photography studio to hand and the UK's volatile weather means shooting outdoors is not always an option. But don't feel defeated; you can still take stunning portraits indoors regardless of what may seem a daunting plethora of problems to tackle, such as low light, mixed light, limited space and cluttered backgrounds. But we promise you, by the end of this guide, you'll recognise more lighting possibilities, know how to make the most of almost any indoor-lighting scenario and be bursting to try out some of our fun shoots for every room in your house.

One big advantage to shooting portraits at home is that few people feel more relaxed when surrounded by familiar home comforts, so you may find getting natural-looking expressions and poses easier and quicker. This type of photography is also very inexpensive; there's no need to pay for a studio or props, as a home has everything you need, and your basic set-up need only comprise of a DSLR, a portrait lens (a 50mm is ideal), tripod and possibly a flashgun. Of course, you can introduce accessories too, such as a reflector or softboxes for your flashguns, but you can always centre your shoot around natural light.

Whether you're shooting in your own home or someone else's, it's a good idea to meander around the house in search of natural light sources and scout out locations. Look for windows and interesting décor, as well as neutral backdrops, white walls and low ceilings to bounce flash off if needed. You may get lucky and have a house with a beautiful glass-roofed conservatory, but you may also find yourself scrounging for glimmers of light in dark, cramped rooms, and if this is the case, look to move the shoot to a garage or even the garden shed!

The number one rule for indoor portraits is that there are no rules: the environment dictates the shoot and you have to work with what light you can find or create. For instance, if a room is dark in colour, you may need to bring in studio lighting or a flashgun, or decide to work with it for a low-key or low-light portrait. Alternatively a light-coloured room can act as a giant softbox, bouncing light off the walls, which is ideal for most shoots and great for high-key images. Available household lighting can offer options too, but be aware of your White Balance as you'll be working with mixed light of different temperatures. The time of day and year also offers benefits and challenges. During winter, most natural light will be gone by 3pm but this just means you can turn your hand to low-light portraits instead. In the summer, however, there is more natural light available, although it will be much stronger too, so it's best to avoid windows in direct sunlight unless you have some heavy diffusion materials handy. The possibilities are endless!

Setting up your digital SLR for indoor portraits

1) EXPOSURE Aperture-priority mode is a good place to start when shooting indoor portraits using available light. By using this semi-automatic mode, you will be able to make the most of limited light by using a wide aperture and shallow depth-of-field to blur distracting backgrounds. If you switch to studioflash, remember to turn your camera to manual mode and dial in the exposure settings having metered the scene.

2) METERING The multi-zone pattern should be more than sufficient for an accurate exposure, but to make sure your shots are sharp when limited lighting is a concern, try raising the ISO rating a couple of stops to increase the shutter speed and avoid shake. Also engage image stabilisation and consider using a tripod, although this will limit your mobility a little. It's better to have a sharp image with some noise than one ruined by blur!

3) FOCUSING While for the most part autofocus will do the job well, it's best to set your camera to central-point focus or to use selective focusing, rather than multi-point AF, as it's likely to pinpoint the nose or eyebrows and not the eyes. Point the central AF point over the eye and half-depress the shutter button to lock focus and then recompose your shot. In very low-light scenarios, you may find that it's easier to switch to manual focus as AF can sometimes struggle in low-contrast situations.

4) WHITE BALANCE While shooting in Raw means you can tweak the White Balance in Photoshop, it's always best to try and get it right in-camera. Working indoors means you may have to tackle mixed lighting and unflattering colour casts. To correct this, take a spot meter reading off a grey card (or white sheet of paper) held in front of your subject's face and use this to set your custom White Balance setting. It will help too if you remember to turn off any indoor lights that are not needed to illuminate the scene, this includes blocking any unneeded windowlight as this can also vary in temperature depending on the time of day.

1
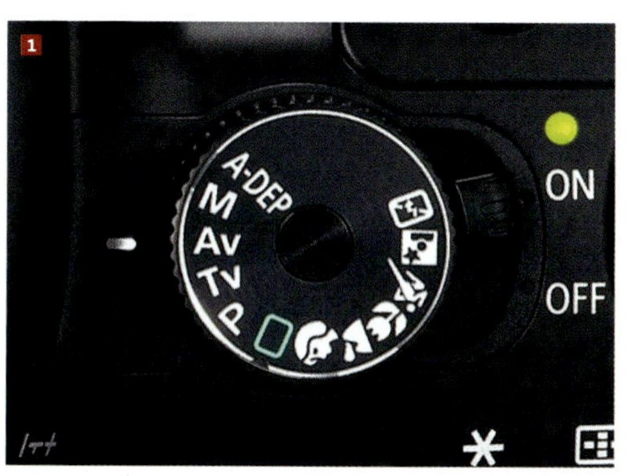

2
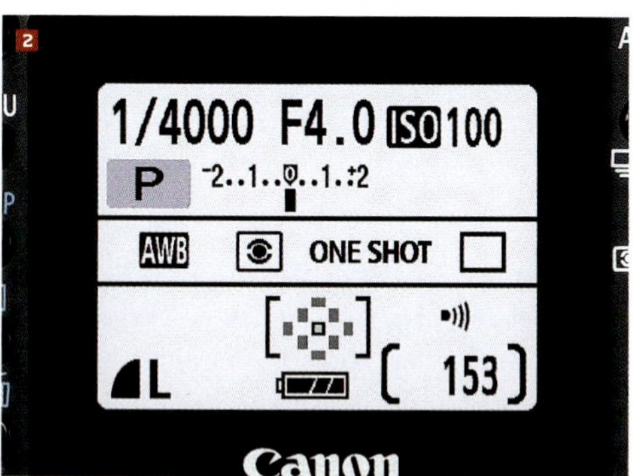

3
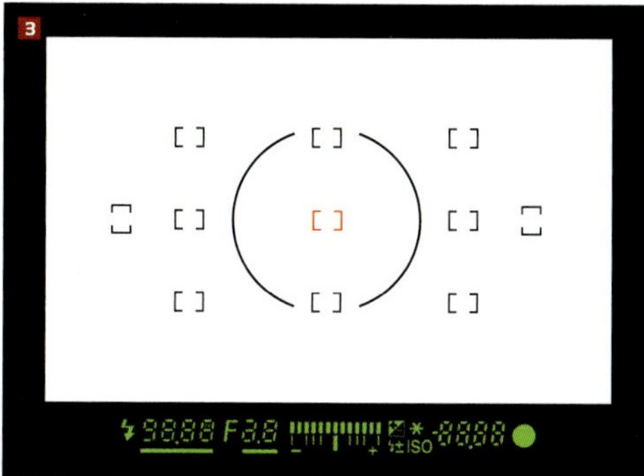

4
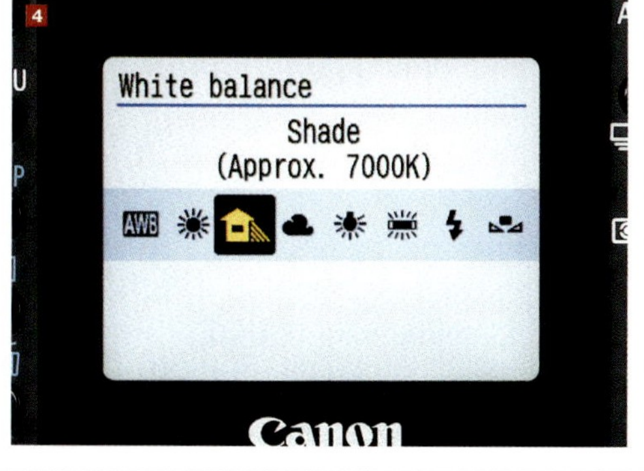

Accessories for indoor portraits

Lenses

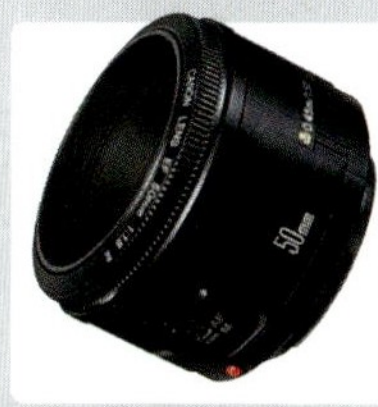

As light levels can be limited, ideally use a portrait lens with a wide maximum aperture, such as f/1.8, so you can make the most of the light and create a shallow depth-of-field to blur distracting backgrounds. A 50mm prime lens or the short end of 55-200mm telezoom are good options. A standard zoom like a 18-55mm kit lens is also usable; the widest focal length is ideal for group shots but any wider and at close range in cramped spaces you risk distorting perspective.

Reflectors

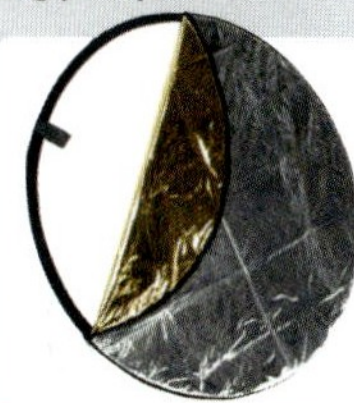

When there isn't enough light or it's just too harsh, reflectors are invaluable for filling in shadows. The 5-in-1 version is a great tool, with a white side to reflect clean, neutral light; a silver side for a cool, strong light and a gold for a warm golden glow. There is also a black side to absorb light and a diffuser to soften harsh rays. A Lastolite Triflector is also a very efficient accessory and with three adjustable sides to control the amount and direction of light, it may be all you need.

Flashgun

Your DSLR's built-in flash is suitable for some techniques, but for the most flattering light and more creative options, it's best to invest in a hotshoe-mounted flashgun, which can be triggered off-camera and held at a 45° angle to your model. A flashgun can also be used with accessories like softboxes to make the most of your light without having to invest in an expensive studio set-up.

Flash meter

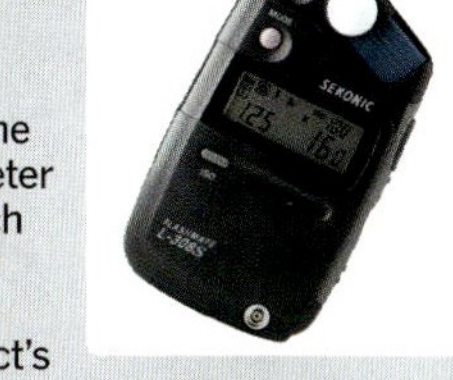

When you want to bring some studioflash into the set-up, a flash meter is essential. Attach the sync lead and hold the meter in front of the subject's face and press the button to find out the aperture you need to input to achieve a correct exposure.

Flashgun diffusion

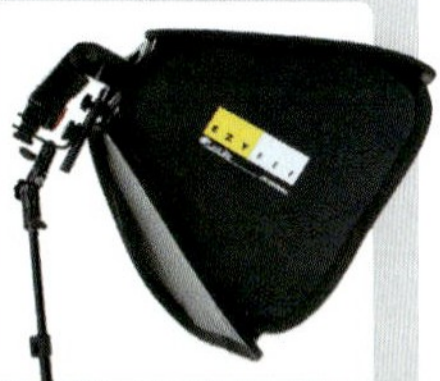

A burst of flash from an off-camera light source could save many indoor portraits from being underexposed, but often the glare is too strong for softly-lit, flattering portraits, which is where diffusion accessories come in. The Lastolite Ezybox is brilliant for portraits shot at home, because it's portable and much easier to prepare and put away than a conventional softbox. It comes in two sizes, with the larger version better for photographing groups. Also check out the Strobies Portrait Kit (www.interfitphotographic.com) for more lighting options. You'll also find a number of flash accessories in the gear section of this guide.

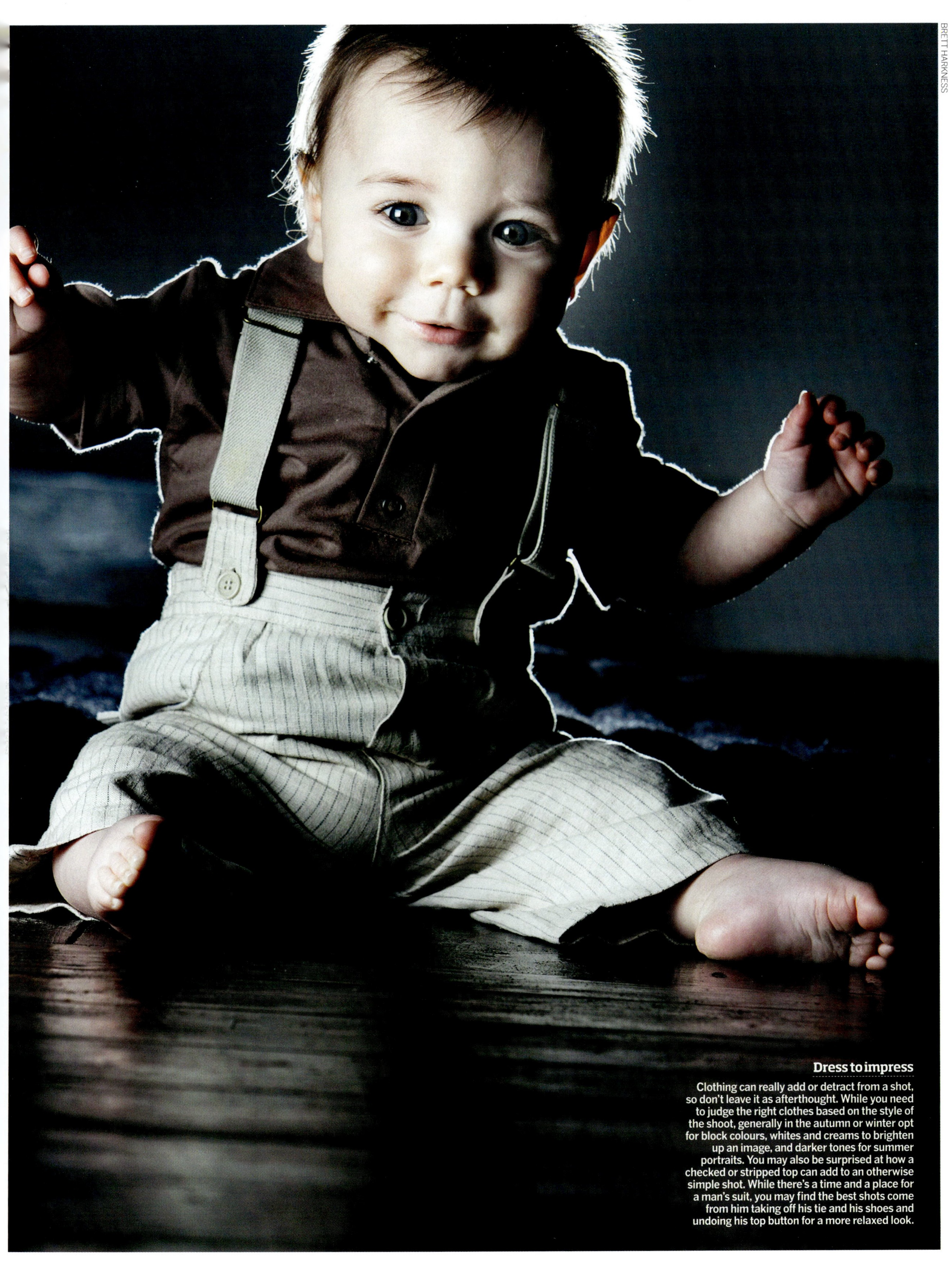

BRETT HARKNESS

Dress to impress

Clothing can really add or detract from a shot, so don't leave it as afterthought. While you need to judge the right clothes based on the style of the shoot, generally in the autumn or winter opt for block colours, whites and creams to brighten up an image, and darker tones for summer portraits. You may also be surprised at how a checked or stripped top can add to an otherwise simple shot. While there's a time and a place for a man's suit, you may find the best shots come from him taking off his tie and his shoes and undoing his top button for a more relaxed look.

Using available light sources

When natural light is in short supply, household lighting may be your only lifeline. We tell you how to make the most of any available light

WHEN YOU'RE SHOOTING INDOORS, you need to make the most of any available light. During the day, this may be in the form of sunlight streaming through a window or patio doors, or the soft diffused light flooding in through a netted window.

Covering all the various options to controlling and manipulating daylight indoors could fill a tome, but there are a few basic lighting principles that if applied properly, pretty much guarantee great results.

The light indoors will usually be diffused and non-directional as it has bounced off walls, the ceiling and floor, which means it's already flattering for portraits. Should you have strong light streaming in, use net curtains, or hang a sheet of muslin or other thin, white, diffusing material over the window to soften the light. Alternatively, move the subject away from the window to soften the light falling on them.

Regardless of the nature of the light or its intensity, the one accessory you should have to hand is a reflector. This lighting aid will help you get the most out of even the smallest amount of light by bouncing ambient light back on to a subject's face. If you haven't got one already, invest in a silver/white reflector or better still, a 3-in-1 reflector that also includes a gold surface.

If you're struggling for a neutral background, stand your model in front of a window for an instant white backdrop and bounce sunlight back onto the face with a reflector. Alternatively, stand with your back to the window and have the model look out to get an even soft light over their face or, if you want more shadow, stand them side on to a window and fill in with a reflector on the other side. Usually the bigger the window the softer the light and, with a big window behind you, it can also be used to give the model's eyes an interesting catchlight.

At night, available light is pretty much limited to room lighting, in particular the traditional tungsten bulb, halogen lights built into ceiling panels, spotlights and, in the majority of kitchens, fluorescent lighting. All have very different characteristics in terms of how they distribute light, from focused beams of a spotlight, to the non-directional spread of a tungsten bulb, which should be explored to find the best way they can be used to light the subject effectively. Also, remember that each has its own colour temperature, so be sure to set the appropriate White Balance preset to get accurate colours, or use a test shot of a grey card to set a custom WB setting on your DSLR (your camera's instructions will explain how).

Another option to try is to use an 'incorrect' White Balance setting to produce images that exhibit a strong cool or warm cast that adds mood to the scene. Whichever method you decide to use, we'd strongly recommend you shoot in Raw as you can then easily tweak White Balance when converting images from Raw to JPEG on your computer.

The bathtub 'reflector'!

Unless you have an avocado or pink suite, a bathroom could be the only room in the house where you have access to clean, white light. It can be a great place to maximise natural light as the white surfaces of the walls replicate a similar effect to a giant softbox. If the light is still limited, however, you could try placing your subject in a white bathtub as light will bounce off the sides to mimic the job of a reflector – this technique is ideal for 'little people'. You could also bounce flash off the sides of the tub for a similar effect.

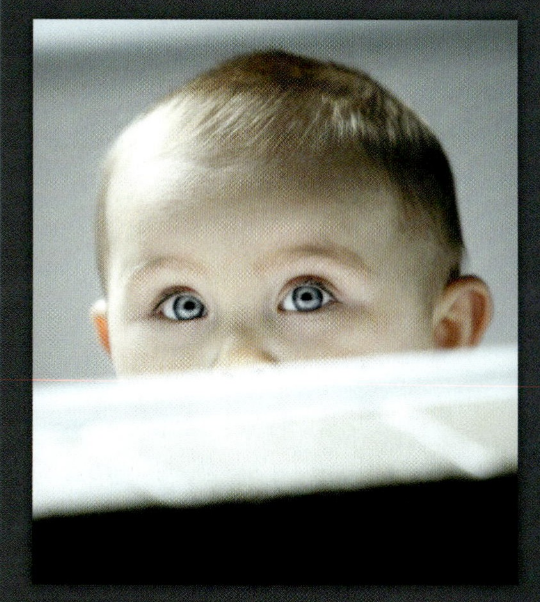

BRETT HARKNESS

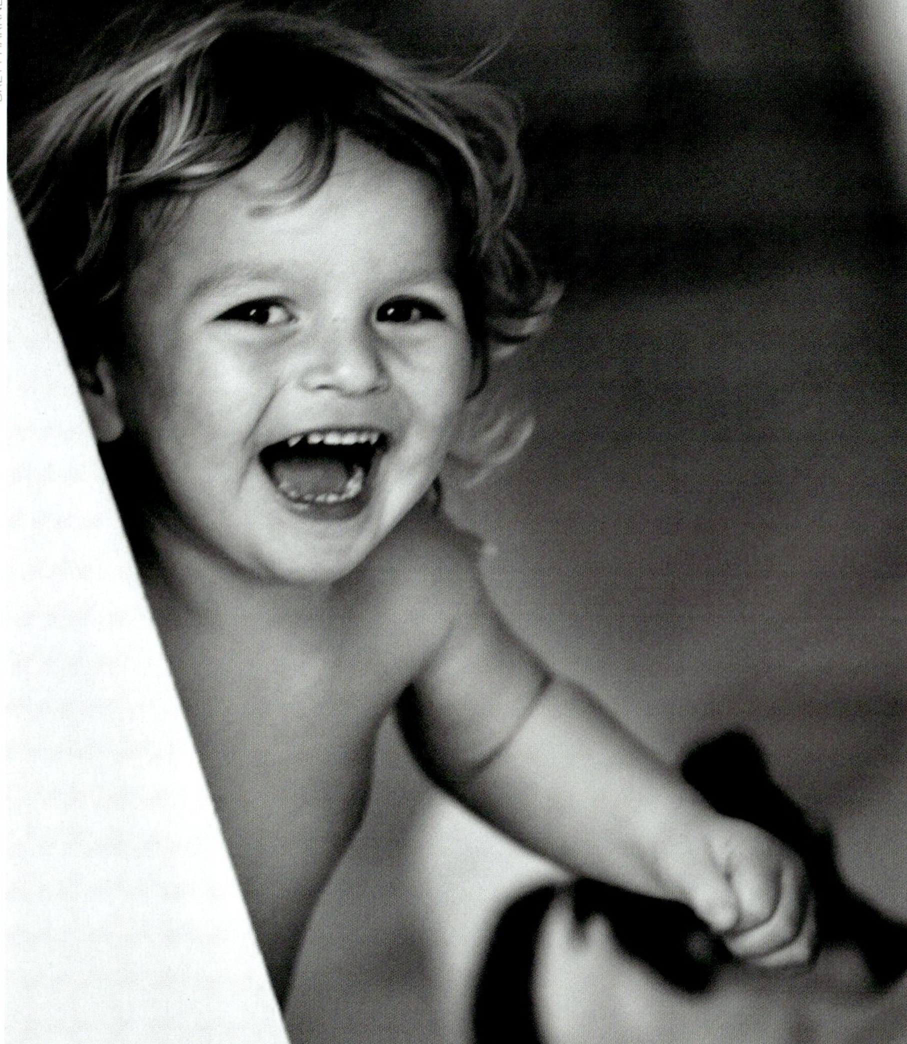

BRETT HARKNESS

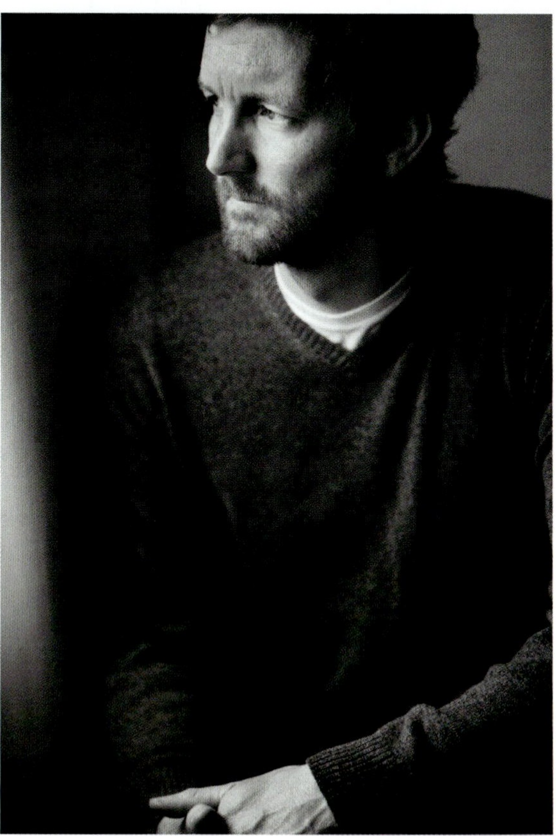

BRETT HARKNESS

Above: Add mood and mystery

Windowlight is perfect for flattering portraits. Try adding an air of mystery to your image by having the subject look contemplative out the window and avoid eye contact. Underexpose the image slightly to darken the subject a little.

Left: Doing it for the kids!

Be prepared for anything when photographing children. Be ready as soon as you step through the front door, so you don't miss any opportunities to take a candid picture.

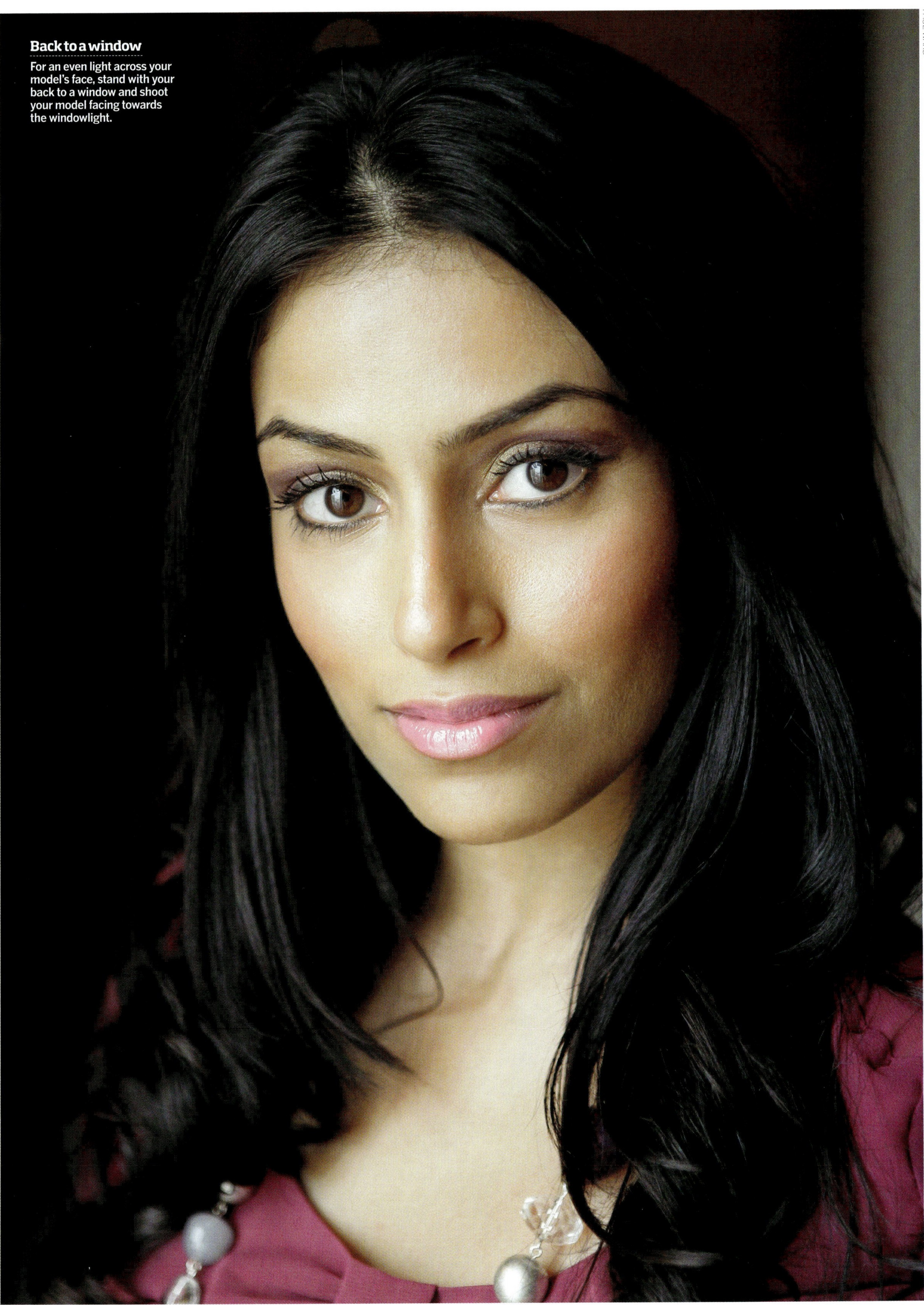

Back to a window

For an even light across your model's face, stand with your back to a window and shoot your model facing towards the windowlight.

PAUL WARD

Shoot a windowlit portrait!

STEWART BYWATER: When the unpredictable British weather prevents you from heading outside, one really easy technique to try indoors is to take a windowlit portrait. Many master portrait photographers have said that they actually prefer windowlight to any artificial light source, as it provides more natural results and can be controlled in a number of ways, such as by diffusing it with net curtains, various kinds of paper, or using a reflector to bounce light back onto your subject. This is one of the most traditional and simple photographic techniques around, and will give you great results, whatever the weather! My subject for the session was Bob, a neighbour of mine, who kindly agreed to sit for me. Bob looks much younger than his age (he's 80), but he has a great deal of character in his face – this is something to consider when choosing your subject, especially if you want to convert it to black & white.

Get ready!

TIME REQUIRED
20 MINUTES

EQUIPMENT NEEDED
NIKON D700 WITH 105MM MACRO LENS & TRIPOD

ALSO USED
5-IN-1 REFLECTOR

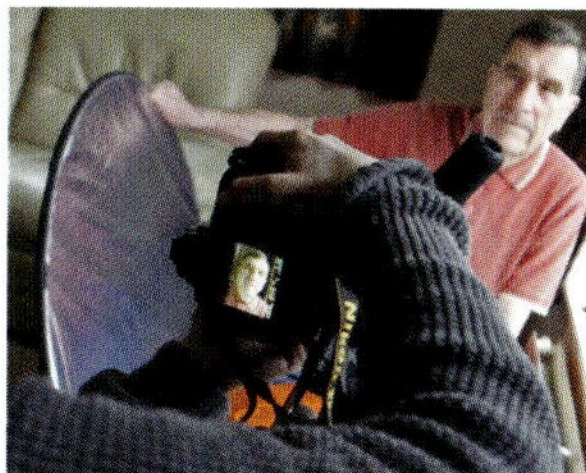

Get a helping hand!
If you're without an assistant, ask your subject to hold the reflector off to the side.

Using a reflector

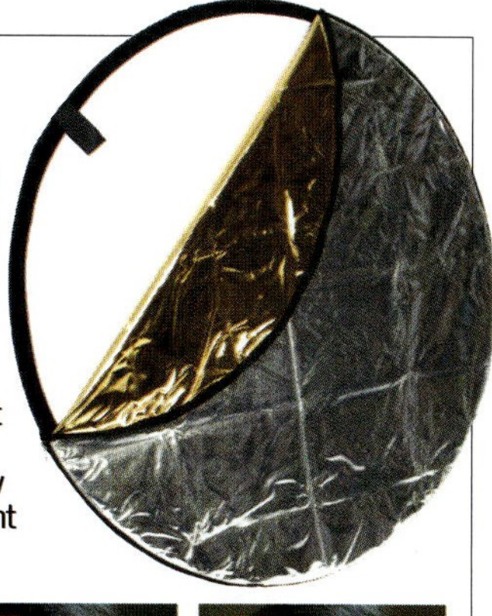

When shooting a windowlit portrait, such as this, with your subject side-on to the window, one side of the face will be brightly lit, while the other will remain in shadow. This can create a very striking, high-contrast look, but that's not always the look that you'll be after. A simple way to compensate for the uneven lighting is to use a reflector, to bounce light back onto the parts of your subject's face that are in shadow. Here, I have used the *Digital SLR Photography's* 5-in-1 reflector, and below you can see the effect that each of the different coloured sides makes to Bob's face.

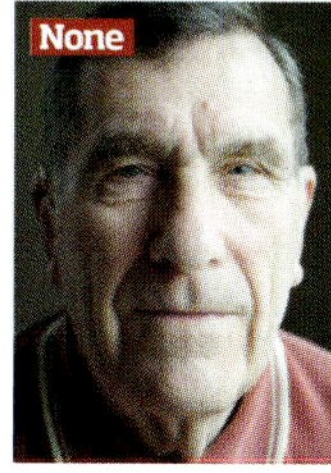

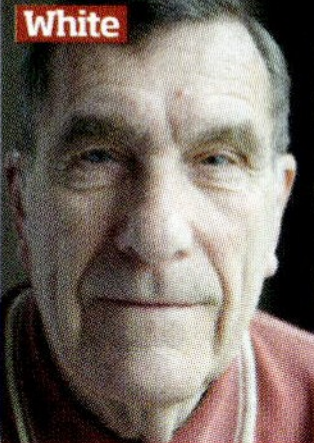

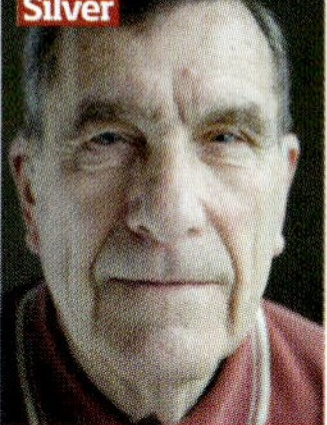

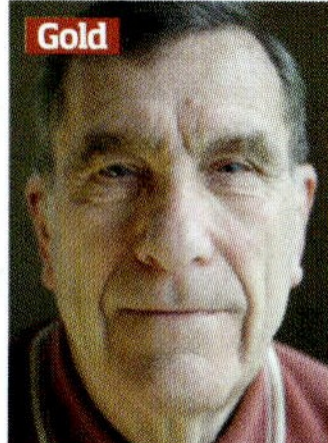

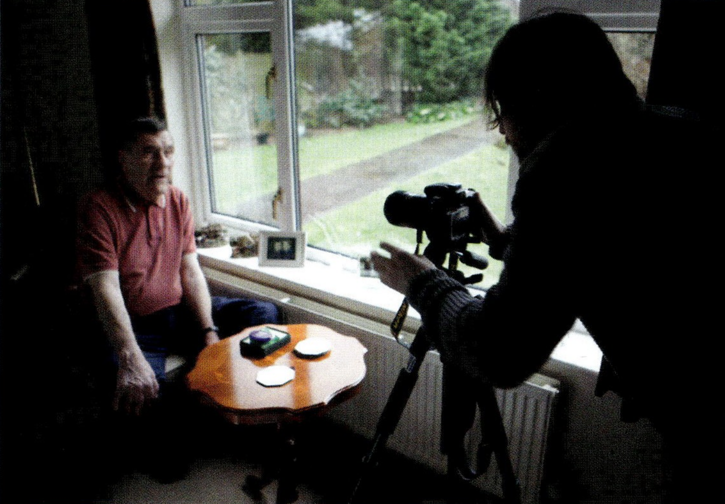

1 **First of all, I placed a stool by the window. It's important to choose the right place, taking into account where the subject's face will be. The trick is to ensure the light falls directly onto the face. I then set up my tripod and mounted the camera on it. I looked through the viewfinder to make sure that the camera was the right distance from Bob for the close-up shot I wanted.**

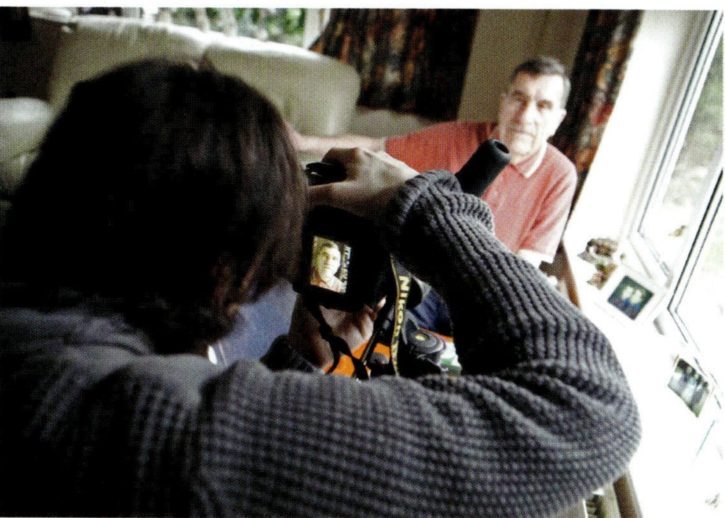

2 **Once everything was in place, I asked Bob to position himself in a comfortable pose. I set the camera to ISO 200 (the lowest native setting on the D700), with an aperture of f/2.8, as I just wanted to keep Bob's eyes and the front of his face in focus, throwing the background into a blur. I then took a few quick shots, and reviewed them on the camera's LCD screen.**

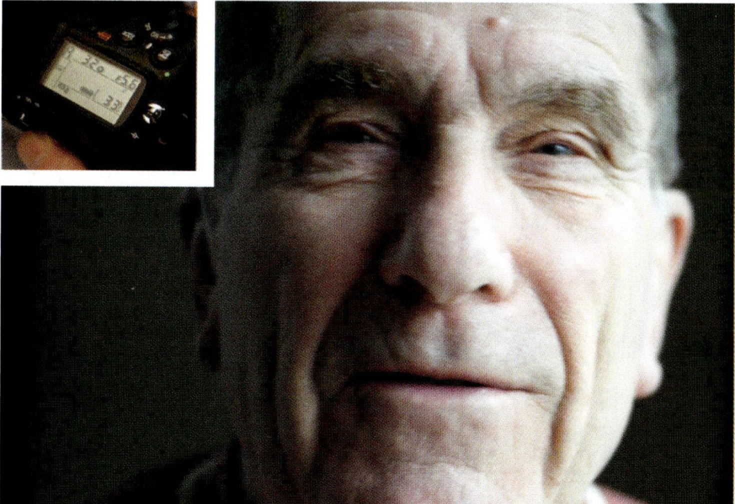

3 **Because of the low light, I was getting longer shutter speeds than I wanted, which made any slight movement on Bob's part really show up. Some of his facial features were also slightly blurred, due to the shallow depth-of-field, so I increased the ISO to 1000, and stopped the aperture down to f/5.6, giving me a slightly faster shutter speed and an increased depth-of-field.**

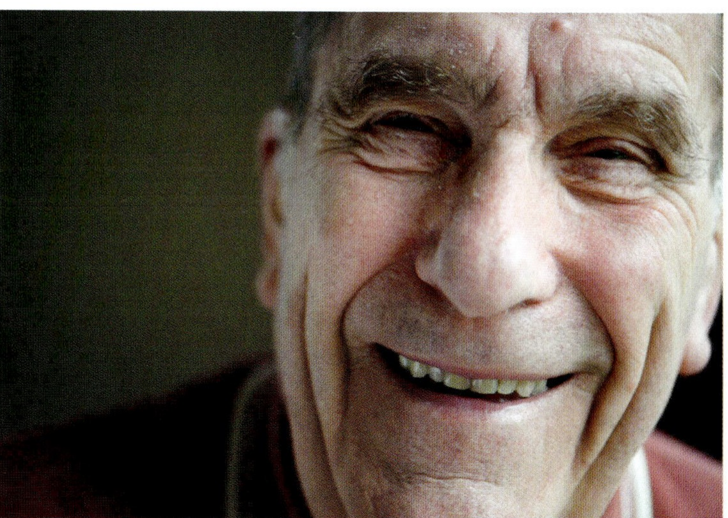

4 **I took a few pictures of Bob looking straight at the camera, but the images didn't capture his vivacious character; so I engaged him in conversation. Bob looks remarkably young for his 80 years, and has a great sense of humour, so by provoking a bit of emotion in his face, it showed up more of his laughter lines and added a bit more interest to the shots.**

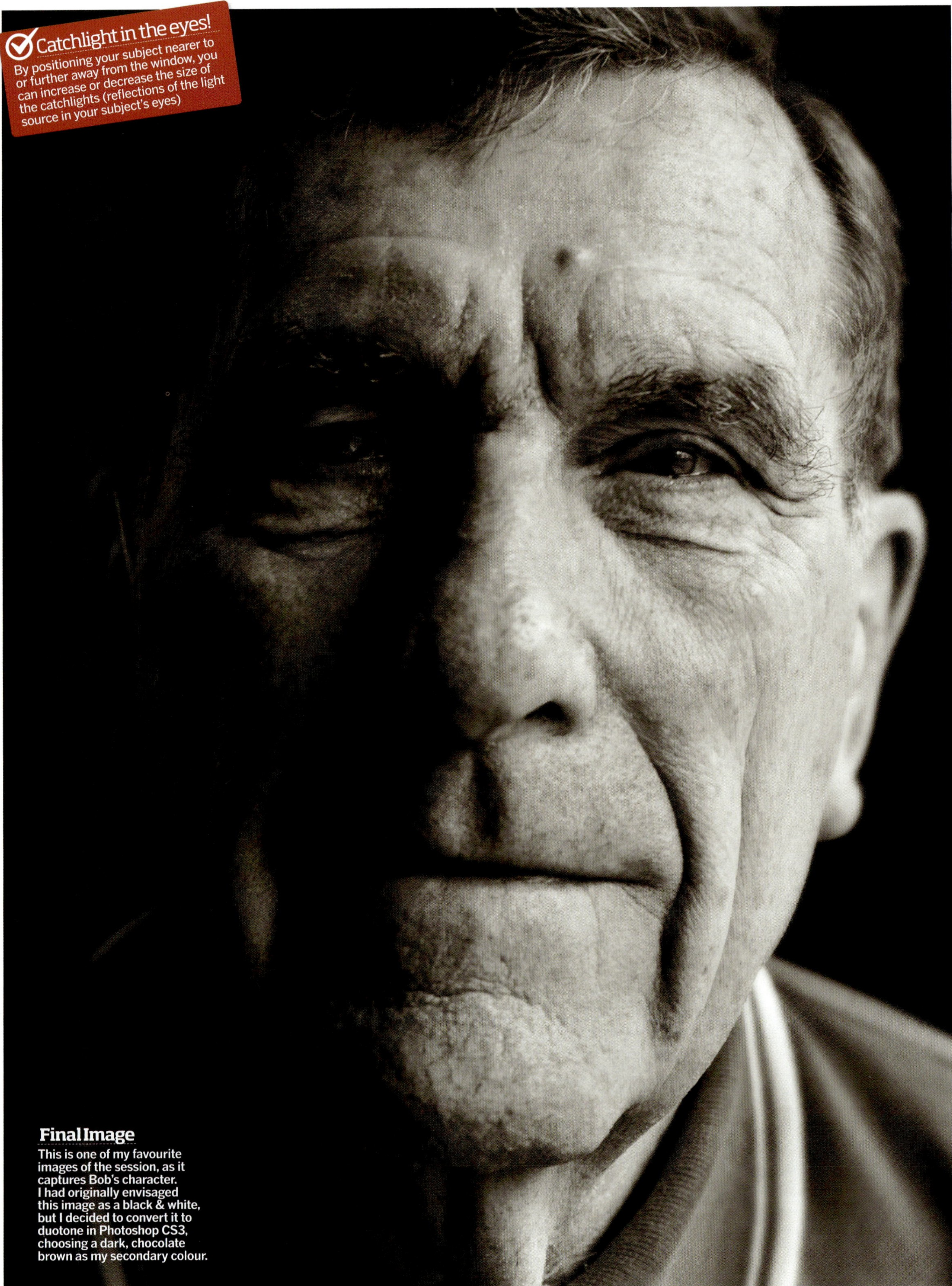

Catchlight in the eyes!
By positioning your subject nearer to or further away from the window, you can increase or decrease the size of the catchlights (reflections of the light source in your subject's eyes)

Final Image
This is one of my favourite images of the session, as it captures Bob's character. I had originally envisaged this image as a black & white, but I decided to convert it to duotone in Photoshop CS3, choosing a dark, chocolate brown as my secondary colour.

How to take the perfect bathtime portrait!

ROSS HODDINOTT: While some photographers might have access to a studio, or own a home studioflash outfit, the majority of us don't. So what can we do when we want to give our portraits a studio-like finish, but lack the equipment at home to do so? Well, have you ever considered using your bathtub? No, not for a relaxing soak, but to reflect light. A white tub will act like a large reflector. It will reflect light entering through an adjacent window, or a burst of flash, evenly around the subject who's sitting in the bath. It will also form a clean, white backdrop helping to create attractive, high-key result. To put this theory to the test, I decided to take some fresh-looking portraits of my two-year old daughter; but would she stay still long enough for me to take a good picture?

Get ready!

TIME REQUIRED
30 MINUTES

EQUIPMENT NEEDED
NIKON D300 & 105MM MACRO LENS

ALSO USED
WHITE BATHTUB

Bathroom set-up

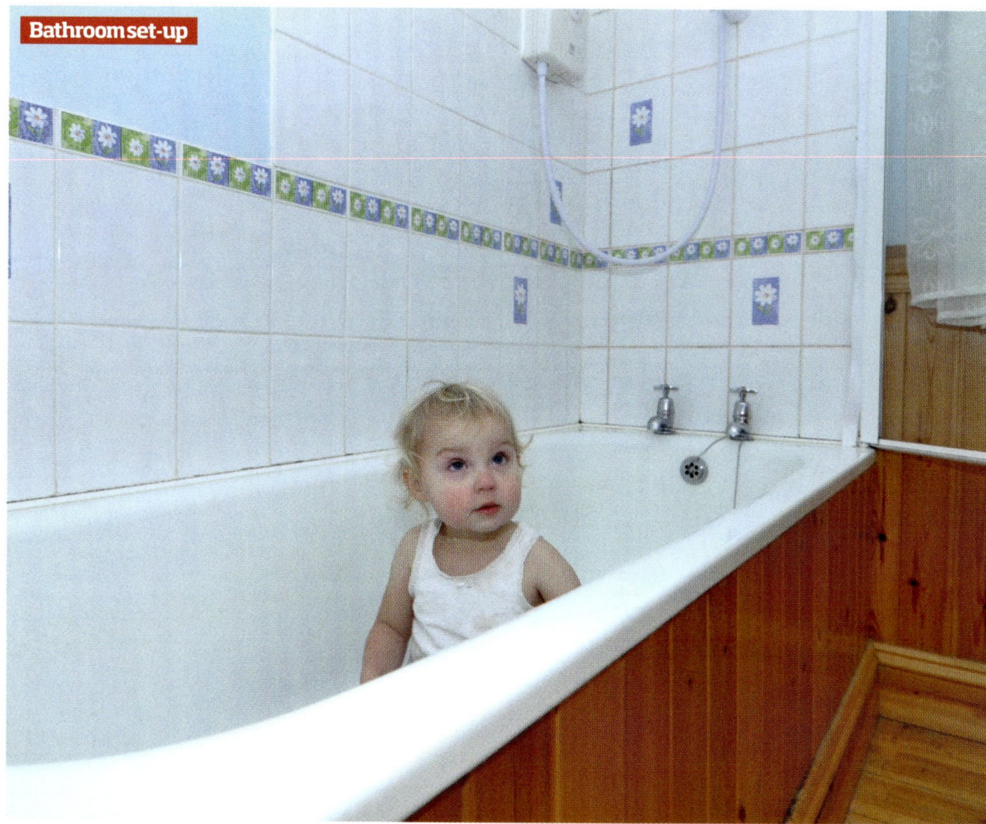

Essential kit: macro lens

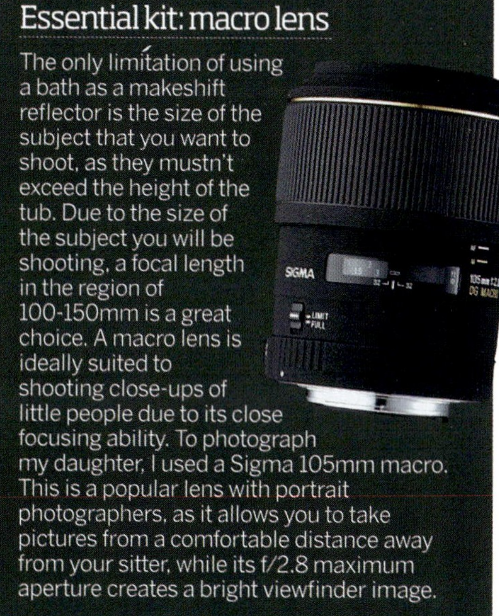

The only limitation of using a bath as a makeshift reflector is the size of the subject that you want to shoot, as they mustn't exceed the height of the tub. Due to the size of the subject you will be shooting, a focal length in the region of 100-150mm is a great choice. A macro lens is ideally suited to shooting close-ups of little people due to its close focusing ability. To photograph my daughter, I used a Sigma 105mm macro. This is a popular lens with portrait photographers, as it allows you to take pictures from a comfortable distance away from your sitter, while its f/2.8 maximum aperture creates a bright viewfinder image.

Checking the histogram

Regularly check your image's histogram to make sure the exposure is accurate. While photographing my daughter in the bath, I relied on the histogram to ensure that the bright, white bathtub wasn't fooling my metering into underexposing the image – something that would have been indicated by peaks to the left of the graph.

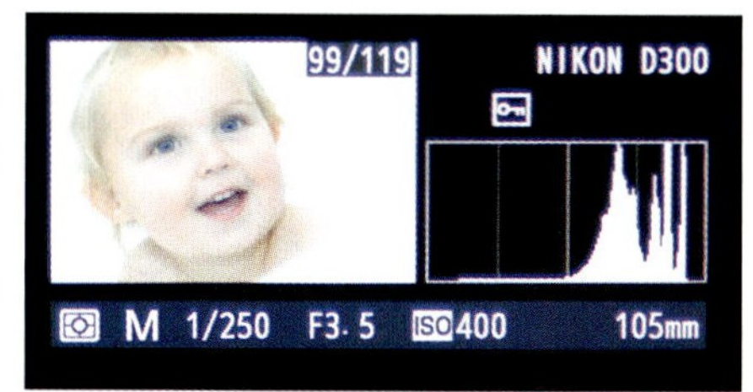

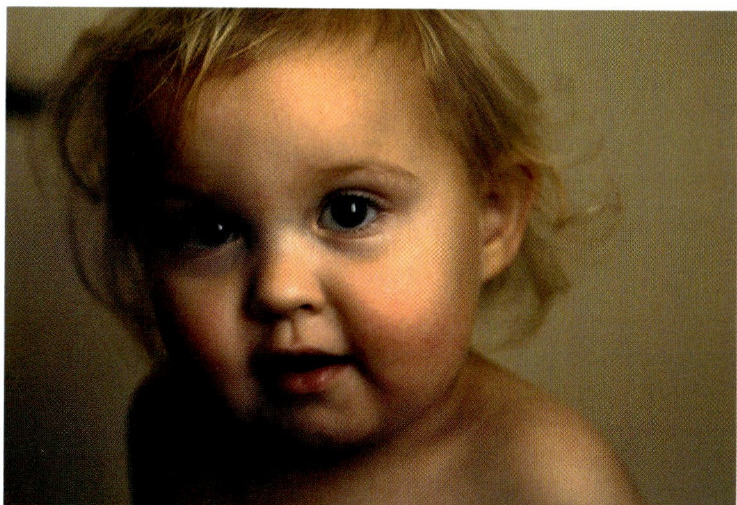

1 I'm not a portrait photographer and don't have access to a proper studio, so when I take pictures indoors, I have to improvise. I wanted to take some fresh shots of my daughter but the initial results were disappointing. When simply taking shots of her in our lounge at home, dark, unflattering shadows formed underneath her eyes, mouth and chin.

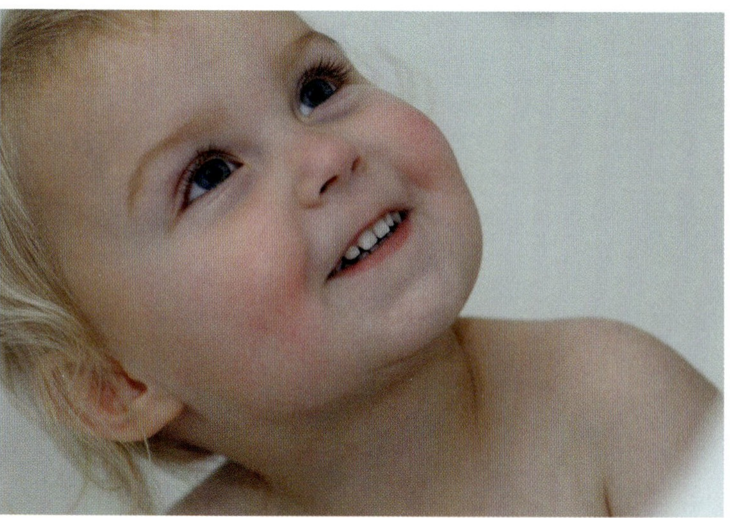

2 With the help of a few chocolate buttons, my daughter sat in the bathtub. Although confused by the lack of water, she happily smiled while I began taking pictures. The light entering through the window bounced around the bath, creating a more flattering light source. The tub formed a clean, simple backdrop, but her eyes lacked a catchlight – vital for creating depth and life.

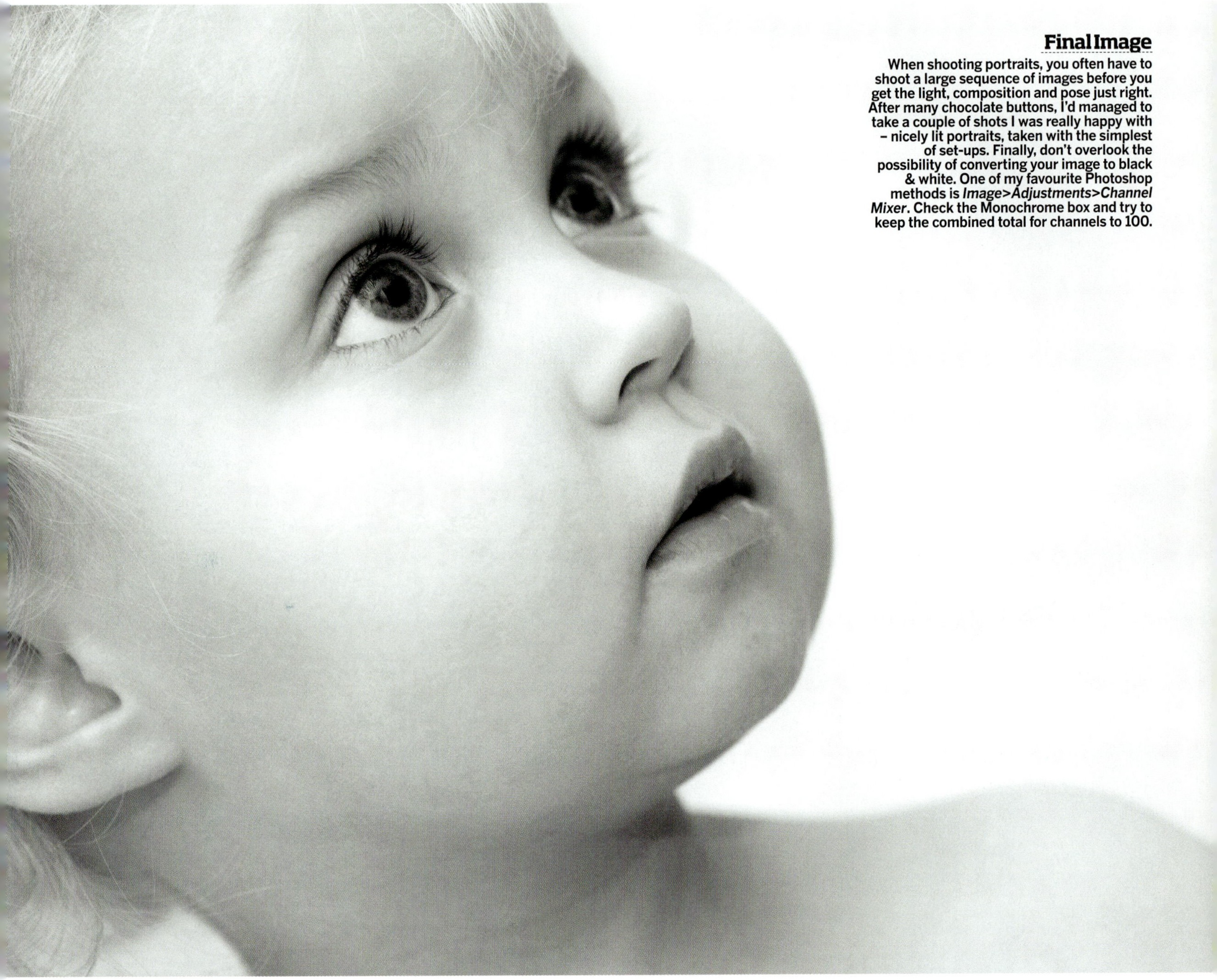

Final Image

When shooting portraits, you often have to shoot a large sequence of images before you get the light, composition and pose just right. After many chocolate buttons, I'd managed to take a couple of shots I was really happy with – nicely lit portraits, taken with the simplest of set-ups. Finally, don't overlook the possibility of converting your image to black & white. One of my favourite Photoshop methods is *Image>Adjustments>Channel Mixer*. Check the Monochrome box and try to keep the combined total for channels to 100.

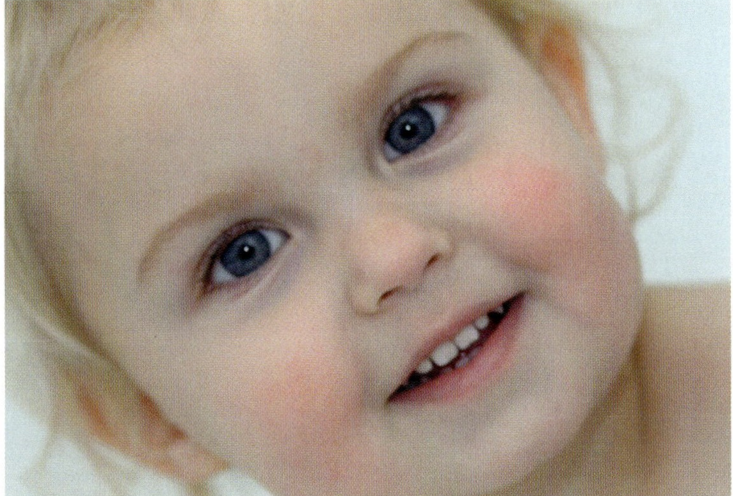

3 To create a catchlight, I used a small burst of fill-in flash. I used my Nikon D300's built-in unit, with a flash exposure compensation of -2 stops, to ensure the burst didn't overwhelm the ambient light. Not only did the burst create a catchlight, but it bounced more light around the bath tub. However, this time my focusing let me down and the eyes are not critically sharp.

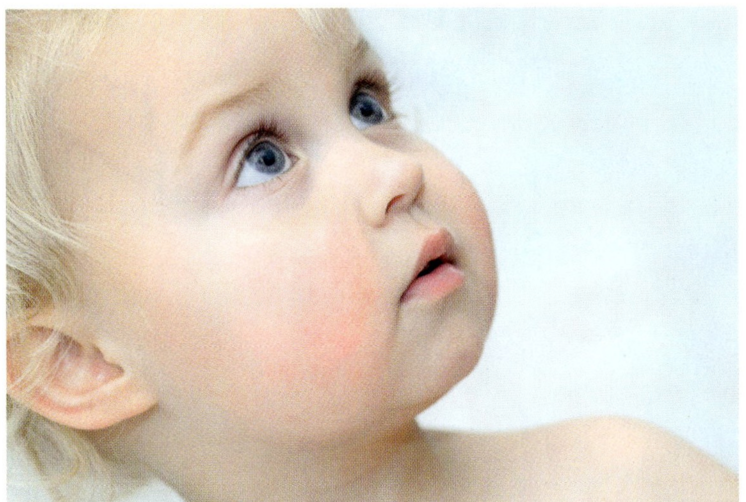

4 I selected the lens's largest aperture of f2/8 to throw the tub out of focus, so it was unrecognisable, and to give a fast enough shutter speed to allow me to work handheld. However, the resulting depth-of-field was narrow, making accurate focusing critical. It is essential that eyes are sharp, so I tried again, taking extra care to ensure the eye closest to me was sharply focused.

Home studio self-portrait

CAROLINE WILKINSON: Studio photography can be an expensive, and daunting, area of photography to test drive, but often the simplest set-ups prove to be the best. Here, I'll show you how to create an attractive hair light using a table lamp, but you can also use wireless flashguns or a studioflash kit.

A hair light is a flattering technique for portraits, created by a strong directional light behind the subject's head, which produces a soft luminous highlight around the hair. If your subject has short hair, directing the light source at the middle of the head can create a subtle halo effect. Whereas, for subjects with long or curly hair, a more dramatic effect can be achieved by positioning the light at the base of the head so it diffuses through more of the hair. It's also worth experimenting with the position of the main light, in this case a second table lamp, to control where the shadows fall on the face. A reflector will also help with this.

I chose to do this technique as a self-portrait. Unfortunately the one person most photographers shoot the least is themselves, but self-portraits are an ideal way to test lighting and creative techniques. Plus it's easier than you might think!

Get ready!

TIME REQUIRED
60 MINUTES

EQUIPMENT NEEDED
NIKON D300, 50MM LENS & MANFROTTO 055B TRIPOD

ALSO USED
TWO HOUSEHOLD LAMPS & A HANDHELD DIFFUSER

Essential kit: Diffuser

In the same way a reflector can fill in shadows or add warmth to a subject's face, a diffuser can soften the strong effects of artificial light – producing a more flattering result. Whether you can get your hands on a diffuser, or an equally effective alternative, such as grease-proof paper, it's worth bearing in mind that not only will it reduce the amount of light that reaches the camera, but will often alter the White Balance too. Normally this won't pose a problem if you're shooting in Raw, as the colour temperature can be easily reset once you have the images on your computer, but if not the White Balance needs to be changed in-camera to compensate for the lighting conditions.

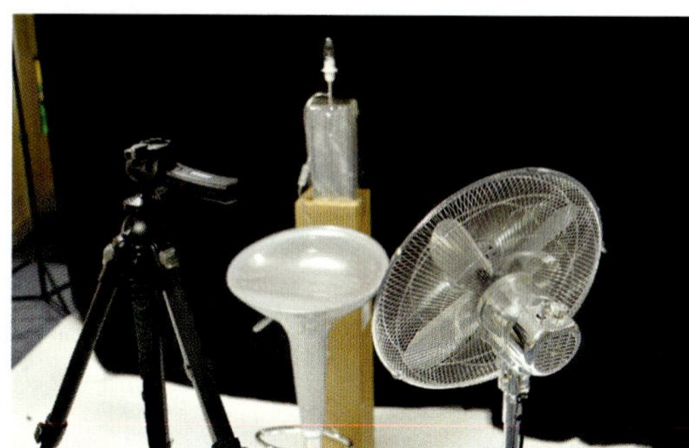

Set-up
I decided to use a black backdrop for this shot to make the effect of the hair light stand out as much as possible. I positioned my main light source, a tungsten desk lamp, off to the side and high up. If this light is too harsh, consider using a diffuser (or a homemade equivalent) to soften it.

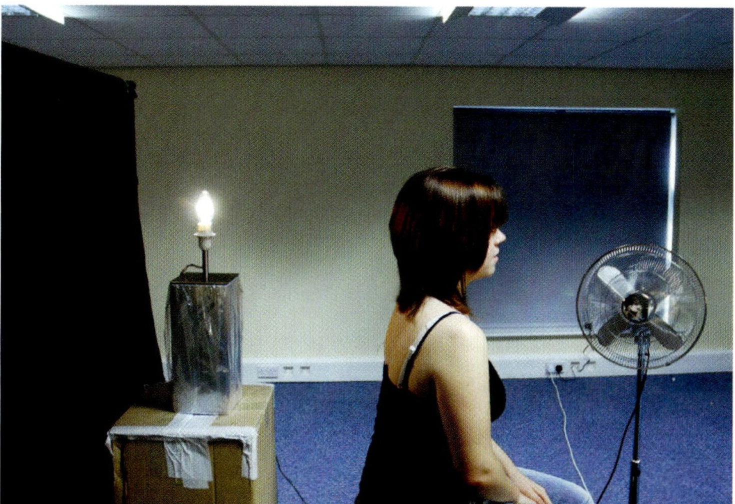

1 HAIR LIGHT I set a standard table lamp, without its shade, between the backdrop and the stool – ensuring the light was directly behind my head and far enough away from the backdrop so not to illuminate it. For optimum highlights, make sure the bulb is level with your head. Use a fan, or have a friend flap a magazine, to lift the hair and add drama to the image.

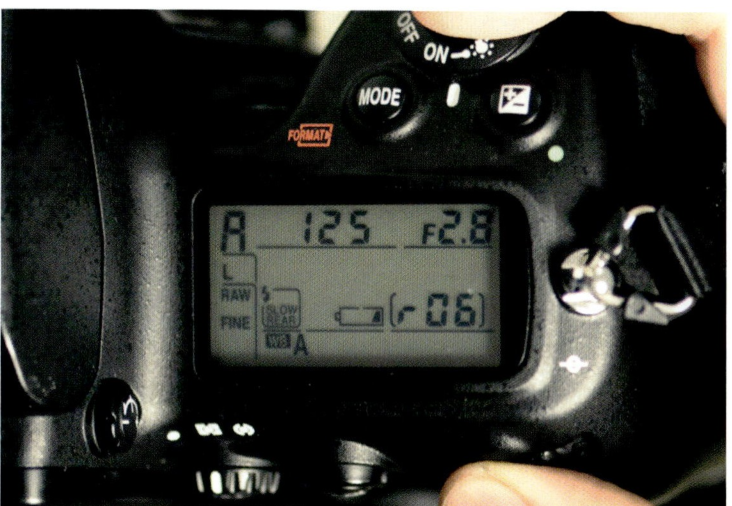

2 EXPOSURE Although I was shooting a head and shoulders portrait, I framed it so there was plenty of room to crop later in Photoshop. I then set the camera to aperture-priority mode at f/2.8 to get a shallow depth-of-field. Having a large mirror placed beside the camera may help you to gauge how the shot looks before it's taken, but I took a few test shots first to assess the framing and focusing.

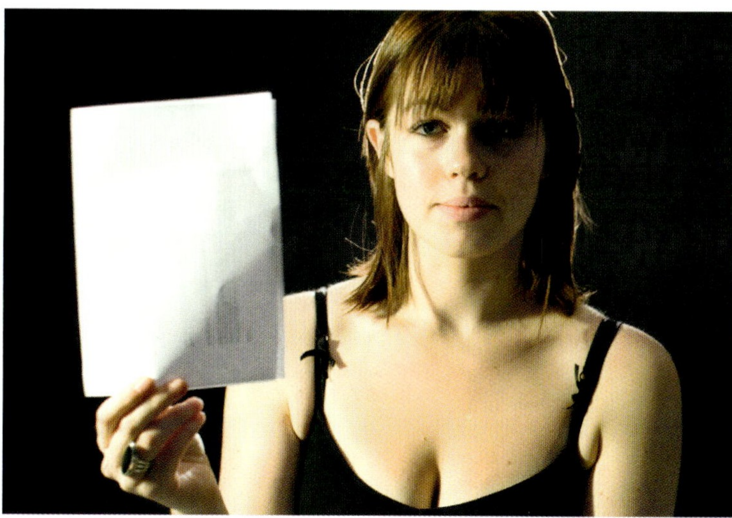

3 WHITE BALANCE Although a diffuser can bathe a subject in softer, more flattering light, it can also alter the colour temperature. As I shot in Raw, the White Balance can be easily changed later in Photoshop's Adobe Camera Raw. I therefore took a photo of me holding a white piece of paper, which I could later use to set the White Balance on my computer.

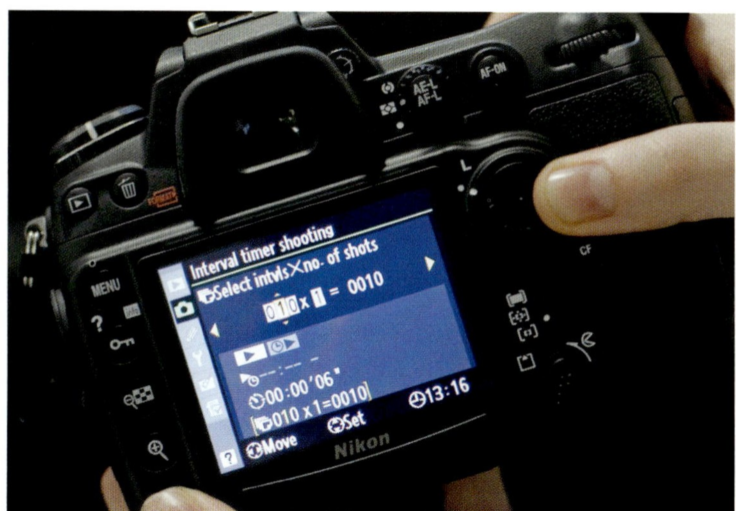

4 INTERVAL SETTING The interval timer is a hidden gem on the Nikon D300. I used it instead of the self-timer as it allowed me to shoot continuous frames at set intervals. A remote trigger would have similar benefits, but the interval timer also adjusts the exposure, focus and metering before each shot. There is a lot of trial and error involved in this technique, so be patient and take lots of shots.

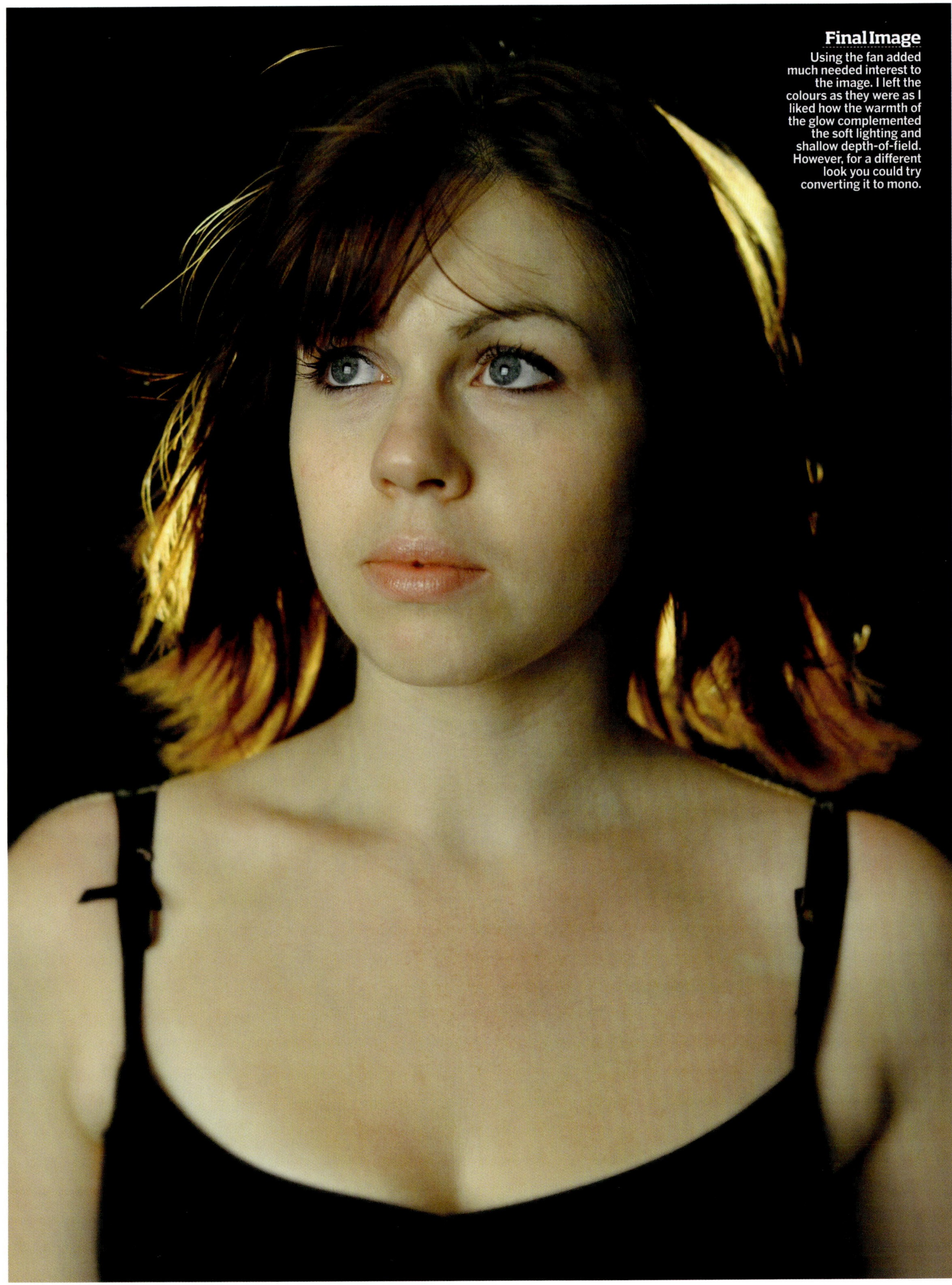

Final Image
Using the fan added much needed interest to the image. I left the colours as they were as I liked how the warmth of the glow complemented the soft lighting and shallow depth-of-field. However, for a different look you could try converting it to mono.

Project: Rooms with a view

Paul Ward shows us the huge potential for shooting portraits in every room in the house

WE CHALLENGED pro-portrait photographer Paul Ward to capture a great portrait in every room of a house within one hour, using different light sources and techniques that showed off what's possible with available light, flash and imagination. As you'll discover, despite the time constraints, Paul managed to creatively use windowlight, flash, candles and even Christmas lights, as well as the humble household light bulb! By the end, you'll have no doubt as to the potential your home offers for you to shoot great indoor portraits. Make sure you give it a go soon!

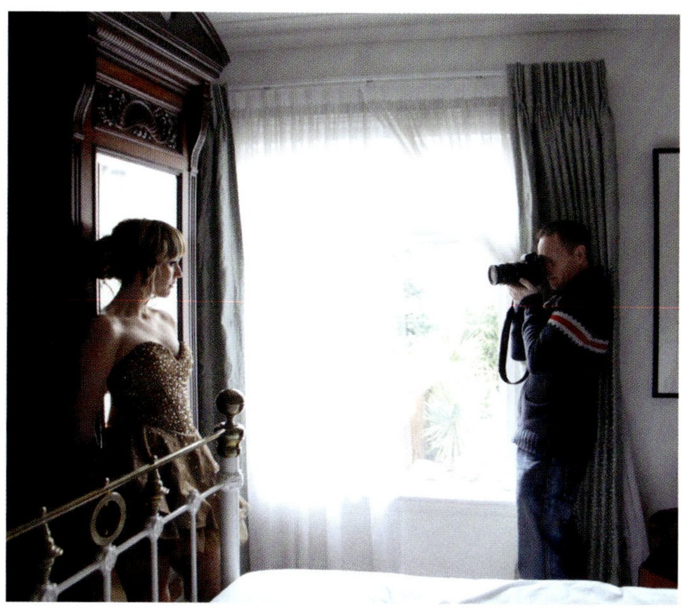

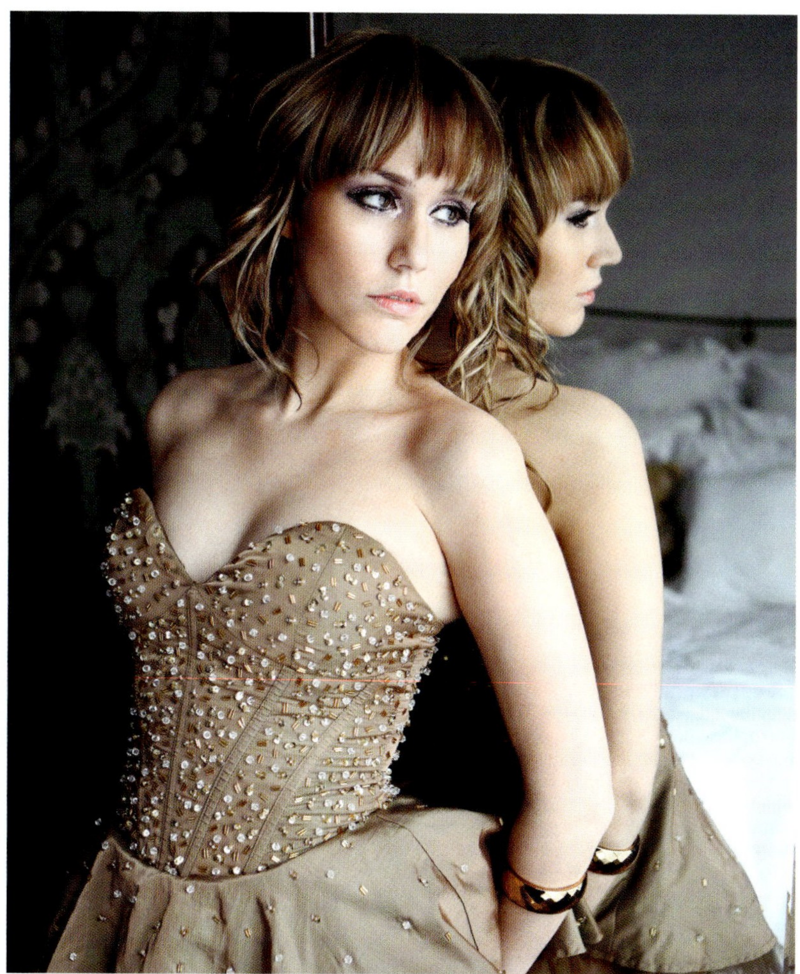

1) Master bedroom: Diffused windowlight

On entry to the bedroom, Paul instantly earmarked the window and mirror as an ambient light source and interesting backdrop, so he positioned Rebecca side-on to the net-curtained window and tried a couple of ideas. Firstly, he asked Rebecca to turn her head away from the window so as to use the light from the window as a white backdrop. By doing this her face fell into shade, so a friend held a reflector to the side of Rebecca to bounce window light back onto her face. Next, he asked her to look towards the window and to create some extra shadow, held the curtain open slightly. As there was limited room for a tripod, Paul set his DSLR to manual mode and set the lens to its widest aperture of f/2.8, which gave a shutter speed of 1/60sec at ISO 800.

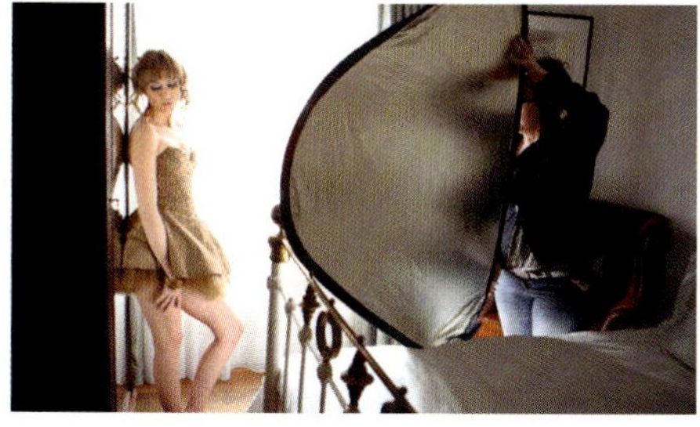

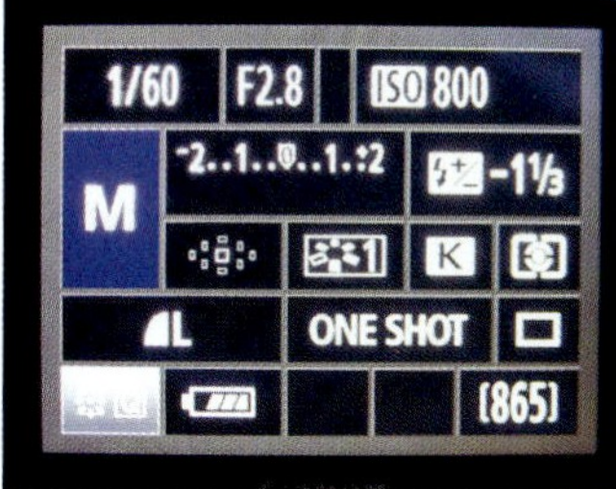

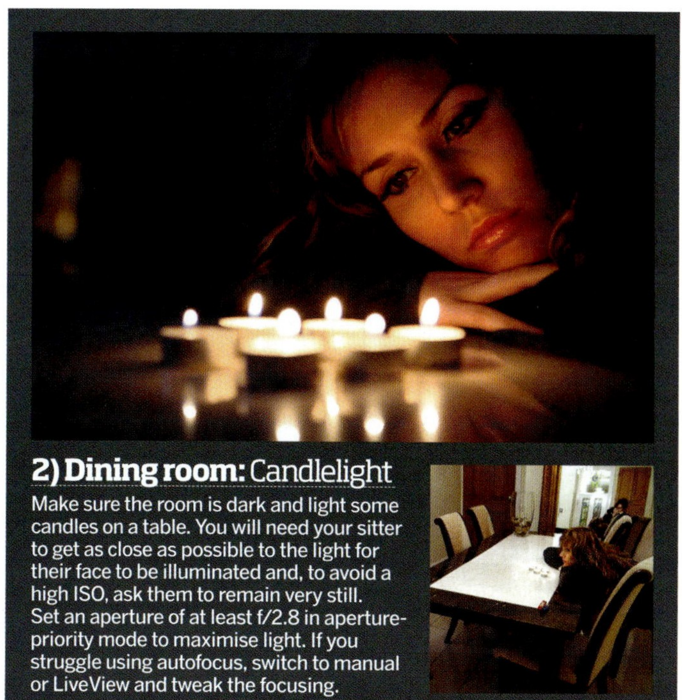

2) Dining room: Candlelight

Make sure the room is dark and light some candles on a table. You will need your sitter to get as close as possible to the light for their face to be illuminated and, to avoid a high ISO, ask them to remain very still. Set an aperture of at least f/2.8 in aperture-priority mode to maximise light. If you struggle using autofocus, switch to manual or LiveView and tweak the focusing.

3) Lounge: One tungsten light bulb

A single light bulb can be efficient in creating shots high in contrast, as it's a sharp light source that will produce harsh shadows. Try and get the light bulb head-height with the model and position it in front of the model's face and the camera to minimise shadows. Either set your camera to a high ISO with an aperture of f/2.8 or wider, or put the camera on a tripod and get your model to stand very still. Remember to switch the White Balance to Tungsten too!

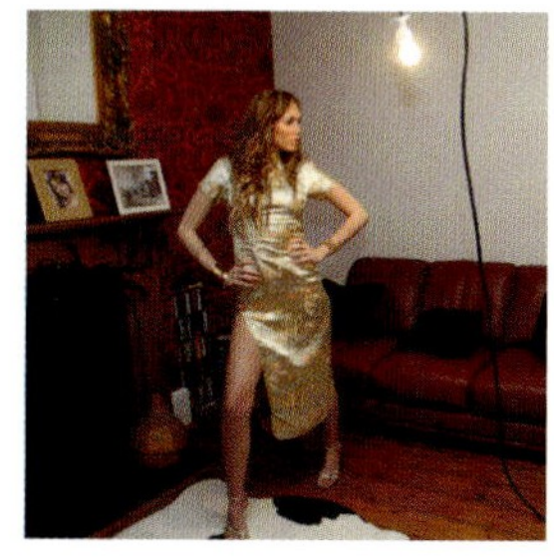

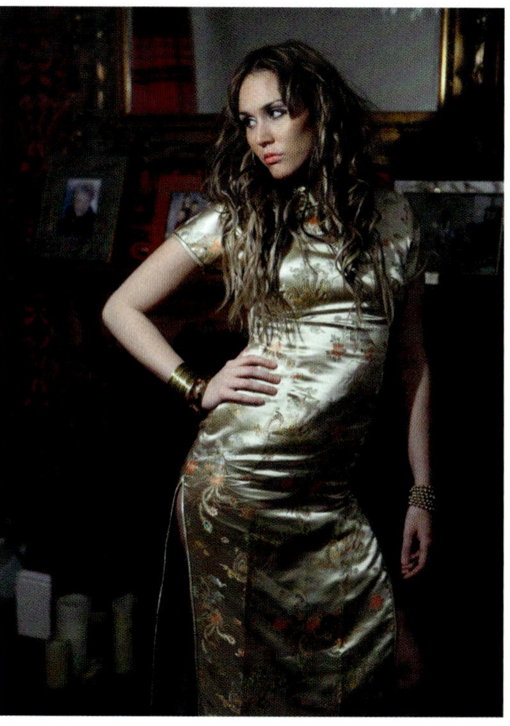

4) Loft: Bounce flash

The principle for this shot can be applied to any room that has white walls or a white ceiling. Paul used this statement wallpaper as a background but, as the rest of the room is white, he was able to bounce one flash off a wall behind him to illuminate Rebecca evenly. Although this can be enough, Paul also fired a second flash into a Brolly to illuminate her at a 45° angle.

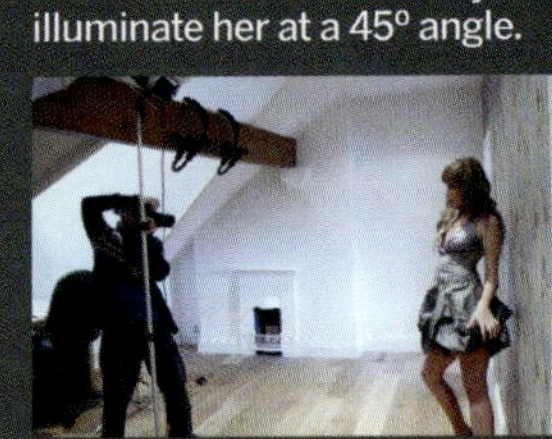

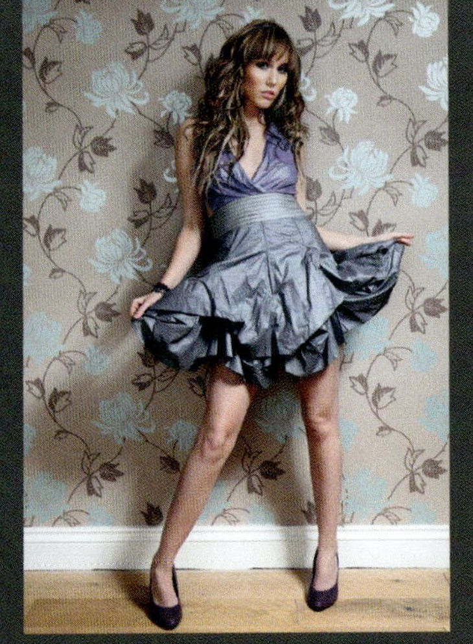

5) Guest bedroom: Christmas lights

This shot can be done in any room that's completely dark. Drape Christmas lights across, or wrap them around, your subject's body. You will need to use a high ISO of at least 800 and a wide aperture, such as f/1.8, so a 50mm lens is ideal. As long as you place some lights on or near the face, your camera's autofocus should lock on to the subject but, if not, switch to manual focus.

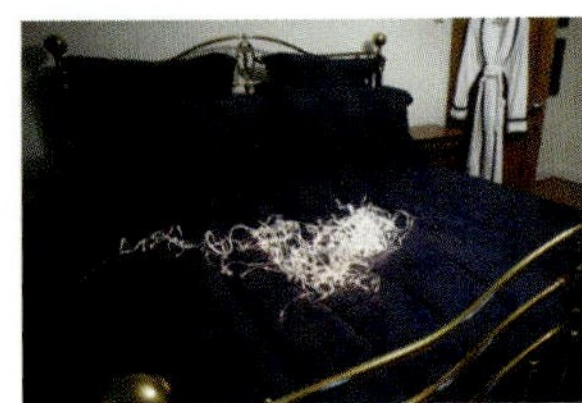

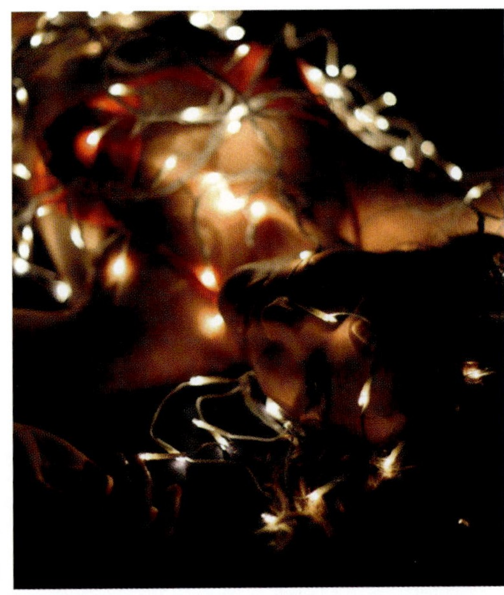

6) Bathroom: Diffused windowlight

Shutters are useful for controlling harsh sunlight and in this bathroom set-up they were necessary as the light increased in strength as the shoot progressed. Having taken a test shot in manual mode, I knew f/6.3 was too narrow an aperture as even at ISO 800 it underexposed the scene. I opened the aperture to f/4 and stopped down from 1/160sec to 1/125sec and ISO 400 to reduce noise. I asked Rebecca to angle herself side-on to the window as space was limited, and this also provided some contrast with the aid of the blinds across her face. While normally altering the White Balance setting to match the lighting (in this case Daylight) turns in the best results, I also tried a Tungsten WB to give a creative blue cast.

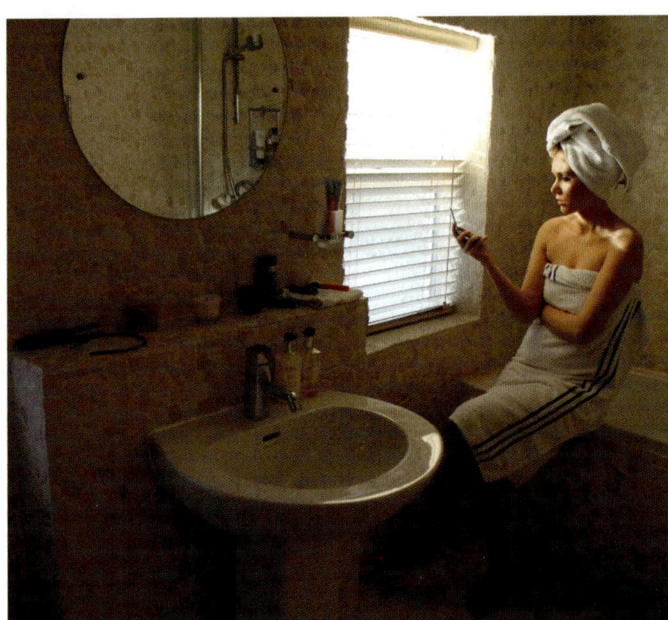

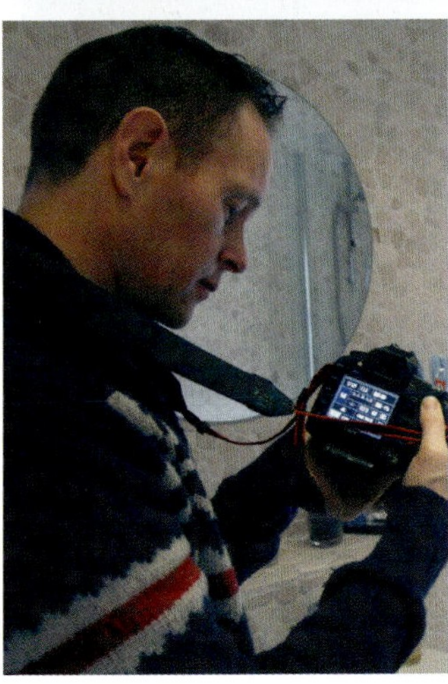

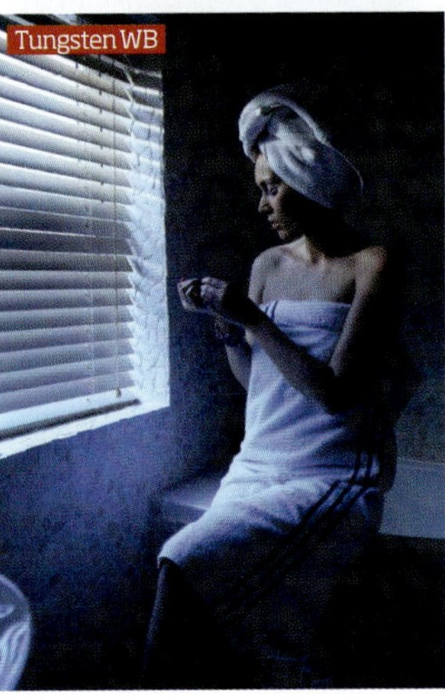

Tungsten WB

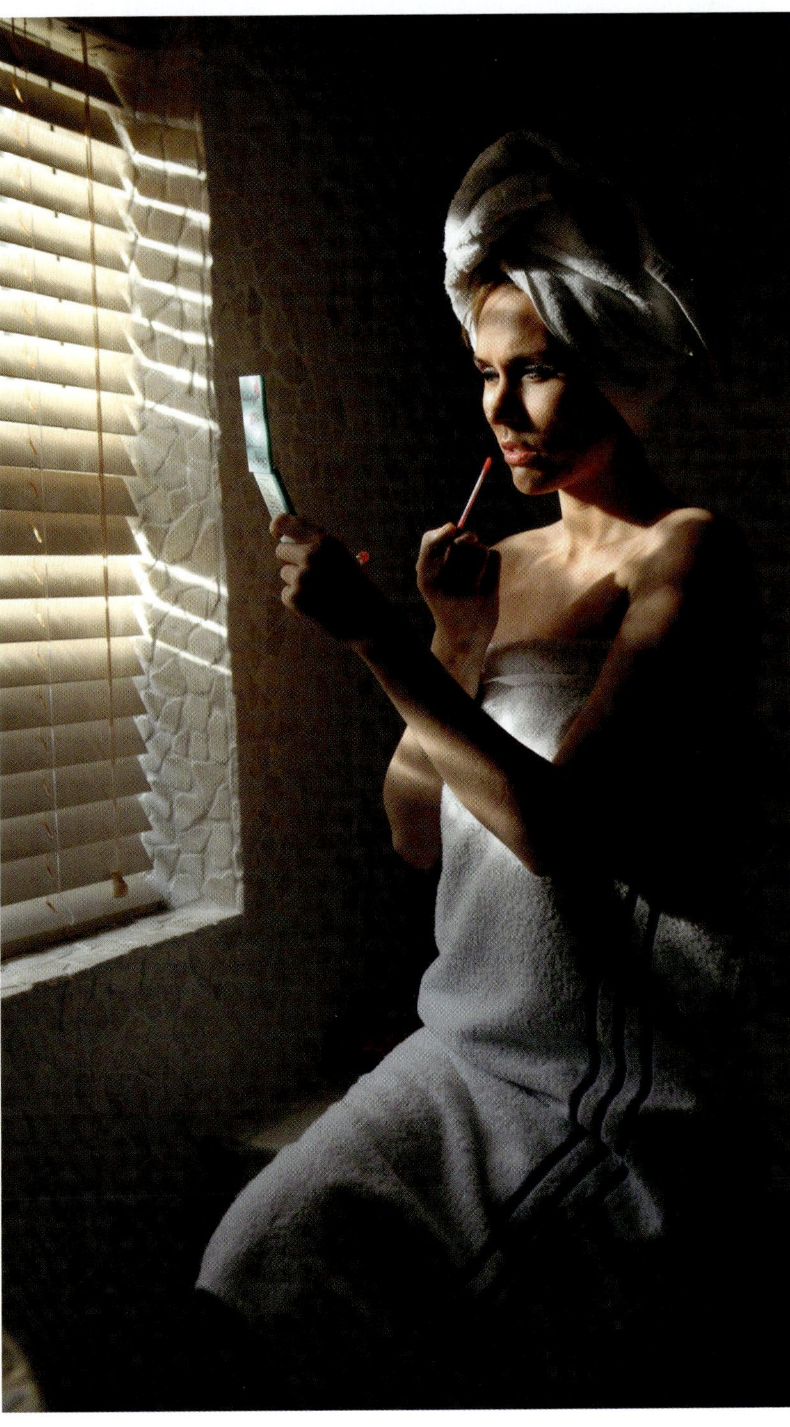

Getting prepared for flash

Flash isn't as frightening as you might think it is. It's just a matter of knowing what to do, when to do it and how

WE'VE ALL BEEN DISAPPOINTED WHEN using a flashgun has produced an image that has failed to capture the mood of a scene. This usually happens when we shoot in auto mode with no real thought for what we are doing or why. The secret to good flash photography lies in using the full range of your camera's exposure modes, and thinking carefully about how light from the flash – and from other sources – affects the final result.

The quality of a flash-lit picture depends on what settings you choose for your camera and flash, for instance whether you use aperture-priority or program exposure mode, or whether you have auto or slow-sync flash set. This is all because, by changing modes, you are altering settings such as shutter speed, which in turn affects the amount of ambient light that reaches the sensor. Additionally, different flash modes command the flash to fire at the beginning or end of the exposure. Either option changes how moving objects will be rendered in the final photograph.

While all this may seem complicated, it isn't. The beauty of digital SLR photography is that you are free to experiment (and learn from your mistakes), and we recommend you do this while following our advice. Take inspiration, try it out yourself, and adapt it with your own ideas. Before long you'll be using flash as an everyday part of your photography – rather than being afraid of it – no matter what your subject matter.

Common flash modes you'll find on DSLRs

The way your DSLR and flash work together is governed by the flash mode that you use. Here are the most common flash modes that you'll find on your digital SLR or dedicated hotshoe-mounted flashgun.

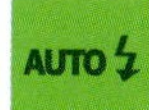

Auto When light levels fall, your DSLR will activate the built-in flash. It calculates aperture via TTL metering, but sets a high shutter speed to avoid camera shake. Convenient, but not very creative.

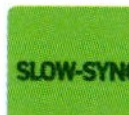

Slow-sync It uses a slower shutter speed to record ambient light properly. Good for night-time portraits where the mood needs to be recorded too, but be careful of camera shake.

Rear/second-curtain sync Works the same as slow-sync mode, except that the flash is fired at the end of the exposure, rather than at the start. Great for leaving a trail of light behind moving subjects.

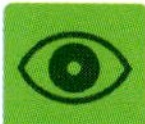

Antired-eye Aims to prevent or reduce so-called red-eye in flash portraits by using a series of pre-flashes to make a subject's pupil narrow before the exposure is taken.

Flash-off Stops a camera from automatically engaging the built-in flash. More useful than you may think, especially when trying to shoot low-light scenes on a tripod.

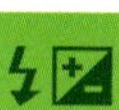

Flash exposure compensation Your DSLR automatically calculates the amount of flash needed for an exposure. Use this feature to increase or decrease the amount of flash output to your liking.

Jargon buster

FLASH EXPOSURE COMPENSATION A feature that lets you increase and decrease flash output, in fractions of an f/stop, as you would adjust ambient light using your DSLR's exposure compensation facility.

GUIDE NUMBER A numerical measure of a flashgun's power. The higher the number, the greater the power. In manual flash mode, divide the Guide Number by the camera-to-subject distance in meters to calculate the required aperture for a decent exposure.

HIGH-SPEED FLASH The ability to use your flash at faster shutter speeds than the camera's standard sync speed. Very useful when trying to work with fill-in flash outdoors in sunny, high-contrast conditions.

PAINTING WITH FLASH The practice of locking open your camera's shutter on a long exposure, and then firing an off-camera flash at your subject multiple times from different angles.

REAR-CURTAIN SYNC A feature that sets the flashgun to fire at the end of the exposure rather than at the beginning. Also called 'second-curtain sync'. Useful when shooting movement with slow-sync flash.

SLOW-SYNC The practice of firing a flash while also keeping a camera's shutter open for a long time, thereby capturing both flash and ambient light.

TTL Through the lens metering, known as TTL, is the way in which a flashgun and camera work together to properly expose a scene. The camera measures flashgun output coming through the lens and tells it when to stop.

WIRELESS FLASH Firing an external flashgun without cables, using an infrared transmitter or integral flash instead.

How to select flash modes on DSLRs

You'll find your camera allows you to select a variety of flash modes for the built-in flash unit. Some cameras also allow you to control the functions of a hotshoe-mounted flashgun too

CANON EOS 500D

(1) Press MENU and scroll to the first tab for red-eye reduction. Below this is a setting called Flash Control with a variety of options including first and second-curtain sync and flash exposure compensation. Custom Functions (seventh tab) has other options.

(2) To deactivate the flash, set the mode dial to Flash-off.

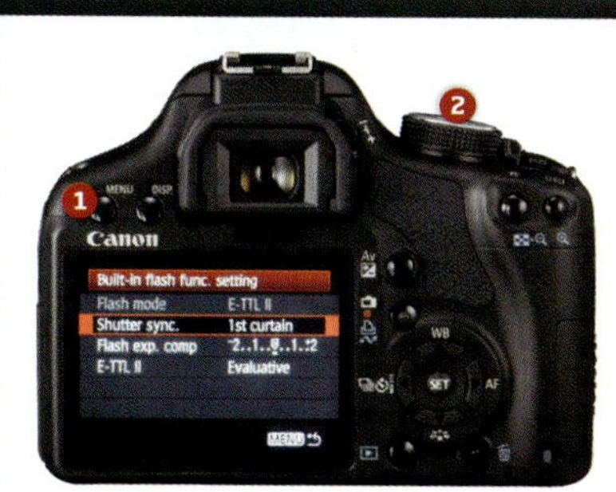

NIKON D60

(1) Press and hold the flash button and turn the input dial to change flash modes.

(2) To set flash exposure compensation, press and hold both the flash and exposure compensation buttons and turn the input dial.

(3) Press MENU, and go to the third tab for Custom Functions and more flash options.

(4) To deactivate the flash, set the mode dial to Flash-off.

OLYMPUS E-420

(1) Press the flash button to pop up the flash and press again to bring up the flash modes on the LCD monitor.

(2) Rotate the thumb dial to choose a flash mode and press OK to set it.

(3) Press MENU and go to the fourth tab for Custom Functions, which has a couple more flash options.

PENTAX K200D

(1) Press the Fn button and then the down button of the four-way control to select flash modes. Use the left/right of the four-way control to select flash modes or the thumb dial to set flash exposure compensation.

(2) Press MENU and go to the Custom Settings (fourth tab) for other flash options.

(3) To deactivate the flash, set the mode dial to Flash-off.

SONY ALPHA 200

(1) Press the Fn button and select the Flash mode box for access to various options.

(2) Press MENU and go to the first tab for other flash options including flash exposure compensation.

(3) To deactivate the flash, set the mode dial to Flash-off.

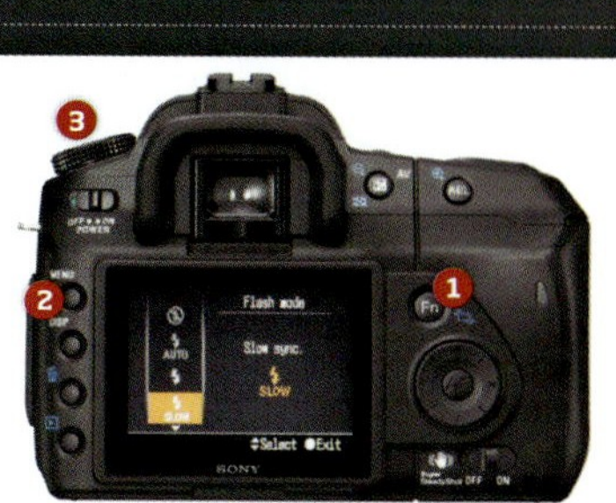

BRETT HARKNESS

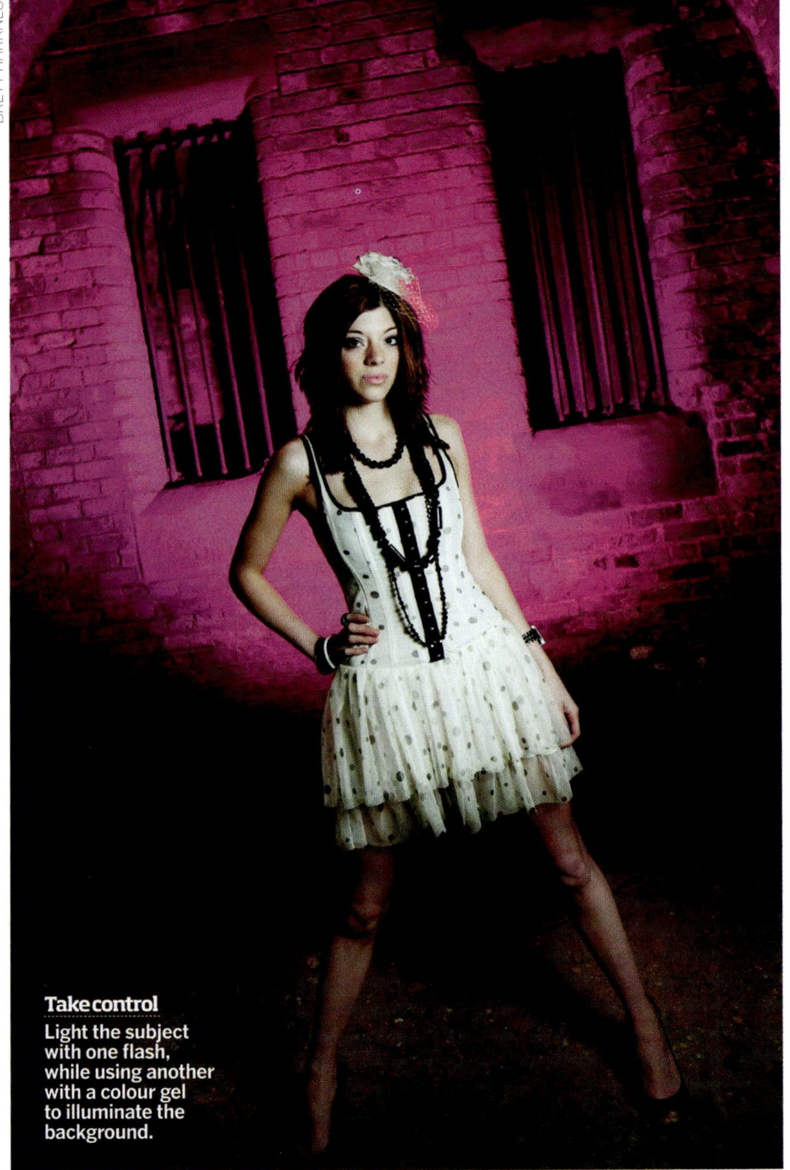

Take control
Light the subject with one flash, while using another with a colour gel to illuminate the background.

Anatomy of a flashgun

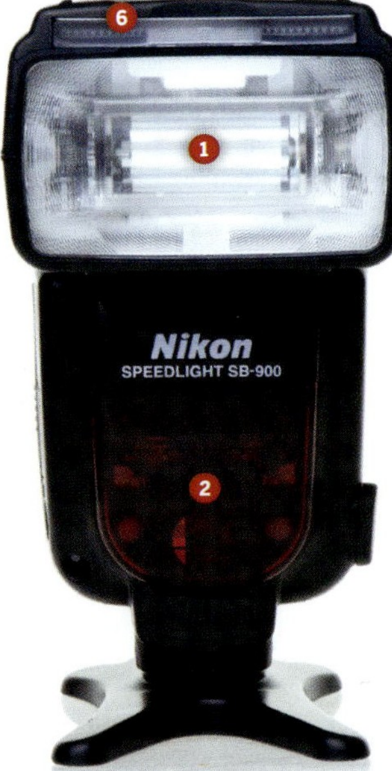

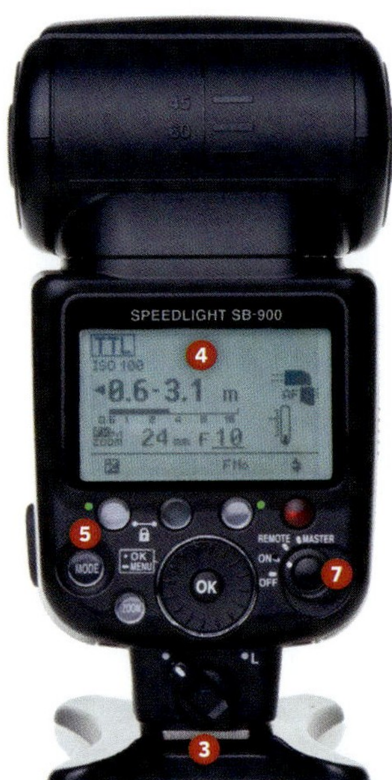

1) FLASH HEAD Can be rotated or flipped to bounce light off walls and ceilings. Most zoom to match light coverage to the lens in use.

2) AF ASSIST Projects an infrared beam to help focus in dim light.

3) HOTSHOE The connection between camera and flash. Used to trigger the flash and communicate data for TTL light metering.

4) LCD SCREEN Shows the status of the flashgun. In this case the metering mode, range, zoom setting and f/stop are all visible. Here, we can see that the unit is set to TTL exposure mode for an aperture of f/10 and a 24mm lens, giving a range of between 0.6 to 3.1m.

5) BUTTONS AND CONTROL WHEEL Used to set advanced features, like flash exposure control, metering mode etc.

6) FOLD-AWAY REFLECTOR AND DIFFUSER The reflector can be used with the gun in bounce mode to direct a small amount of light towards the subject. The diffuser is used to disperse light over a wider area when shooting with ultra wide-angle lenses.

7) POWER AND MODE SWITCH Turns on power to the flashgun and, in this case, dictates how the unit behaves when used off-camera in wireless TTL mode.

Exposure modes and flash

How exposure modes and overrides affect flash for different brands of DSLRs*

BRAND	CANON	NIKON	PENTAX	OLYMPUS	SONY
PROGRAM MODE	Camera sets shutter speed and aperture, but raises shutter speed to avoid camera shake. Background may be dark.	Camera sets exposure, but raises shutter speed to avoid camera shake, unless slow-sync mode is set. Background may be dark.	Camera sets exposure, but raises shutter speed to avoid camera shake, unless slow-sync mode is set. Background may be dark.	Camera sets exposure, but raises shutter speed to avoid camera shake, unless slow-sync mode is set. Background may be dark.	Camera sets exposure, but raises shutter speed to avoid camera shake, unless slow-sync mode is set. Background may be dark.
APERTURE-PRIORITY	User picks aperture; camera calculates flash exposure accordingly. Shutter speed is picked to render ambient light correctly. Be aware of camera shake.	User picks the aperture and the camera selects flash exposure accordingly. Shutter speed is limited to prevent camera shake, unless slow-sync mode is selected.	User sets aperture and camera sets shutter speed to correctly expose background, up to the maximum sync speed. Risk of camera shake in low light.	User picks aperture and camera selects flash exposure accordingly. Shutter speed limited to prevent camera shake, unless slow-sync mode is also selected.	User picks aperture and camera selects flash exposure accordingly. Shutter speed limited to prevent camera shake, unless slow-sync mode is also selected.
SHUTTER-PRIORITY	User picks shutter speed and camera picks corresponding aperture for ambient light, then calculates flash output according to this aperture.	User picks shutter speed and camera picks corresponding aperture to expose ambient light correctly, then calculates flash output according to this aperture.	User picks shutter speed and camera picks corresponding aperture to expose ambient light properly, then calculates flash output according to this aperture.	User picks shutter speed and camera picks corresponding aperture to expose ambient light correctly, then calculates flash output according to this aperture.	User picks shutter speed and camera picks corresponding aperture to expose ambient light correctly, then calculates flash output according to this aperture.
EXPOSURE COMPENSATION	Affects ambient light exposure only.	Affects both ambient and flash exposure.	Affects both ambient and flash exposure.	Affects ambient light exposure only.	Affects both ambient and flash exposure.
FLASH EXPOSURE COMPENSATION	Affects flash exposure only.	Affects flash exposure only.	Affects flash exposure only.	Affects flash exposure only.	Affects flash exposure only.

* Please note that the stated information relates to most general shooting conditions. However, in certain situations, the camera and flash will operate differently.

Flash exposures with an easy twist!

DANIEL LEZANO: While virtually every technique you'll encounter has instructions to keep your DSLR as steady as possible, this particular effect involves you doing the complete opposite and moving your camera during the exposure. The principle behind flash swirls – or flash twirls as they're also commonly called – is simple. You rotate the camera smoothly while shooting a long exposure with a burst of flash. The flash output will illuminate the main subject while the ambient light in the scene is recorded as a blur due to the camera movement. The effect is unusual and not suited to every situation, but works a treat when you need to use flash but you want to add more visual impact and energy than you'd get from a normal flash exposure. Try it the next time family or friends visit your home and see how you get on. It's pretty easy to do!

Get ready!

TIME REQUIRED
15 MINUTES

EQUIPMENT NEEDED
CANON EOS 450D & 17-40MM LENS

ALSO USED
FAIRY LIGHTS

Preparing to twirl

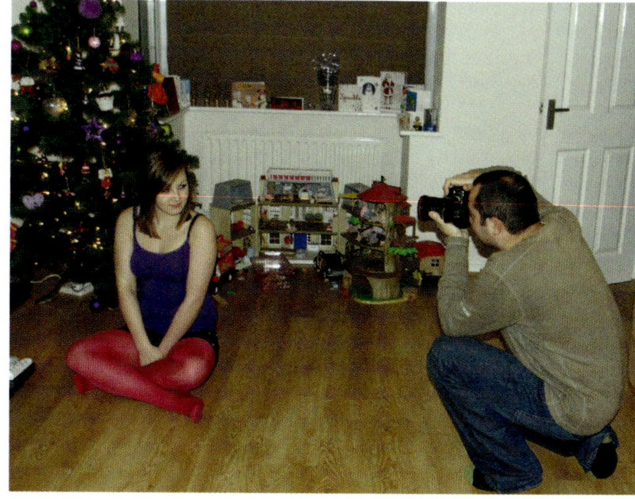

There are a few things to bear in mind when you want to give this technique a try. The first is even though the technique is called flash swirls, the streaks of light are not the result of the flashgun's exposure: it's the ambient light being recorded during the exposure. The longer the exposure, the longer the twirl and the brighter the ambient light, the more pronounced the twirls appear. Including bright light sources, such as lamps, light bulbs or even sunlight streaming through windows, can lead to very bright streaks. And of course, if the light is coloured, then the streaks will be too. So if shooting indoors, with the White Balance set to Flash or AWB, the flash-lit subject will appear correctly exposed and colour-balanced, while ambient light sources such as table lamps or ceiling lights will appear as warm orange streaks. And while you can use a hotshoe-mounted flashgun for added power, your built-in flash is more than suitable, as this step-by-step proves.

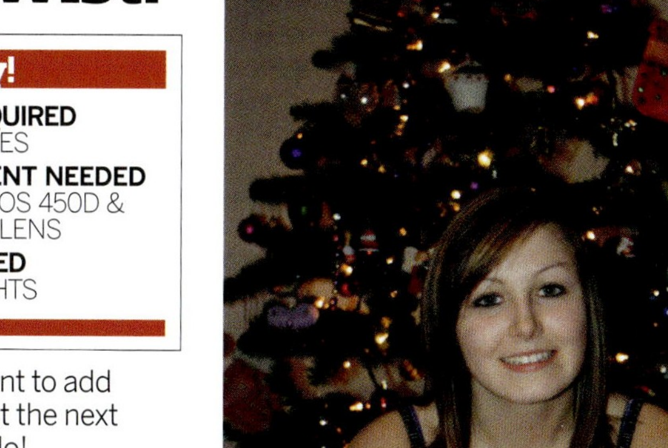

1 You can try this technique indoors or outdoors, all you need is a backdrop with bright light sources to create the swirls. Here's my chosen scene, an indoor portrait taken with the subject sat in front of a Christmas tree.

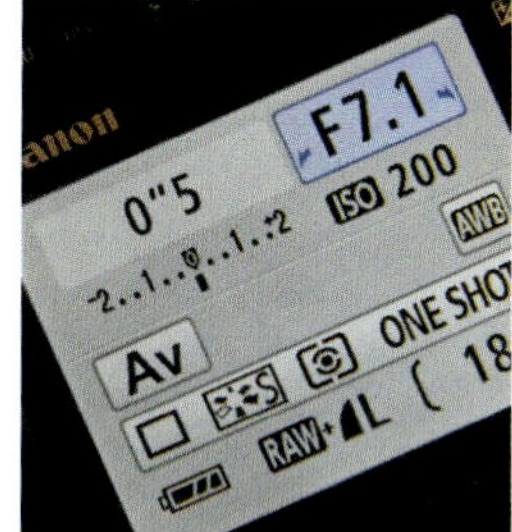

2 To create the swirl effect, you must set a long exposure so that once the flash has fired, you have time to rotate the camera to create the swirls. Set your camera to Av or Tv and set slow-sync mode on your flash. You'll need to experiment with the shutter speed, but start by setting 0.5 seconds.

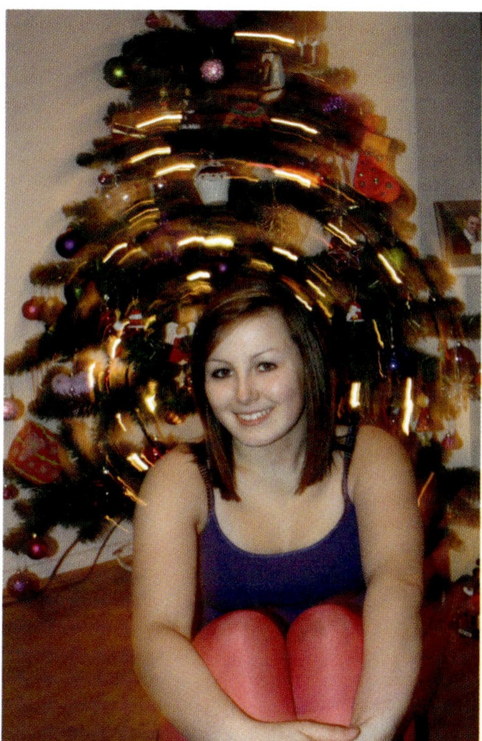

3 To create the swirl, you need to fire the shutter and as soon as the flash fires, start turning the camera slowly in a circular motion. With this first attempt, the light streaks are too short because the exposure is too short and I turned the camera too slowly.

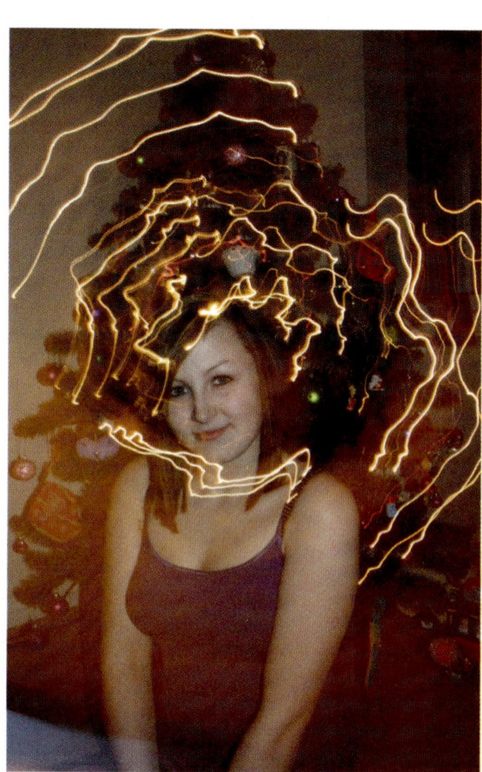

4 I increase the shutter speed to two seconds and try again. This time I've rotated the camera too quickly and by doing this it has resulted in the light trails being too long and erratic. I also have the problem that the streaks are cutting across my subject's face and upper body.

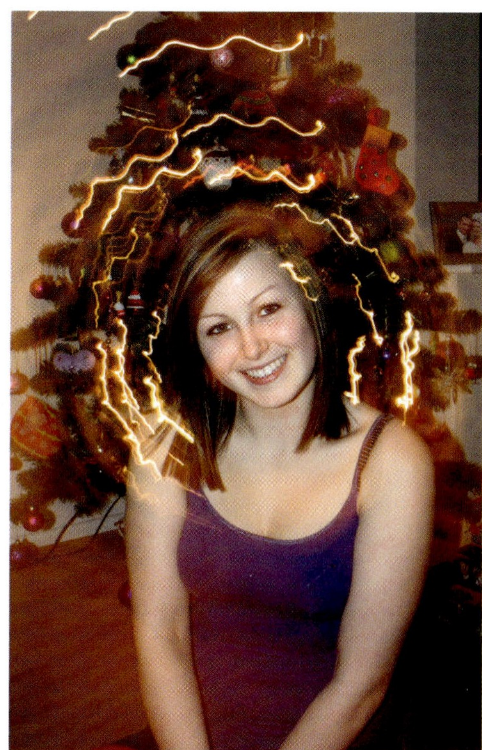

5 I adjust the shutter speed by halving it to one second and try again. The shortened exposure results in better light swirls that aren't as long and don't cut across my subject too much. With the exposure sorted, I can now concentrate on improving the composition.

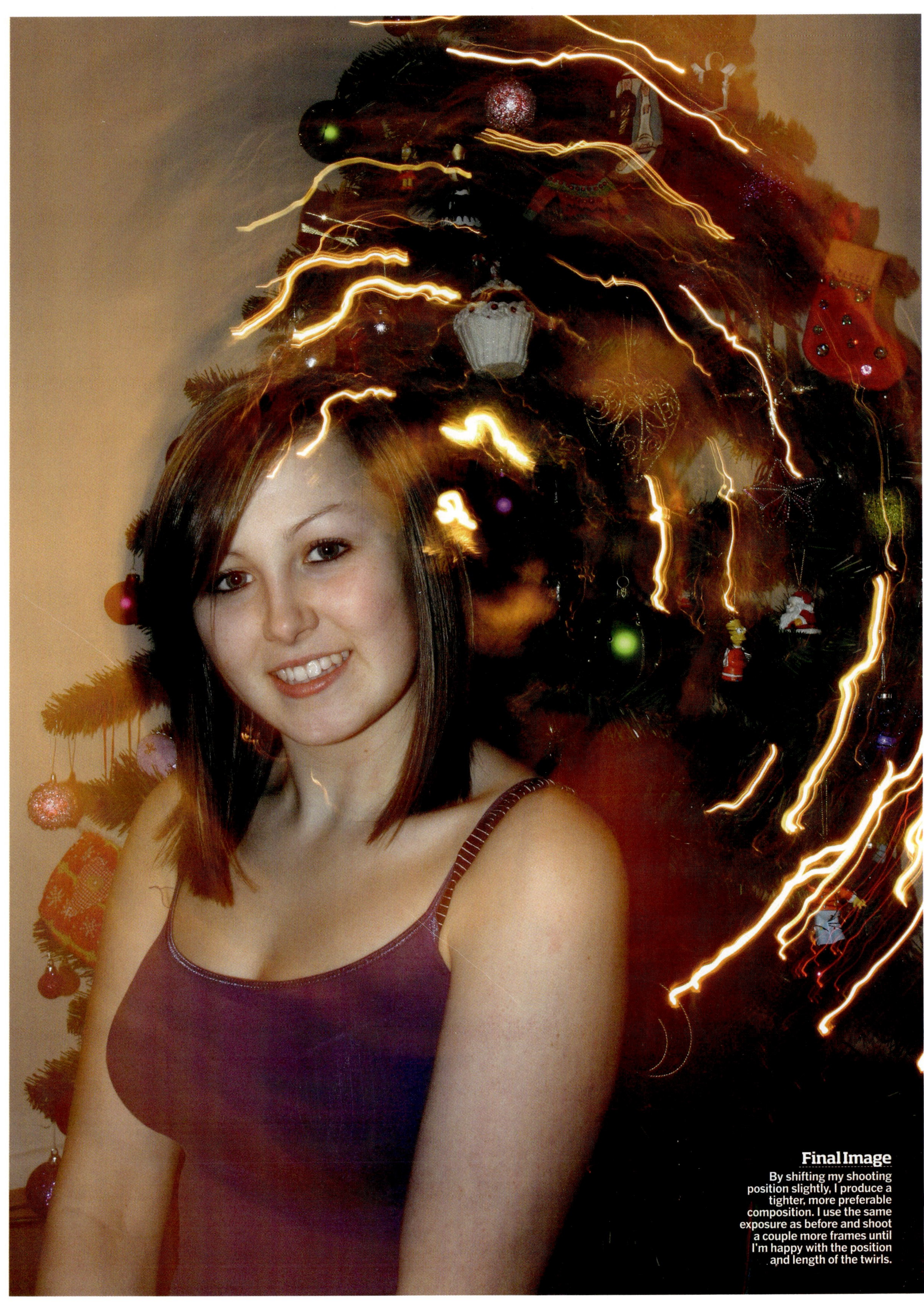

Final Image

By shifting my shooting position slightly, I produce a tighter, more preferable composition. I use the same exposure as before and shoot a couple more frames until I'm happy with the position and length of the twirls.

Using a wireless flash set-up

THE CREATIVE OPPORTUNITIES OF WORKING with off-camera flash are endless. By positioning a flashgun where you like, you can control the direction and strength of the light on your subject. You can use more than one flash too, meaning you can light the foreground and background separately, or fire flashes in different directions to create special effects.

Measuring exposure with off-camera flash becomes more complicated if you want to do things manually, and a nightmare if you have more than one flashgun, so it's a blessed relief that modern flash systems retain their TTL auto setting, even under these circumstances. You can also change the power of individual flashes independently of one another, and buy additional light-modifying accessories, such as softboxes to make a multiple TTL flash set-up an alternative to studio-lighting kits.

If you take your flash off-camera and use it wirelessly, the camera communicates with the flashguns via a series of pulses that happen before the main exposure. These pulses come from either a separate infrared unit, a radio transmitter, or your DSLR's built-in flash. If opting for this latter method, turning down the power of the integral flash will minimise the effect it has on the scene.

Wireless flash is extremely intelligent. After you press the shutter release button, the following happens: the infrared trigger or pop-up flash tells each group of off-camera flashes to fire a metering pulse. Using its TTL flash metering, the camera measures the amount of light coming from each strobe, then mixes it with the ambient light coming through the lens. The TTL system then transfers data that tells each strobe how much light to put out for the main exposure, triggering them to fire when the shutter is opened. This is triggered via a series of very short pulses of light, but they are so rapid that you won't recognise any appreciable delay.

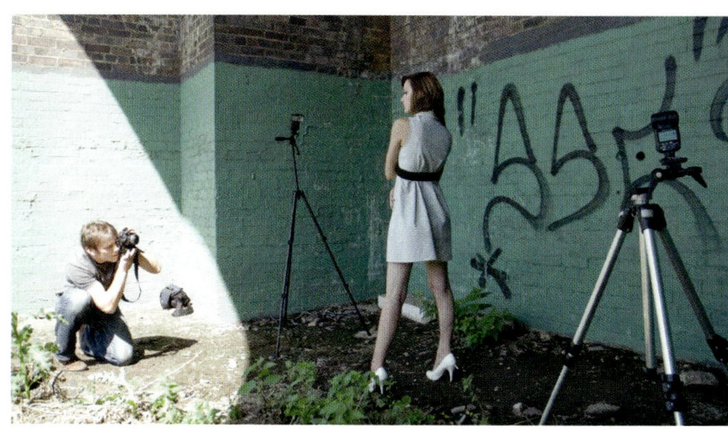

Wireless flash step-by-step guide

Ian Farrell: I've previously used off-camera TTL flash with one flashgun and been pleased with the results. But now, in an attempt to be more daring, I'm going use three Nikon Speedlight SB-900 flashguns simultaneously.

My subject, Lauren Worby, is a local up-and-coming model who has kindly agreed to pose for me. I want to photograph her outside in a gritty, urban scene to create a fashion-style shot by mixing flash with daylight.

I'm going to use my Nikon D700 in manual mode and use the pop-up flash to trigger the off-camera flashguns. This is done by setting the flashes to Remote mode and the camera's flash to Commander mode. I'm turning down the built-in flash to 1/128th power so it doesn't affect the exposure.

Step 1 **Here's how Lauren looks on location with no flash. I like the background, pose and the clothes we've chosen, but the lighting is boring! Some flash will help Lauren stand off the background and bring some mood and drama to the proceedings. Once the flash is added, the image should look more like an editorial fashion shoot, rather than a quick snap from a day out.**

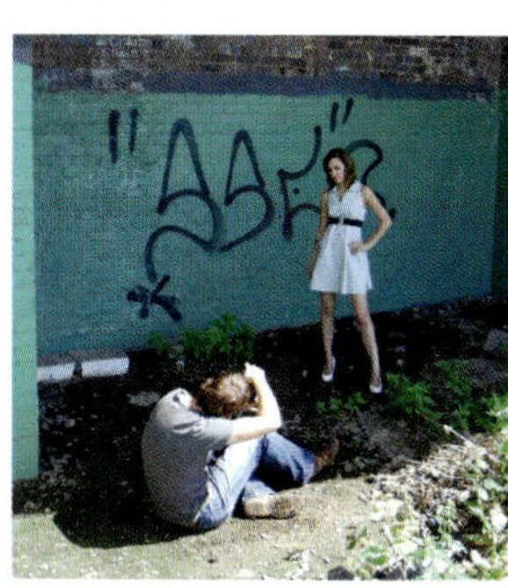

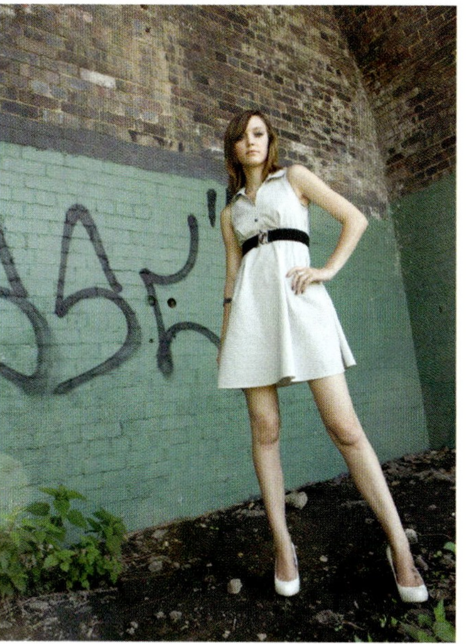

Step 2 **Let's add the first SB-900 flashgun. I'm mounting it on a tripod using the supplied hotshoe mount and have set it to TTL Remote mode. I'll start by pointing it at Lauren from the side to balance the daylight coming in from the other side. Here's how Lauren looks lit by one flash, with the camera balancing the flash with daylight, using an exposure of 1/60sec at f/11 (ISO 200).**

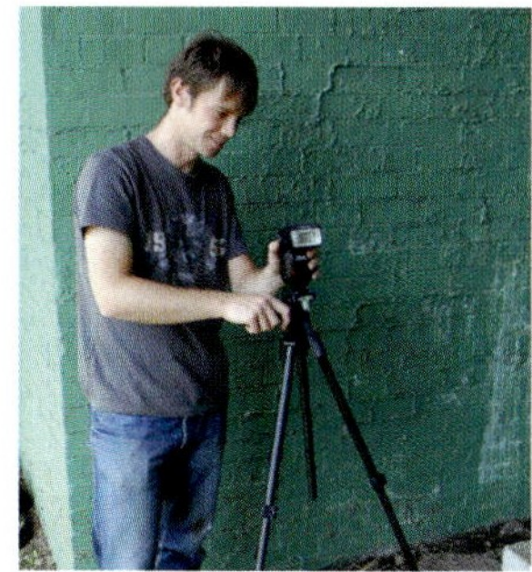

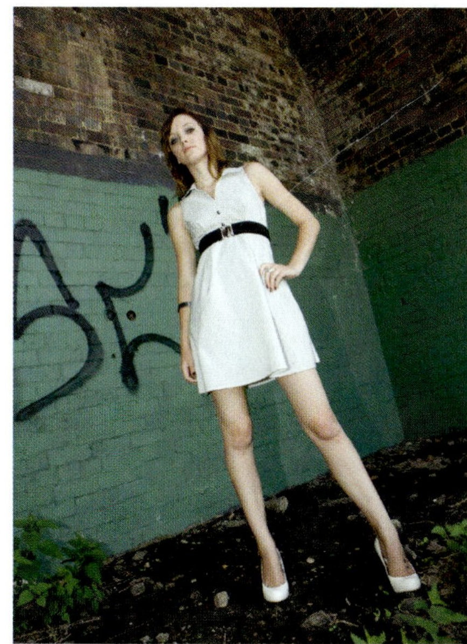

Step 3 **I'm adding another flash to light up the background, again mounting it on a tripod and setting it to TTL Remote mode. I'm also reducing the amount of ambient light in the mix by raising the shutter speed one stop to 1/125sec. Adding more flash to the picture has changed the look again. The wall is the same brightness thanks to the second flash, but the scene has more contrast.**

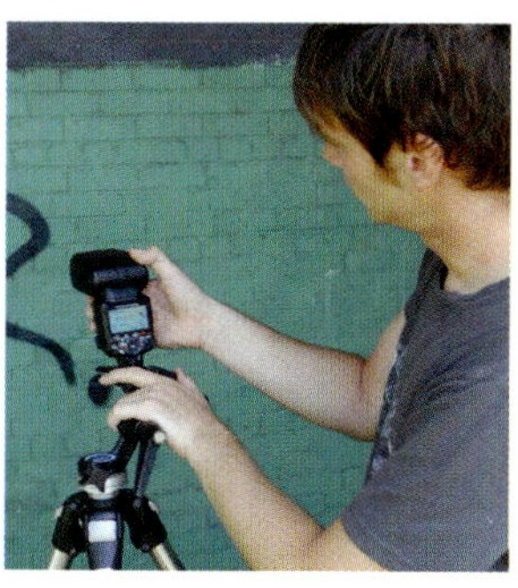

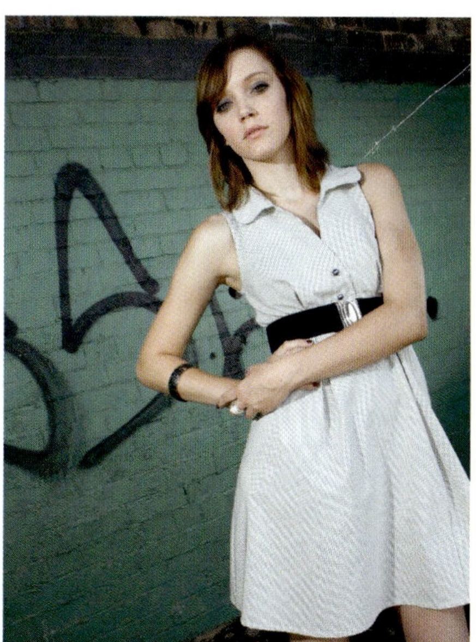

Step 4 **I want to create some hair light by positioning a third flashgun to point at the back of Lauren's head. I haven't brought a third tripod with me, but I do have a willing assistant to hold the third flashgun for me. The hair light has done its job and illuminated the back of our model's head, brightening her hair slightly as well as helping to define the skin on her left arm.**

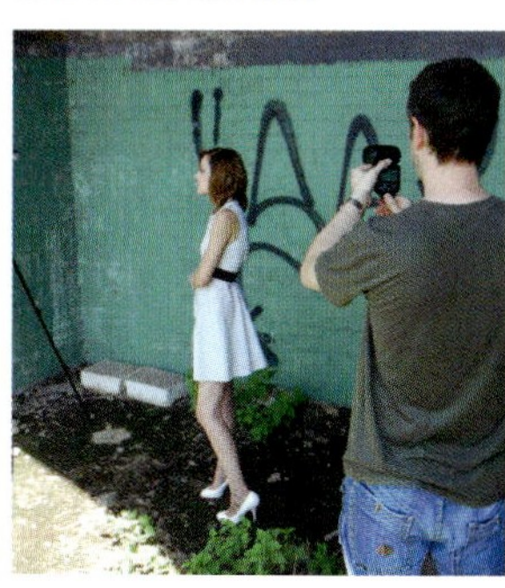

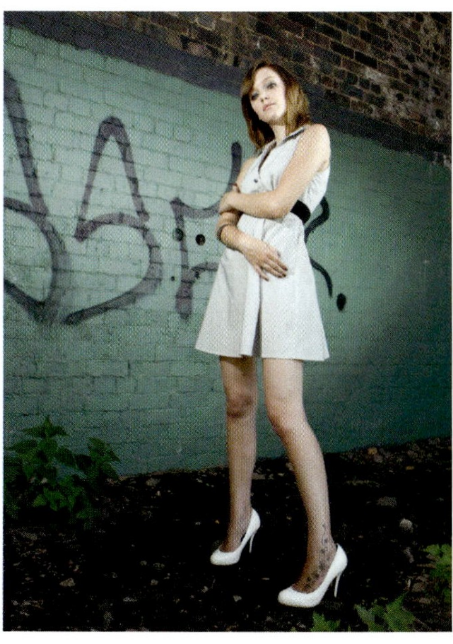

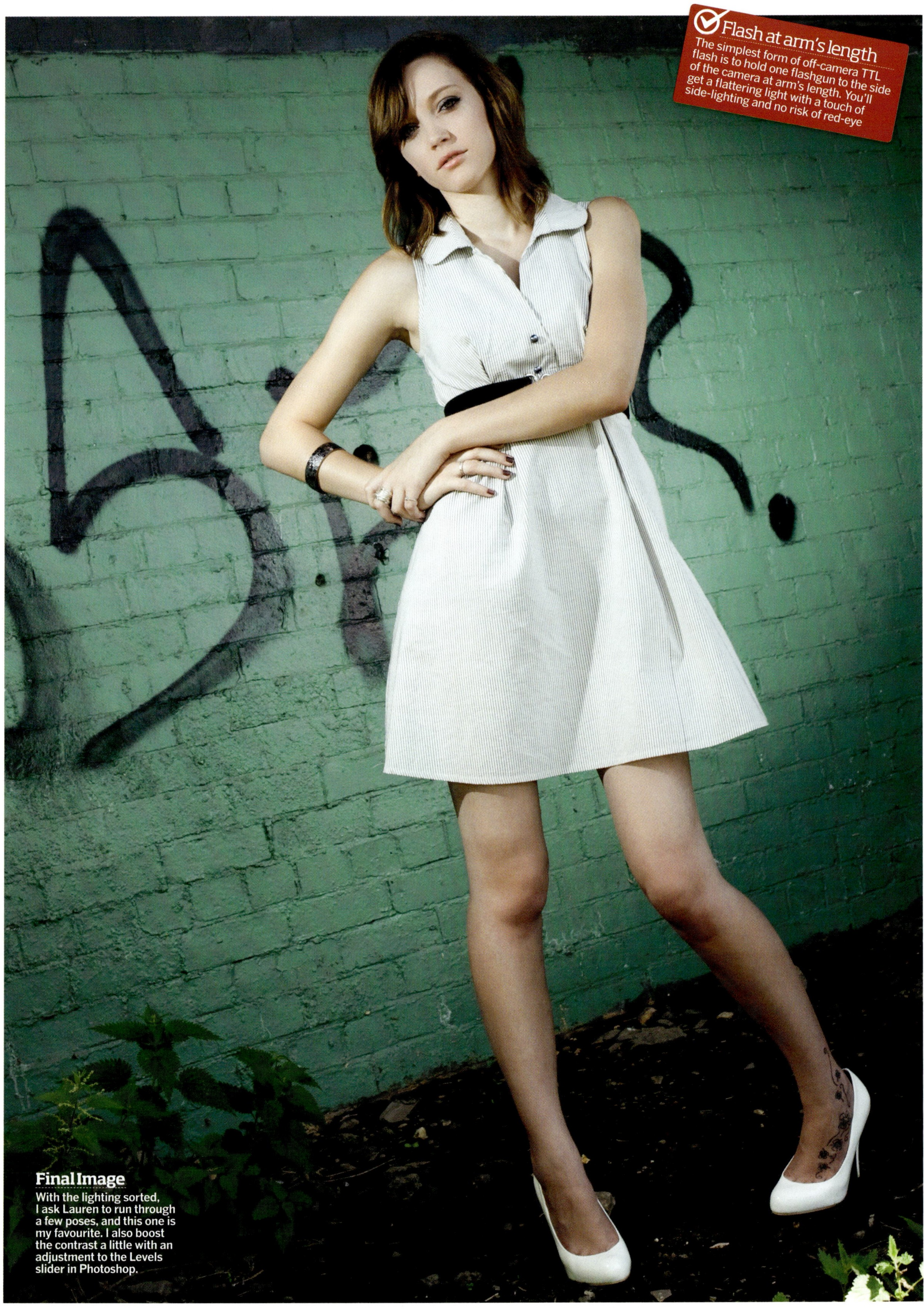

Final Image

With the lighting sorted, I ask Lauren to run through a few poses, and this one is my favourite. I also boost the contrast a little with an adjustment to the Levels slider in Photoshop.

Studioflash outfits

While newcomers may find studioflash intimidating, the truth is that using it isn't as difficult as you may think

Although there are various studioflash kits available, ranging in price from under £200 to several thousand, the fact is most of them have very similar characteristics and features, and so all follow similar operating principles. A studioflash head is basically designed to fire a burst of flash at a given power setting – the extra functions and accessories are all geared to allow the photographer more control of the flash output. Learning how a studioflash system works and how it can be controlled is something that can take years of dedication and experience, but thankfully, getting to grips with the essentials is relatively easy. Much like using ambient light, the key factor behind your success with studioflash is learning how best to control it so that your subject is lit the way you'd like it to be. The big difference between studio and ambient light is the level of control you have – you are able to fine-tune the lighting's intensity and direction, as well as the nature of the light falling on the subject, far more than you could ever achieve with available light. This makes it an incredibly versatile form of lighting, but, obviously, one that does need time to use properly. In this section of the guide, we cover the basic workings of a studioflash system and how the various attachments, such as softboxes and brollies, can be used to control how your subject is lit.

Anatomy of a studioflash head

The following anatomy illustration is based on the rear of an Interfit flash head, but most will have a similar set-up, with easy-to-use and well-labelled controls.

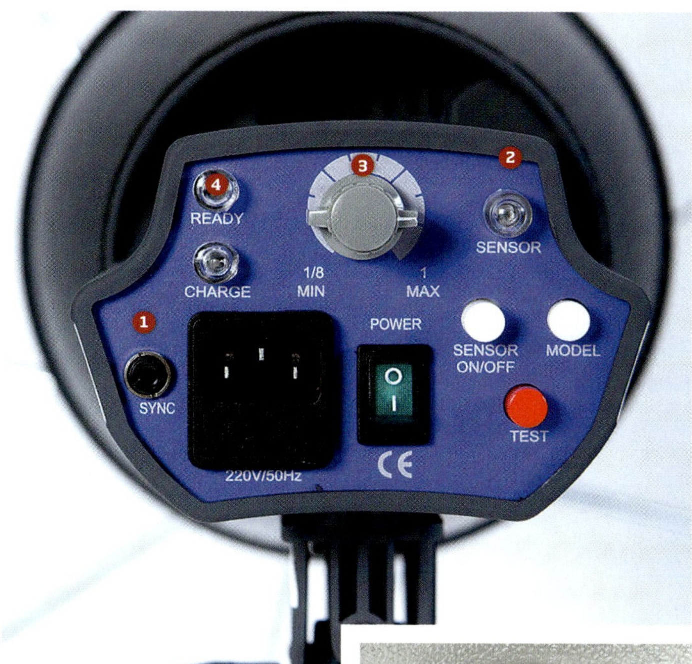

REAR OF LIGHT

You'll normally find controls on the rear of the head, but some models have them on the side, too.

1) SYNC SOCKET Most studioflash outfits are supplied with a sync lead, which connects your camera to your flash head, allowing the flash to fire when you press the shutter button.

2) SLAVE CELL This sensor detects any flash output, so if your camera is connected to one light in a multiple set-up, its output will trigger the slave cell on other lights, making them fire.

3) POWER SETTINGS A key function of studioflash heads is being able to adjust the power of the output. Basic heads have fixed power settings e.g. ¼, ½ etc, while most advanced heads have step-less variable settings.

4) STATUS LIGHTS/BEEPS Most heads have lights or beeps to indicate the head has sufficient charge to fire.

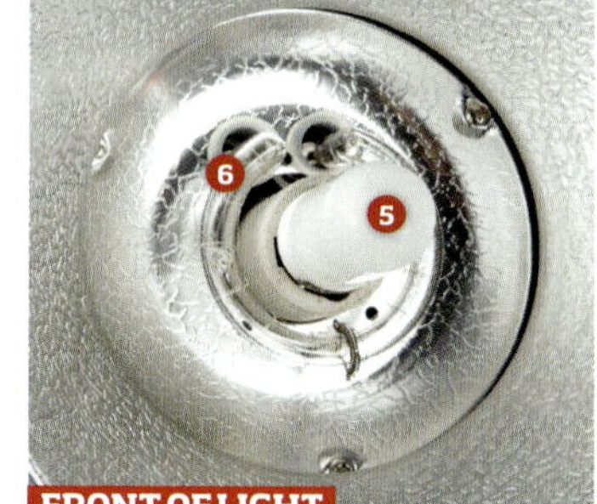

FRONT OF LIGHT

Removing the lighting attachment will usually reveal two bulbs, each with different uses.

5) MODELLING LAMP This tungsten bulb remains switched on, to allow you to compose the image, focus on the subject and predict the flash effect.

6) FLASH BULB These provide the powerful flash output. Most brands have specialised bulbs to fit certain heads or studioflash series. They're very fragile, so handle them with care.

Setting up your DSLR for using studioflash

When you're ready to shoot with studioflash, the key things to do are to set the camera to Manual and set the correct flash sync speed

CANON EOS 400D/500D

(1) Set the main control dial to M to select manual mode

(2) Turn the input dial behind the shutter button and set the flash sync speed (1/200sec on most Canon DSLRs)

(3) Once you've taken a flash meter reading, press and hold down the +/- button, then turn the input dial to set the aperture you require

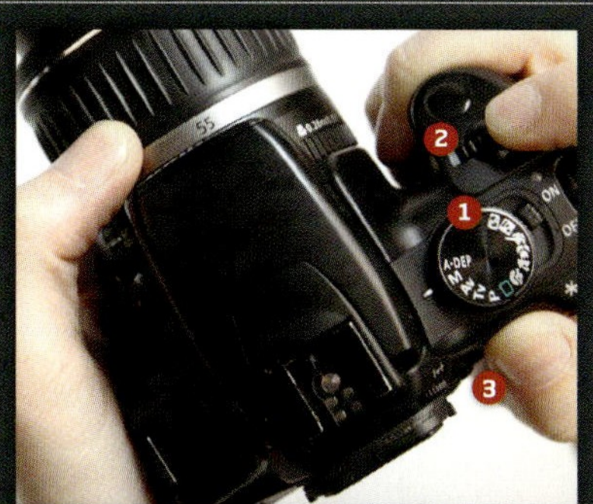

NIKON D60/D80

(1) Set the main control dial to M to select manual mode

(2) Turn the input dial behind the shutter button and set the flash sync speed (1/200sec on most Nikon DSLRs)

(3) Once you've taken a flash meter reading, turn the input dial on the front of the hand grip to set the aperture

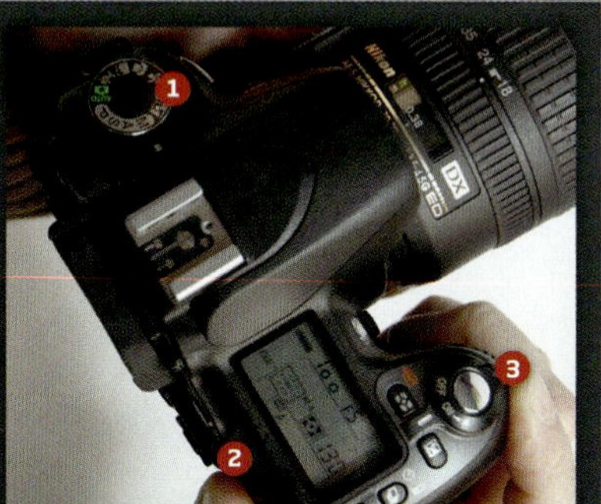

OLYMPUS E-400/E-410/E-420

(1) Set the main control dial on the top-plate to M to select manual mode

(2) Turn the input dial behind the shutter button and set the flash sync speed (1/200sec)

(3) Once you've taken a flash meter reading, press and hold down the +/- button, then turn the input dial to set the aperture you require

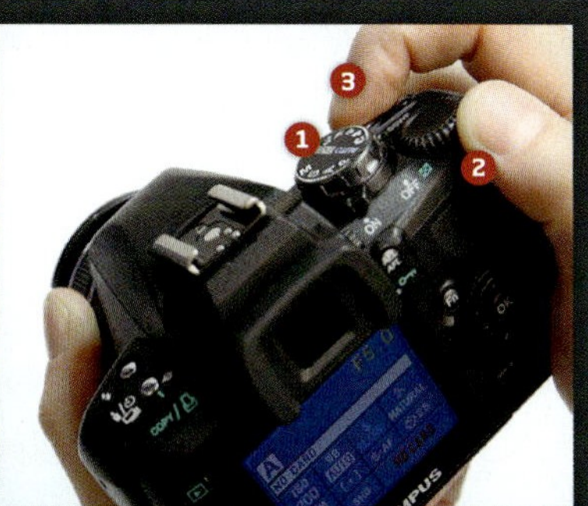

PENTAX K100D/K200D

(1) Set the main control dial on the top-plate to M to select manual mode

(2) Turn the input dial behind the shutter button and set the flash sync speed (1/180sec on most Pentax DSLRs)

(3) Once you've taken a flash meter reading, press and hold down the +/- button, then turn the input dial to set the aperture you require

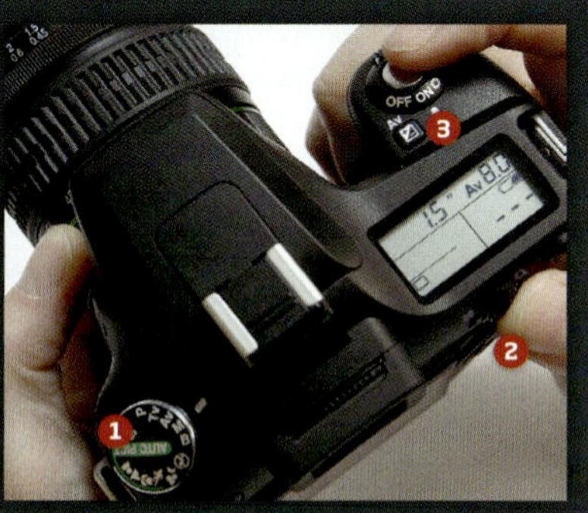

SONY ALPHA 100/200

(1) Set the main control dial on the top-plate to Tv to select shutter-priority mode

(2) Turn the input dial in front of the shutter button and set the flash sync speed (1/160sec on most Sony DSLRs)

(3) Once you've taken a flash meter reading, press and hold down the +/- button, then turn the input dial to set the aperture you require

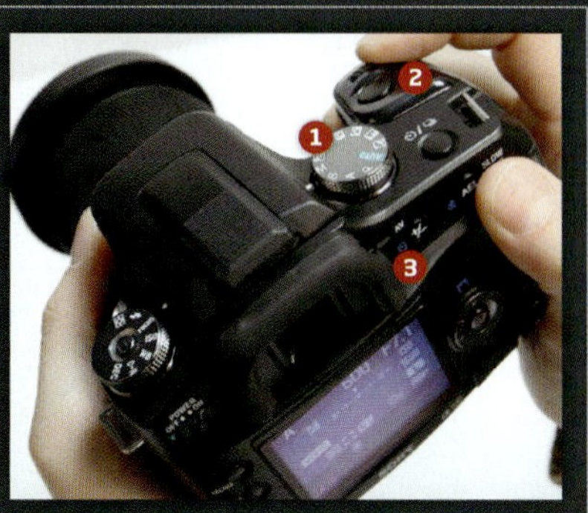

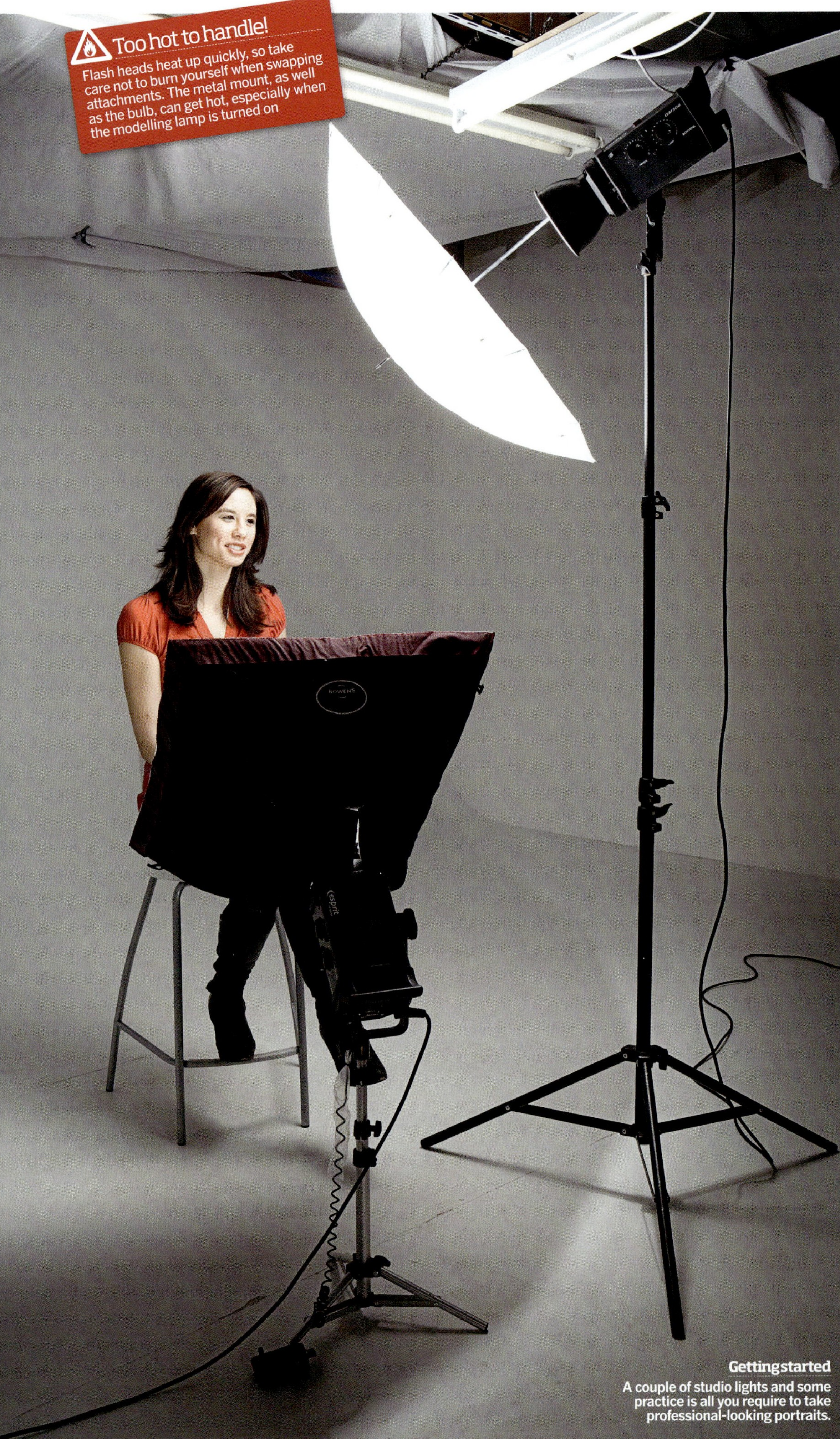

Too hot to handle!
Flash heads heat up quickly, so take care not to burn yourself when swapping attachments. The metal mount, as well as the bulb, can get hot, especially when the modelling lamp is turned on

Getting started
A couple of studio lights and some practice is all you require to take professional-looking portraits.

Studioflash Q&As

Q How much should I spend on a studioflash system?
A We would recommend you start with a two-head system, with a softbox and umbrella being good starter attachments. After extensive tests, we found the £250 Interfit EX150 MkII and the £560 Elinchrom D-Lite 4 IT to be excellent budget studioflash outfits for beginners.

Q What advantages do more expensive outfits offer?
A General build quality and reliability will be better, but the key benefits are power, features and performance. More power is useful as you can set the lights up further away from your subject, while relative light loss from attachments like softboxes is reduced. You'll find that more expensive heads allow more control over flash output and faster flash recycling times.

Q Are attachments from different systems compatible?
A In general, different brands have their own fittings so aren't compatible. However, Chimera make speed rings for their softboxes, which are compatible with just about any system. *www.chimeralighting.com*

Q How should I set up my DSLR to use studioflash?
A You will need to set it to manual mode as the metering system is only set up for ambient light. Set the shutter speed to the flash sync speed and the aperture to whatever the flash meter states.

Q How do I take an exposure reading with studioflash?
A Simply use a flash meter connected to a light via a sync lead. Once you've set up the lights, hold the meter in front of the subject's face, take a flash reading and set the meter's recommended aperture on the camera. Don't forget to ensure that the flash meter and DSLR are set to the same ISO rating!

Q How do I connect my DSLR to my studioflash system?
A The plug at the end of the studioflash sync lead connects to your DSLR's PC socket. If your camera hasn't got a PC socket, buy a PC adaptor (around £10) that slots on your camera's hotshoe and connect the lead to this. A more expensive option is to buy a wireless trigger that sits on your hotshoe and triggers a receiver on the flash head.

Lighting accessories

Your studioflash system is only as good as the lighting attachments you choose to use with your flash heads

Flash heads are designed to produce a high-power burst of light, but it's the lighting attachment that you have fitted to it that dictates the effect of the light on the subject. If you've ever looked into buying a studioflash system, you'll no doubt have seen the various types of attachments on the market, each having their own unique way of affecting the intensity and nature of the light that reaches the subject and/or the background. While most basic kits are often supplied with a simple brolly or two and spills, there are a huge number of optional accessories available, and getting to know which are best suited to your needs is important. In our comprehensive comparison set below, we have used the most common types of attachments available for most studioflash kit systems to give you a better idea of how each affects the light.

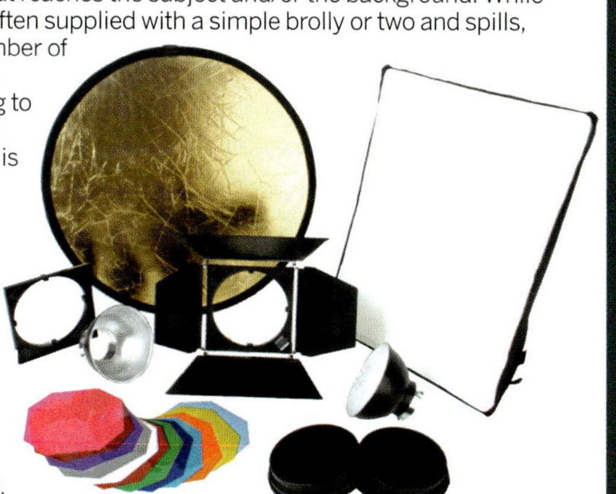

Other accessories

FLASH METER Attach the sync lead, hold the meter in front of your subject and press the button to take a reading to discover what aperture you need to set your camera to for a perfect exposure.

BACKGROUND There are a variety of backgrounds available, from plain to coloured patterns. As well as paper rolls that fit on frames, there are several collapsible backdrops that offer the benefit of portability.

HOTSHOE PC ADAPTOR If your DSLR lacks a PC socket, this inexpensive adaptor slips onto your hotshoe and can be connected to the sync lead to trigger the studioflash.

REFLECTOR Using a reflector to bounce light back onto part of the subject or background is an alternative to using an additional light. Silver is the most efficient, white provides a softer and more natural effect, while using a black reflector can really accentuate cheekbones!

Umbrella (Brolly)

Available in white, silver and translucent, a brolly is one of the cheapest options available. Silver is very efficient at bouncing light, white gives a soft, natural effect, while translucent brollies provide the most diffused light.

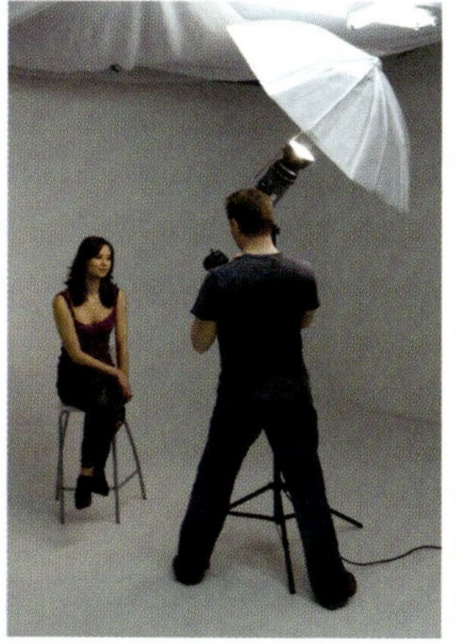

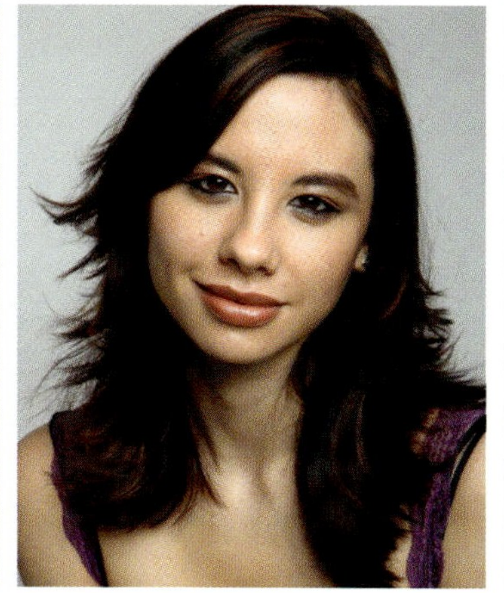

Softbox

A real favourite, as it provides a very diffused light that's ideal for flattering portraits. The larger the softbox, the softer the light it produces. The majority are square, but some are rectangular and thin (also called strip lights).

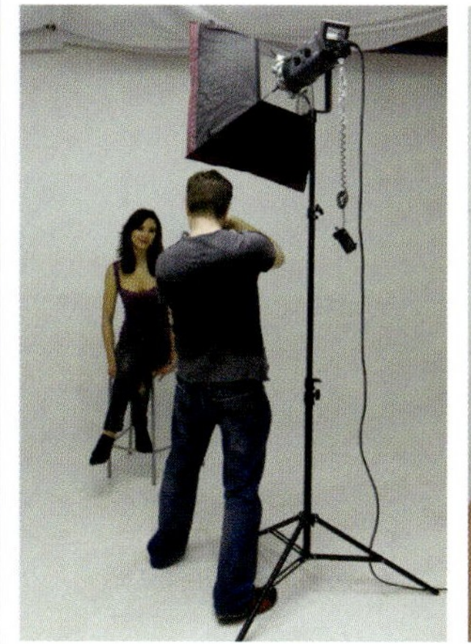

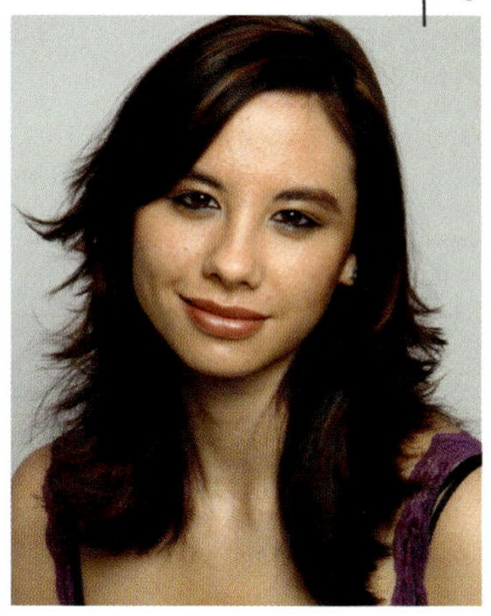

Beauty dish

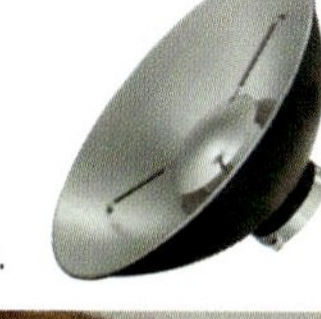

Beauty dishes are often used, as you may expect, for close-up 'beauty' and make-up shots. They give off a very harsh light in the centre, which enhances make-up, but also highlights flaws on a subject's skin.

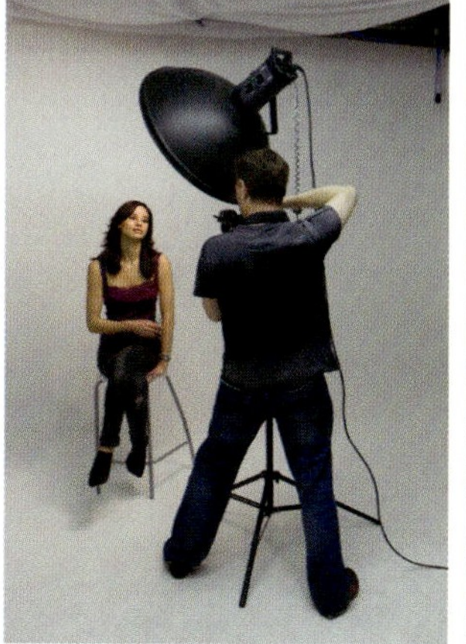

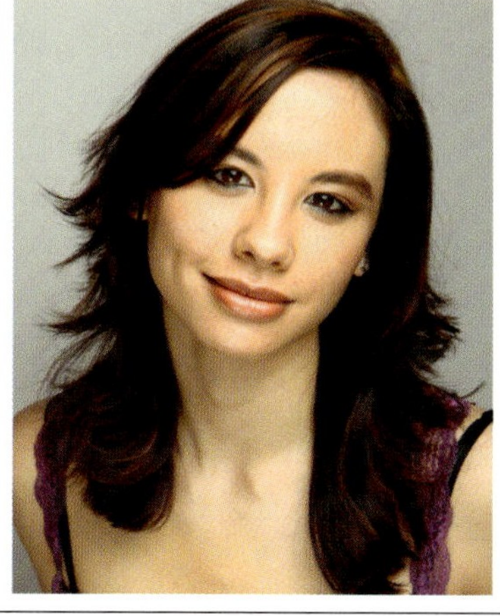

Spill (Spill Kill)

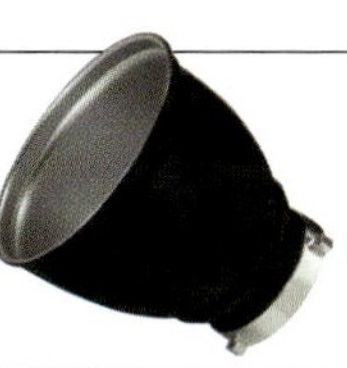

Often supplied with the flash head, spills provide a concentrated beam of light. With portraits, they're useful for lighting backgrounds, but quite harsh when aimed directly at a subject's face.

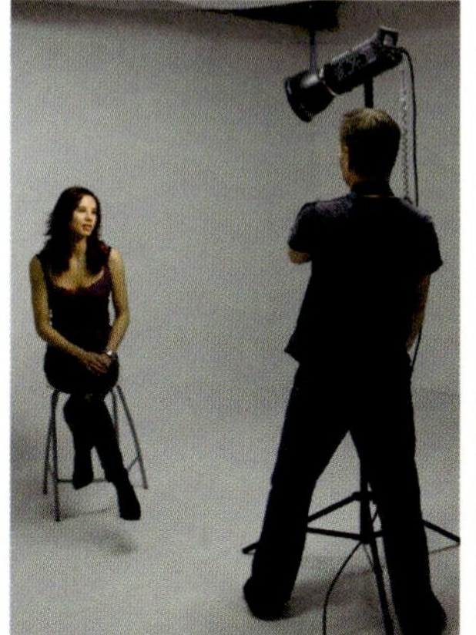

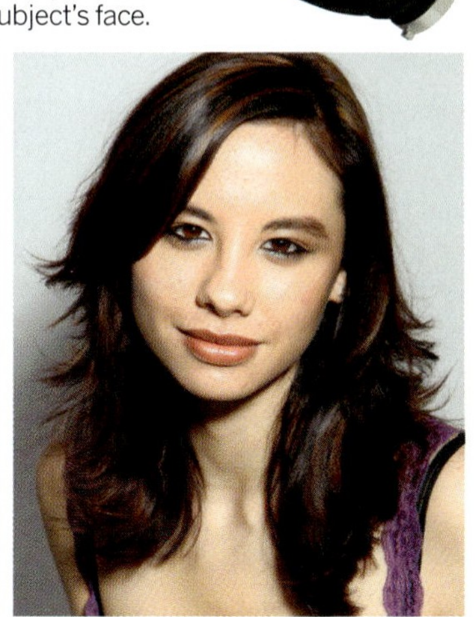

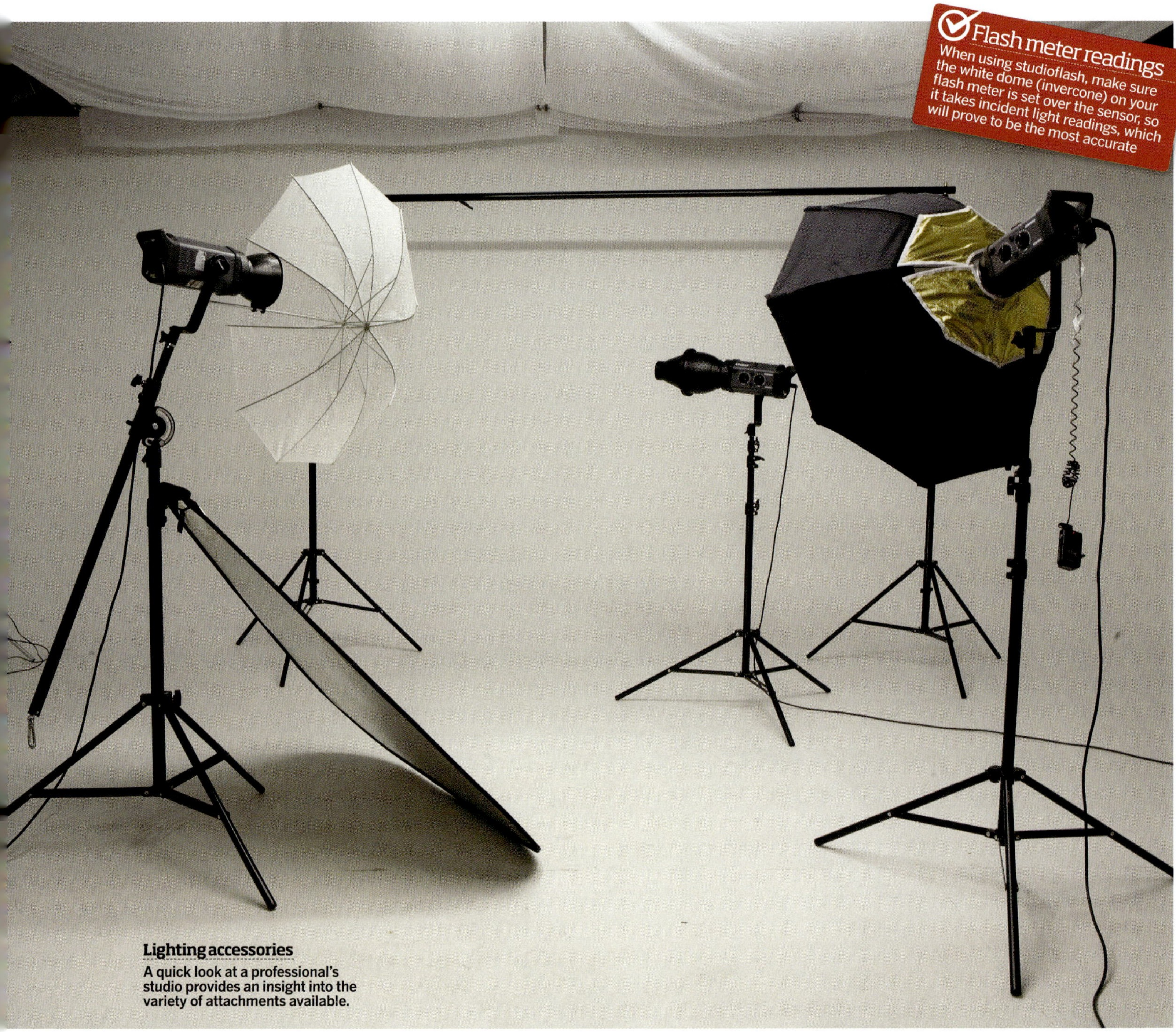

Flash meter readings
When using studioflash, make sure the white dome (invercone) on your flash meter is set over the sensor, so it takes incident light readings, which will prove to be the most accurate

Lighting accessories
A quick look at a professional's studio provides an insight into the variety of attachments available.

Snoot

This conical attachment provides a hard-edge and directional beam of light that's better suited for backlighting or as a hairlight than providing the key lighting for your portraits.

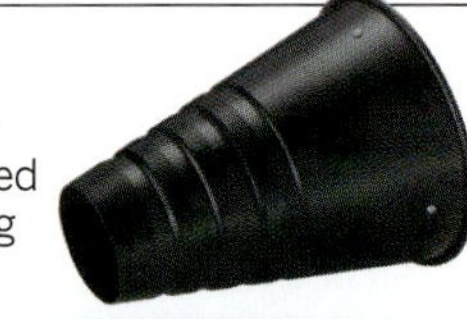

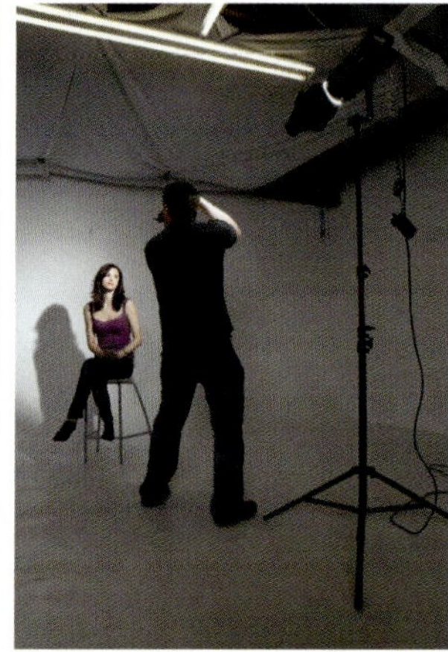

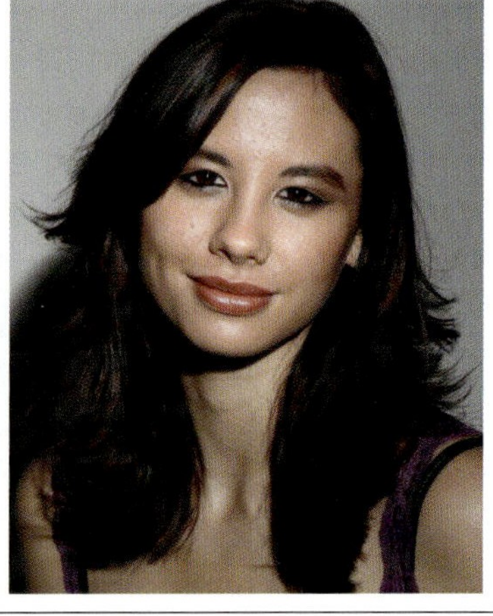

Honeycomb grid

These provide a soft-edged circle of light and are a popular alternative to a snoot. They act in a similar way to a spotlight, but provide a wider spot effect. Honeycombs are available with various sizes of grids.

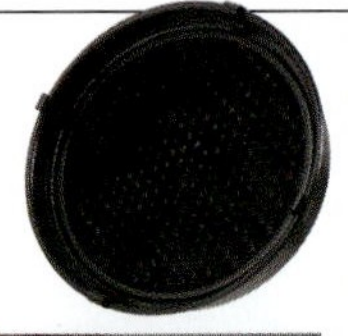

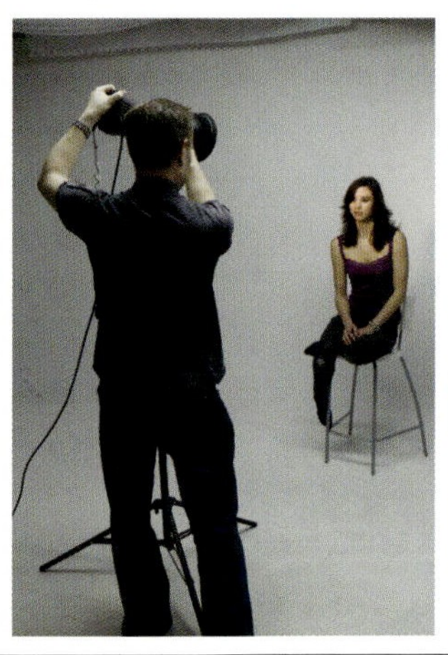

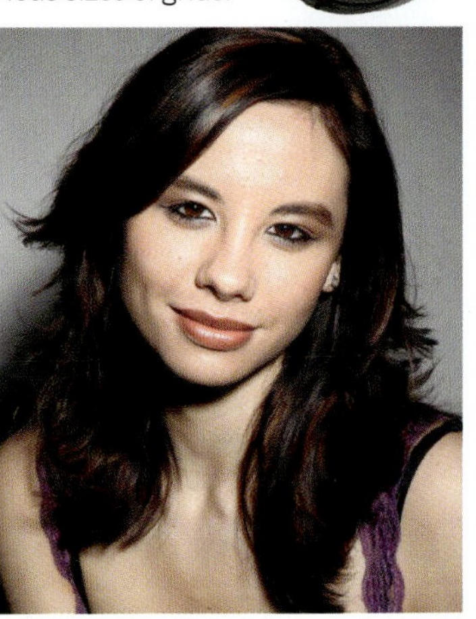

Studio set-up: One light

The most basic studio set-ups involve using just one light, so here are five techniques to get you started

If you want to learn how to control your lighting, you're best off starting with just one light. It's more than sufficient to produce stunning results and many great photographers still use a single head for their work. After all, outdoors we only have a single light source – the sun – so one light can deliver all we need. This set-up is very easy to control and the smallest adjustment to the light on your subject has a clear effect. This forces you to fine-tune the light's angle and diffusion method. And while you'll only have one source of illumination, you can also use reflectors in your set-up to bounce light and fill in any shadows.

The set of images below shows what happens when you position your single light (and softbox) at different heights and angles. As you can see, it's crucial that you learn the do's and don'ts of how to set up your single studioflash head to avoid some of the unflattering results shown below.

As mentioned earlier, you need to set your DSLR to manual mode and set it to the flash sync speed (if you don't know it, use 1/125sec as a safe bet or check your camera's manual). The aperture is determined by the meter reading you take, which is easy to do with a one light set-up. With the sync lead from the light attached, hold the meter in front of the subject's face and press the button to fire the flash and take a reading. Adjusting the power setting on the flash head allows you to effectively change the aperture you work with to in turn achieve the depth-of-field you're after. Add power to set a smaller aperture and reduce power to use a wider aperture.

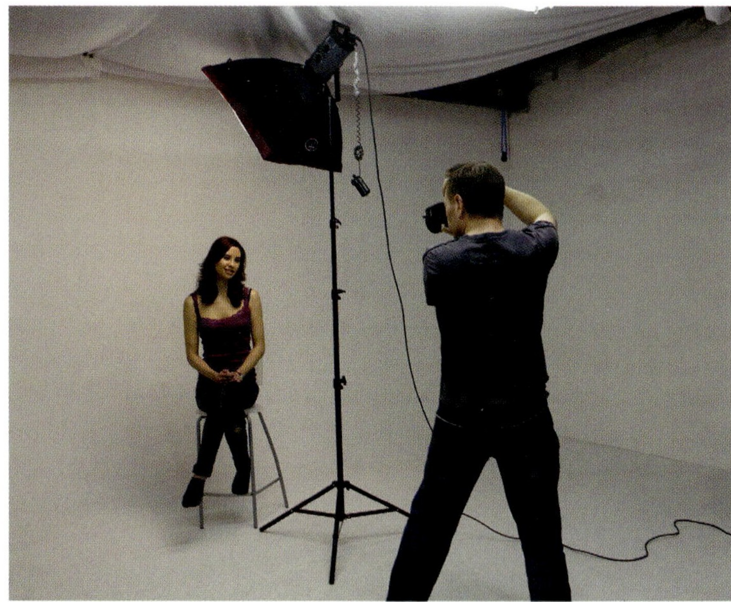

ONE LIGHT: All you need to get started is your DSLR and a single flash head. With a bit of practise, you will soon find yourself getting great results!

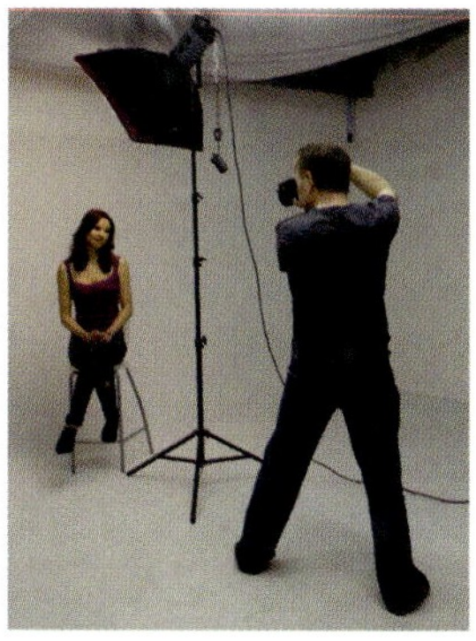

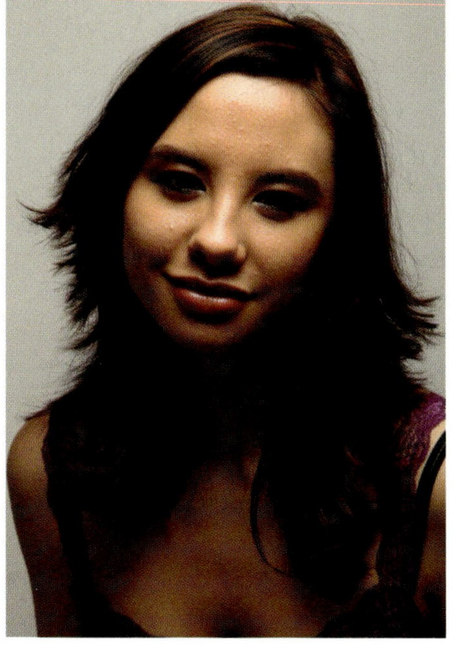

1) Lit from above

With the light positioned high above the model's head, you get a more natural-looking light, though the shadows can be rendered harsh under the nose and chin. For the best results, get the model to look towards the light. You could also ask her to hold a reflector to fill the shadows.

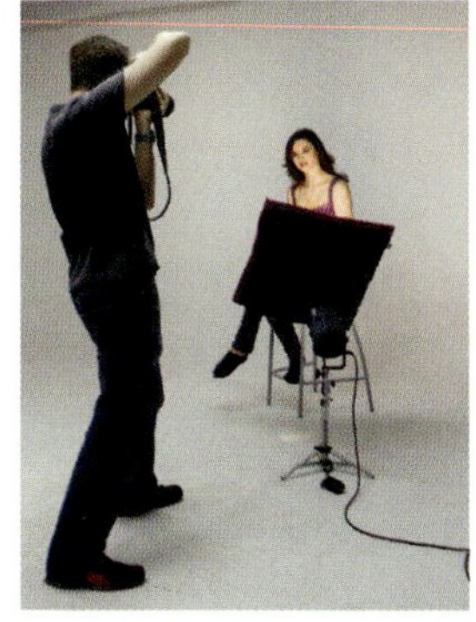

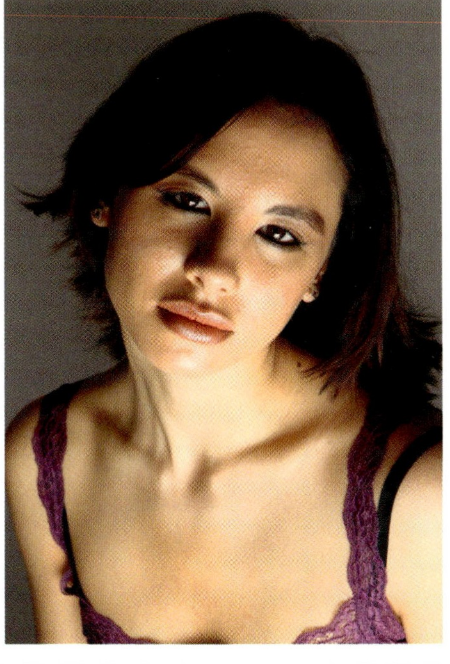

2) Lit from below

Placing the light lower than the model's head, pointing upwards will eradicate any unsightly shadows under the nose and chin. For best results get the model to look down towards the light, which as you can see also makes catchlights appear in the subject's eyes.

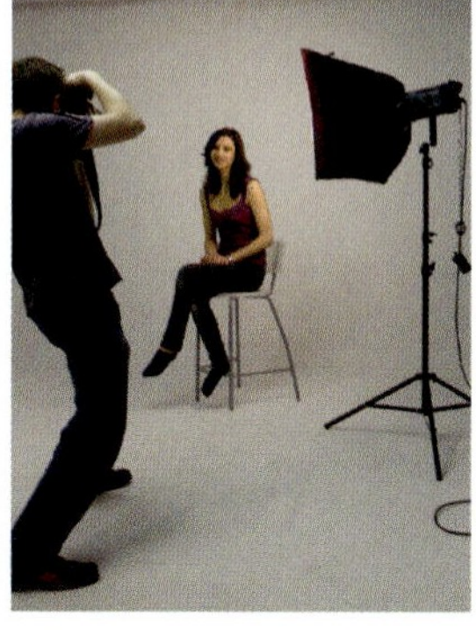

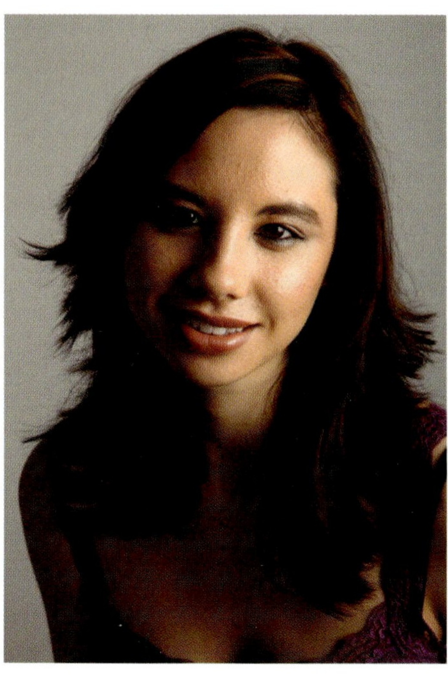

3) Lit from the side

Place the light to either the left or right-hand side of your model's face for a strong, directional light, keeping half of the face in shadow. To increase your chances of capturing the catchlights in your subject's eyes, it is important to make sure the light is far enough forward.

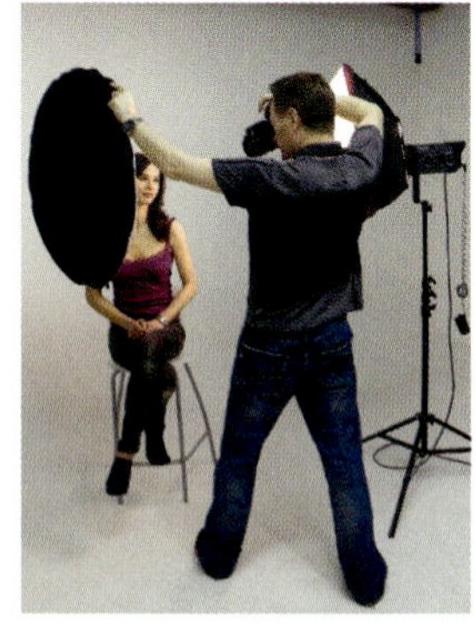

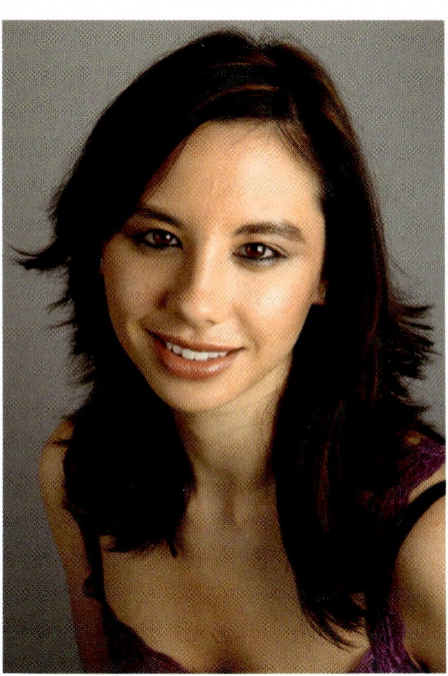

4) One light & reflector

By holding a reflector close to the face, on the opposite side from the light, you will be able to even up any harsh shadows, much like using a second head. The closer you place it to the model, the stronger the reflection will be. For this technique it definitely helps to have an assistant!

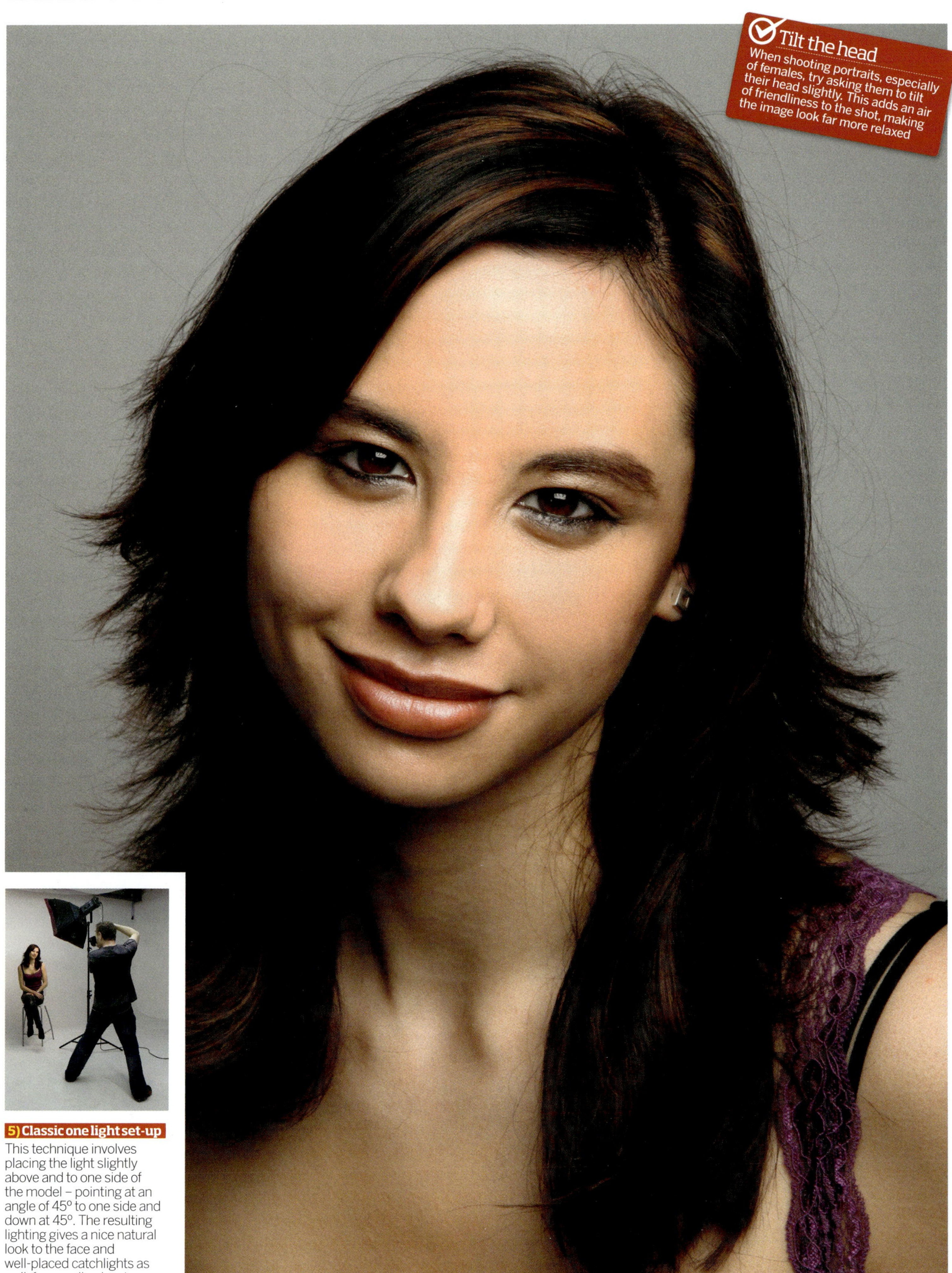

Tilt the head

When shooting portraits, especially of females, try asking them to tilt their head slightly. This adds an air of friendliness to the shot, making the image look far more relaxed

5) Classic one light set-up

This technique involves placing the light slightly above and to one side of the model – pointing at an angle of 45° to one side and down at 45°. The resulting lighting gives a nice natural look to the face and well-placed catchlights as well, for a really pleasing, flattering result.

Studio set-up: Two lights

When you feel ready, you can extend your creative options by introducing a second flash-head into the mix

Many kits come with two heads, so once you've mastered lighting subjects with a single light, experiment with a second one. Often, when shooting with a single light, a reflector is used to fill shadows and provide an even lighting for your subject, but, without an assistant, they can be difficult to position.

A second head can be used instead, with the benefit that you can control the power output and add attachments to diffuse or precisely focus the light. The second light is usually called the 'slave', and is triggered when it detects the flash from the primary flash head. Using two lights gives you much more scope for different scenarios: you can light the model from different angles, or aim one light at the model and the other at the background.

So how do you meter for two lights? The simplest way is to set up the lights how you would like them, then take a meter reading from the subject's face and take a test shot at the recommended aperture. You can then consider moving the lights' position, adjusting the light ratio between the two or changing the power. Whatever you decide to do, take another reading to see what aperture you need and fire another test shot. A more accurate way of taking a reading is to check the exposure of each light in turn (i.e. only one light on at a time) and make adjustments accordingly. This will allow you to control the balance of flash between the two lights more accurately, but is a more involved process, so we would recommend using the simplest method first and try the second method once you have a bit of experience behind you.

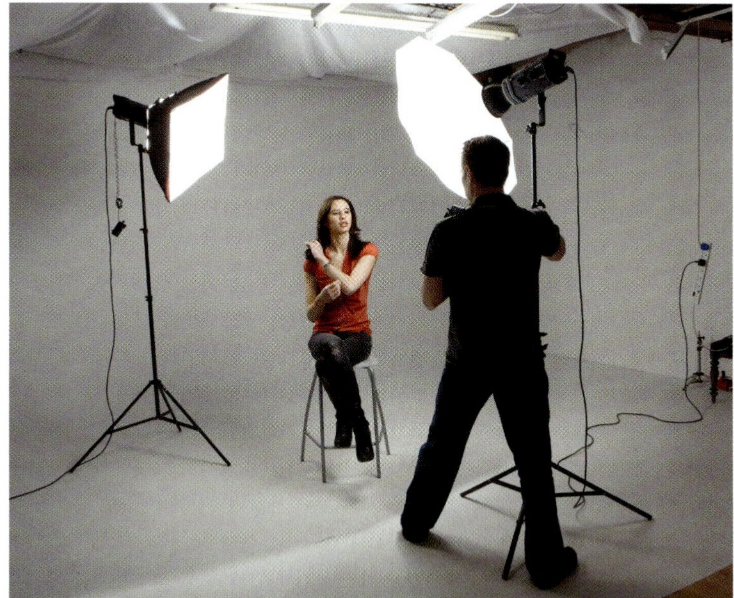

TWO LIGHTS: This is a typical two-light set-up. The lights are fitted with a softbox and an umbrella to produce a diffused flattering light.

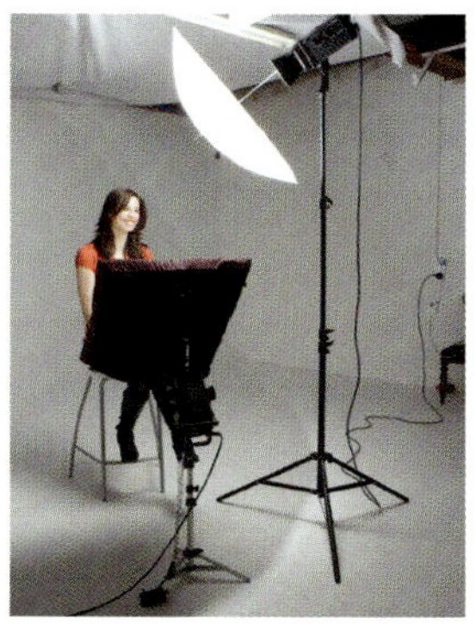

1) Lit from above & below

This is a typical headshot set-up, with the key light at 45° to the subject to give the most flattering light. The second light fills the shadows under the chin. This technique works for almost any subject. Set the key light two stops brighter than the second light.

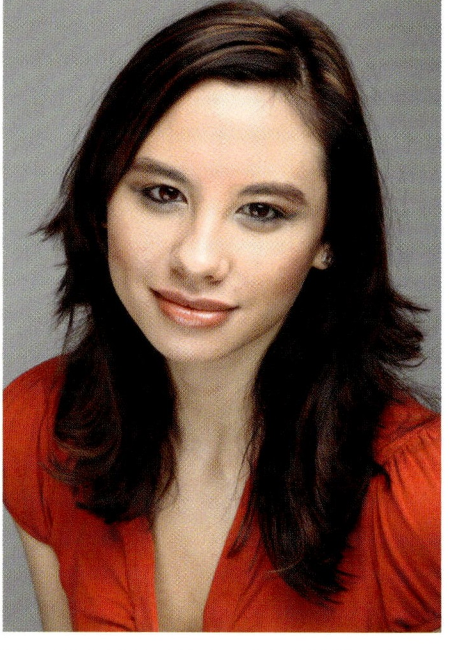

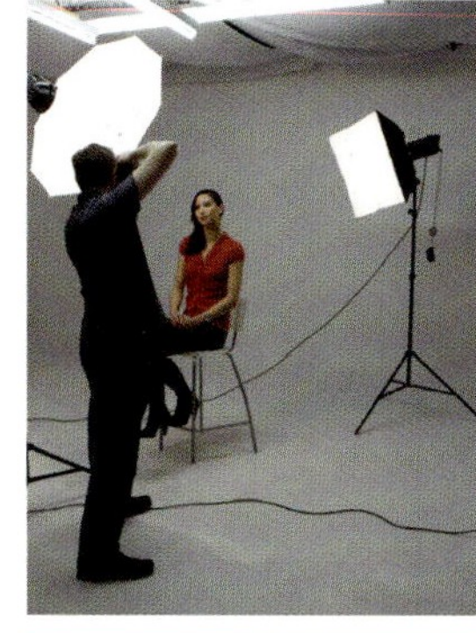

2) Lit from above & rim light

The key light is above and to the right of the model. The slave light is positioned behind the model, opposite the key light. This throws light over her shoulder, adding a touch of light to her cheek. It adds interest to the shot, and gives her face more of a three-dimensional feel.

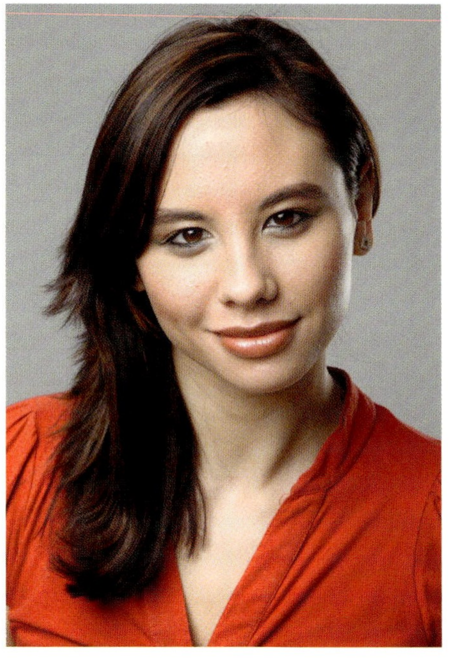

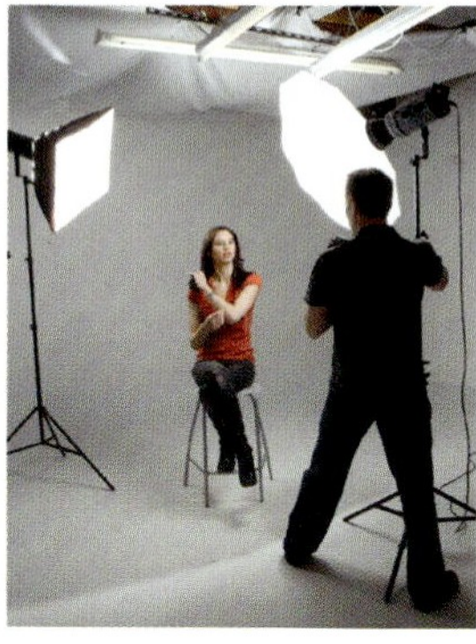

3) Lit from back & front

Here, we have one light in front of the model to light her face, and another behind her to light her hair, adding a bit of shine to it. This works well if your model has silky or colourful hair, and is a technique commonly used for 'hair' shots used in magazine advertisements.

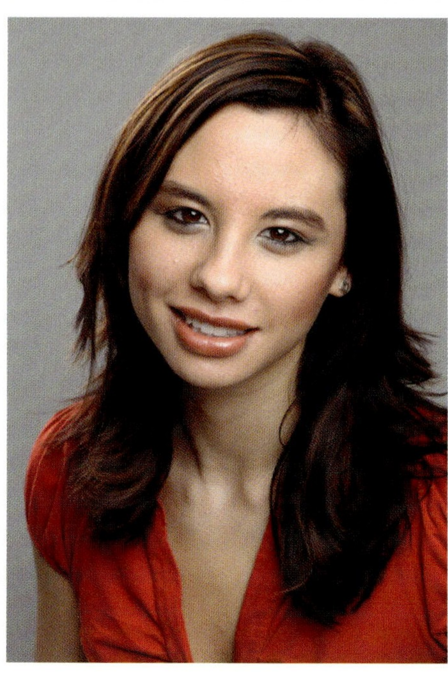

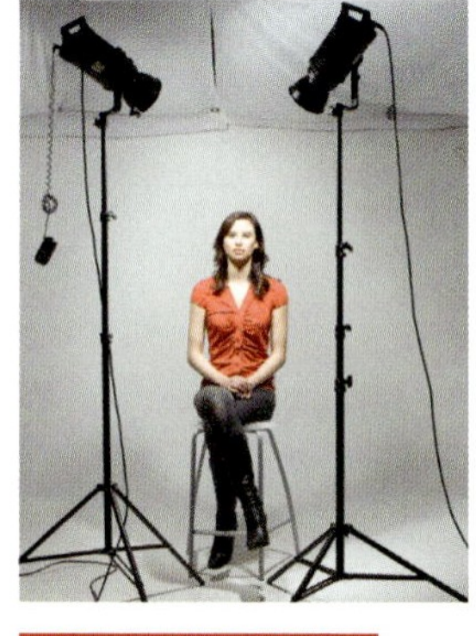

4) Butterfly lighting

This is an old-fashioned technique that is not used very much in contemporary photography. By placing both lights above the model, pointing down at a sharp angle, to cast the shadows on her face, you create an interesting 'butterfly' shape under the model's nose.

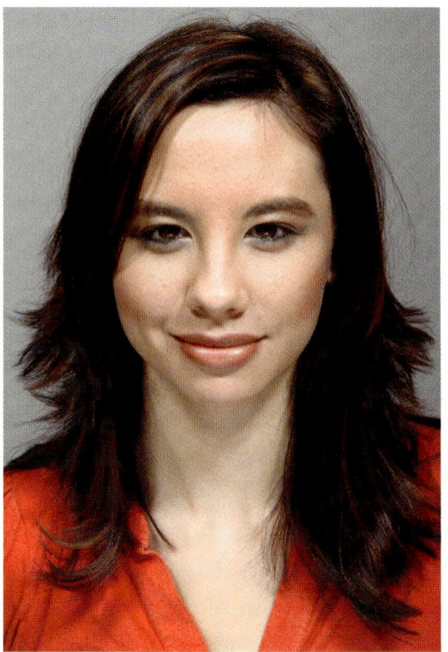

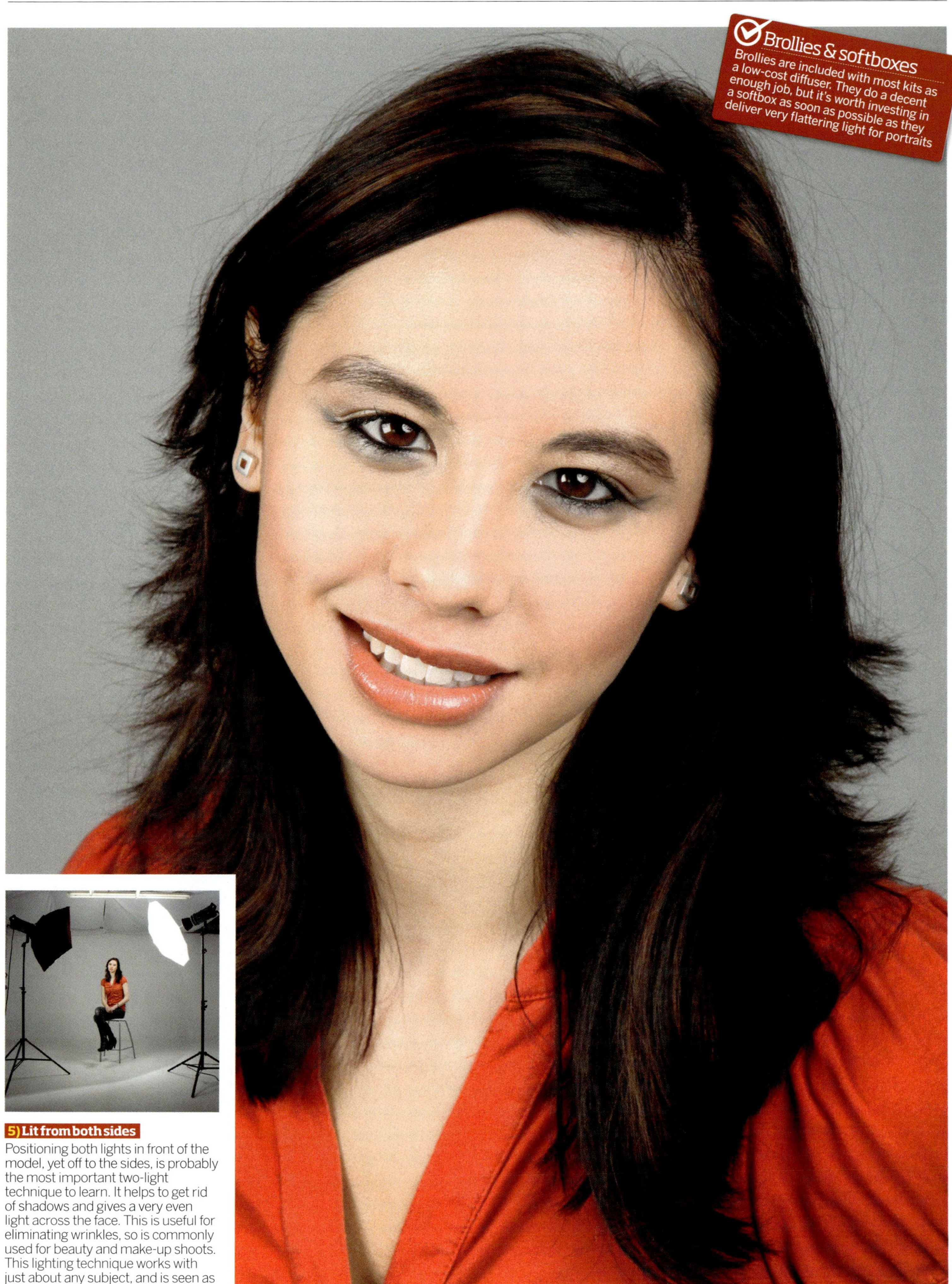

Brollies & softboxes
Brollies are included with most kits as a low-cost diffuser. They do a decent enough job, but it's worth investing in a softbox as soon as possible as they deliver very flattering light for portraits

5) Lit from both sides
Positioning both lights in front of the model, yet off to the sides, is probably the most important two-light technique to learn. It helps to get rid of shadows and gives a very even light across the face. This is useful for eliminating wrinkles, so is commonly used for beauty and make-up shoots. This lighting technique works with just about any subject, and is seen as a 'safe bet' for studio portraiture.

Studio set-up: High-key lighting

High-key lighting is one of the most popular techniques used by contemporary portrait photographers, and it's surprisingly easy

For a number of years, commercial portrait studios have been making a fortune out of their 'modern-lifestyle' portraits, often taken with wide-angle lenses and almost always shot against a white background. For the technique to work, the lights need to be turned up so high that any skin flaws become bleached out. The term high-key, although meaning different things to different photographers, generally refers to images with a very low contrast ratio so there's little difference between the areas of shadow and highlight. The results look fresh and clean, and with a bit of experimentation, it is easy to achieve good results. The shadows you can see are so subtle that the skin often looks flawless without the need for much, if any, post-processing. You will probably find that a lot of modelling agencies use this type of technique for their models' main headshots, as it's flattering and hides a multitude of blemishes and imperfections.

Contrary to what many beginners to studio lighting believe, this is a very simple technique to set up, and could even be achieved using only windowlight and a single reflector. While a reflector and a single studioflash can also work, for the best results you should use at least two studio lights. In this part of the guide, we're going to show you how to create a high-key lighting effect for your portraits using a two-light and a four-light set-up from your budget studioflash outfit.

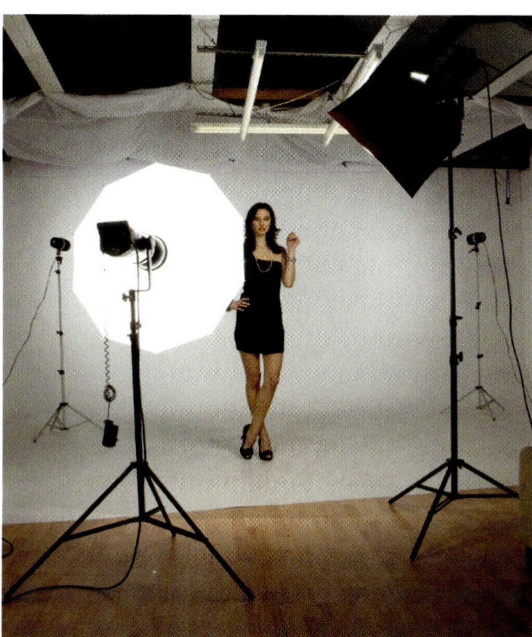

1) The four-light set-up

This involves two diffused lights pointing at the subject and two lights, with no attachments fitted, pointing at the background. The principle is simple: your subject needs to be correctly exposed, whereas the background should be so grossly overexposed that it's rendered as pure white. To do this, with the background lights off, set up the two main lights so that they illuminate your subject and work out the correct exposure. Then, switch on the background lights and ensure the power setting for them is two stops brighter or more than it is for the subject's lighting. Just remember to take care that the background light isn't so bright that it spills off the backdrop and creates flare that spoils the overall result.

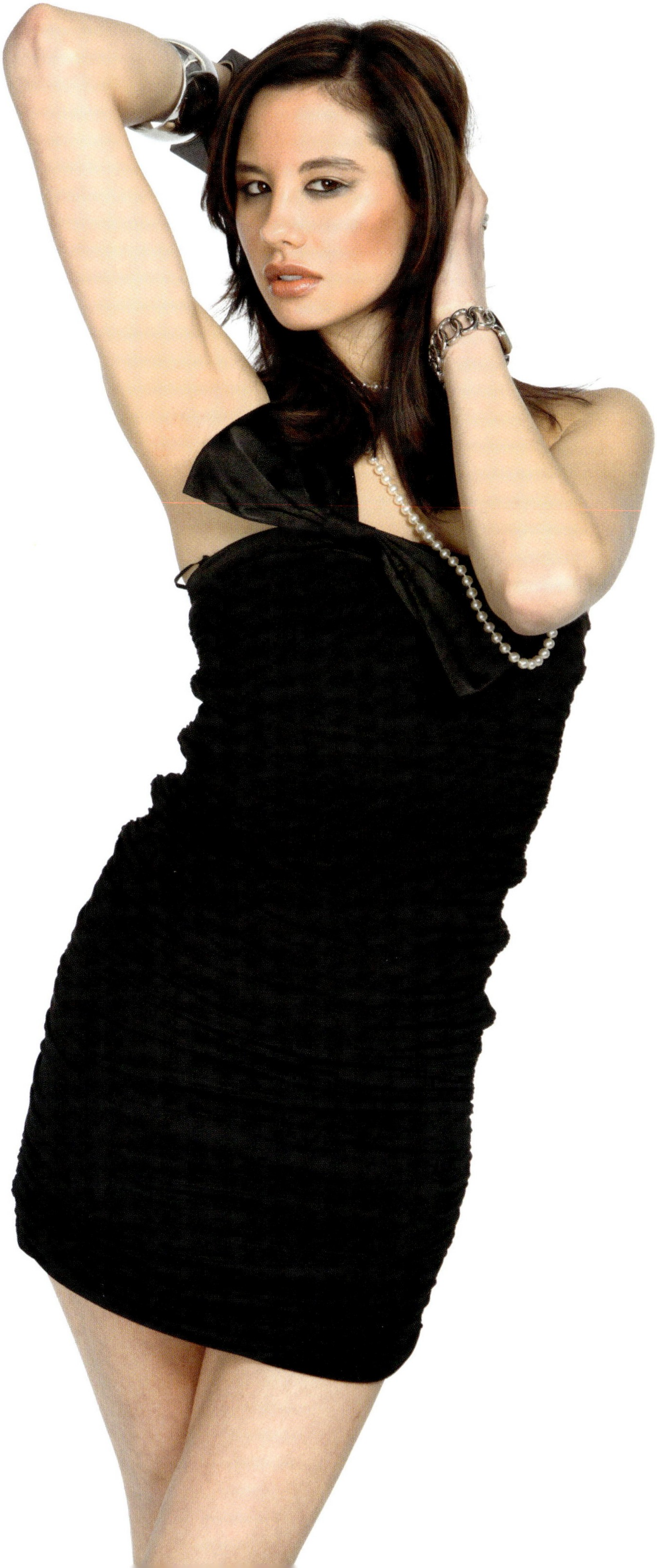

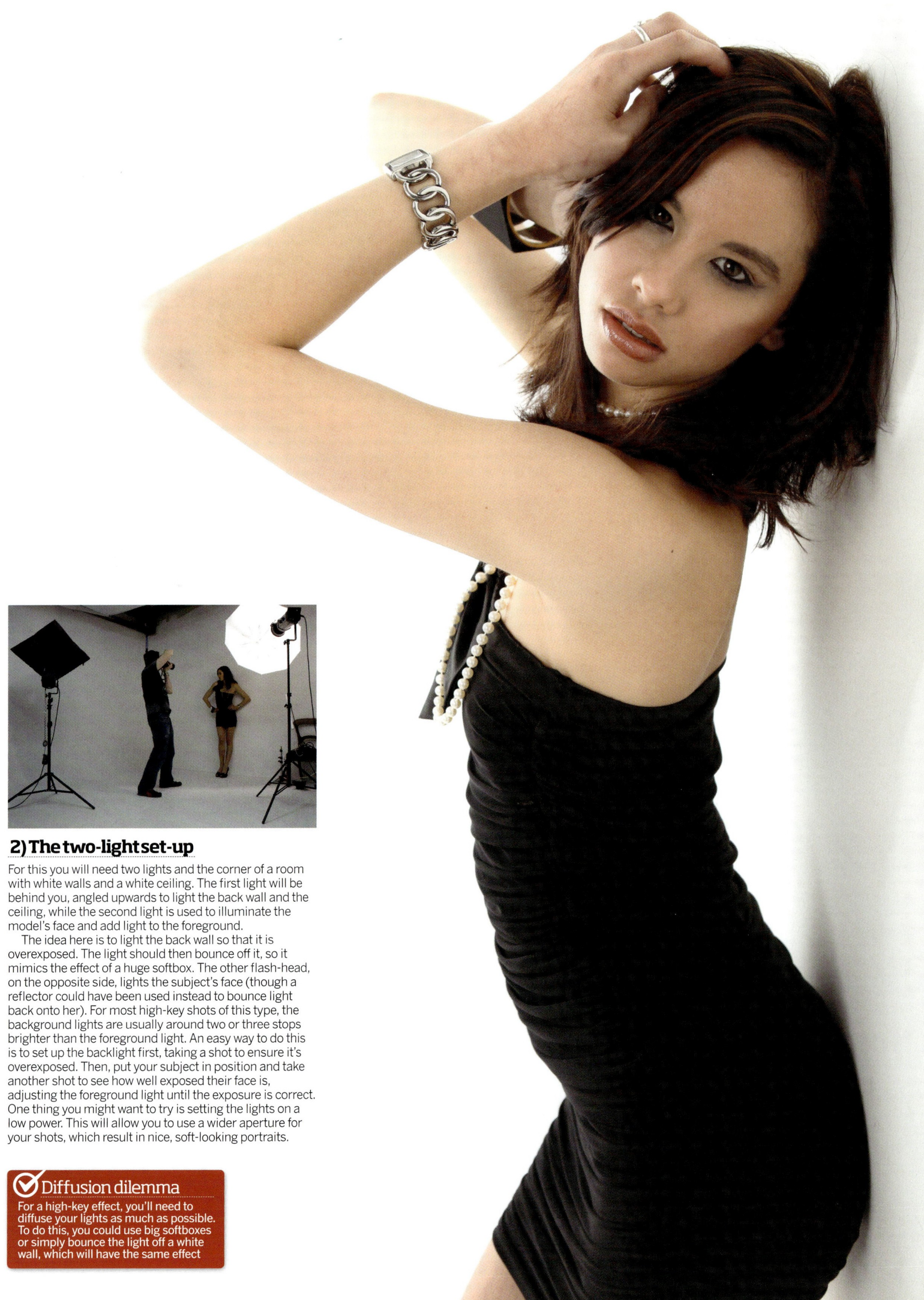

2) The two-light set-up

For this you will need two lights and the corner of a room with white walls and a white ceiling. The first light will be behind you, angled upwards to light the back wall and the ceiling, while the second light is used to illuminate the model's face and add light to the foreground.

The idea here is to light the back wall so that it is overexposed. The light should then bounce off it, so it mimics the effect of a huge softbox. The other flash-head, on the opposite side, lights the subject's face (though a reflector could have been used instead to bounce light back onto her). For most high-key shots of this type, the background lights are usually around two or three stops brighter than the foreground light. An easy way to do this is to set up the backlight first, taking a shot to ensure it's overexposed. Then, put your subject in position and take another shot to see how well exposed their face is, adjusting the foreground light until the exposure is correct. One thing you might want to try is setting the lights on a low power. This will allow you to use a wider aperture for your shots, which result in nice, soft-looking portraits.

Diffusion dilemma

For a high-key effect, you'll need to diffuse your lights as much as possible. To do this, you could use big softboxes or simply bounce the light off a white wall, which will have the same effect

Isn't it time you lost your head?

DANIEL LEZANO: There are numerous reasons for taking pictures, but sometimes you should do it just because it's fun. With this in mind, I decided to recreate an image I'd seen in a magazine that showed a headless body holding a head under one arm. It was quite a high-end image, so there was plenty of Photoshop involved to make it appear realistic, but I wanted to shoot a far more attainable image for anyone wanting to recreate a similar shot without having to spend ages in post-production. While this image does include a little Photoshop work, the emphasis is on careful composition and lighting to give the impression that there's only one person in the frame, and that they're holding their own head!

Setting the scene: There was no glamorous location for this portrait shoot, just the inside of a garage! The subjects, Hayley (the headless torso) and Katie (the head) were placed a metre or so from the white garage wall, with Hayley standing and Katie sat on top of a couple of sofa cushions. Both had been asked to wear black, as this would help with merging the two figures together to give the impression of a floating head. The windows of the garage had to be blocked off with parcel paper to minimise ambient light. For this image to work, I had to illuminate Hayley's neck and torso with one flashhead and Katie's head with the other. I fitted the softbox to the 500W studioflash and, with it at Hayley's head height, tilted it upwards slightly to reduce the amount of light reaching Katie's head. I fitted a spill to the 250W flash and placed this low and close to Katie, so that the light was concentrated on her head, with as little lighting as possible on her shoulders. A snoot or spotlight would have been a better option, but I lacked both. You can see the optimum position of the lights on the image on the right.

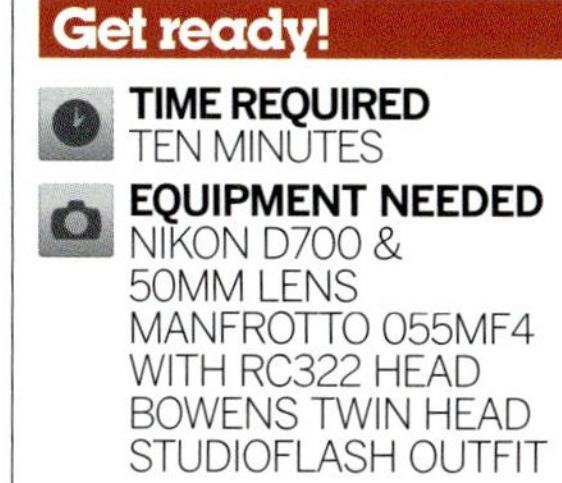

Get ready!

TIME REQUIRED
TEN MINUTES

EQUIPMENT NEEDED
NIKON D700 & 50MM LENS
MANFROTTO 055MF4 WITH RC322 HEAD
BOWENS TWIN HEAD STUDIOFLASH OUTFIT

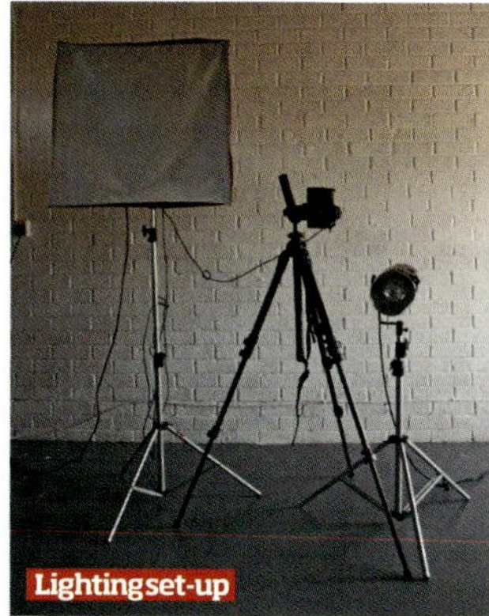

Lighting set-up

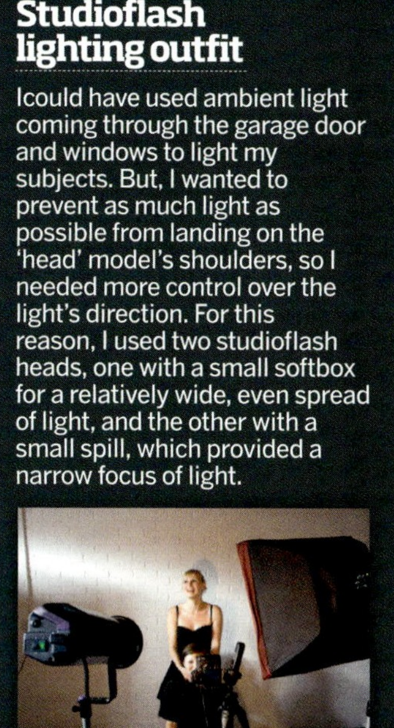

Studioflash lighting outfit

I could have used ambient light coming through the garage door and windows to light my subjects. But, I wanted to prevent as much light as possible from landing on the 'head' model's shoulders, so I needed more control over the light's direction. For this reason, I used two studioflash heads, one with a small softbox for a relatively wide, even spread of light, and the other with a small spill, which provided a narrow focus of light.

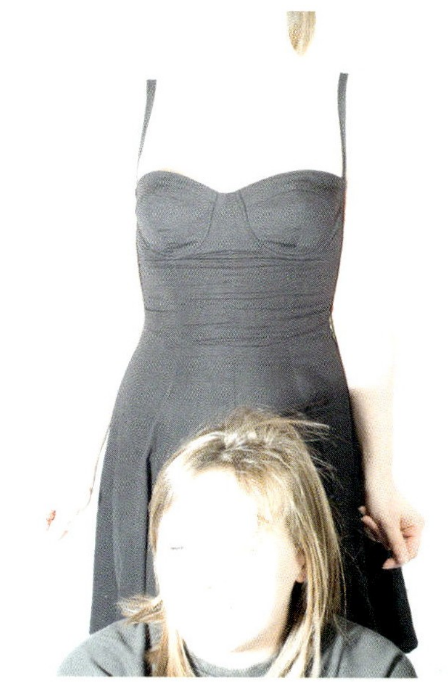

1 METERING FOR THE SCENE The best way to calculate the exposure is to use a handheld flash meter, taking readings from the neck of the 'torso' and the face of the 'head', adjusting the power of each studioflash light so that both have the same exposure. For those without a flash meter, the simplest way is, with your camera set to manual exposure mode, put the shutter speed to the flash sync speed, choose a small aperture (in this case f/8) and take a picture, then review the image on the LCD. This first test shot was grossly overexposed.

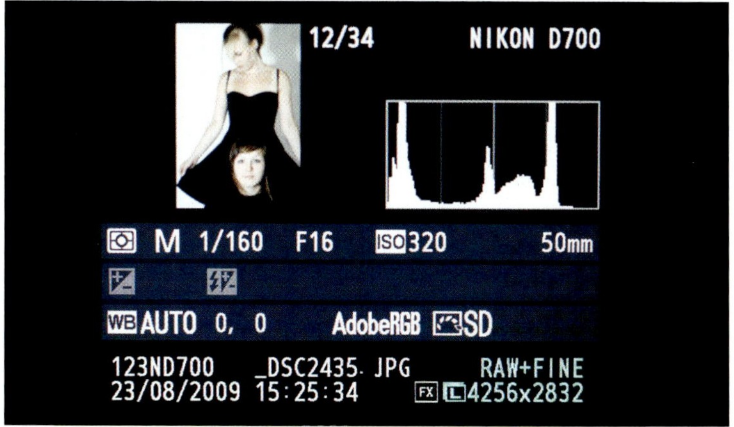

2 FINE TUNE THE EXPOSURE To adjust the exposure, you can open or close down the aperture, change the ISO rating and/or adjust the power of the studioflash (do this by changing the power values and/or moving it closer or further away from the subject). I kept ISO 320, set the aperture to f/16, then lowered the power of both flashheads, taking care to keep the ratio of both the same. A couple more test shots and minor adjustments to the power gave a decent exposure, which I confirmed by checking the histogram.

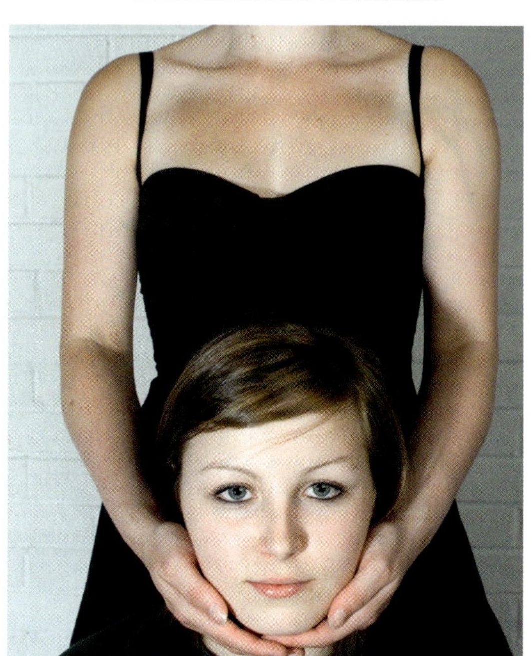

3 COMPOSING THE SCENE With the lighting and exposure sorted, it was time to position the models so that the image was as realistic as possible. The key area I had to keep an eye on was getting the head's height correct so that the arms looked natural and not stretched out. It was also important to have the hands positioned so that they appear to be holding up the head, as well as also covering up as much of the neck area as possible. I asked Hayley to keep her chin up so that her neck is stretched out. Once I was happy with the set-up, I fired off a few different images, getting Hayley to adjust her hands to find the best position.

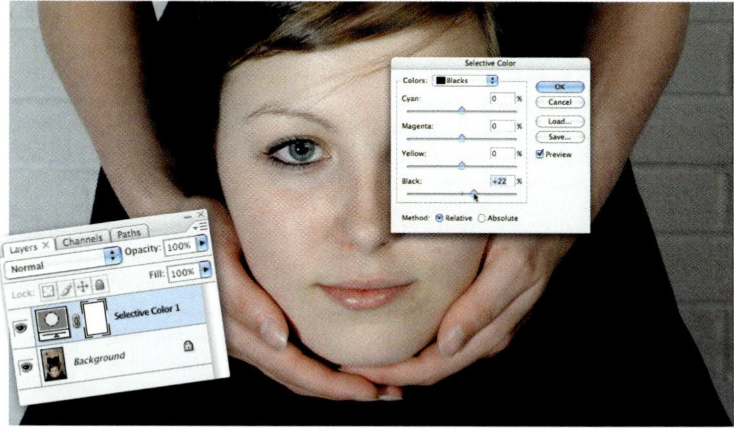

4 TIME FOR PHOTOSHOP Work is needed to remove the visible neckline and detail from the T-shirt. For the neckline, using the Polygonal Lasso Tool, I make a selection around the neckline area. Now I select the Paint Brush Tool and, while holding down the *Alt* key, click on an area of black, which selects that colour, and begin to paint out the skin. To merge the dress and T-shirt detail, I go to *Layer>New Adjustment Layer>Selective Color*, creating a new layer and preserving the original image. I select *Blacks* in the drop-down menu, then move the Black slider until all the detail has merged. Finally, using the Erase Tool, I delete any areas where wanted detail has been lost, such as the face and arms, restoring detail still preserved on the layer beneath.

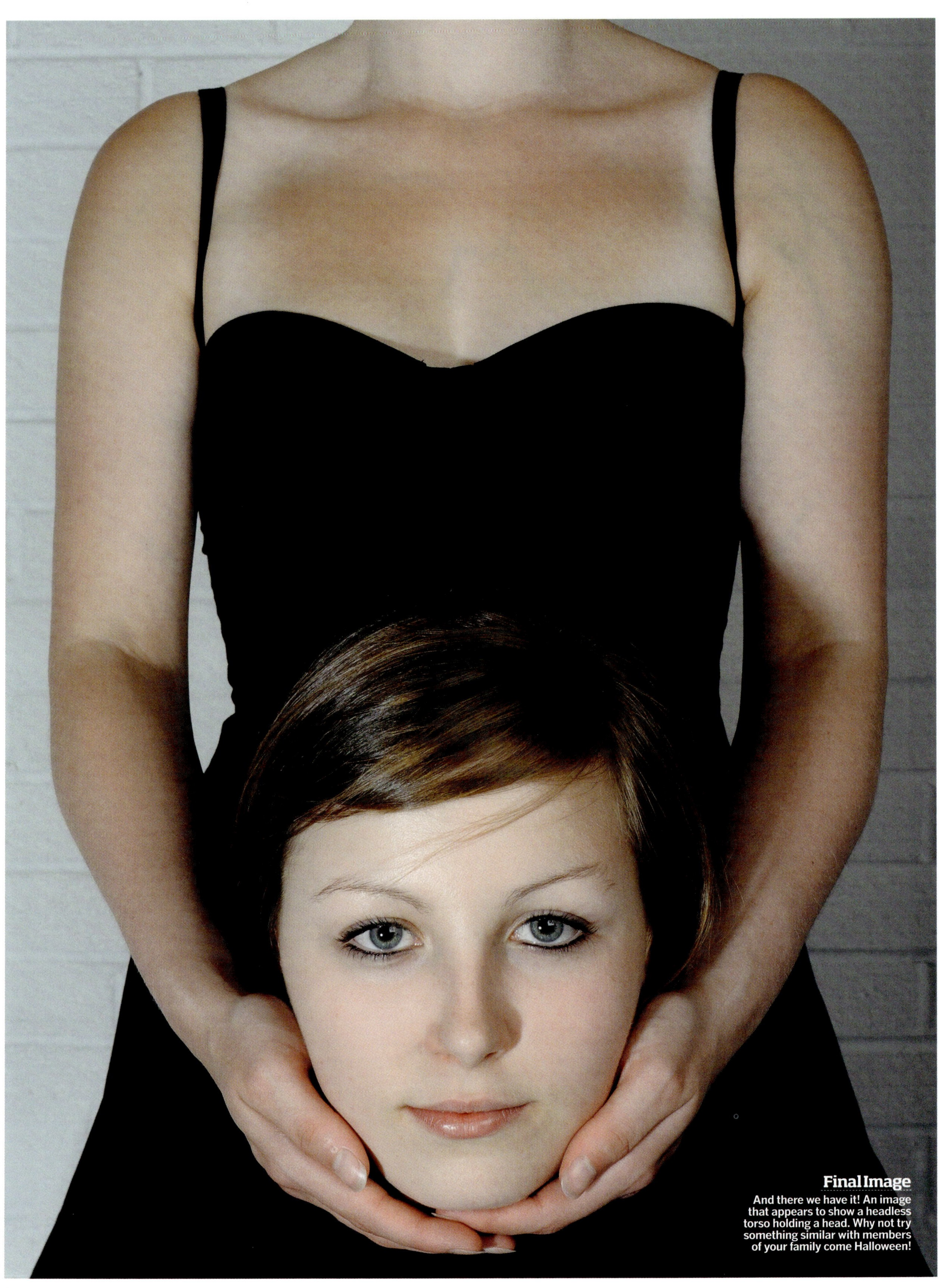

Final Image

And there we have it! An image that appears to show a headless torso holding a head. Why not try something similar with members of your family come Halloween!

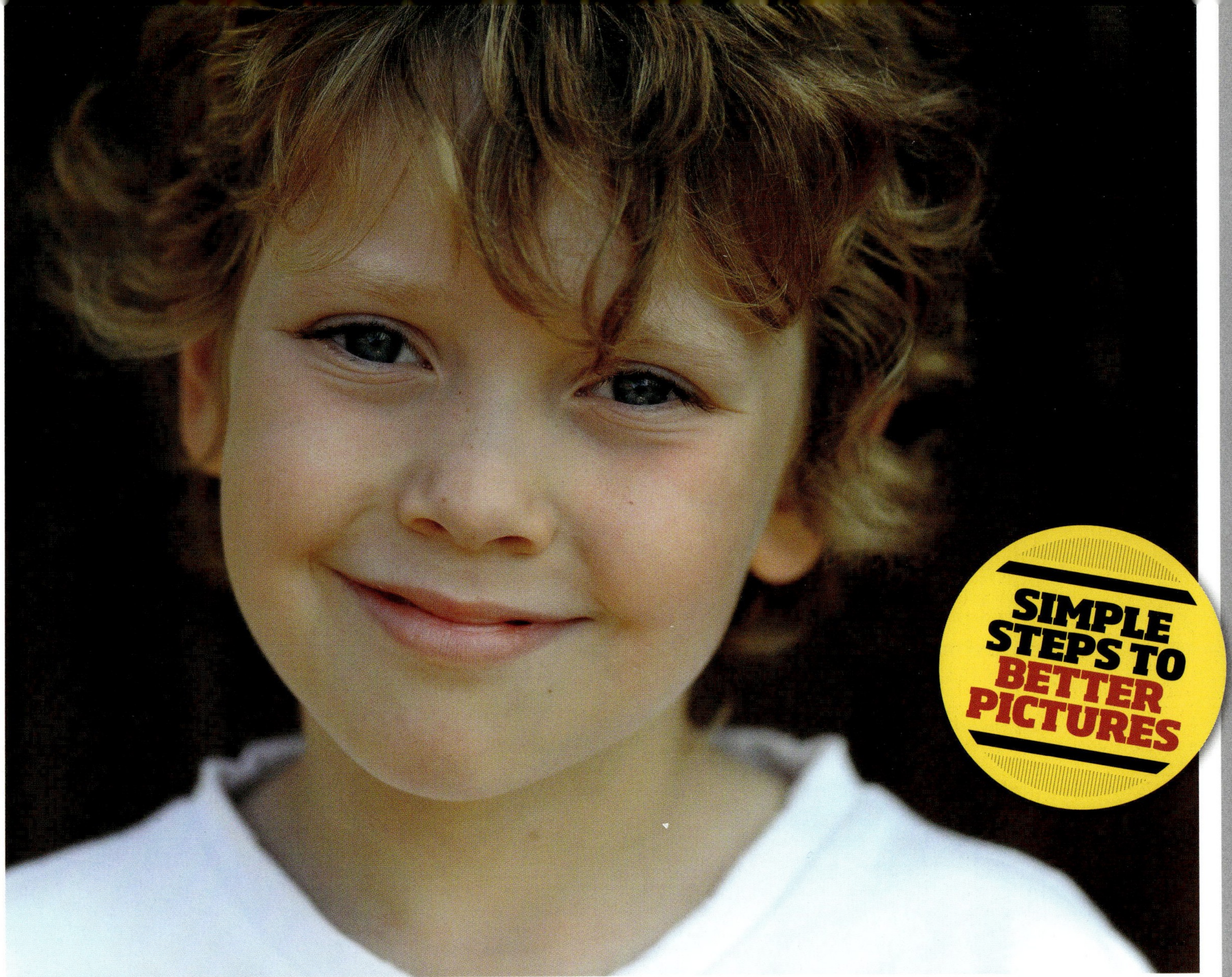

SIMPLE STEPS TO BETTER PICTURES

FAMILY PORTRAITS

IDEAS & INSPIRATION TO HELP YOU TAKE FAMILY PICTURES YOU'LL TREASURE FOREVER

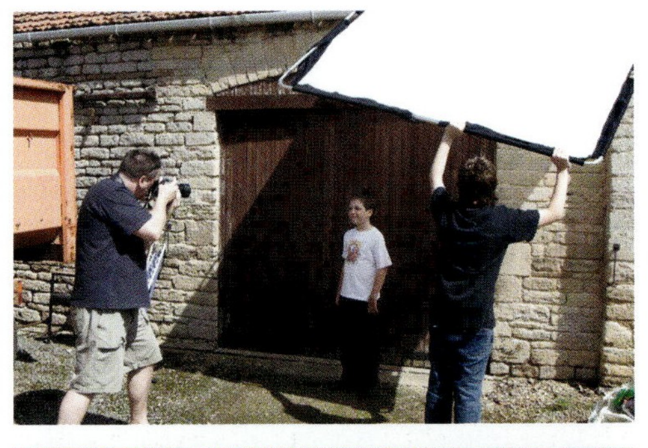

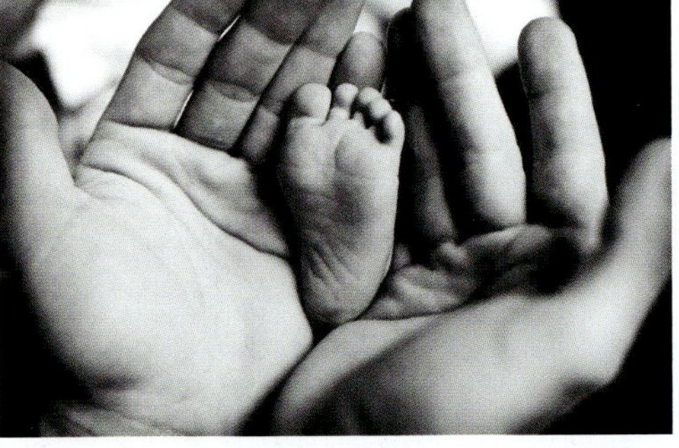

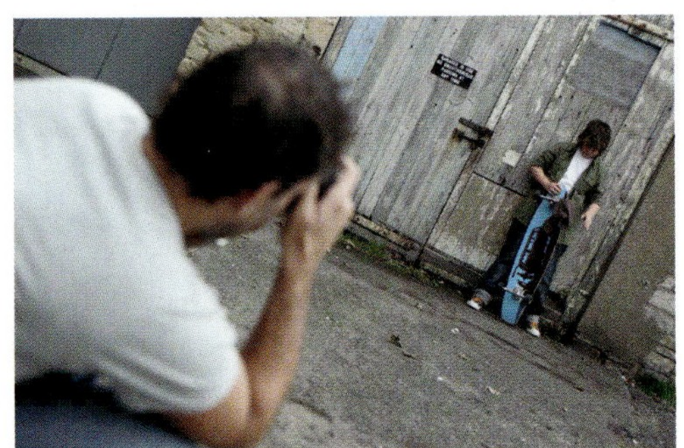

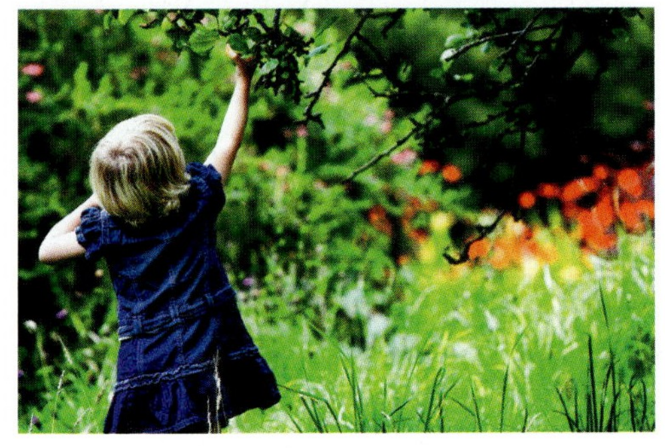

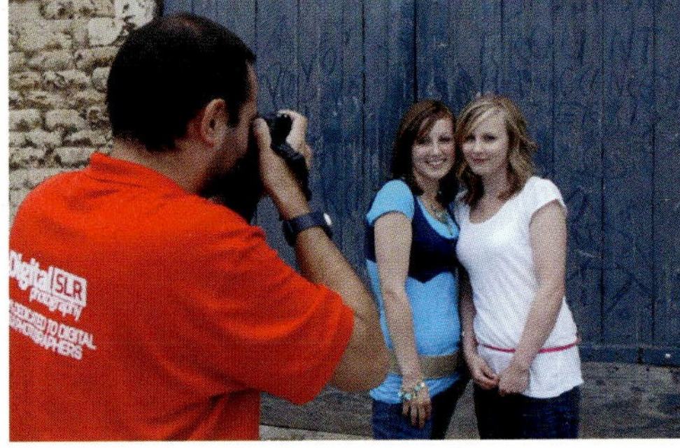

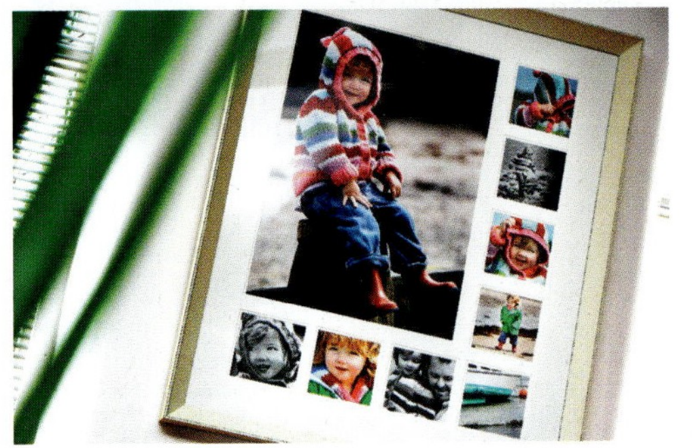

The basic principles to photographing kids

Every child is unique and each has to be handled in their own special way. But there are certain steps to follow that can help you take your best ever pictures

IT ISN'T ALWAYS EASY, but capturing great shots of kids is one of the most rewarding moments in photography. Because they're often a law unto themselves, children often prove a real challenge to photograph. However, by learning a few basic skills and knowing how to make the most of their exuberant nature, you should be able to build up a nice collection of images. Strangely enough, when shooting kids, one of the key factors for success isn't anything to do with photography, it's actually all to do with how well you interact with the subject. It's essential that your subject feels comfortable and relaxed having their picture taken by you, otherwise they just won't look natural in the shots. Ideally, for at least the first ten minutes, keep any camera gear out of sight and spend the time chatting to the child and the parents. Only once they've got used to you should you think about getting out your DSLR and taking pictures. You'll normally find that younger children are generally the easiest to get on with and teenagers can be the most difficult, as they're more self-conscious about their image, and so often more reluctant to have their picture taken.

What sort of pictures should you aim to take?

Well, that's something that you, the parents and (in the case of shooting older children), the subjects themselves can decide. In the past, portraits were very formal and staged but thankfully things have moved on and the most pleasing portraits are those that capture relaxed subjects with happy and natural expressions. Shooting in the sitter's home is usually a very good starting point for various reasons. They'll obviously feel very comfortable in their surroundings and you'll also have the opportunity to have them change outfits or include different props, such as sunglasses, headbands etc if required. One more thing on clothing – don't get the children to wear their Sunday best as they won't feel comfortable, but instead have them dress in casual clothes or a favourite outfit.

As good as the home is, there is much to be said about heading out and shooting on location. Virtually anywhere is suitable – local parks, open countryside, industrial areas, beaches and city centres each have different attractions and moods that they can add to a portrait, so try as many as possible. And remember, there are countless ways to compose the subject in the frame, from head shots to full-length body shots and images where they're relatively small in the frame. The options are endless, so use your imagination and our expert advice to help you take your best ever pictures of children.

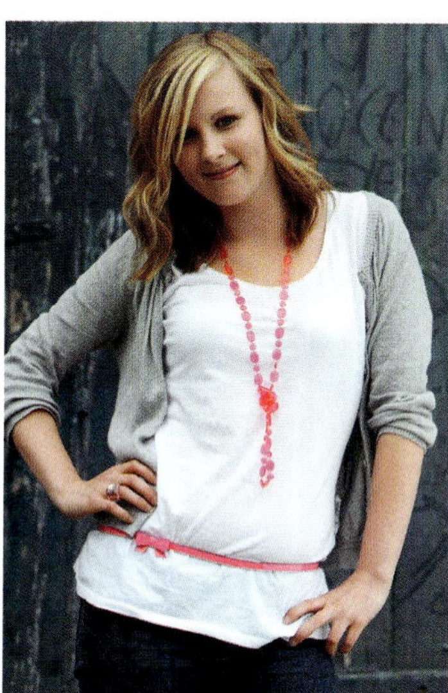

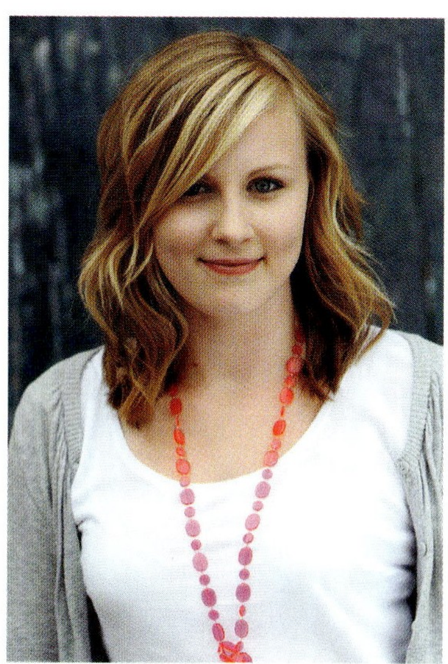

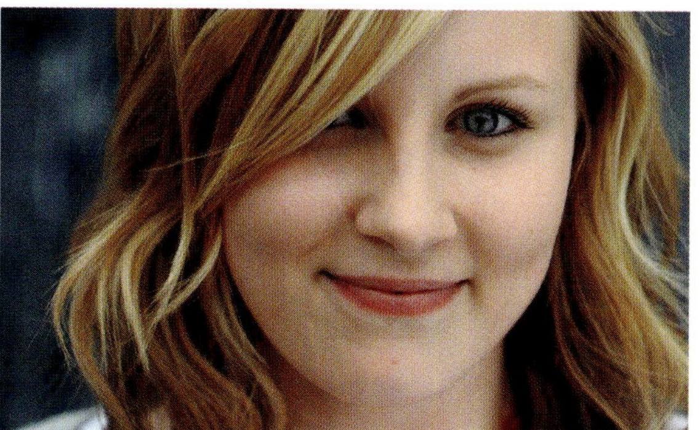

Vary your composition
As well as asking your subject to adopt different poses, you can dramatically alter your portrait by the way you frame your subject. Try close face crops, head and shoulders and full-length body shots.

How should you set up your DSLR?

When shooting portraits of kids, you'll need to be able to think on your feet and work fast, as while there will be moments where they're posing nicely, most of the time you'll be trying to keep up with their antics. Here's how we recommend you set up your DSLR

1) EXPOSURE MODE: The best bet is to use aperture-priority mode. We'd suggest you start off by setting f/5.6 and, to be honest, you can more or less leave it set to f/5.6 for the entire time. At this setting, you're working with a shallow depth-of-field that ensures your subject's face is sharp, but the background is thrown out of focus. What you'll need to keep your eye on is the shutter speed as you want to ensure it's fast enough to avoid shake. Increase the ISO rating (to a maximum of ISO 800-1000) when the shutter speed drops too low. Try to keep it at 1/200sec or faster and you should be fine if you're using a 50-200mm, or 1/300sec if it's a 70-300mm that you're using.

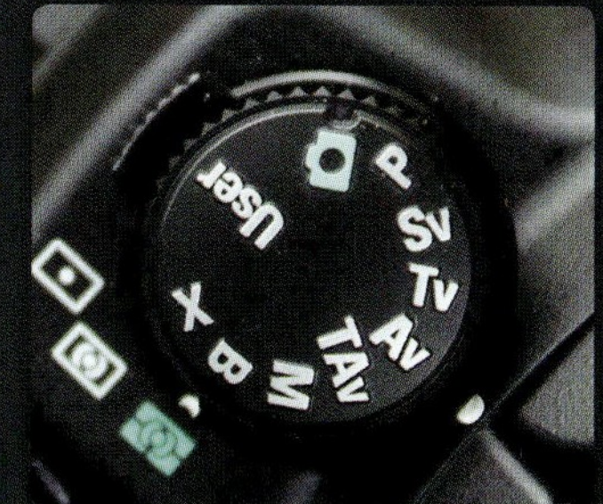

2) AUTOFOCUS: You can leave your camera set to multi-point AF mode if you want, but you run the risk of focusing on a shoulder, forehead, tip of the nose etc and not on the eyes, which is what you want to ensure is pin-sharp. We'd suggest you set your AF to single-point AF and use the central focusing sensor, which offers the best sensitivity. Set your AF mode to S (S-AF, AF-S) so that when you focus on the eye, you can lock the focus by pressing the shutter button halfway down, then recompose and take the shot.

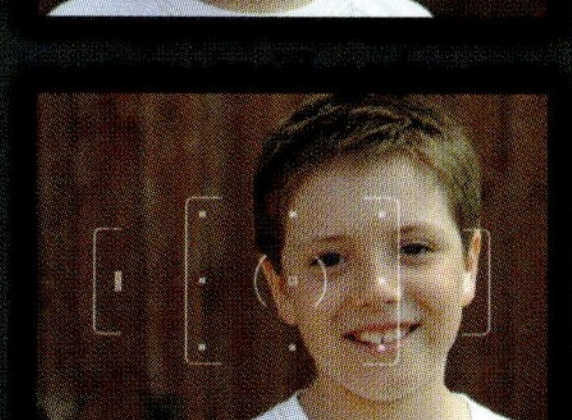

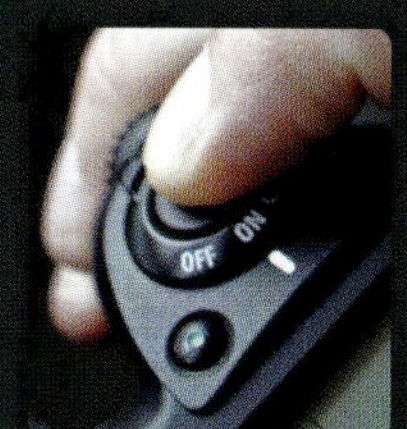

3) METERING: Stick to multi-zone metering and you shouldn't have any problems. If your subject is predominantly dark, take one shot and check the LCD monitor, if detail is missing, add +1EV using the exposure compensation facility.

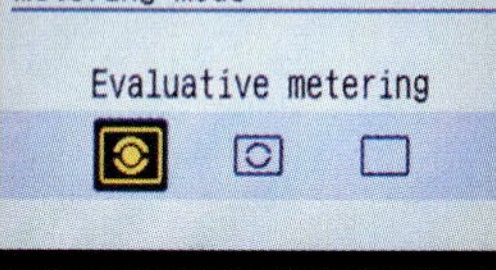

CANON

NIKON
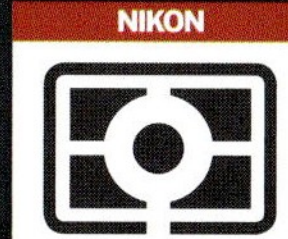

OLYMPUS
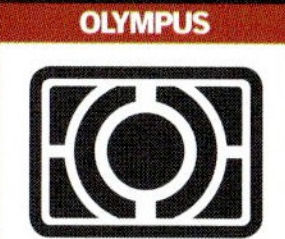

PENTAX
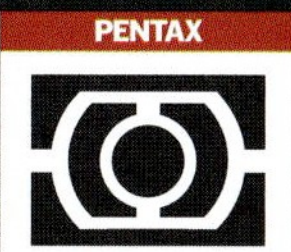

4) FILE FORMAT: Shoot in Raw for the maximum control over image quality and colour balance. However, when shooting fast sequences, it can slow your shooting rate because the buffer has to handle more data. Shoot JPEG only if you're not confident about converting Raw to JPEG or when memory space on your card is limited.

Remaining Count : 99
Picture Wizard
File Format — JPEG / RAW / RAW+
JPEG Size
JPEG Quality
Colour Space
Set RAW Button
Liveview
OK : Set — MENU : Cancel

5) WHITE BALANCE: Ideally, set White Balance to suit the lighting conditions. If you're unsure what to use, set Auto White Balance (AWB). Bear in mind though, if you're shooting in Raw, you can easily change settings once you have the images on your computer.

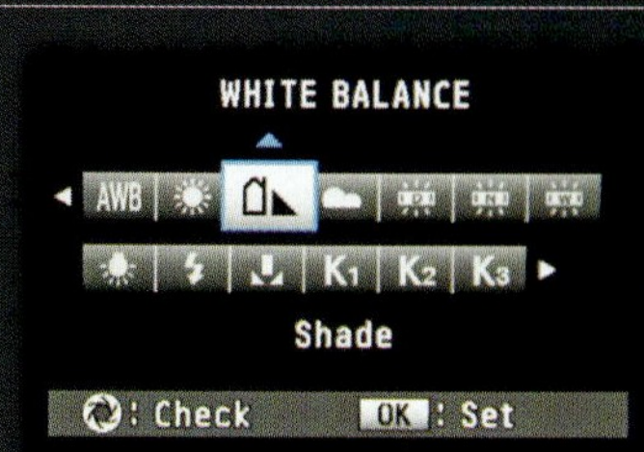

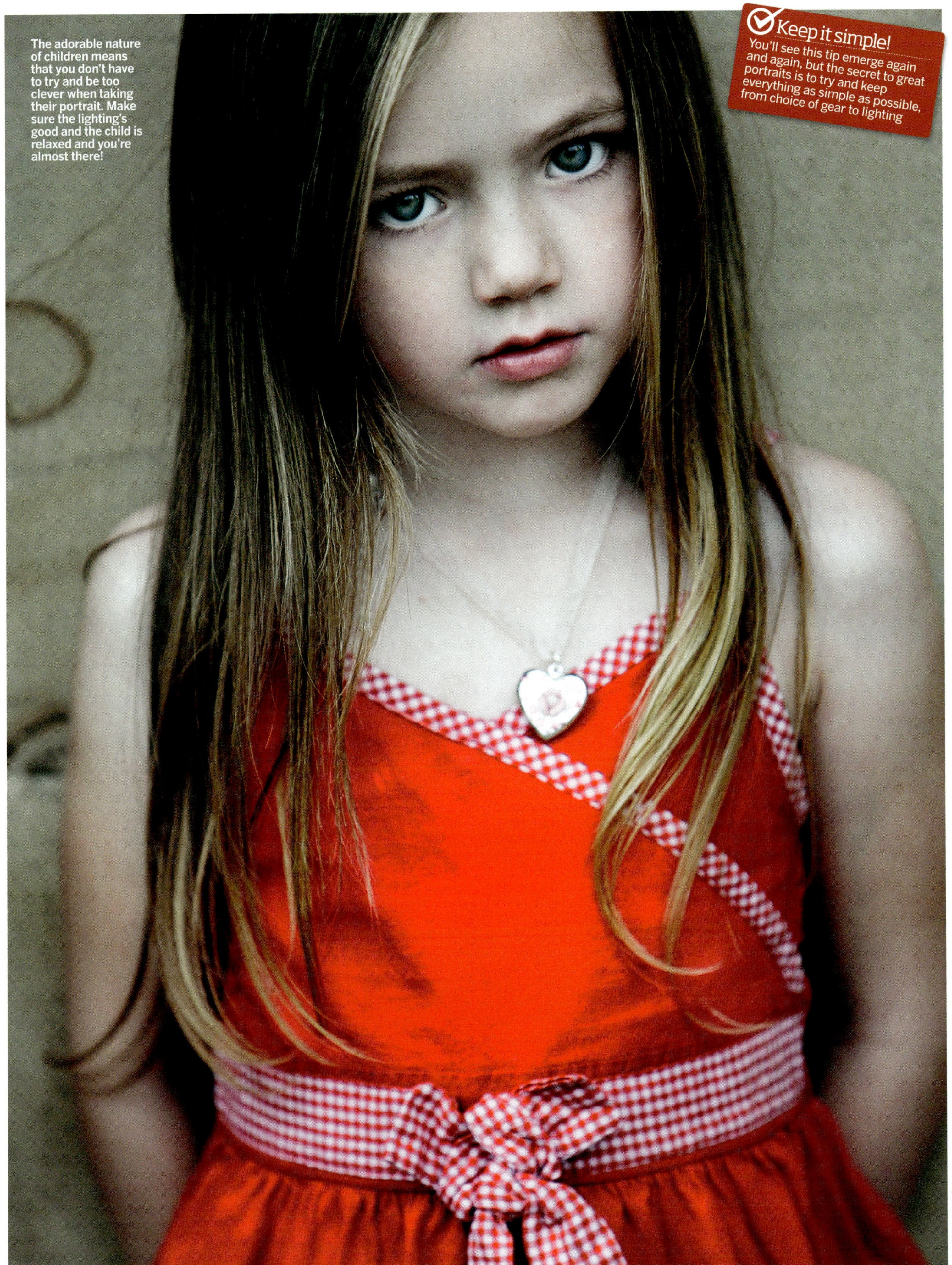

The adorable nature of children means that you don't have to try and be too clever when taking their portrait. Make sure the lighting's good and the child is relaxed and you're almost there!

Keep it simple!
You'll see this tip emerge again and again, but the secret to great portraits is to try and keep everything as simple as possible, from choice of gear to lighting

BRETT HARKNESS

Photographing the kids: Be prepared

You can improve your chances of success by being ready in advance!

Get permission

If you're photographing other people's children, make sure you gain permission from one or both parents. Make sure to get a model release form signed too if you plan to have any published

WHAT KIT SHOULD YOU USE? Your choice of kit will largely be influenced by the type of pictures you're taking and the location of your shoot. If you're looking to shoot natural portraits and working with natural light, it's often best to keep your kit to a minimum – a DSLR fitted with a zoom, along with a reflector, is often all you need to capture a decent portrait. Sometimes you'll find you need additional lighting and while your camera's integral flash can provide fill-in, a hotshoe-mounted flashgun with bounce facility is better, while a basic studioflash set-up offers more scope for creative lighting. However, the more artificial lighting you add to a scene, the more effort you'll need to put into making sure the shots appear natural.

USING NATURAL LIGHT From a beginner's perspective, working with natural light is a far easier proposition than having to use studioflash. But while there are not any power settings to twiddle with, there are still a number of factors that have to be considered when working with ambient light. For instance, the nature of daylight varies according to the weather conditions and time of day. On a sunny day, light is harsh and unflattering, on very overcast days it is dull, while shooting in the shade can give cool, flat results. By knowing how to control the various lighting conditions using a reflector, whether it's the gold, silver, white or black side, diffusers or flash, you can manipulate the light to help produce high-quality portraits. As you'll see mentioned time and again, a reflector is an indispensable accessory for virtually every form of lighting, while a diffuser is ideal for strong sunlight (see panel for details).

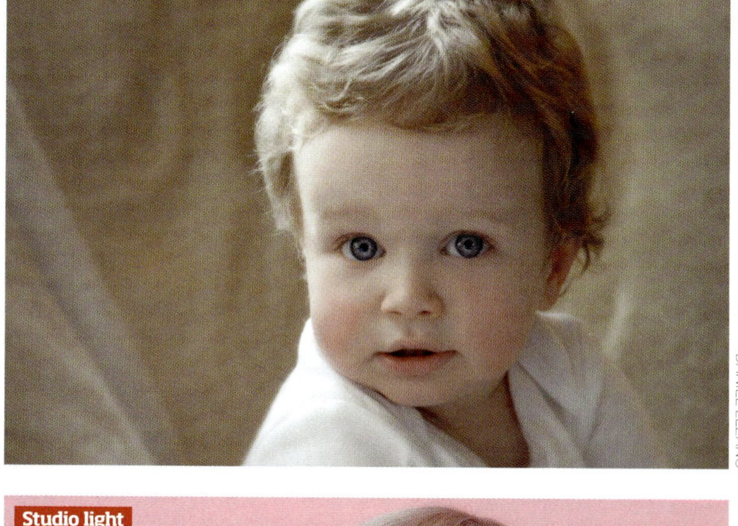

Natural light

DANIEL LEZANO

USING STUDIOFLASH While daylight makes a fantastic source of portrait lighting, it's not always available when and where you need it. Being able to use studioflash offers you the chance to shoot when the weather's poor, at night, or when you're indoors. Using one or two flash heads with a brolly or softbox and a reflector can give you great results with minimal effort, once you've established how to position the lights and how to adjust the power of the flash heads. In the past, studioflash kits were usually only available to the wealthier amateurs and professionals, but there are now a number of kits available at very affordable prices that allows many amateurs the chance to try their hand at studioflash photography. And because you're able to instantly review your images on the LCD monitor, it's far easier to check lighting set-ups and make adjustments than ever before. If you decide that you would like to try out studioflash, then check out the studioflash sections of this guide for expert advice on the best studioflash kits, accessories and techniques to buy and try.

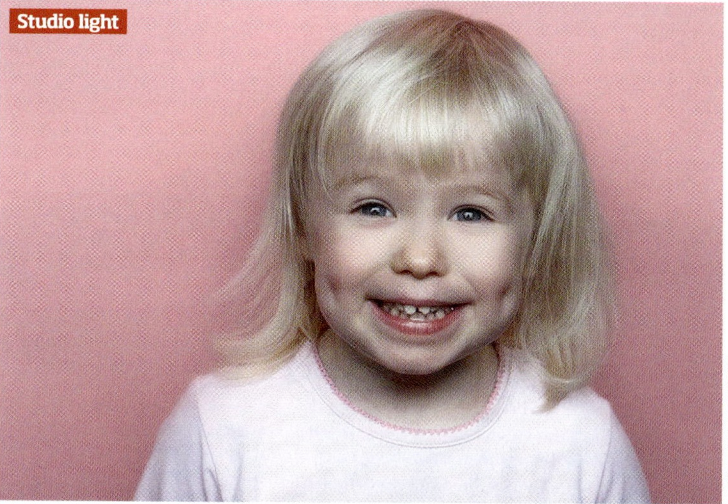

Studio light

BJORN THOMASSEN

Ideas for outdoor locations

Stuck for ideas on where to photograph great images of the kids? To be honest, almost any location is suitable, but here's a selection of tried and tested backdrops...

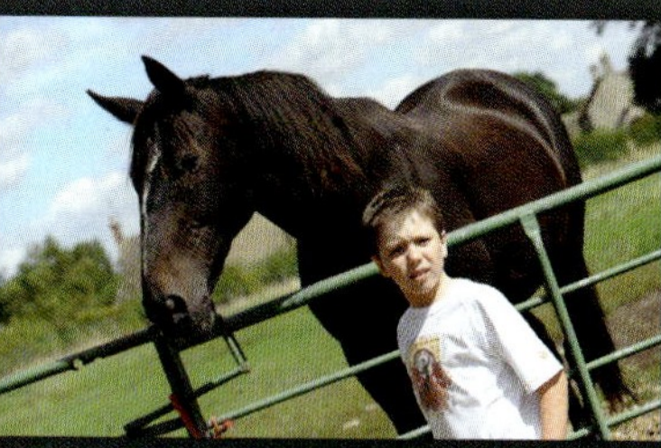

INDUSTRIAL AREA Large corrugated doors, graffiti, warehouses with broken windows and skips have distinctive character. It may sound dodgy to some but we reckon its the perfect place to shoot some great portraits of the kids.

FARM If you can visit a local farm and you're able to wander safely around it, you'll find that the barns, farmhouses, bales and general scenery can make for really interesting pictures.

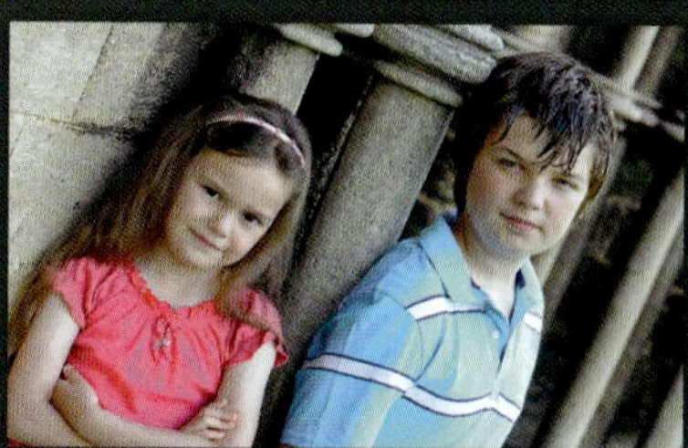

PILLARS OR COLUMNS You'll find the pillars and columns outside some museums, cathedrals and large libraries make great backgrounds. If you've more than one child in the scene, have them poking their heads around different pillars.

WEATHER-BEATEN DOORS The texture of old wooden doors makes an ideal portrait backdrop. As well as brown, splintery wood, look for painted doors where the paint is old and flaky.

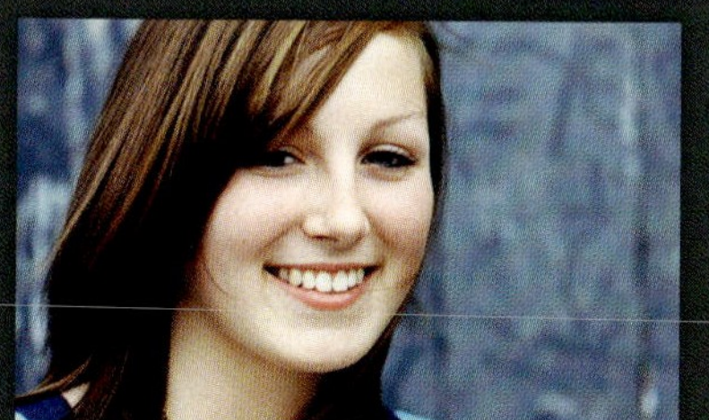

THE LOCAL PARK Feeding ducks, sat on a bench munching sandwiches or enjoying an ice cream, sat beneath a tree shaded from the sun. The picture-taking possibilities are endless!

Lighting accessories

Ideal accessories to help you control and manipulate light are as follows:

REFLECTORS A handheld reflector is a must. Ideally, go for one with a white side and a silver side. White reflects less light than silver but its effect is more subtle and natural. Silver is more efficient but should be used with care as its effect can be overpowering. Gold has a similar efficiency to silver but gives a warm glow, making it a good choice if your subject is a little pale or you're shooting in shade or on a cool winter day.

DIFFUSERS These are worth considering if you plan to shoot outdoors in direct sunlight. Place a diffuser between the sun and subject to bathe your subject in a soft, diffused light that is ideal for flattering portraits. Diffusers are available in different sizes and diffusing 'strengths'. Some can be supported on stands but the majority are handheld, although you'll need a friend to assist as they're easily blown around in the wind.

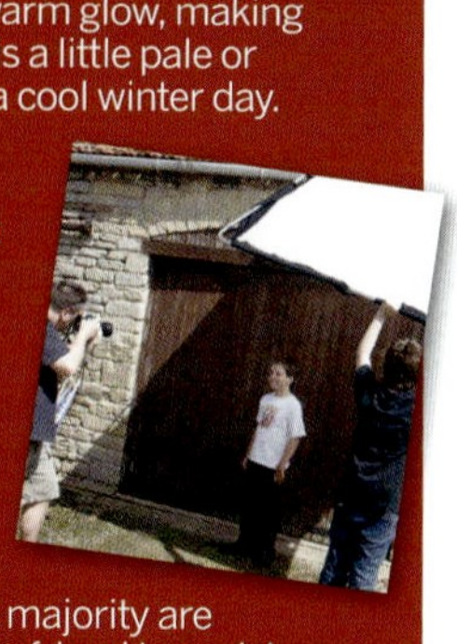

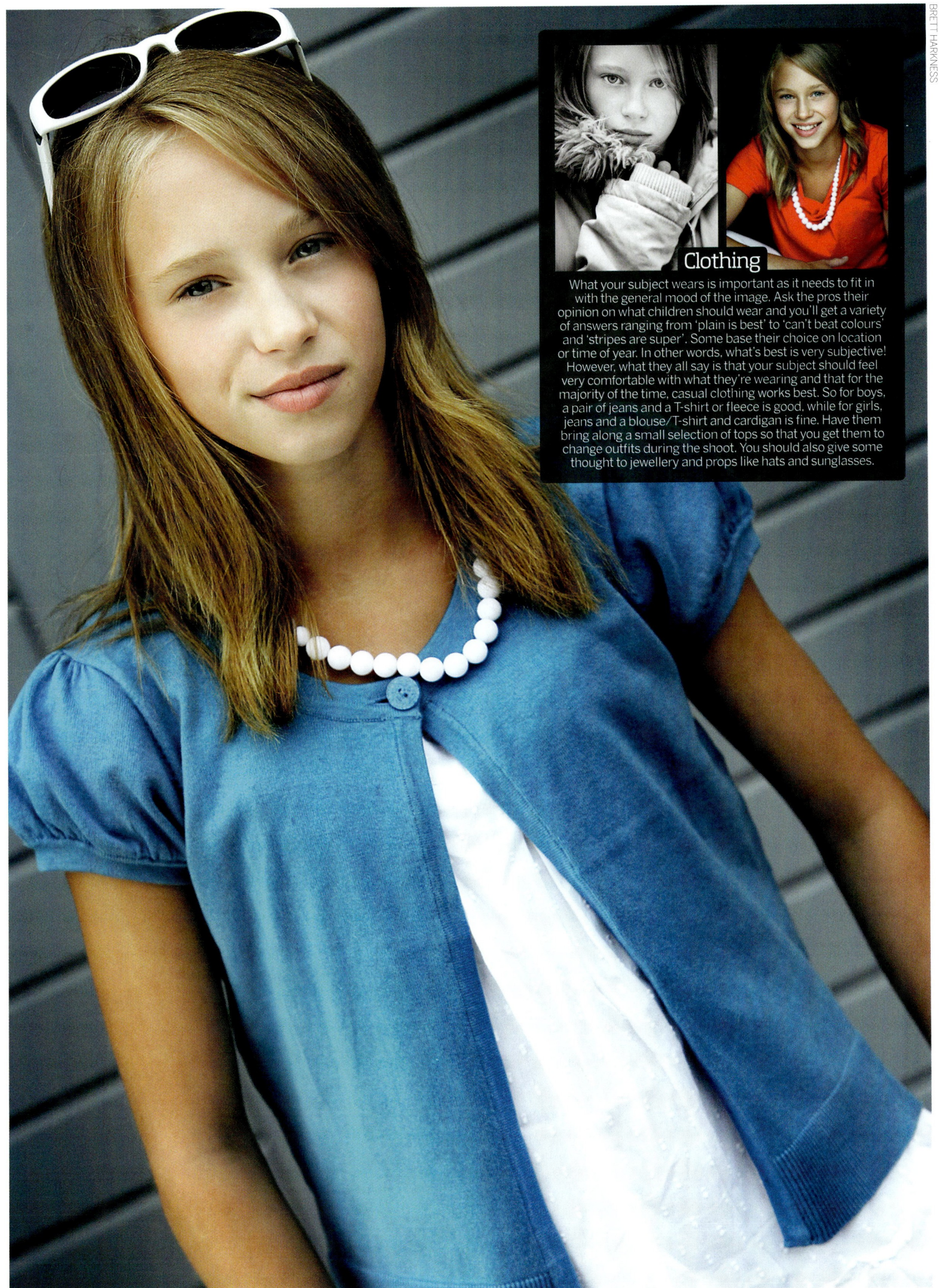

BRETT HARKNESS

Clothing

What your subject wears is important as it needs to fit in with the general mood of the image. Ask the pros their opinion on what children should wear and you'll get a variety of answers ranging from 'plain is best' to 'can't beat colours' and 'stripes are super'. Some base their choice on location or time of year. In other words, what's best is very subjective! However, what they all say is that your subject should feel very comfortable with what they're wearing and that for the majority of the time, casual clothing works best. So for boys, a pair of jeans and a T-shirt or fleece is good, while for girls, jeans and a blouse/T-shirt and cardigan is fine. Have them bring along a small selection of tops so that you get them to change outfits during the shoot. You should also give some thought to jewellery and props like hats and sunglasses.

Bright, beautiful babies

The arrival of a new member of the family is one of the main reasons people buy a DSLR. Follow our advice for some great baby shots!

FEW THINGS HAVE AS MUCH OF AN 'Aah' factor for cuteness as a baby. Those chubby cheeks, oversized eyes and toothless smiles are the perfect ingredients for wonderful portraits. However, as photogenic as babies are, they're not the easiest of subjects to shoot. For one, they're not going to pay any attention to what you're saying, so forget asking them to look out of the window or smile and thinking they'll oblige. Instead, expect lots of dribbling, snoozing, crying and looking everywhere except at the camera. Another obstacle you'll need to overcome, especially with babies just a few months old, is that they'll still not be strong enough to support themselves, so you'll have to shoot them lying down or being supported.

For that reason, many parents and family members are left frustrated that they can't capture the latest addition to the family as well as they'd like to. It's no surprise when you consider many get too close with a wide-angle lens and pop up the integral flash. The result is a distorted baby grimacing after the nth flash burst of its short life.

So, you've got a hard task ahead of you but there are several things in your favour. The first is that your subject isn't very mobile, so isn't going to run off anywhere. And because one or both parents will be present, they'll generally be comfortable and happy – especially if you plan to shoot after one of their regular naps or feeds.

Before taking any pictures, it's worth spending a few minutes with the baby so that they can get used to you. Talk to the baby, wave toys around, let them hold your finger, anything that puts them at ease. Make sure you smile a lot and don't feel daft for making silly noises or talking in a cutesy voice, it all works at establishing an initial bond.

If you're shooting indoors, aim to place your subject near patio/french doors; if outdoors, look for an area of well-lit shade. You'll want to work fast and be able to hand-hold the camera, so set a high ISO (400-800) and use a wide aperture. Look to shoot against as plain a background as possible – try shooting against light and dark backdrops, reviewing your LCD monitor to see which is most suitable.

A baby's eyes are relatively large in relation to the rest of their face so ensure at least one is sharply in focus. Change your viewpoint, shooting from above and then lying down to shoot from the baby's eye level or even lower.

Once you start taking pictures, you'll need to work fast. If you want, set the frame rate to continuous and shoot sequences whenever your subject is looking directly at you. You'll find the majority of images aren't worth keeping, but with any luck you'll get a handful of good shots that the parents will love. The better alternative is to leave the drive to single-frame advance and opt for less pictures taken with a little more craft and purpose.

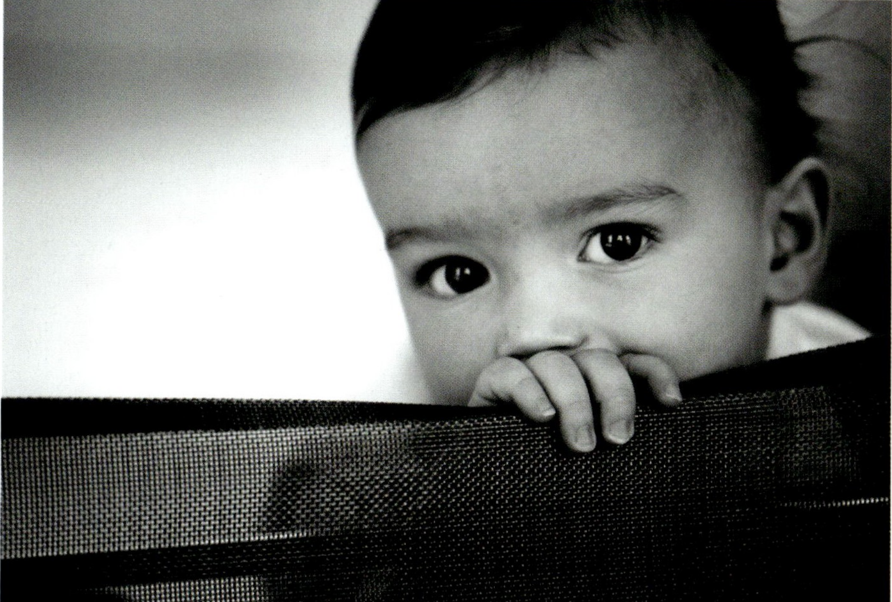

ALL IMAGES: BRETT HARKNESS

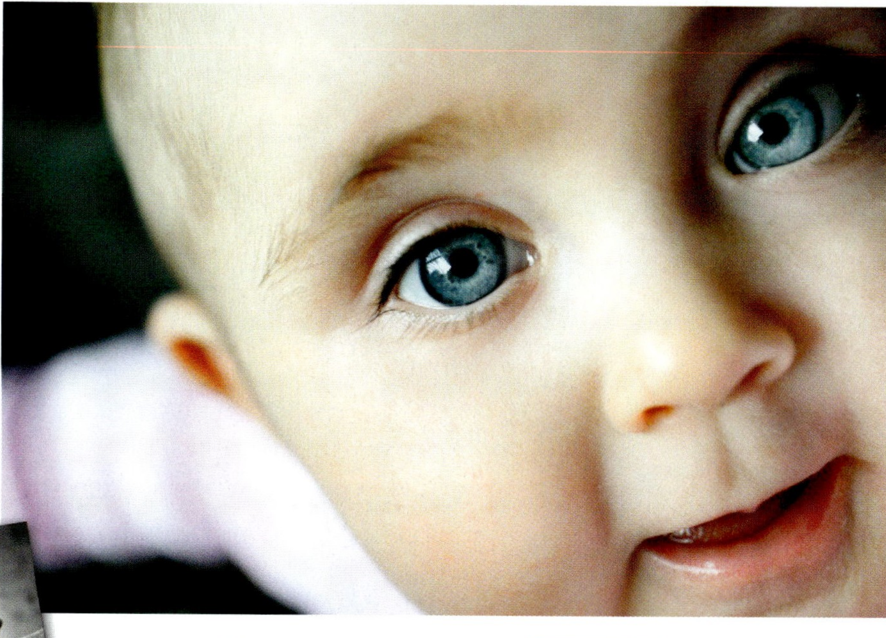

TOP: Young babies are often too weak to support themselves, so use furniture as an aid and, if possible, have a parent or assistant close by to prevent any accidents!

ABOVE: Be bold and try unusual compositions. Babies usually have very large eyes and so close crops and a very shallow depth-of-field allow you to emphasise this.

Top tips: Babies

1) GRAB THEIR ATTENTION You can usually get them to look at you if you hold a toy and give it a shake or a squeeze just before you plan to fire the shutter.

2) DON'T OVERDO IT! A ten-minute session is long enough. Take a tea break, then try again!

3) KEEP YOUR COOL You should not get frustrated or annoyed if the shoot's not going to plan. Accept that there's always the chance that you won't get any, let alone many, suitable pictures.

4) EXPECT MESS! Keep a kitchen roll handy for wiping away any baby-sick and some tissues for dribble or mucus from noses. Babies produce surprisingly large amounts of both!

5) GET CREATIVE If the baby's not looking at the camera, try unusual angles and compositions that might make a good shot, or concentrate on shooting hands, feet or other small details.

Hands & feet

You should make sure you take some shots of the baby's hands and feet. This is a good picture to try when the baby is only a few days old as they'll be sleeping most of the time and their wrinkly skin adds to the effect. Use soft light and keep colours pale and neutral, set a wide aperture for shallow depth-of-field and experiment with different angles and viewpoints. Try images in colour and black & white.

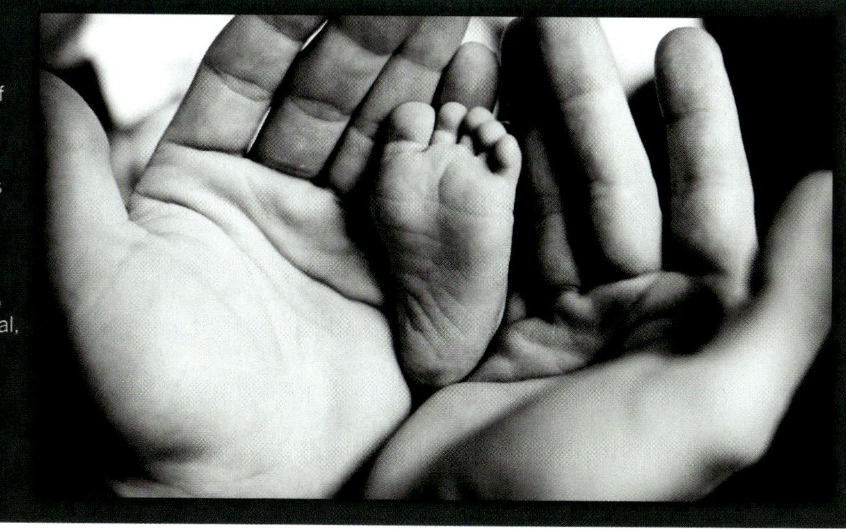

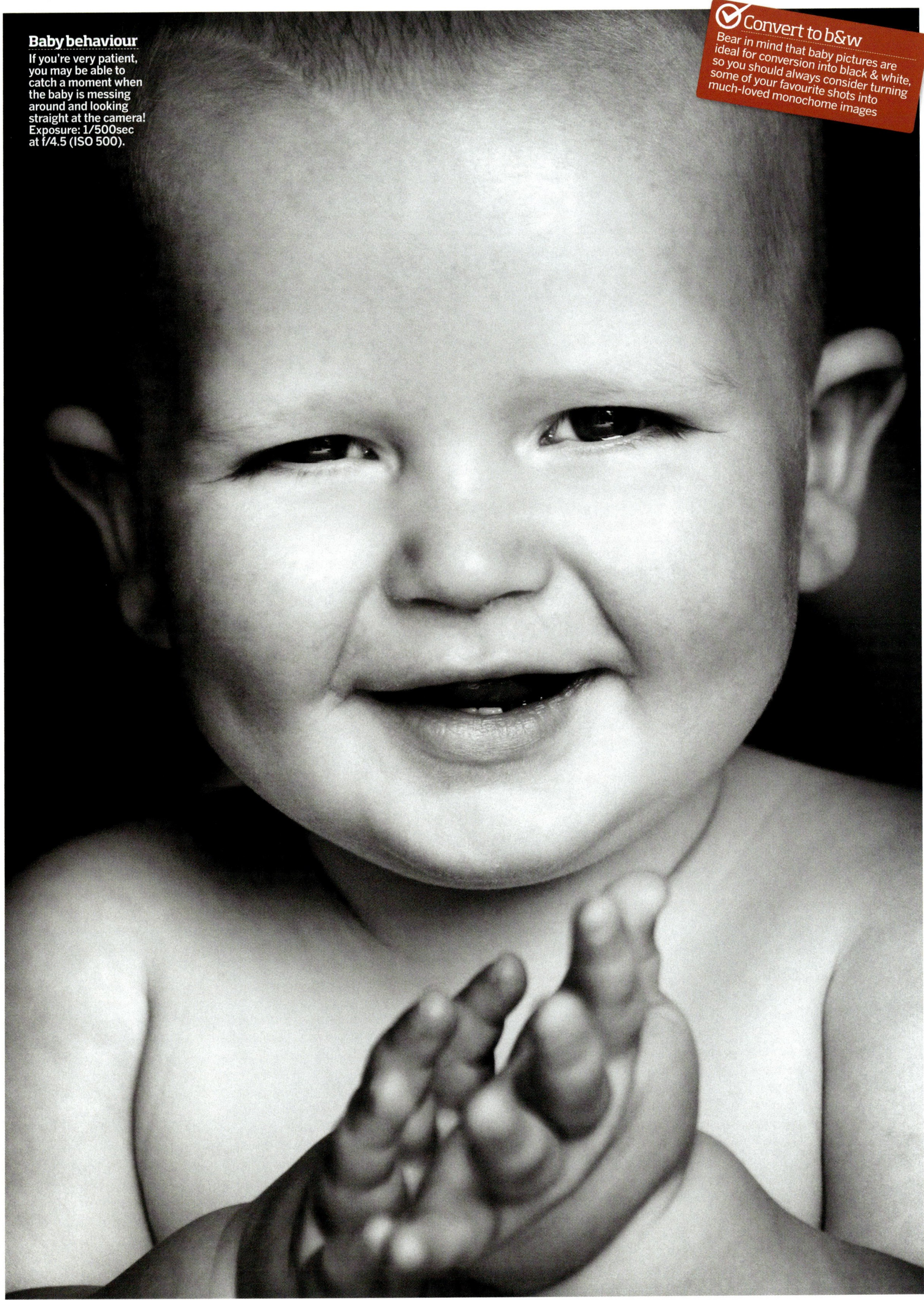

Baby behaviour
If you're very patient, you may be able to catch a moment when the baby is messing around and looking straight at the camera! Exposure: 1/500sec at f/4.5 (ISO 500).

Convert to b&w
Bear in mind that baby pictures are ideal for conversion into black & white, so you should always consider turning some of your favourite shots into much-loved monochome images

An hour with Ivy

So how easy is it to photograph a little baby using the minimum of kit? As Daniel Lezano discovers, a happy subject works wonders!

I HAD ONLY MET SIX-MONTH-OLD IVY once before – a week before I went to take her picture. She is a very happy baby, with a near-permanent smile, so I knew that she had the potential to be a great subject to photograph. Having photographed a few babies in the past, however, I knew that I couldn't take anything for granted.

Arriving at her home, her wide gummy smile greeted me and so the signs looked good. Before I started taking any pictures, I had a quick brew, chatted with Ivy's mum Keely and played a little with Ivy. I explained to Keely what I aimed to do, to keep her fully in the picture. To keep things as simple as possible, I was only using one fixed lens (105mm) and a reflector.

Having a quick look around Keely's home, it was her sitting room, with its french doors, that offered the best ambient light for the shoot. We placed Ivy in her small rocker seat and positioned it close to the window but at an angle, so to create some side-lighting. I took a few shots of her this way, then turned the chair so that her face was more evenly lit. After a few more frames, we placed a white sheet over the seat to cover its pattern and give a neutral background. This was followed by removing Ivy's top and vest to give a more natural baby shot. During this entire process, Ivy was looking around with a variety of expressions, from big smile to deep frown. Only rarely did she look directly at the camera and smile, but this didn't put me off taking pictures as, even without direct eye contact, the shots were working.

The large, round reflector really grabbed Ivy's attention and again made her smile, especially when using the shiny silver or gold side, but unfortunately this also meant she looked at the camera even less. However, by shifting her position and that of the reflector, I was able to shoot from above it and grab a few shots with her looking at the camera.

Having Keely with me meant I had an extra set of hands to hold the reflector in position, which proved essential. It also meant that she could pick up Ivy every now and then to give her some attention, breaking up the routine, which was important to keep Ivy interested and in a good mood. It also allowed me to take some shots of Ivy 'leaning' against the sofa arm, with Keely supporting her from behind. These shots proved to be the best of the shoot, as Ivy's upright position meant her face had a more natural shape and also because the background was thrown out of focus and was less distracting. Towards the very end of the shoot, Ivy started crying and while Keely cuddled her and bounced her up and down to cheer her up, I took a few side profiles of Ivy to get a different perspective. One of these was my favourite shot of the day.

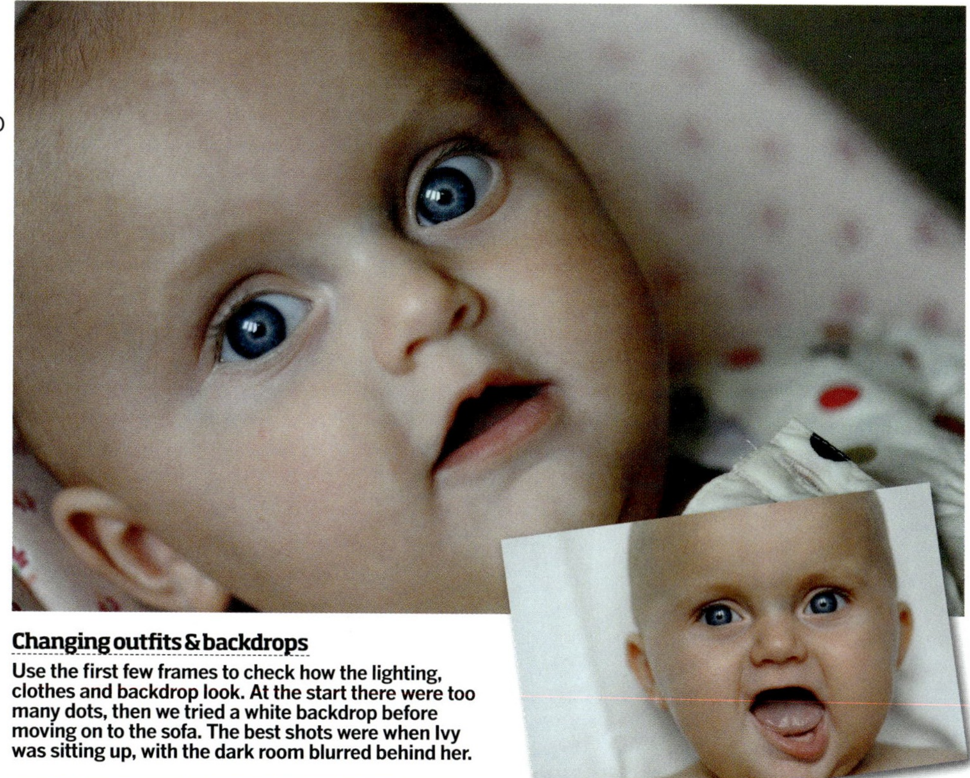

Changing outfits & backdrops

Use the first few frames to check how the lighting, clothes and backdrop look. At the start there were too many dots, then we tried a white backdrop before moving on to the sofa. The best shots were when Ivy was sitting up, with the dark room blurred behind her.

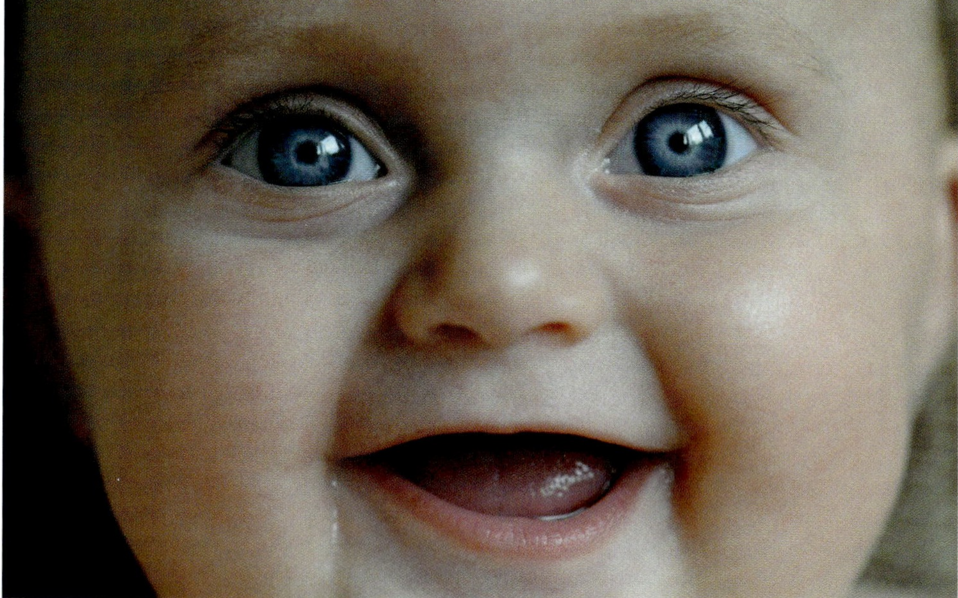

Include mum!

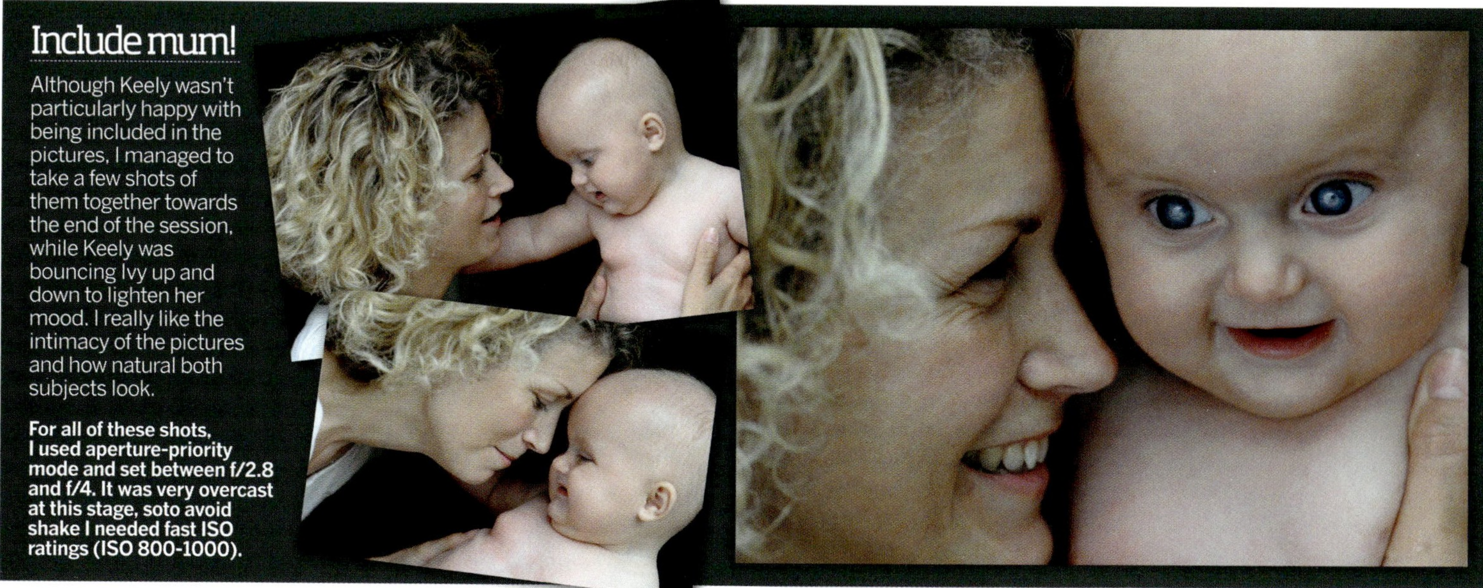

Although Keely wasn't particularly happy with being included in the pictures, I managed to take a few shots of them together towards the end of the session, while Keely was bouncing Ivy up and down to lighten her mood. I really like the intimacy of the pictures and how natural both subjects look.

For all of these shots, I used aperture-priority mode and set between f/2.8 and f/4. It was very overcast at this stage, soto avoid shake I needed fast ISO ratings (ISO 800-1000).

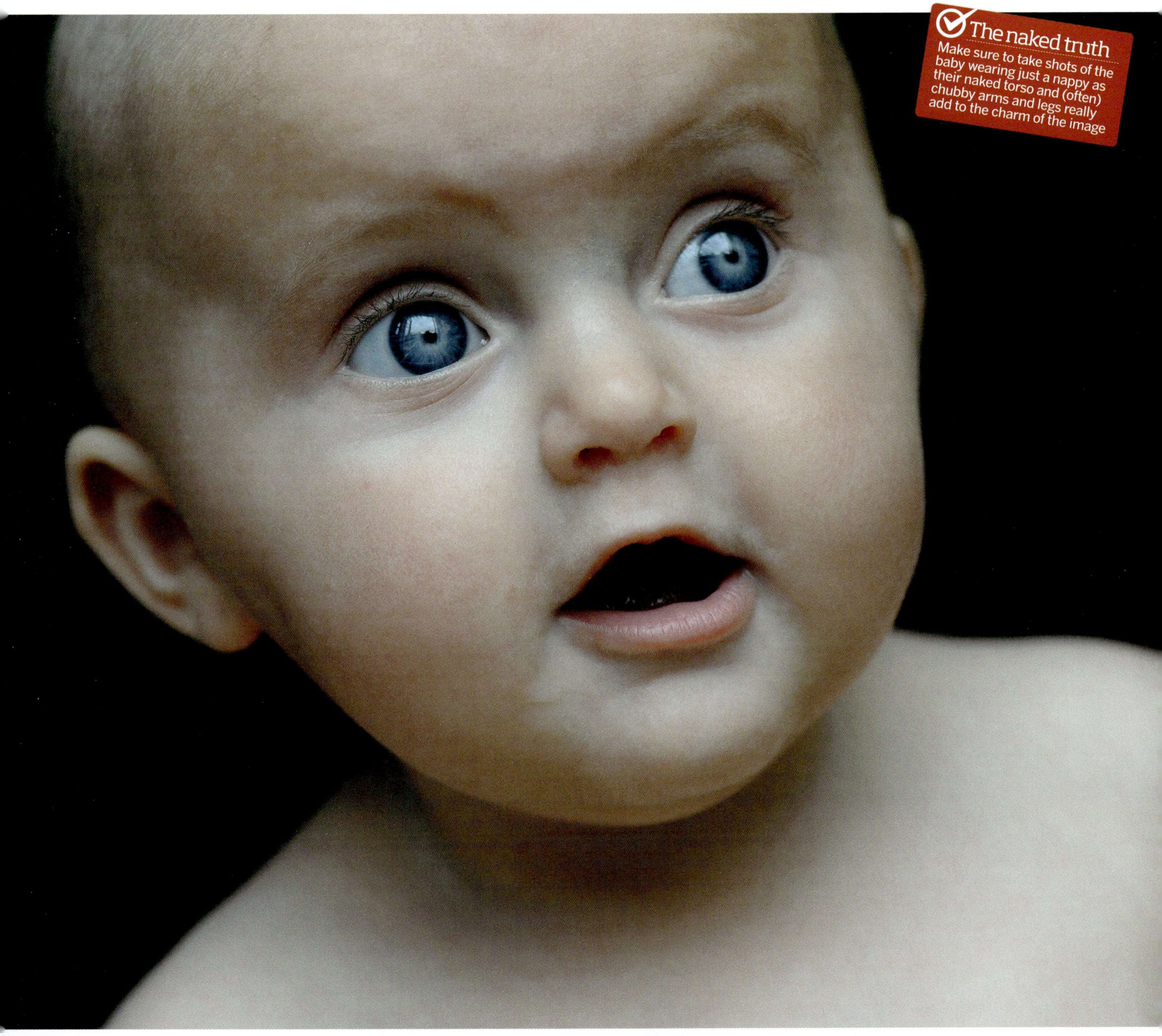

The naked truth

Make sure to take shots of the baby wearing just a nappy as their naked torso and (often) chubby arms and legs really add to the charm of the image

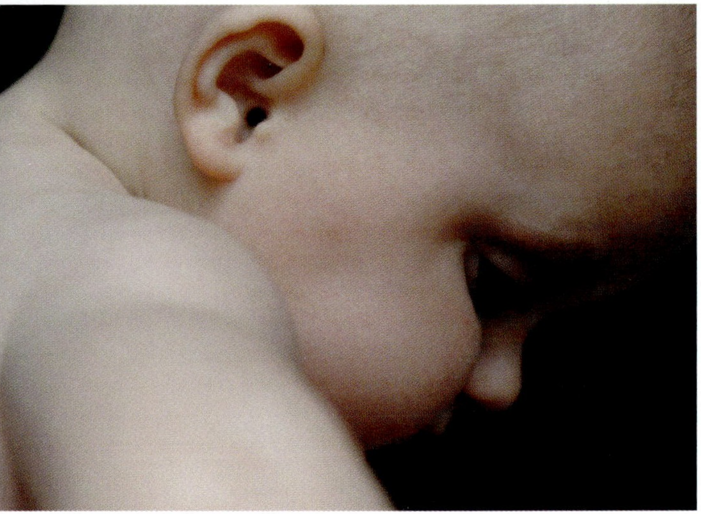

RIGHT: As well as lots of cute smiles, Ivy went through a whole repertoire of funny faces. Here are a couple of them. If you get a nice selection, think about how you can use them to create a set of images, such as a triptych or a quad.

LEFT: This unconventional portrait, captured right at the end of the session, is one of my personal favourites from the day's shoot.

All shots were taken using windowlight.

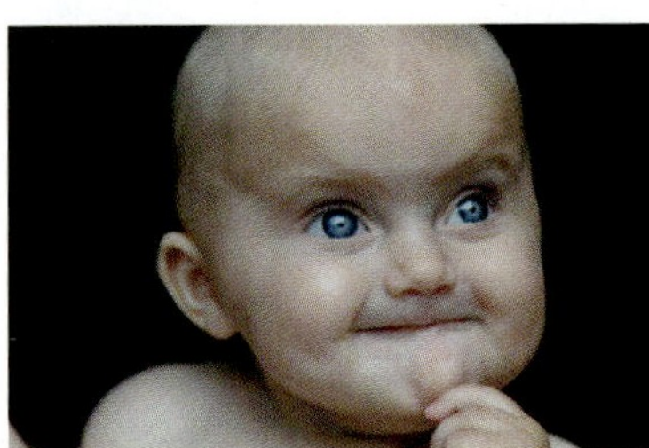

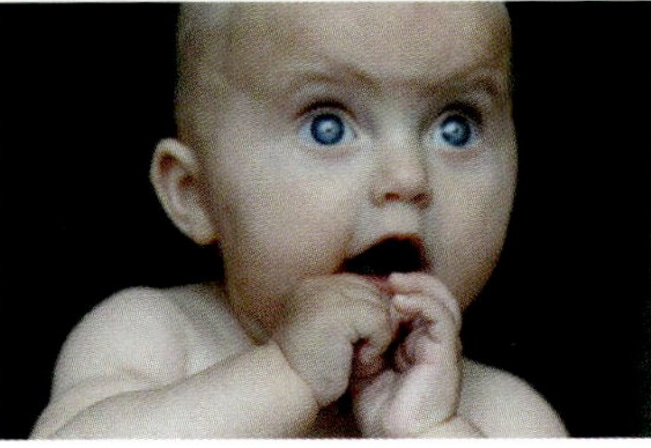

Baby shoot: Summary

- ✓ Be very patient. You'll rarely get great pictures straight away.
- ✓ Snapping fingers and squeezing toys works at getting a baby's attention at first, but its effect soon wears off.
- ✓ Include a parent in the shoot to keep the baby happy and smiling!
- ✓ Don't be afraid to change positions, viewpoints, clothes and backdrops. Keep experimenting and don't stop taking pictures!

Photographing: Toddlers

The early years of childhood, when a baby finally finds its feet, are exciting times for both parent and child, so be ready to capture these special moments with your DSLR

IF YOU HAD TO SUM UP TODDLERS IN ONE WORD, it would most likely be 'unpredictable'. From the moment that babies discover the mobility of their own two wrinkly little feet, they're up and about with a mind of their own, exploring a whole new world. It's something that they'll continue to do for a number of years, so you've plenty of time to get some great shots of them in their first years of discovery. That said, kids grow up extremely quickly at this stage of life, so you don't want to miss out on never-to-be-repeated moments. You need to be prepared for anything they're likely to do, so if they pull a face, fall over, break into fits of giggles, or anything else that kids of this age often do, you'll have your camera ready to capture every treasured moment.

It's really important that you spend a bit of time getting to know the kids and more importantly, give them a chance to get to know you too. If you're photographing your own kids or your family or friends' children, this isn't such an issue, but if it's a child you don't know, imagine how they'll feel if a complete stranger starts taking their photos. Spend ten to 15 minutes in the company of the parents chatting to the child and gaining their trust and you'll find that they're far more relaxed and responsive.

A telezoom like a 50-200mm is without doubt the best choice of lens, as you can shoot at a distance without your subject even knowing that they're being photographed, allowing them to behave completely naturally. If your images aren't completely candid, make sure that you spend a little time playing games and talking to your subject before you start taking pictures, so that they get used to you being around. They'll soon lose interest in you, allowing you to shoot more freely. Look to use a reflector if shooting indoors – you'll find many toddlers see the reflector as a large, fun, shiny toy, so if they're playing with it, aim for tight portraits while their faces are well lit! Remember not to carry around too much kit, it will get in the way and you'll invariably be switching lenses when the best photo opportunities happen!

You need to have a lot of patience when photographing young children. Don't try to manipulate them, if they decide that they've had enough of having their picture taken, then let them roam around for five minutes, and then try and coax them in to a few more shots. But always be ready. When the chance comes to grab a shot, your camera should be correctly set and you should be able to capture the moment before it's gone.

BRETT HARKNESS

BRETT HARKNESS

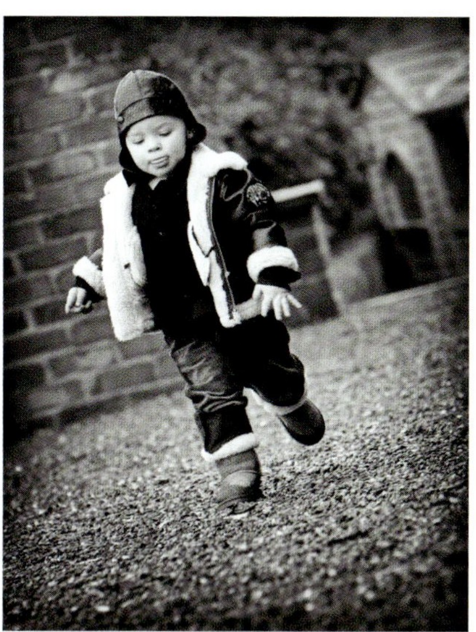

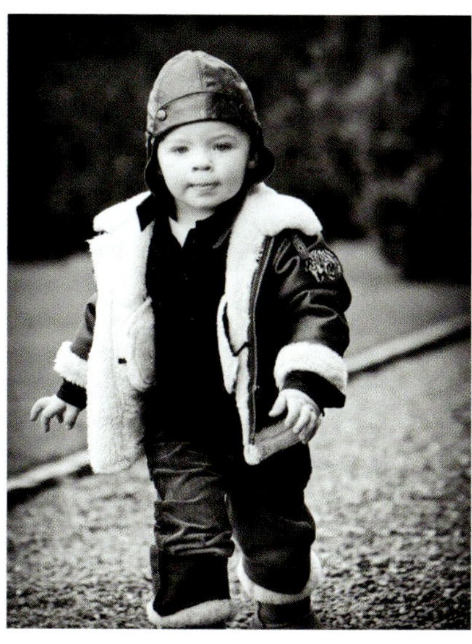

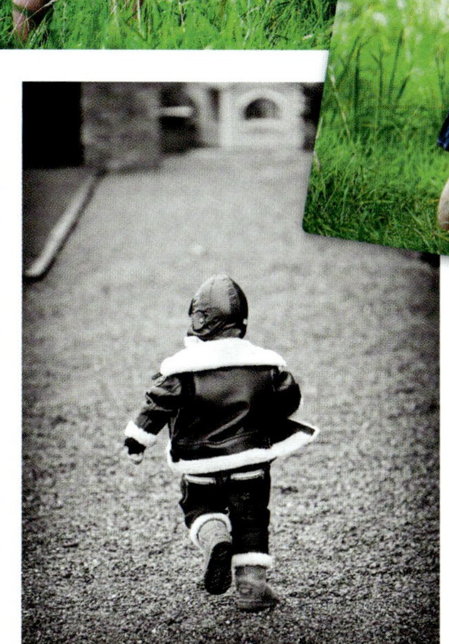

ABOVE: Allow toddlers freedom and it won't be long before they forget about the camera, allowing you to capture very natural candids.

LEFT: Always keep in mind that you can create sets of images that tell a story. Triptychs (a set of three images) are very popular and worth trying out.

Make the studio fun!

If you're using studioflash, it's not unusual for toddlers to get a little anxious, so find things that easily distract them. It's natural for parents to bring some toys with them, but you can have some of your own there too as young kids love to try out new toys. Contributor Bjorn Thomassen has another solution: "I've found that bubbles can really work at capturing their attention and they'll usually widen their eyes and smile when bubbles are near. I also have a Disney CD playing quietly in the background as these familiar songs help put them in a 'happy place'."

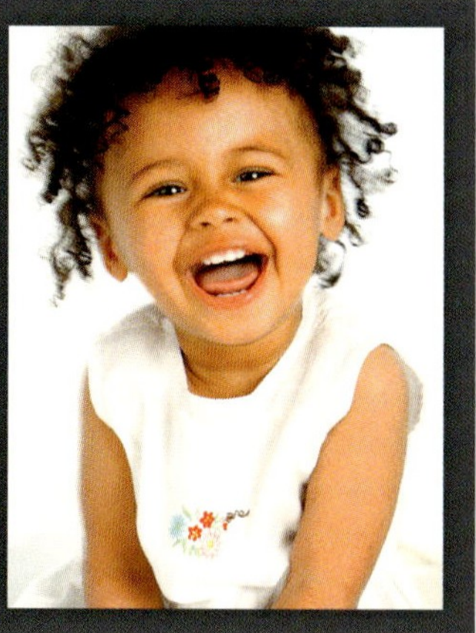

BJORN THOMASSEN

GIFT IDEAS

Framed photo-story

Producing framed prints that are made up of a multiple of images is a great way to provide a photo-story of the day. You'll find many photo outlets and art stores, as well as some large department stores, sell frames with mounts for holding several images. It makes an interesting and eye-catching variation to the normal method of mounting a single image within a frame.

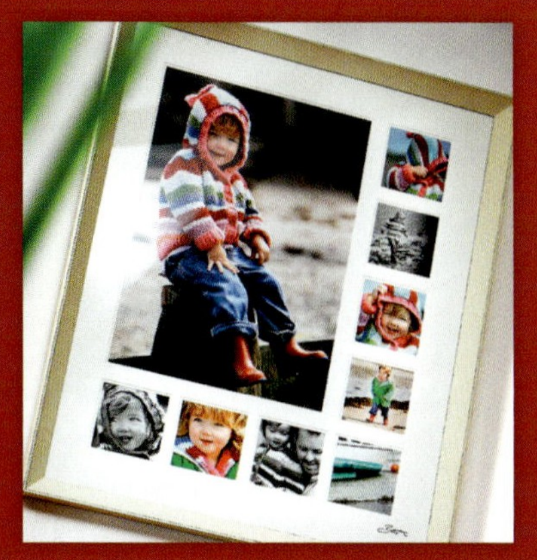

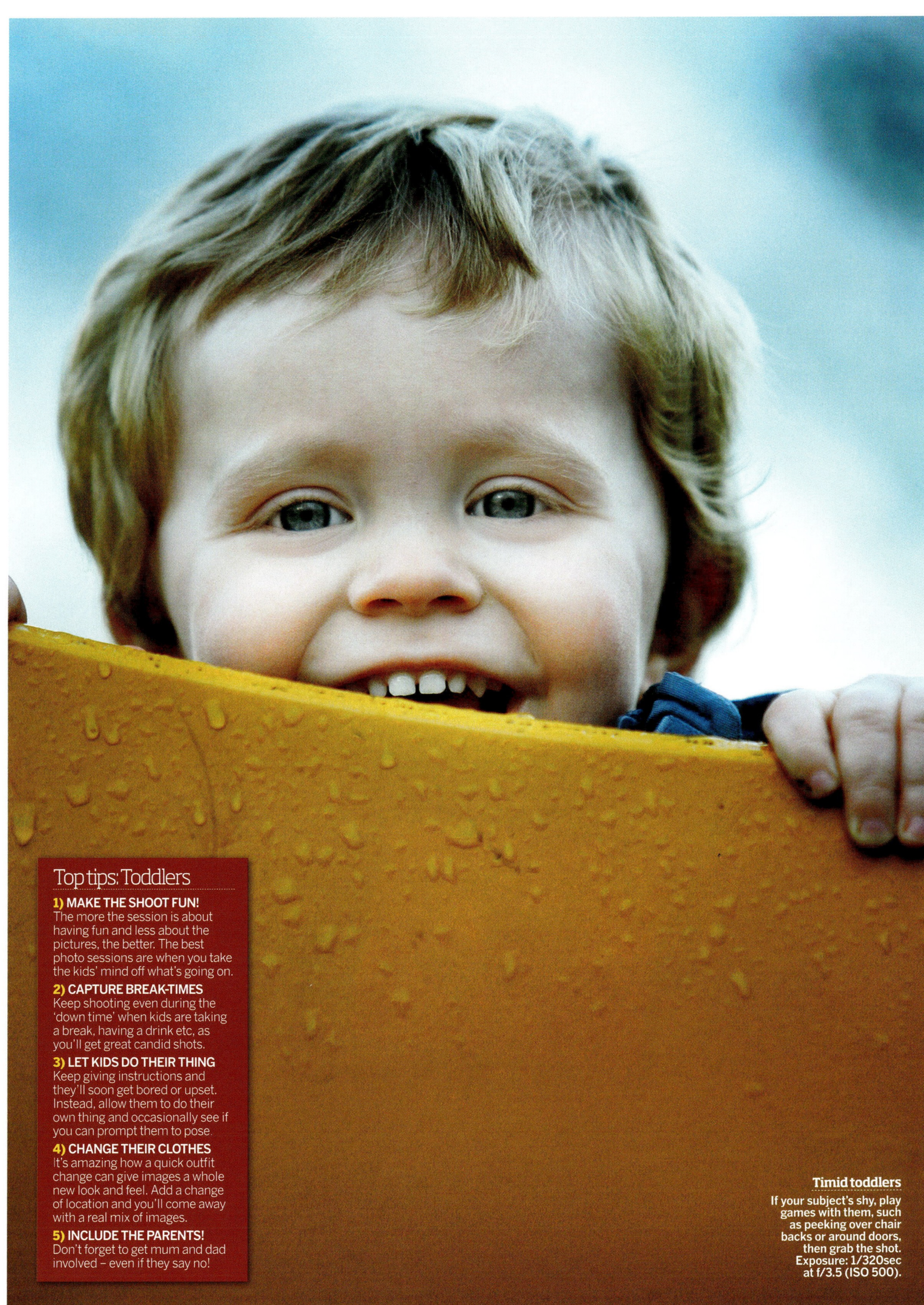

Top tips: Toddlers

1) MAKE THE SHOOT FUN!
The more the session is about having fun and less about the pictures, the better. The best photo sessions are when you take the kids' mind off what's going on.

2) CAPTURE BREAK-TIMES
Keep shooting even during the 'down time' when kids are taking a break, having a drink etc, as you'll get great candid shots.

3) LET KIDS DO THEIR THING
Keep giving instructions and they'll soon get bored or upset. Instead, allow them to do their own thing and occasionally see if you can prompt them to pose.

4) CHANGE THEIR CLOTHES
It's amazing how a quick outfit change can give images a whole new look and feel. Add a change of location and you'll come away with a real mix of images.

5) INCLUDE THE PARENTS!
Don't forget to get mum and dad involved – even if they say no!

Timid toddlers
If your subject's shy, play games with them, such as peeking over chair backs or around doors, then grab the shot. Exposure: 1/320sec at f/3.5 (ISO 500).

BRETT HARKNESS

Photographing youngsters

They can be precocious, naughty and downright cheeky. But at this age, kids are often at their most photogenic, too!

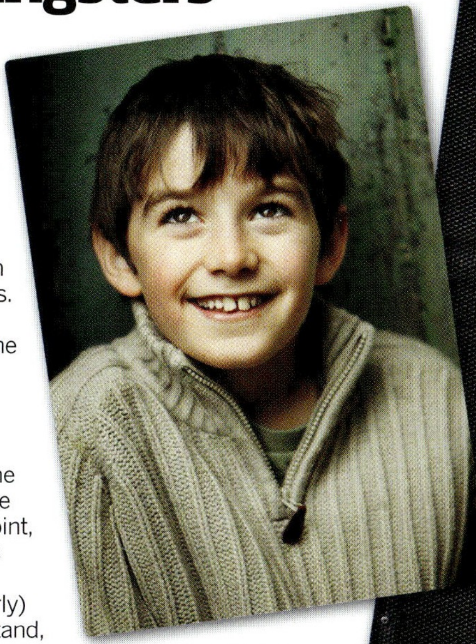

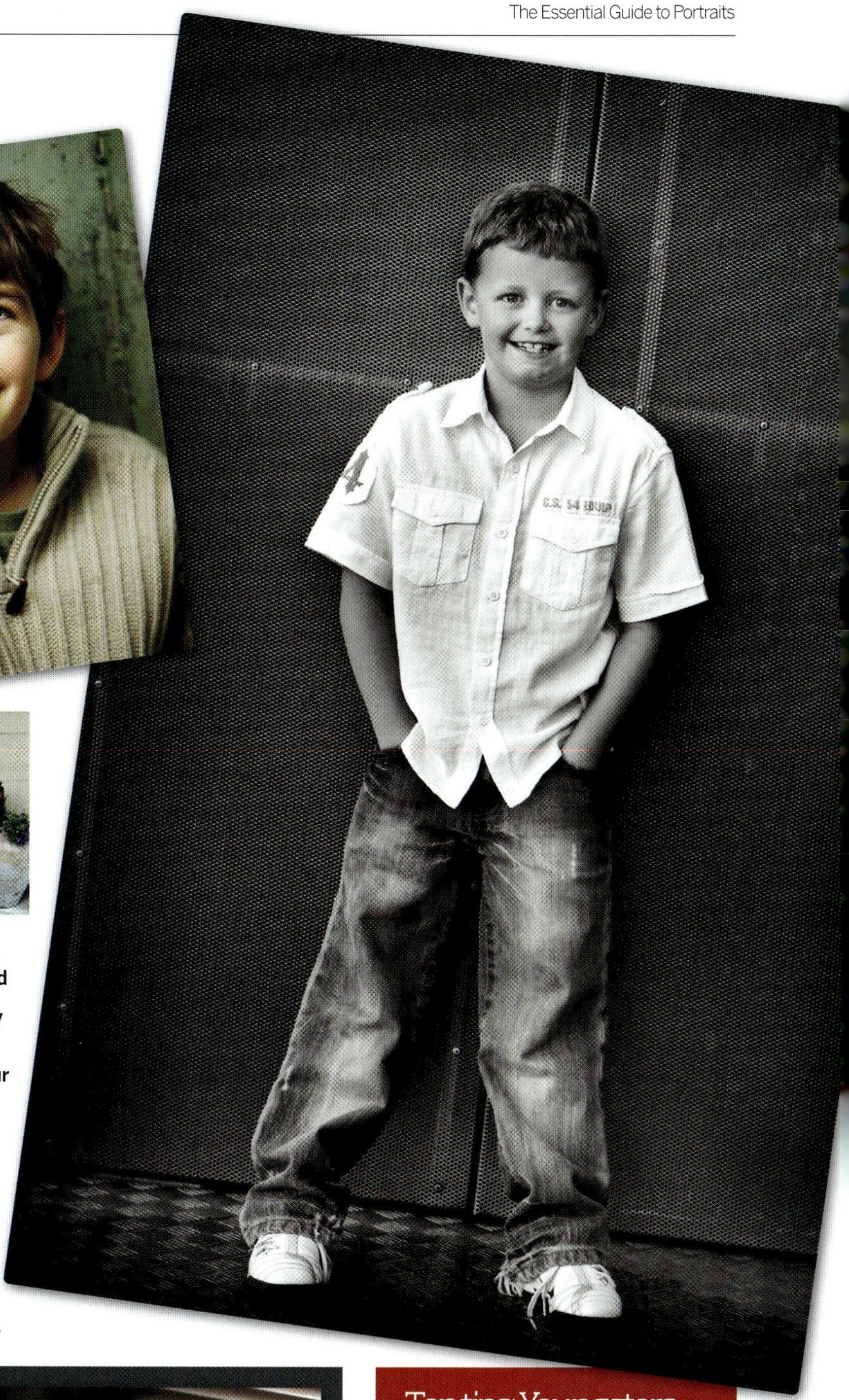

IT'S GENERALLY ACCEPTED BY MANY PARENTS that the most enjoyable years of childhood are when their kids are aged between five and ten. These are the years when children develop their personality and a small sense of independence, which can lead to some fantastic photographic opportunities.

In many respects, these younger years have the potential to deliver the best child portraits. Because the kids are able to run around and play on their own, you've got plenty of scope to capture some excellent candids. Fit a telezoom to your DSLR (50-200mm or 70-300mm are good options) and you can keep your distance so that your subject carries on oblivious to the fact that they're having their picture taken. After you've taken a few shots, a good idea is to find a good viewpoint, call their name and, with your DSLR set to continuous drive, rattle off a few frames when they look over.

A great benefit of kids at this age is that they're (fairly) responsive to instruction, so if you need them to sit, stand, turn around etc, they're more than likely to do so. This allows you to shoot a good mix of pictures, from candids to more staged shots, in a relatively short space of time. And, because your subject will start to get a little bored after a few minutes and begin messing about again, you can expect a few silly faces and poses towards the end of the session.

You should aim to be very relaxed about how you 'pose' your subjects. A good method to try is to ask them to stand/sit by a particular place and then take a couple of shots. If they look tense, get them to shake their arms and head to get them to relax and laugh as they do this, so they feel like they're having fun. Take a couple more shots, tell them they're doing great and get them to raise/drop their chin, tilt their head and so on until you get the shot you're after. Try a variety of viewpoints and crops to really mix up the shots. And at the end of the shoot, tell them to go crazy for a couple of minutes and capture them at their least sensible!

Kids' fashion has come on in leaps and bounds so as well as head and shoulder shots, be sure to take some full-length body shots to include the fashion of the time. If they have a unique sense of style, use it and show it! It might be they like to wear hats, bright colours or dress up as Superman. Your ultimate goal should be to take a good mix of images that together captures various aspects of your subject's nature.

As always, if you can, have an 'assistant', (i.e. a friend or family member) handy as they can hold a reflector or diffuser to give you added control of the lighting.

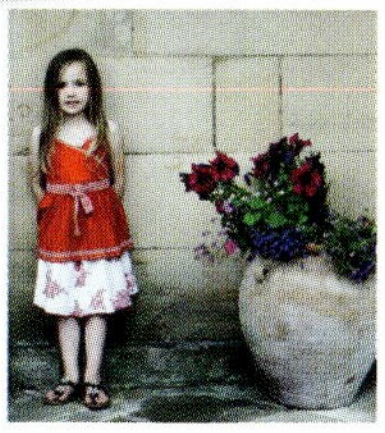

Doorways are ideal for getting a youngster to stand or sit in front of and pose candidly for pictures. Choose clothes that suit the colour of the door and if the youngster's wearing layers of tops, get them to lose the fleece/jumper after a bit and pose in their T-shirt. And we do keep saying it, but you can't beat the extra bit of light that a reflector can give.

GIFT IDEAS

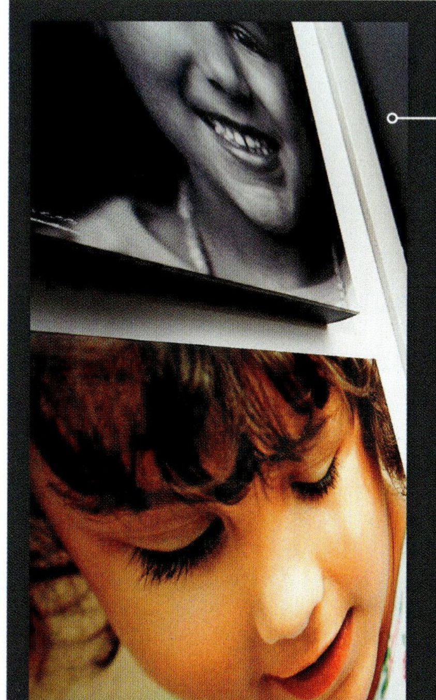

Canvas blocks

They've been around for a few years but there is little sign of their popularity diminishing. Having a child portrait on a canvas block is a distinctive way of displaying your best shots and a great photo gift idea.

Inkjet prints

If you fancy producing your own range of photo art, then check out the wide range of fine art papers available to use with inkjet printers. Some good names and types to try are Hahnemuhle Photo Rag Satin Glossy Fine Art and Permajet Royal Fine Art.

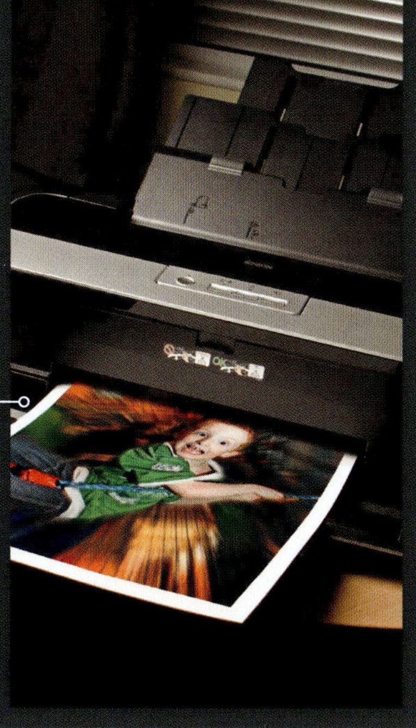

Top tips: Youngsters

1) WORK QUICKLY
A telezoom (e.g. 50-200mm) allows you to quickly change the composition from tight head shots to full body shots.

2) ENSURE THEY'RE AT EASE
Before you start taking pictures, explain to them what you plan to do and get them to relax, as it will be easy and over with quickly.

3) BE POSITIVE! Constantly tell them they're a natural at having their picture taken and that they look really good in the shots. Even at a young age, kids will benefit from this encouragement.

4) LET THEM PLAY! If they start messing around, let them play and capture some candids, before stopping them to get ready for the next shoot.

5) REWARD THEM! A bribe (toy, sweets etc) always works a treat and a reward for their efforts will help them say yes again!

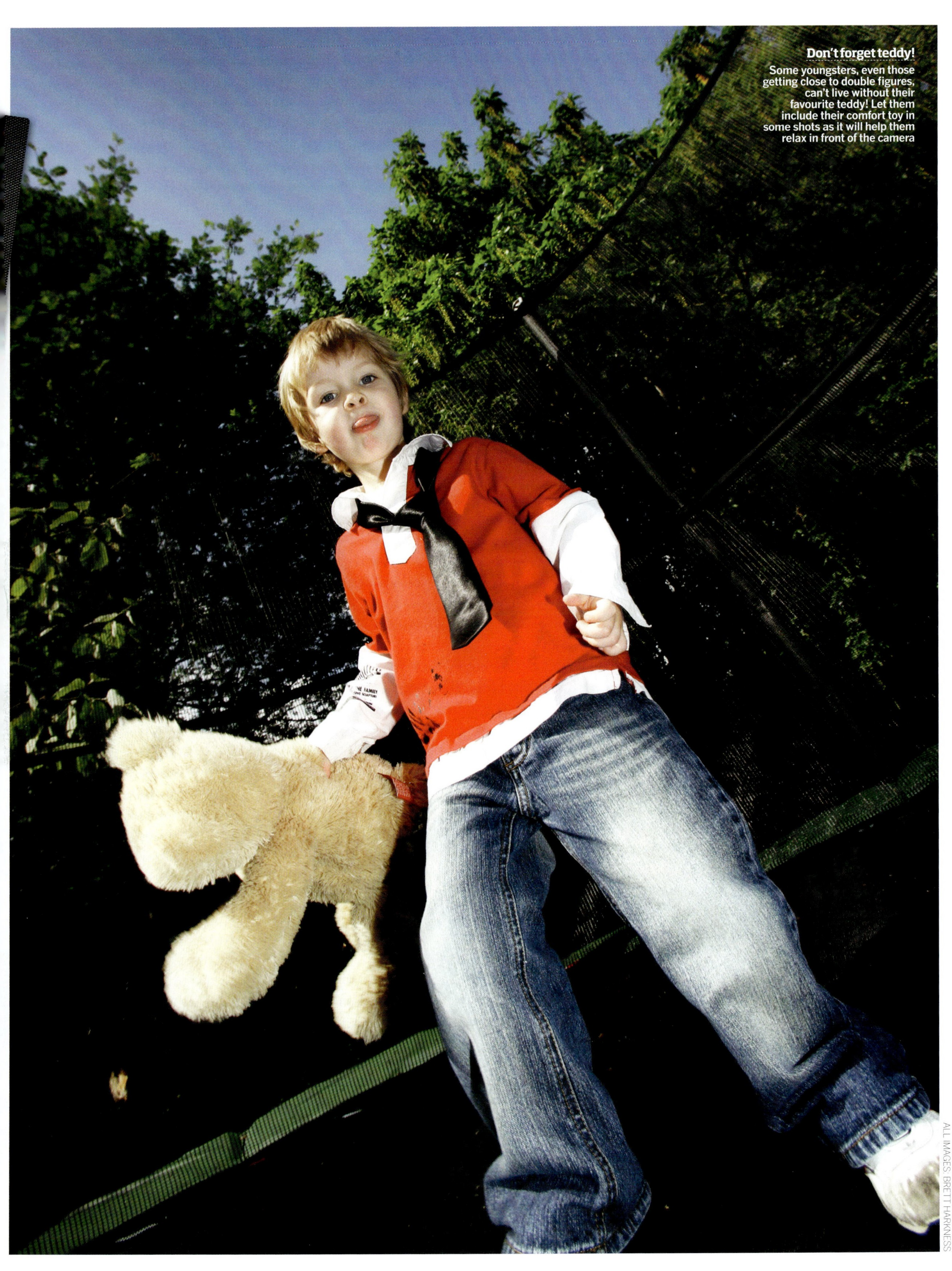

Don't forget teddy!

Some youngsters, even those getting close to double figures, can't live without their favourite teddy! Let them include their comfort toy in some shots as it will help them relax in front of the camera

ALL IMAGES: BRETT HARKNESS

Photographing youngsters: Brothers Caleb & Miles at the farm

Daniel Lezano heads to a local farm with *Digital SLR Photography* reader Sean Norris and his two sons, Caleb (9) and Miles (6), to see what was possible in an hour at an unusual location that most parents wouldn't even consider for a portrait shoot

I'VE DRIVEN BY A LOVELY FARM on my way to and from work every day and always fancied shooting portraits there. So a week before the arranged shoot, I visited the farm to meet with the owner Harry to get his permission, rather than turn up unannounced.

Sean is a subscriber to *Digital SLR Photography* and is also a good family friend, so I know his two boys well. After discussing the shoot with him, he had a good idea of what I wanted to do and on arriving at the location, we left the camera gear in the car, and had a walk around to seek out potential spots to take our pictures. Within a couple of minutes, we'd earmarked a stone wall, some wooden doors, large steel containers, metal horse-boxes and hay bales as all potential locations.

It was a sunny day, so as well as a reflector, I took along a large Lastolite Skylite diffuser in case I had to work in direct sunlight. We started off using the brick wall as a backdrop, with Caleb and Miles standing in front of it or leaning against it. I tried a number of viewpoints, with my favourite being to shoot the wall at an angle, so that it vanished off into the distance. I also shifted Miles and Caleb, so that sometimes they were in contact with the wall, then moved them forward to put some distance from the wall to help throw it out of focus. As well as shooting from the kids' eye-level, I also knelt and lay on the ground to get different perspectives. I took a shot with no reflector, followed by a couple with the white then silver sides of the reflector (and occasionally the gold side), to see how this affected the light falling on the subjects.

Next, we took pictures against some metal tanks, which were bathed in bright sunlight. We rested a large diffuser against the tanks and had each of the boys stand beneath it in turn. After taking a number of portraits of the boys from different angles, we headed to the wooden doors and used the diffuser panel in much the same way to soften the light. We also tried shots against some horse-boxes parked in deep shade. Setting a high ISO of 1000 and a wide aperture, we used the silver and gold sides of the reflector to bounce some light back on to the boys. The lads were in a playful mood, so I didn't try to stop them and shot away as they messed about, before heading for the hay bales for the final shots of the day.

I took a series of images of the two boys on their own and together. We went through a variety of relaxed poses, from sitting to lying down and standing on the bales and captured some great shots. Again, relatively low-light levels meant care was needed to avoid camera shake and to make sure that the reflector was bouncing enough light onto the boys' faces. Despite using a very similar set of skills and techniques at each of the different shoots while at the farm, each of the backdrops had a profoundly different effect on the result. And don't forget, each of the shots are open to black & white conversion as another creative possibility. In an hour, I'd taken around 200 shots and, having reviewed the LCD monitor, knew there were several that would please their parents.

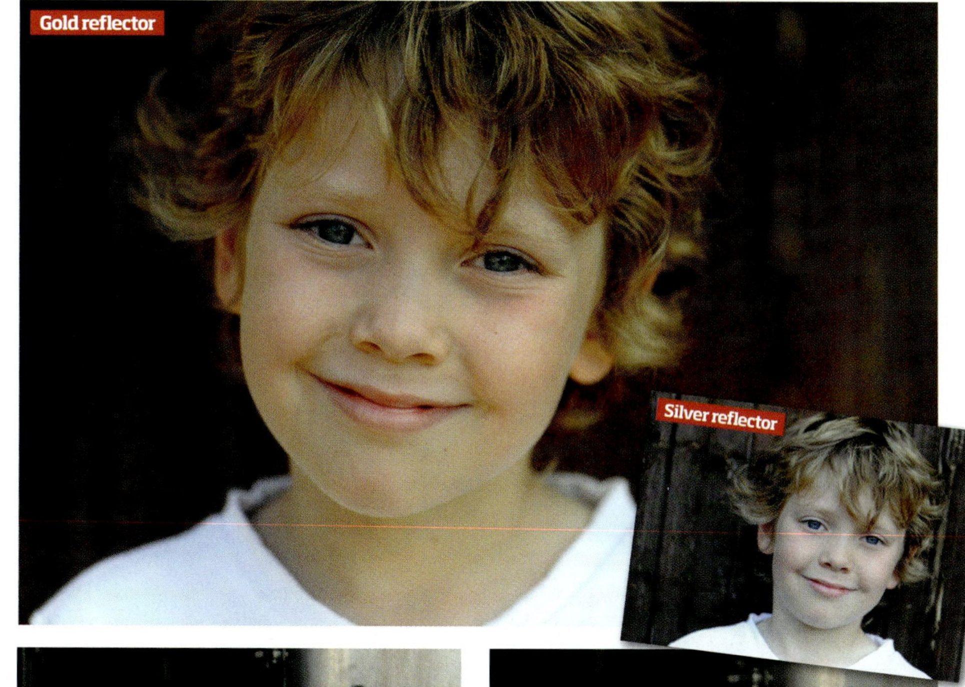
Gold reflector

Silver reflector

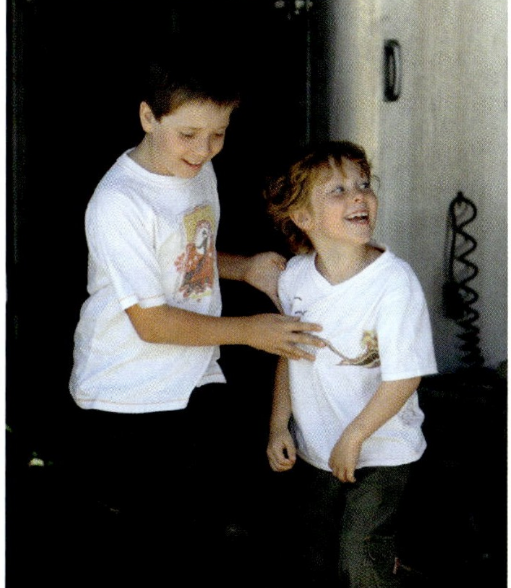

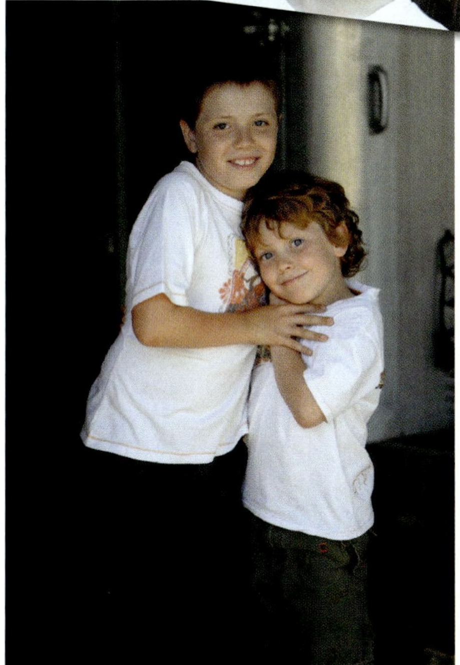

An hour is more than enough time to wander around a location and take pictures. Any longer and the youngsters will start getting bored. Remember to take a reflector (and if possible a diffuser) with you, but use the gold and silver sides carefully as their effect can be overpowering.

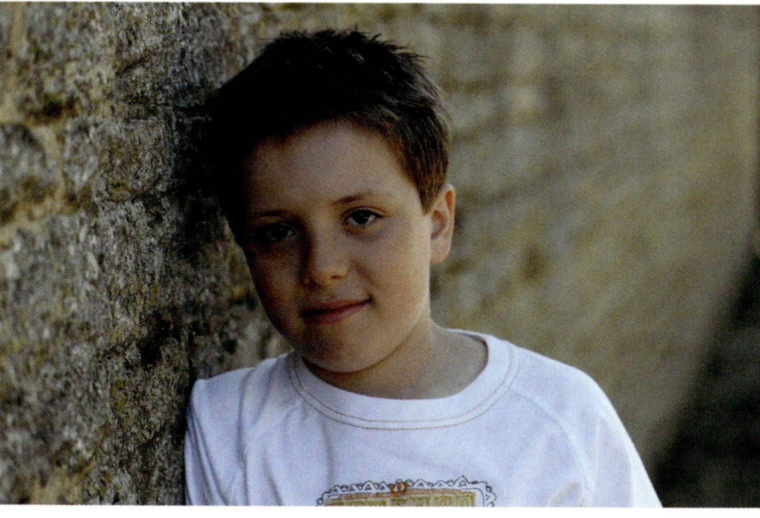

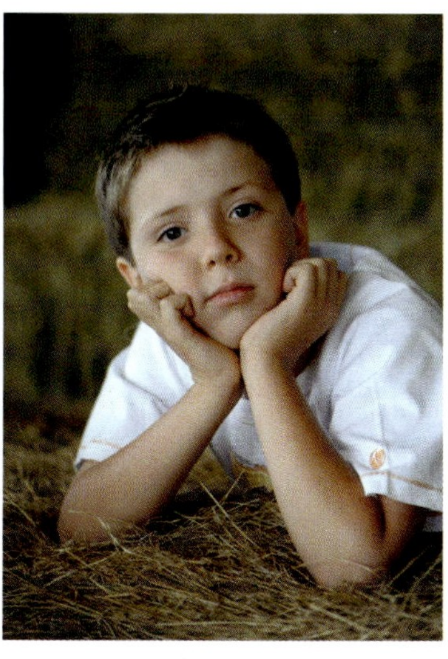

Youngsters: Summary

- ✔ Regular reassurance and praise will help nervous kids relax in front of the camera.
- ✔ **You'll find a single location has the potential for several types of backdrop.**
- ✔ Older brothers are less likely to want to 'cuddle' their younger siblings as sisters are.
- ✔ **If you plan to use a large diffuser, make sure you have an assistant to help!**
- ✔ Take care with gold and silver reflectors in bright sunlight as their effect can be overpowering.

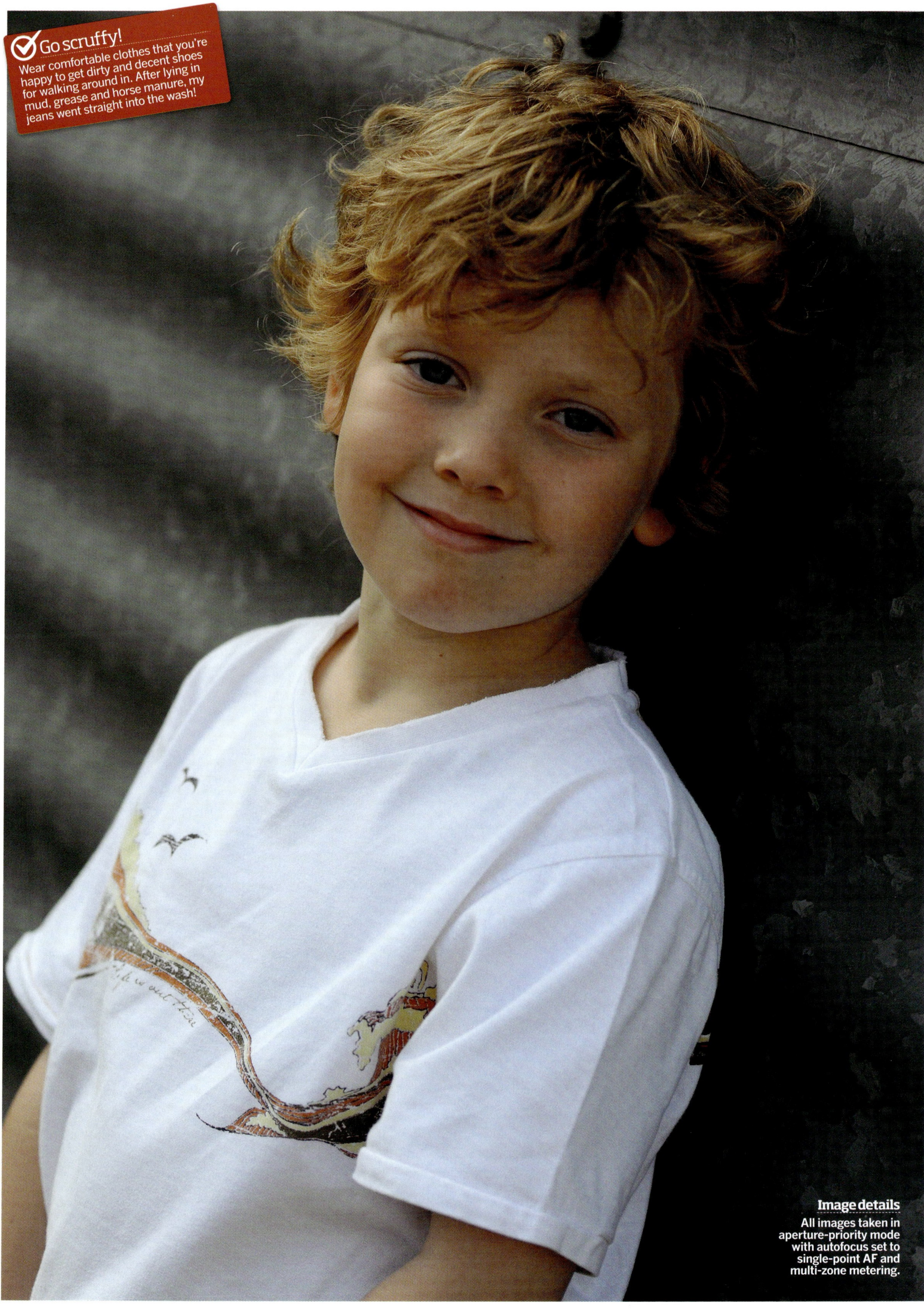

Go scruffy!
Wear comfortable clothes that you're happy to get dirty and decent shoes for walking around in. After lying in mud, grease and horse manure, my jeans went straight into the wash!

Image details
All images taken in aperture-priority mode with autofocus set to single-point AF and multi-zone metering.

It's time for the teenagers!

Be careful not to call them kids – teenagers need to be treated like adults if you want to get the very best from them!

AS EVERY PARENT WILL testify, kids rapidly develop far more independence when they reach secondary school and each year as a teenager sees them develop both mentally and physically at a startling rate.

As a photographer, what this generally means is that your subjects will need to be treated more like adults than as children if you're going to have any chance of getting them to perform in front of the camera. So while you may want to offer some advice on what they should wear, for instance, don't be negative if they turn up wearing the complete opposite of what you've asked them to. Work with them and when you've taken a good selection of shots, ask them to change outfits and see if they'll go with what you want them to wear.

You'll generally find that they have a short attention span and act as if they have better things to do than have their picture taken. But if you're friendly, interested in what they have to say and listen attentively to ideas on how they want to be shot, you'll find it goes a long way to keeping them on your side. If you can get your subjects to enjoy what they're doing, you'll find them literally shift from pose to pose after every shot!

Kids are at their most self-conscious when they're in their teens and while some are pure exhibitionists, the majority are worried about how they'll look in pictures, especially if their hormones are playing havoc with their skin. Your aim should generally be to capture them in flattering light, make them look like 'grown-ups' rather than kids and try to get them to enjoy the experience while being themselves in front of the camera.

Teenagers can be real fun to work with, so try and capture this in your images. Have your assistant or a friend try and make them laugh and be ready to capture the moment. Many teenagers have strong interests so try and incorporate this into the image where possible, either through what they wear or what you include with them in the frame, e.g. a skateboard, car etc.

BRETT HARKNESS

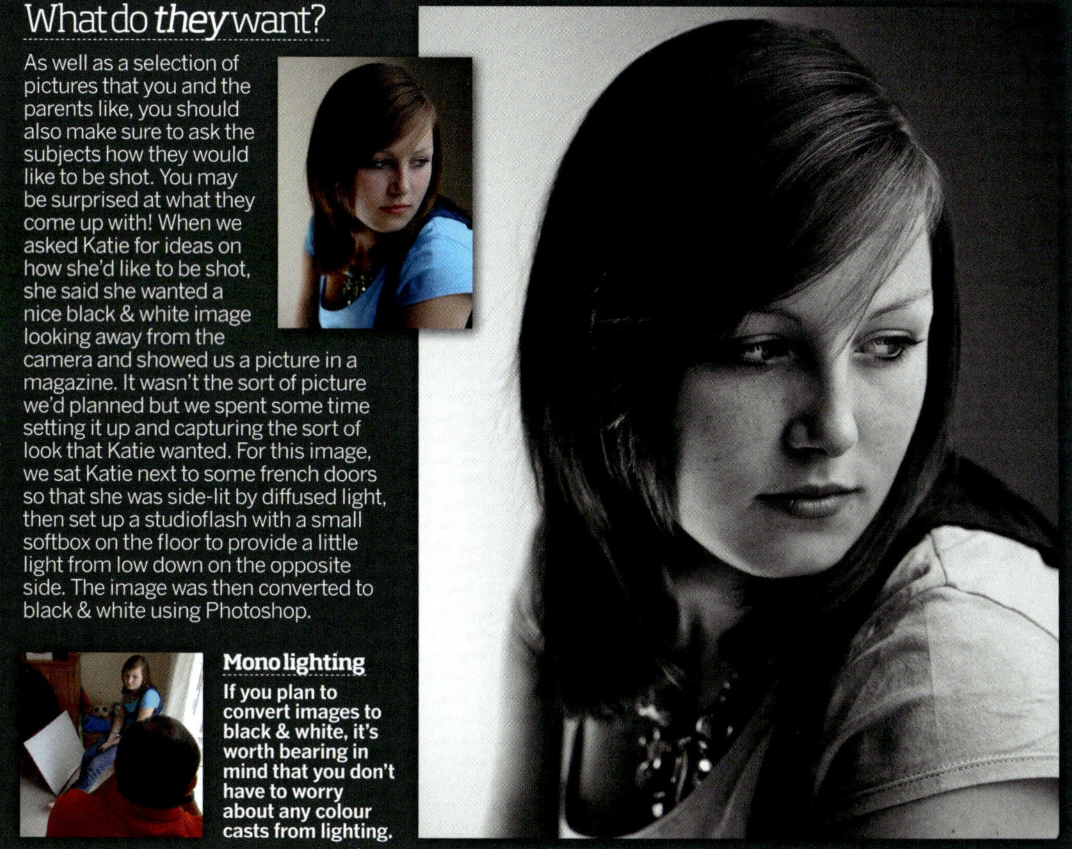

What do *they* want?

As well as a selection of pictures that you and the parents like, you should also make sure to ask the subjects how they would like to be shot. You may be surprised at what they come up with! When we asked Katie for ideas on how she'd like to be shot, she said she wanted a nice black & white image looking away from the camera and showed us a picture in a magazine. It wasn't the sort of picture we'd planned but we spent some time setting it up and capturing the sort of look that Katie wanted. For this image, we sat Katie next to some french doors so that she was side-lit by diffused light, then set up a studioflash with a small softbox on the floor to provide a little light from low down on the opposite side. The image was then converted to black & white using Photoshop.

Mono lighting

If you plan to convert images to black & white, it's worth bearing in mind that you don't have to worry about any colour casts from lighting.

Top tips: Teenagers

1) Make sure they're happy, relaxed and having fun. You'll end up with far better images than if they're bored and uninterested.

2) Ask them if they've any favourite photos of some of their heroes and see if you can shoot them in a similar style.

3) Give them a rough idea of what you'd like them to wear (e.g. plain T-shirt, jeans, etc) but make sure they're happy with your choice.

4) Try not to sound too formal when talking to them, but be careful not to use words like 'cool' if you think it could backfire!

5) When you've got a good shot, show it to them on the LCD screen. If they like what they see, you'll give them the needed interest to continue.

6) Don't shoot with their parents or friends watching as they'll probably feel intimidated, so ask those who aren't being included to leave the room!

7) Make sure to give them a small gift (e.g. £10 iTunes voucher) as a thank you and send them some prints of the best shots. It's a small price to pay for their time and will also mean they're more likely to say yes next time.

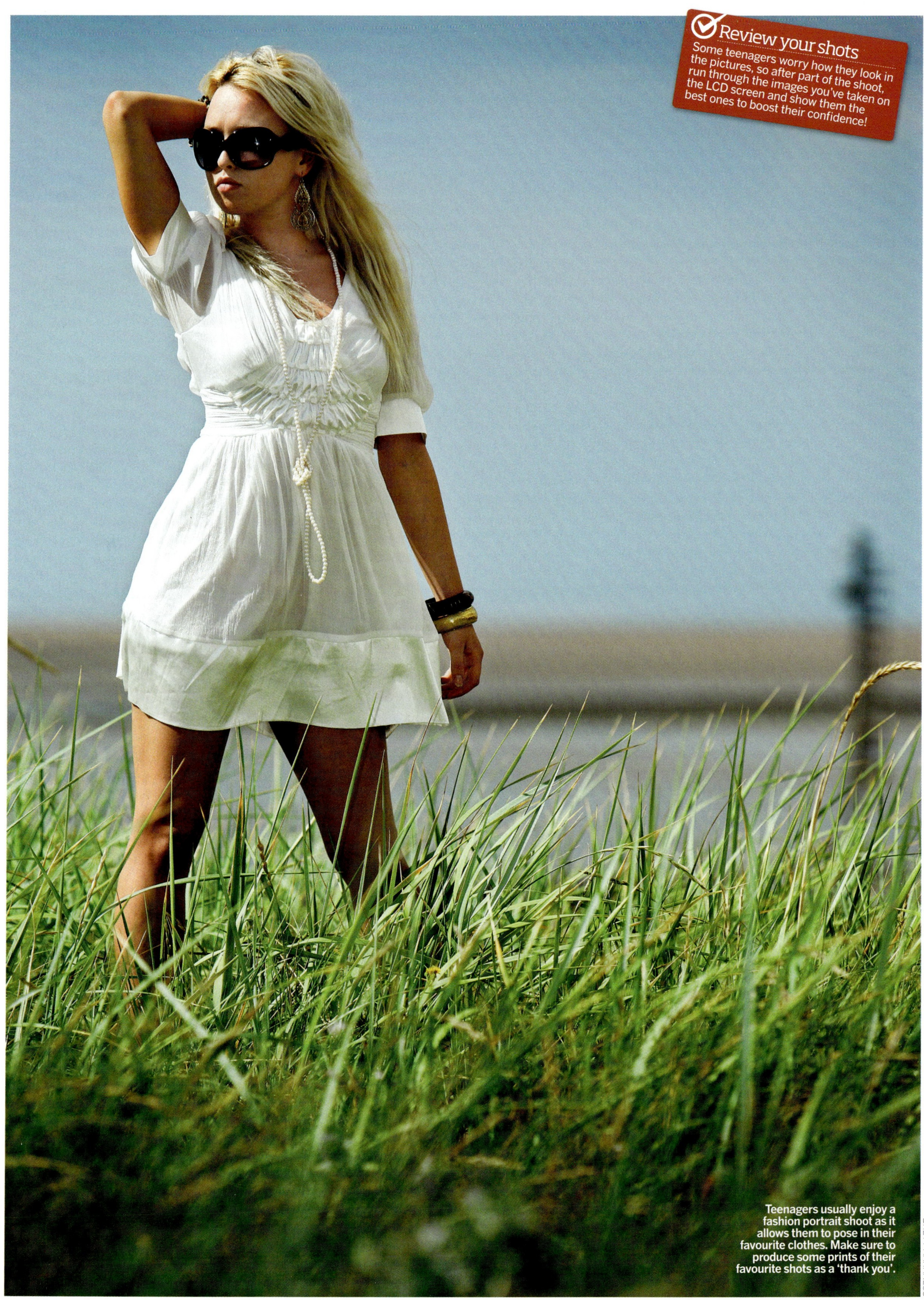

Teenagers usually enjoy a fashion portrait shoot as it allows them to pose in their favourite clothes. Make sure to produce some prints of their favourite shots as a 'thank you'.

BRETT HARKNESS

A fun lifestyle shoot with teenage sisters

Daniel Lezano sets out with two sisters for an outdoor photo session. As he discovers, if they're having plenty of fun, it's not difficult to capture lots of great shots!

HAYLEY (16) AND KATIE (14) ARE PART OF my extended family and I've known them for around ten years. They're no strangers to having their pictures taken by me, often for various features in the *Digital SLR Photography* magazine, but this was the first time they'd been asked to pose 'as themselves', rather than to show specific techniques or as part of a camera test. A few days before the session, I had asked them how they wanted to be shot and they didn't really have any clear ideas, so I asked them to have a look through various fashion titles and back issues of *Digital SLR Photography* to see if any type of portraits took their fancy. They came back with plenty of ideas, ranging from nice black & white portraits to a 'fashion lifestyle portrait' similar to the type taken by contributors Brett Harkness and Bjorn Thomassen. As for their parents, the request was simple – produce a nice deries of images of the two of them together.

I had already scouted out a location full of character in the centre of their home town, Stamford in Lincolnshire and on the day, the overcast conditions were ideal. A set of large blue doors provided the ideal backdrop to take some 'fashion portraits' of Hayley. First though, we asked the two sisters to mess around a bit and make the whole photo experience more fun. I snapped away while they pulled faces, pushed each other about and gave each other piggybacks and after a couple of minutes, they realised the shoot had the potential to be lots of fun, so they were lively and responsive to my instructions. I shot the two of them leaning against each other, hugging and so on and the results were excellent, as the two of them looked like they were really enjoying themselves!

Next, it was time to shoot Hayley on her own. Running through a few poses and shooting from various angles resulted in several nice shots within minutes. The silver side of the reflector was ideal for bouncing light on to Hayley and filling in unwanted shadows. I asked Katie to hold the reflector to keep her involved and interested. As well as full-body poses, we took some head and shoulders shots and tight crops of her face. During the shoot, I tried to let things flow with minimal interruptions, but kept an eye out for small details, asking Hayley to move stray hairs away from her eyes and also removing her pink necklace. We also added a bit of fun to proceedings by having Katie use the reflector as a makeshift fan, blowing Hayley's hair in all directions while I fired away. The results were very hit and miss as her hair was flying everywhere, but it kept their enthusiasm high, which was important as I still had more shots to take. With both very relaxed, I took some more of the two of them together by a blue door, this time with an assistant holding the reflector. In the space of only 20 minutes, we had captured a real mix of pictures and having reviewed them on the LCD screen, it was pretty clear that there were several images from the shoot that could be printed and framed.

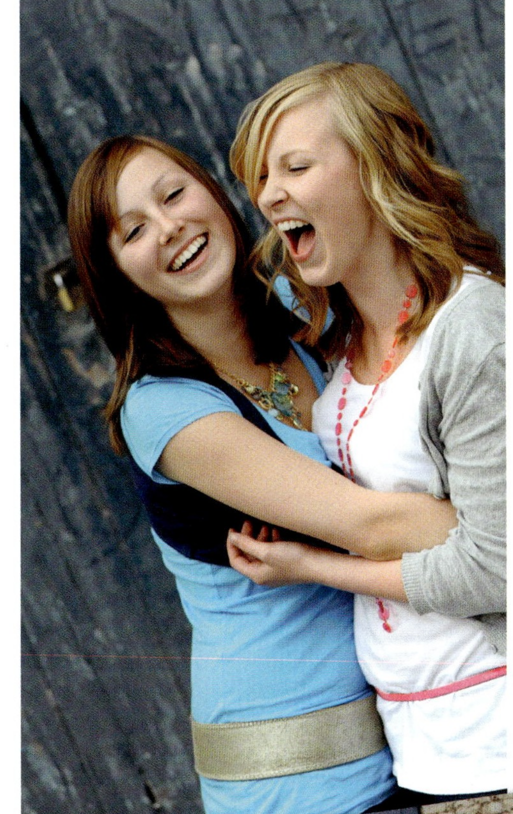

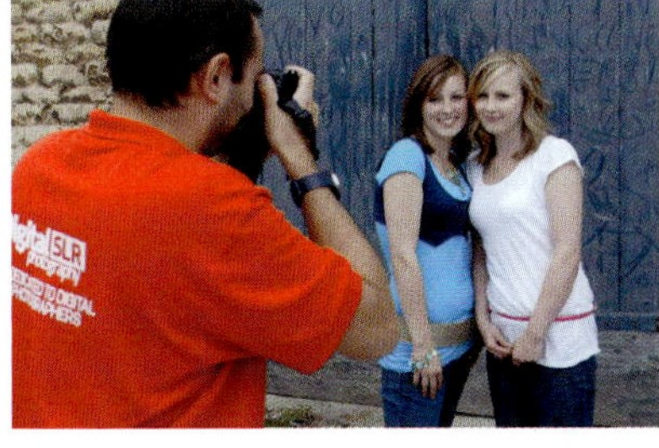

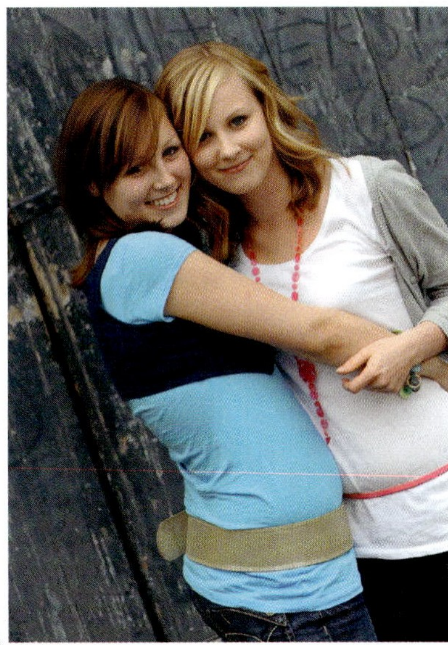

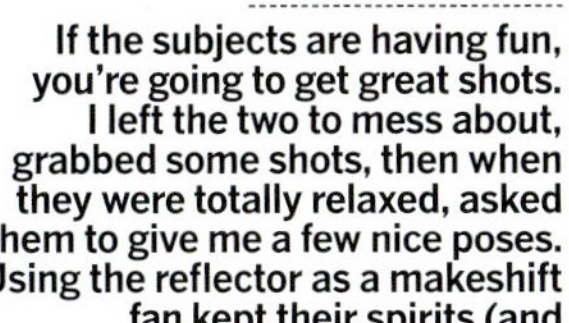

Have some fun!

If the subjects are having fun, you're going to get great shots. I left the two to mess about, grabbed some shots, then when they were totally relaxed, asked them to give me a few nice poses. Using the reflector as a makeshift fan kept their spirits (and Hayley's hair) flying high, too!

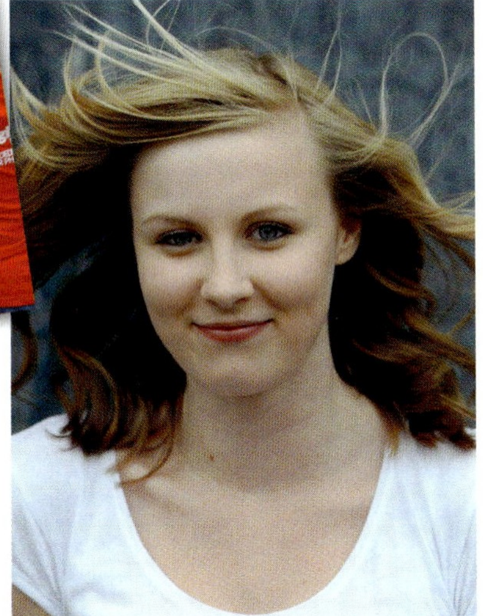

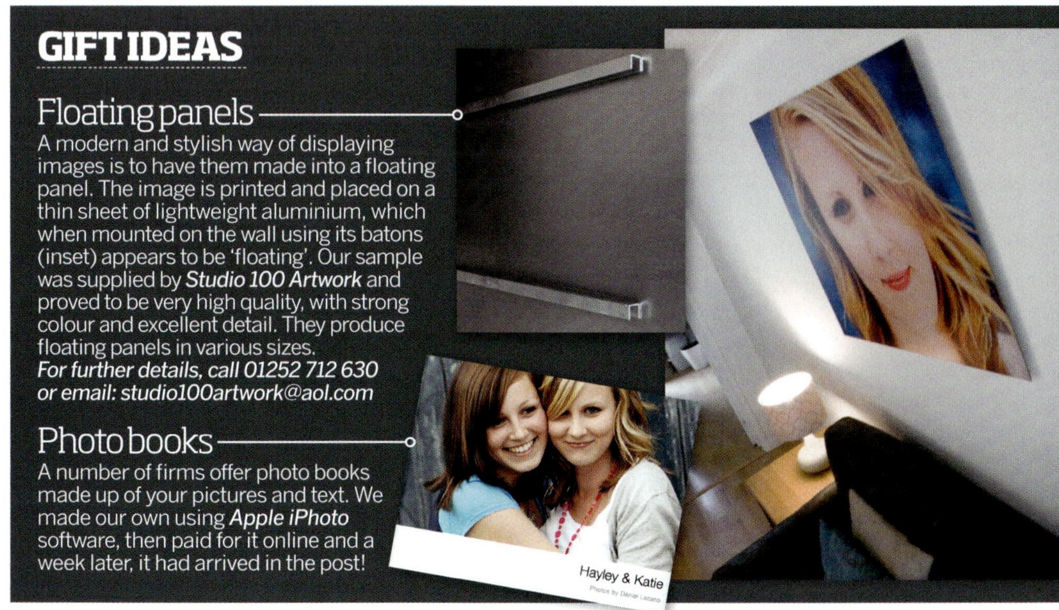

GIFT IDEAS

Floating panels

A modern and stylish way of displaying images is to have them made into a floating panel. The image is printed and placed on a thin sheet of lightweight aluminium, which when mounted on the wall using its batons (inset) appears to be 'floating'. Our sample was supplied by ***Studio 100 Artwork*** and proved to be very high quality, with strong colour and excellent detail. They produce floating panels in various sizes.
For further details, call 01252 712 630 or email: studio100artwork@aol.com

Photo books

A number of firms offer photo books made up of your pictures and text. We made our own using ***Apple iPhoto*** software, then paid for it online and a week later, it had arrived in the post!

Teen shoot: Summary

- ✔ Formal settings are nowhere near as much fun as the outdoor for a lifestyle shoot. The latter is also far better for revealing more of the subject's personality.
- ✔ **Having two (or more) teenagers together means they have more fun during the session and this makes for much better pictures. And when each is being shot on their own, the other can be kept involved by assisting with holding the reflector.**
- ✔ Don't believe the stereotype of teenagers as grungy, sulky and introverted. Most are intelligent, streetwise and fun to photograph.
- ✔ **Before the day of the shoot, be sure to mention make-up if you're photographing girls. Make sure they only apply a small amount to cover blemishes and don't go over the top!**

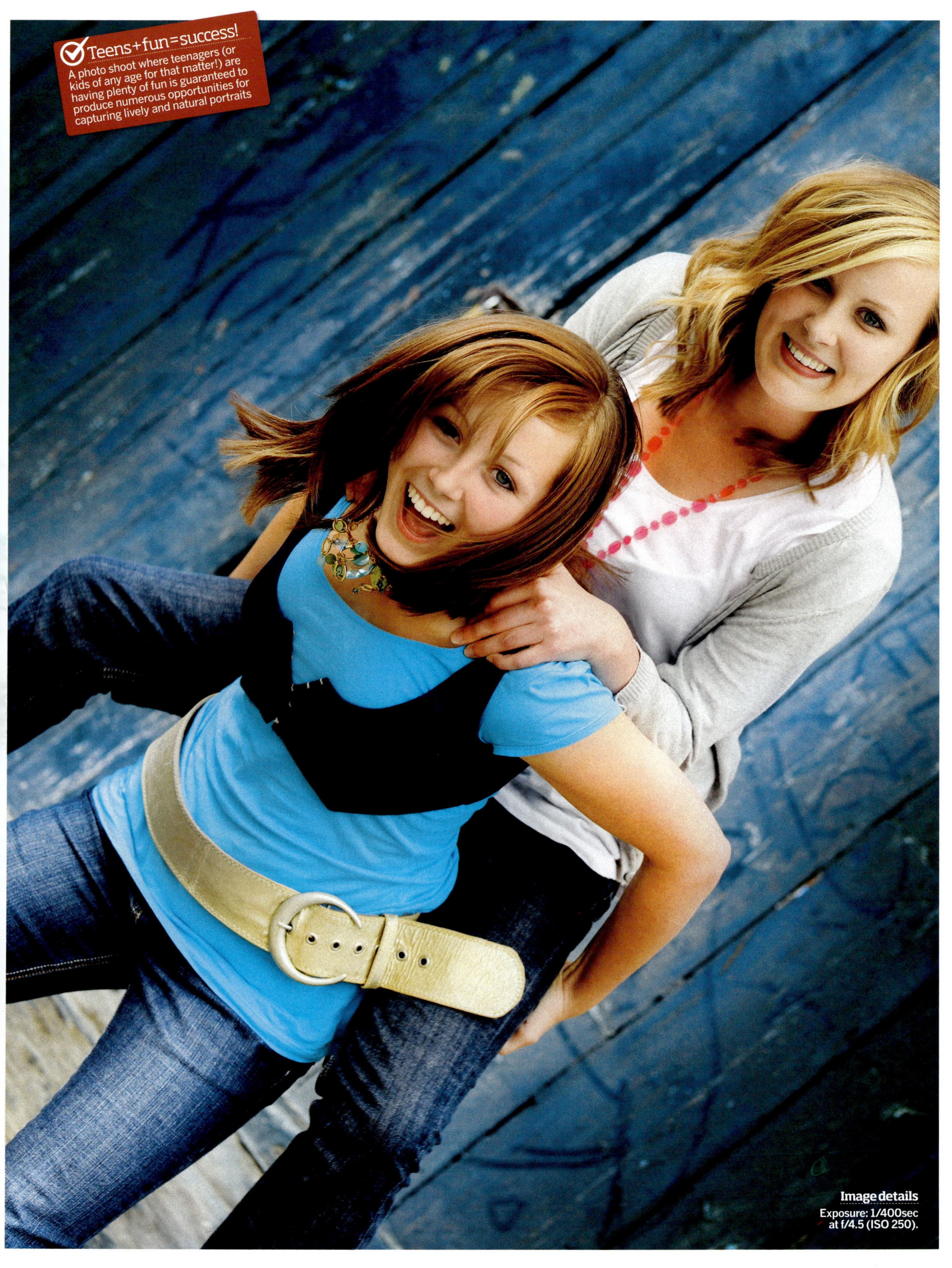
Teens+fun=success!
A photo shoot where teenagers (or kids of any age for that matter!) are having plenty of fun is guaranteed to produce numerous opportunities for capturing lively and natural portraits
Image details
Exposure: 1/400sec at f/4.5 (ISO 250).

Shoot the perfect family album

Daniel Lezano heads out with *Digital SLR Photography* reader Shaun Smith to see how well he can capture candid portraits of his wife Tracy, their 12-year-old son Connor and their family four-legged friend, Benson, in a one-hour camera challenge

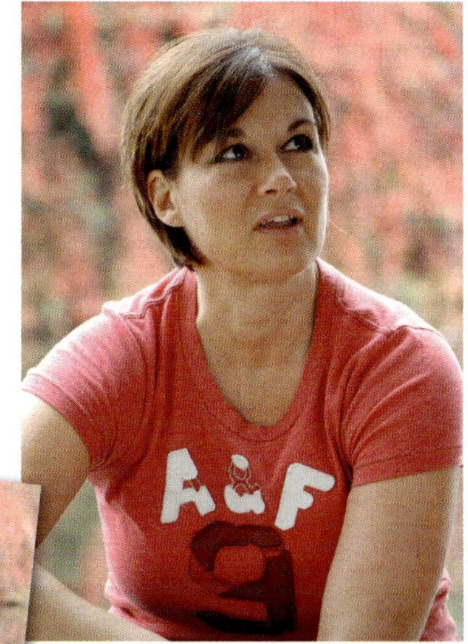

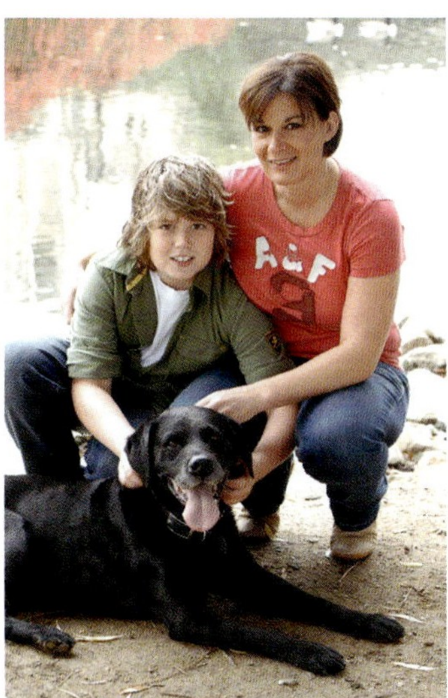

THE OLD ADAGE 'never work with kids or animals' is one you'll often hear muttered by photographers who are struggling to control excited and distracted subjects, be they on two legs or four. So the task that awaited *Digital SLR Photography* reader Shaun Smith was a tough one, not only had he to direct and shoot his better half, their hyperactive son and the family pooch, Benson, he also only had one hour to capture some great pictures. No pressure then!

The photo challenge took place in the scenic surrounding of the Meadows in the Lincolnshire market town of Stamford. This beautiful park, surrounded by the river Welland and its meandering streams, makes for an idyllic setting to capture some wonderful candid outdoor portraits. The aim is to use nothing but natural light, and apart from a Lastolite Tri-Grip silver/white reflector, we've no lighting aids or accessories of any type to work with.

I meet up with Shaun and his family and we head to a favourite photo haunt of mine, where a large willow tree sits close to the river's edge with the town bridge as a backdrop. We're extremely lucky with the weather as it's a grey overcast day, meaning that the light is bright but flat and diffused; perfect conditions for outdoor portraits. I run through the brief with everyone and Shaun removes the Nikon D80 from his gadget bag in preparation to begin.

"I've set the camera to aperture-priority mode, but what would you say are the best settings to use?" enquires Shaun. I suggest he sets f/5.6 as it will deliver images with good sharpness but in conjunction with a shallow depth-of-field so to create blur in the background, especially if he uses the zoom at the telephoto end. Looking at the conditions, it wasn't overly bright so I advise him to set ISO 400 rather than anything slower to help keep the shutter speed reasonably high – even with the telezoom offering Vibration Reduction, it's worth taking a few precautions as I didn't want him ruining his images with shake. We check the LCD panel and see that we're working with an exposure of 1/250sec at f/5.6, which is ideal.

So it's time to start the clock and begin shooting. The key to successful portraiture is as much the relationship between the photographer and the subject as it is their technical proficiency. Shaun has the advantage of knowing his subjects, so there's no problem with trust, but this familiarity can also present its own problems, especially when it comes to getting subjects to pose as the novelty wears off and they get bored of the camera.

The hour starts well with Shaun taking some simple shots of Tracy and Connor side by side. It's OK, a little posed, but it builds a little rapport between the three of them and also helps Tracy, who's not that keen on being photographed, to feel more at ease. It is quite dark under the shade of the willow tree, so we ask Connor's friend Max to help out by holding the reflector to bounce some light back on to the subject. It's a lighting technique that is used throughout the hour, with the silver side bouncing enough light to lift skin tones and fill in any shadows.

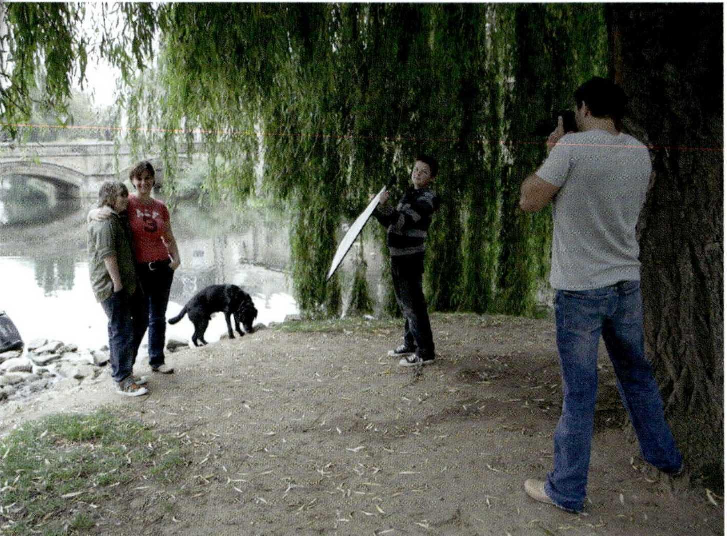

The initial part of the challenge took place by the river's edge beneath a large willow tree. The silver side of a Lastolite reflector helped throw extra light into the scene. Careful composition excludes the bin in the water.

The scene behind them is thrown out of focus by the choice of aperture, with the lovely red Virginia creeper, bridge and water adding an interesting but not distracting backdrop. After a couple of minutes shooting, Shaun asks them to kneel down so that Benson – their dog – can be included in the frame. Placing the subjects carefully by the water's edge ensures that a black wheelie bin resting in the water is obscured from view. We spend a few minutes taking

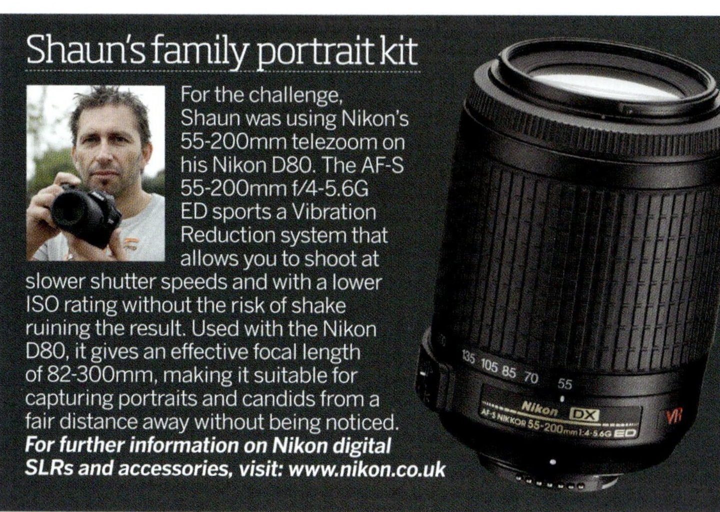

Shaun's family portrait kit

For the challenge, Shaun was using Nikon's 55-200mm telezoom on his Nikon D80. The AF-S 55-200mm f/4-5.6G ED sports a Vibration Reduction system that allows you to shoot at slower shutter speeds and with a lower ISO rating without the risk of shake ruining the result. Used with the Nikon D80, it gives an effective focal length of 82-300mm, making it suitable for capturing portraits and candids from a fair distance away without being noticed.

For further information on Nikon digital SLRs and accessories, visit: www.nikon.co.uk

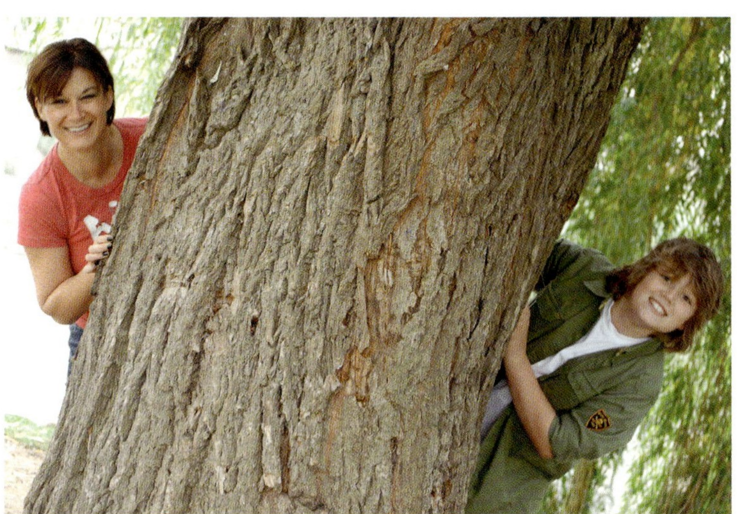

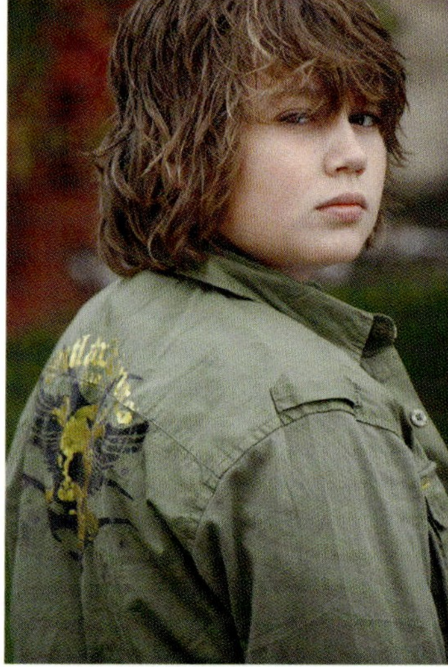

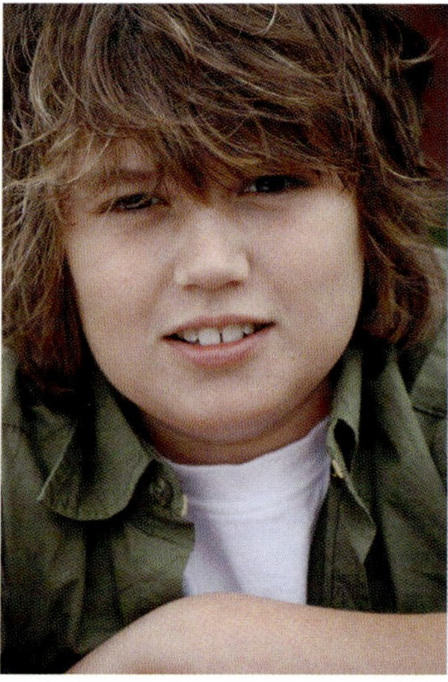

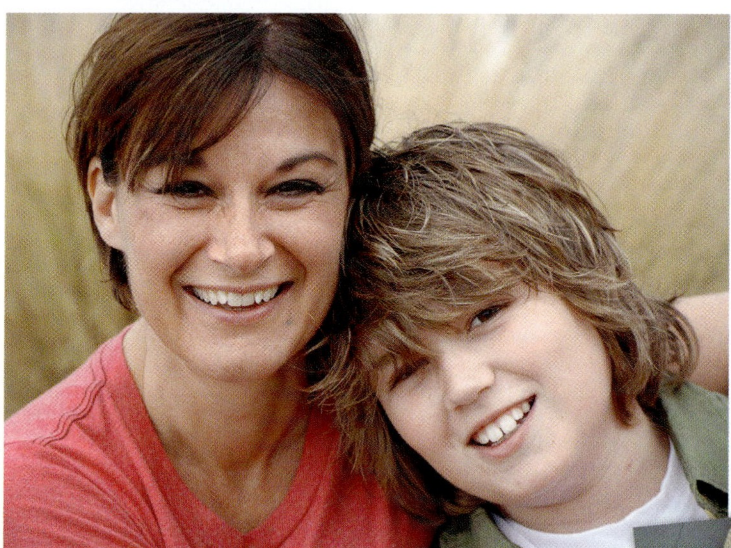

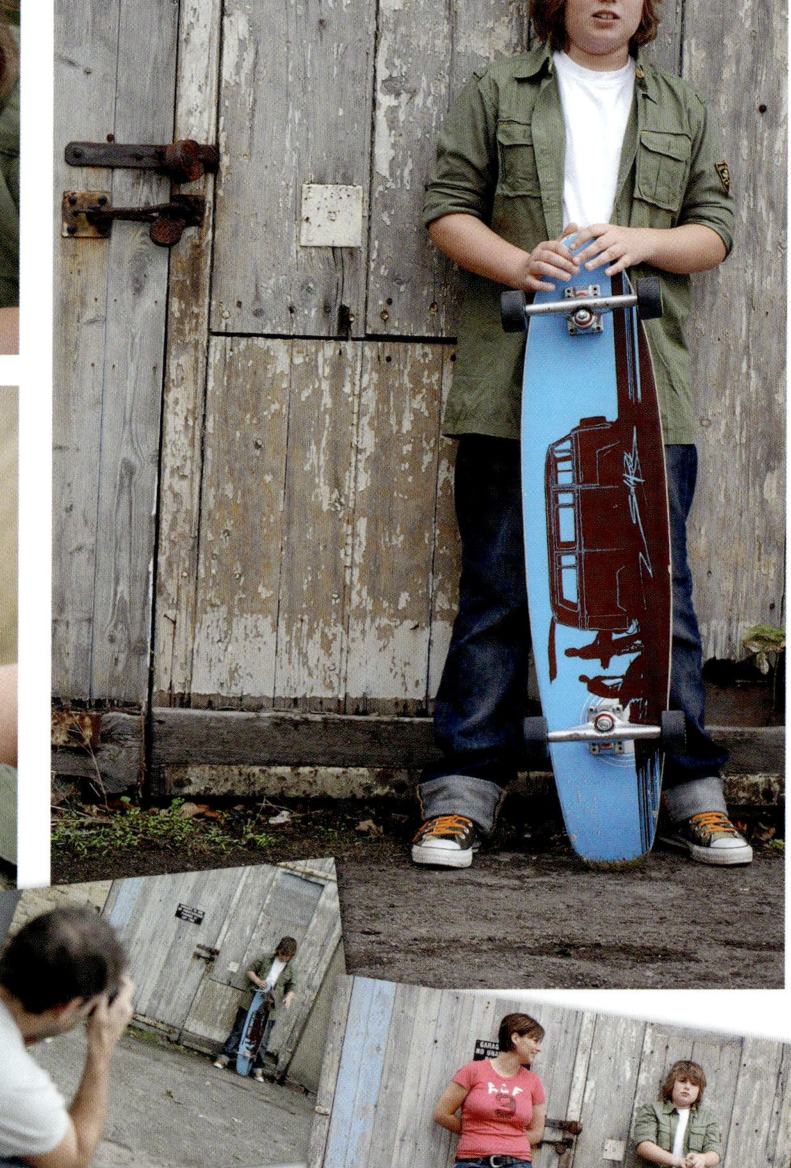

The versatility of the 55-200mm made it an excellent lens for our portrait session, allowing for a wide variety of images to be captured, from close crops to group shots.

pictures and then decide to move away from the water's edge. Shaun uses the trunk of the willow tree as a prop from which Tracy and Connor peek out from either side for a fun result. I tempt Shaun to angle the camera rather than shoot with the horizon level. This small shift in angle adds a little extra drama to the picture.

We're almost halfway through the hour and Shaun asks his family to sit at a picnic table. The next ten minutes sees him shoot them both individually and together. It starts to become clear that Connor is tiring of the shoot – we've done well to keep his attention for over half an hour, as children lose interest notoriously quickly. I'm impressed with how Shaun never loses patience though and keeps cracking jokes and making conversation to keep the shoot moving along.

As well as the 'posed' shots, he continues to shoot when the subjects aren't looking at the camera and as a result catches some nice, candid moments. One thing I notice is that he's often shooting at the 200mm end of the zoom, so I suggest he set the lens to around 105mm. At this setting the optics will deliver sharp results, and physically moving closer to the subjects means Shaun is able to communicate more easily with them too.

With 15 minutes left, Shaun asks if we can head to a set of old doors he's seen on the opposite side of the river. It's a good call, as the flaked paint makes for a fantastic backdrop. Shaun spends ten minutes shooting from different angles and viewpoints and capturing a real mix of images, from 'wide' shots at 55mm that include the door and both subjects, to close head and shoulders images at 200mm. Shaun planned to use the skateboard and incorporates this in the images to add interest to the frame and reveal a little more about his son's personality and interests.

The hour's almost up and we start heading back to the car park. As we go, Shaun spots some ornamental grasses growing by the road. He reckons there's potential there for a final shot or two but I'm not so sure. As it turns out he's absolutely right, as he cracks a joke, makes them laugh and fires off a brilliant series of candids. It makes a great end to a good hour and I'm impressed with the selection of shots that Shaun's managed to take in such a short space of time. I'm sure that a few of the shots from the day will find its way into the Smith family album or maybe even on the wall.

The last 15 minutes were spent taking pictures with some old, flaky garage doors providing an interesting backdrop.

Shaun's verdict

"I admit I was a little nervous as, in my job, I'm directing photo shoots rather than taking the shots! I didn't want to come across as being stupid; I've got a good eye for taking pictures but find that I let myself down technically. So usually my pictures are good when the light's perfect!

So for Dan to suggest leaving my DSLR on aperture-priority was a great relief for me. The last thing that I wanted to do was to be fiddling around with settings while trying to capture natural candid moments, especially with a child and dog! I was also concerned that Benson, being black, would fill in. The reflector was brilliant and bounced enough light back at the subject to give a lovely natural quality. After ten minutes I relaxed, but I wasn't too keen on the first location, so was eager to move on. I had seen the old garage doors months ago and thought they would provide an excellent backdrop. Also, including Connor's skateboard would add something to the pictures. Although I now like the pictures taken near the river more than I did at the time, my favourites are these, but for purity, I think that the last few capture Tracy and Connor best.

Not bad for a two-minute session grabbed just before the hour was up. I didn't know the one-hour challenge was so precisely timed!"

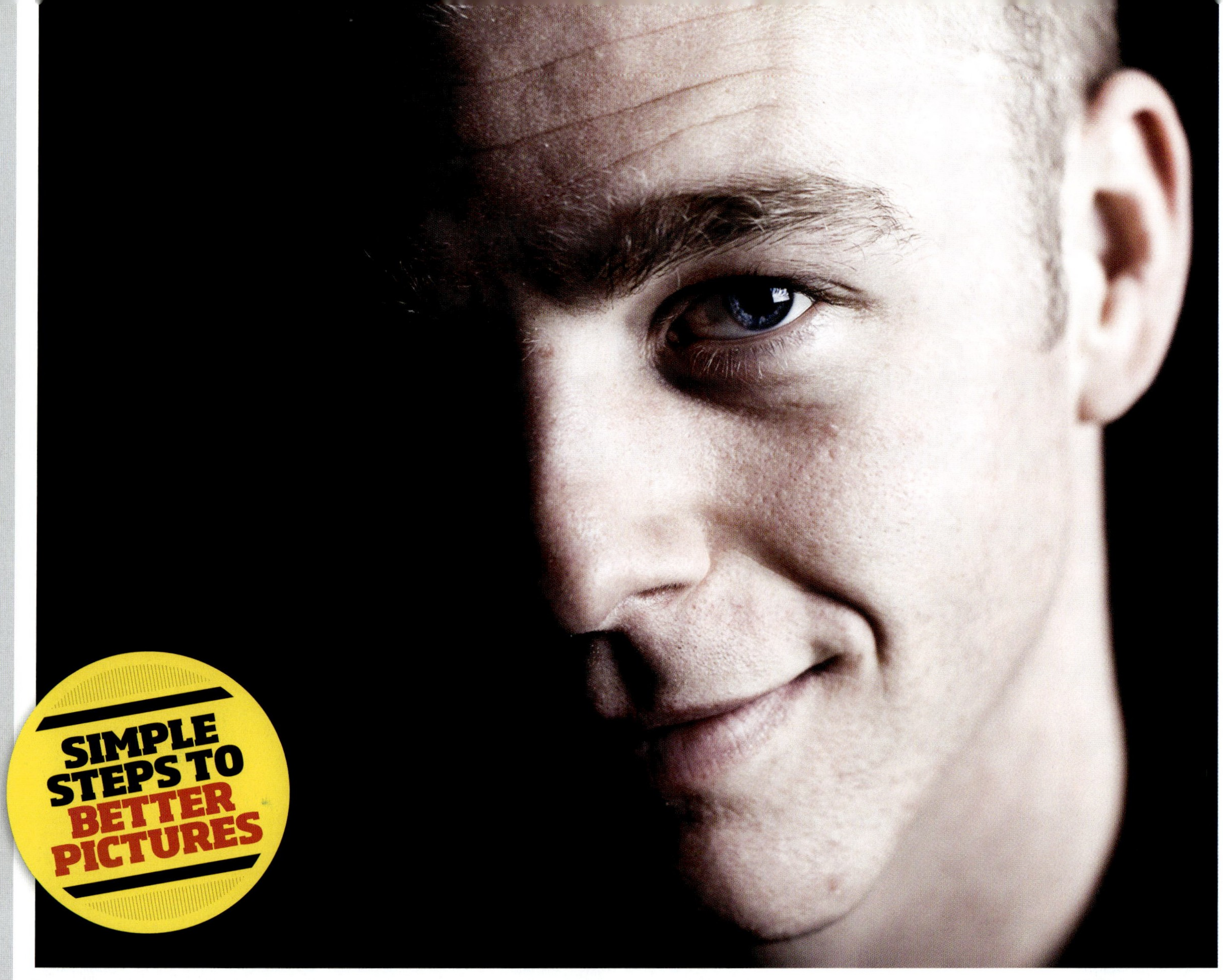

SIMPLE STEPS TO BETTER PICTURES

DIGITAL TECHNIQUES

IMPROVE YOUR IMAGES & ADD CREATIVE EFFECTS WITH OUR POST-PROCESSING TUTORIALS

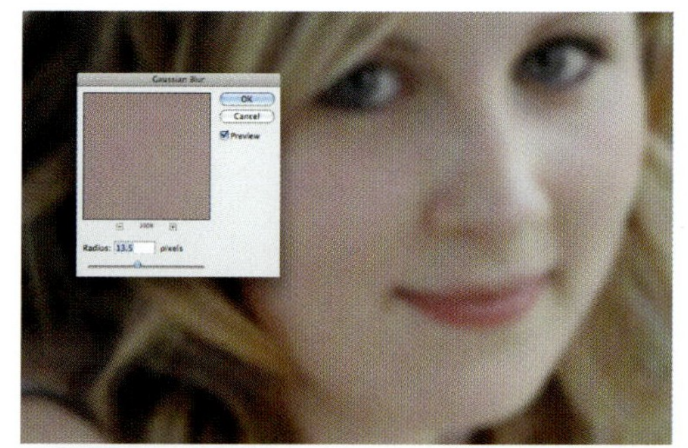

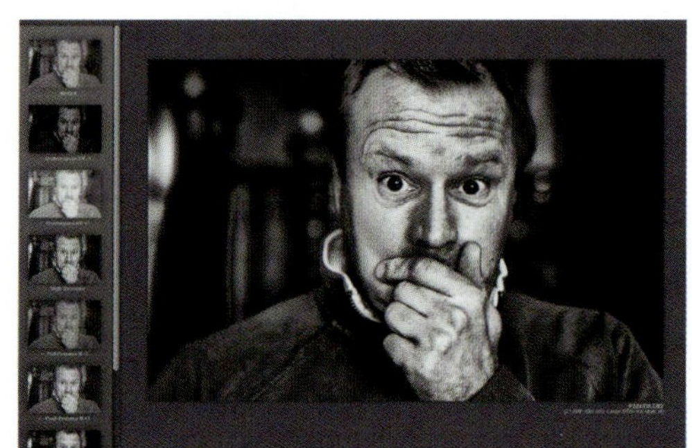

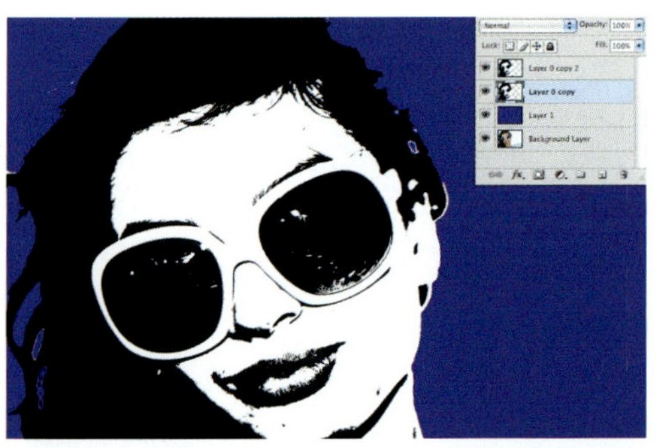

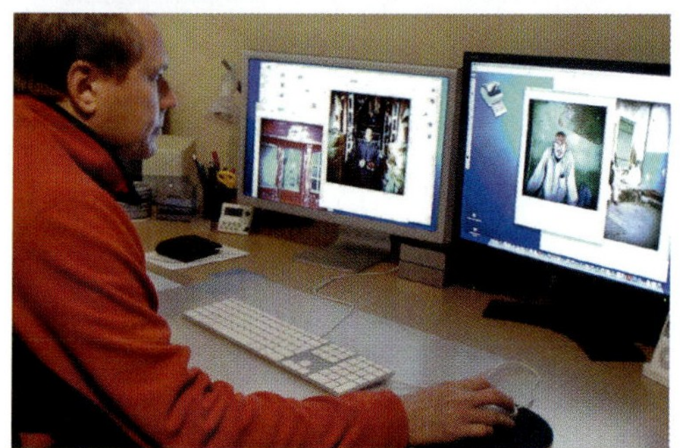

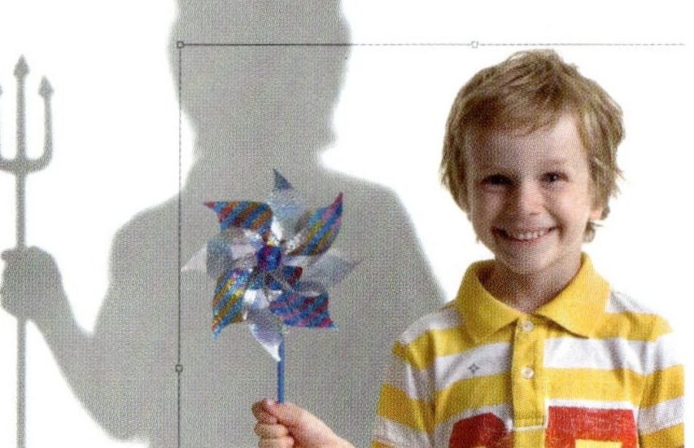

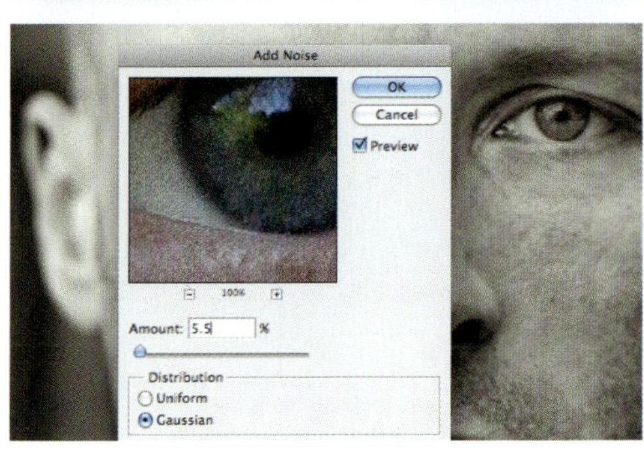

Give your portrait a perfect digital makeover

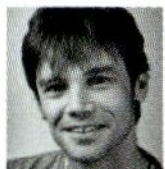

IAN FARRELL: The subject of digital retouching in portraits, fashion and advertising photography always provokes mixed reactions. Some think it's unnecessary and over the top, while others think that digital post-production is the making of a photograph. One fact, however, is undeniable: you won't find a commercial shot in a magazine or advert that hasn't been retouched. Editorial photography is so routinely touched up that it's now the norm. Eyes brightened, teeth whitened, skin smoothed and blemishes removed. And if you are looking at a glossy magazine right now and can't tell, it just means it's been done really well.

The secret to doing this type of retouching is to take your time and be as precise as possible. Use a graphics tablet and set aside an hour for a single image. The Photoshop techniques themselves are actually quite simple, it's just the way in which they are applied that is important. Let's have a look what's involved.

Get ready!

TIME REQUIRED
60 MINUTES

EQUIPMENT NEEDED
ADOBE PHOTOSHOP CS OR ELEMENTS

ALSO USED
GRAPHICS TABLET

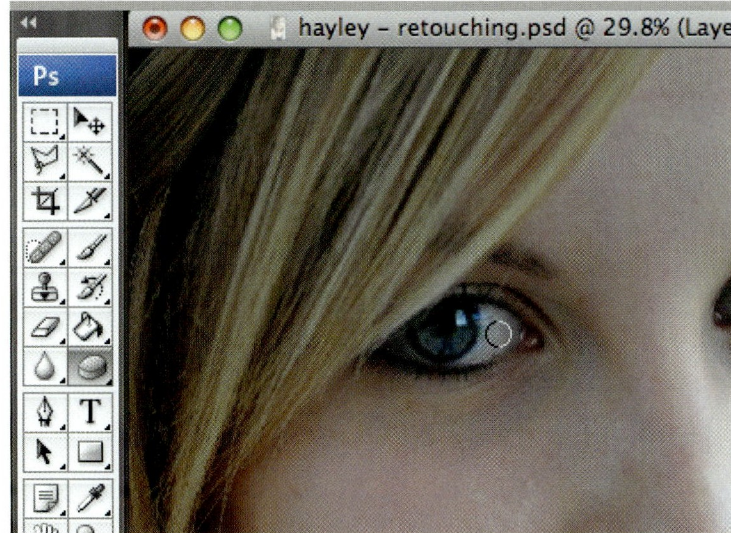

1 Eyes can be brightened to add impact. Use the Sponge Tool set to Desaturate, which you'll find in the tool box under the same square as the Dodge and Burn tools. Select a small, soft-edged brush at an opacity of 20%, go over the whites of the eyes removing colour. We've deliberately oversaturated the eye on the left to show how effective this tool can be.

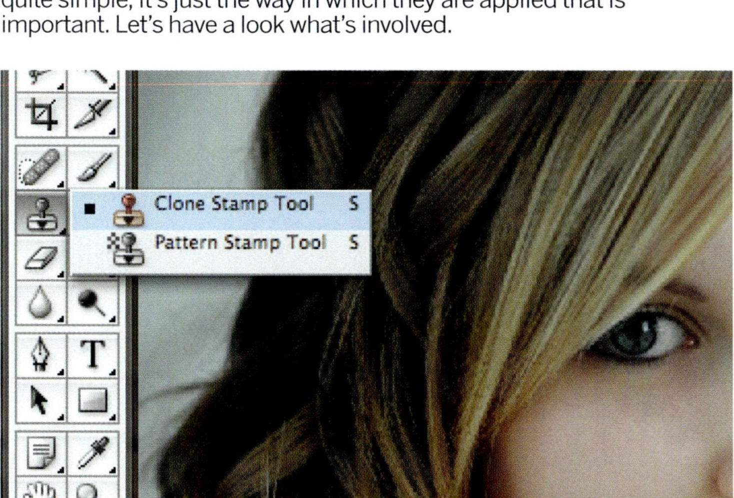

2 Everyone has wrinkles, spots and pimples, even supermodels. These are easily removed with the Clone Stamp Tool or Healing Brush Tool, and it's best to do this on a separate layer to avoid spoiling the original image. Create a new working layer by clicking *Layer>New>Layer.* Whether using the Clone Stamp or the Healing Brush Tool, start with the opacity around 15% and build it up.

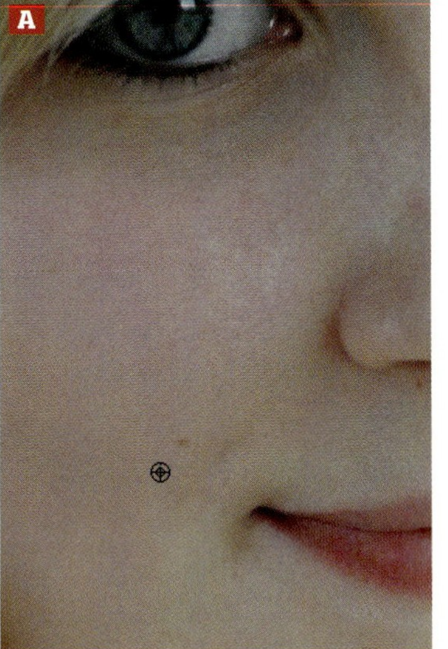

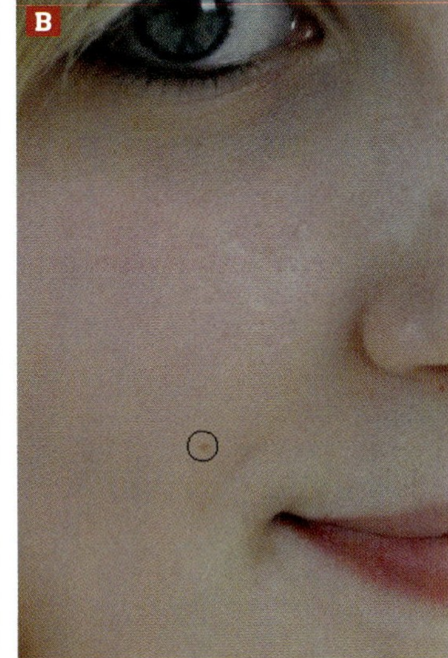

3 Select the Clone Stamp Tool and find an area of clean skin near to the spot you want to improve. This is important as it will most likely have a similar tone. Holding *Alt* will make a crosshair appear. Click on the clear area before moving the mouse over to the pimple. Then position your cursor circle over the pimple, hold the mouse down and slowly 'paint' over the area until it fades.

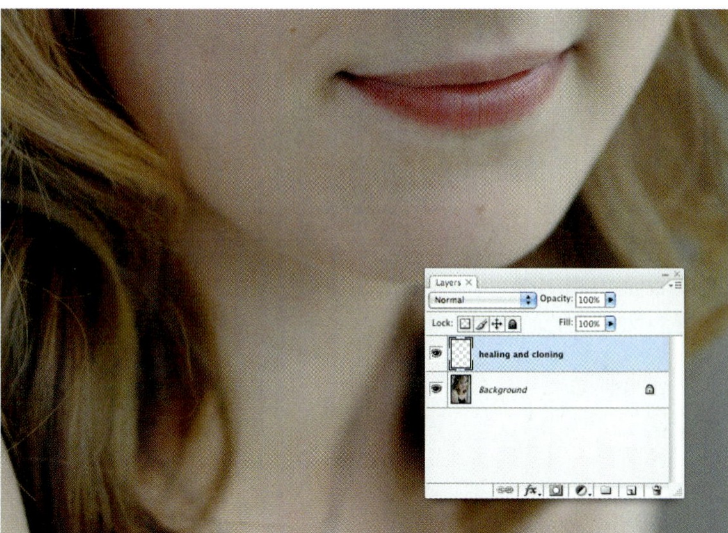

4 With the obvious skin blemishes removed, it's time to smooth out the rest of the texture in the skin. We'll go overboard first, then pull some of the original texture back to make things look more natural. Start by merging the layers by selecting the original image, the cloning and healing edits and then clicking *Layer>Merge Down.* Then duplicate the layer (*Layer>Duplicate*).

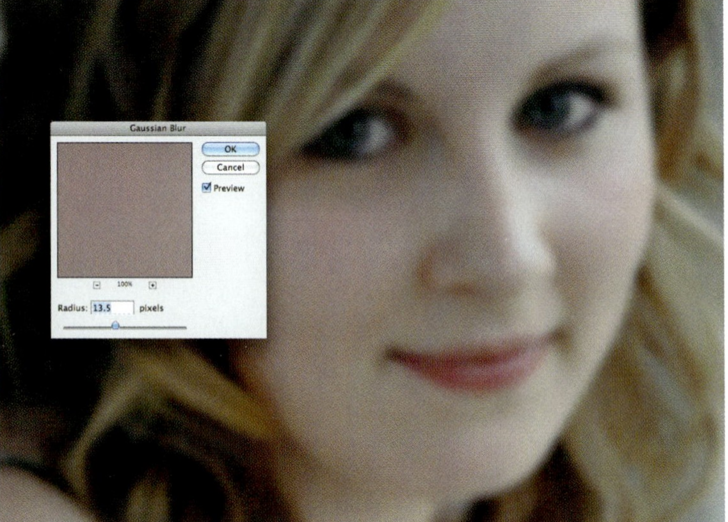

5 Apply some blur to this duplicated layer using the Gaussian Blur filter (*Filter>Gaussian Blur*): 10-15% should do it. The next step depends on which software version you are using. If you use Elements then you need to erase portions of the blurred layer so it only shows on your model's skin. Use a soft-edged brush and take your time. This is where a little bit of patience will really pay off.

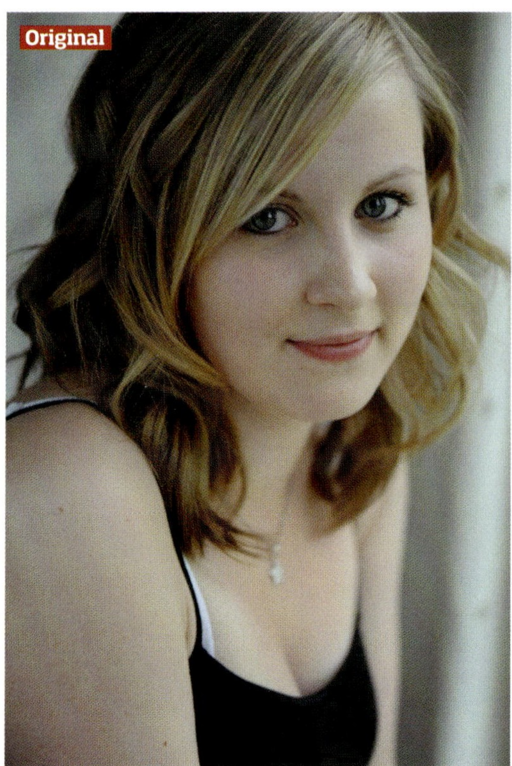

ABOVE: The original image was shot with the model's face illuminated by soft daylight, although these techniques are equally applicable to pictures taken outdoors or with sources of artificial light such as studioflash.

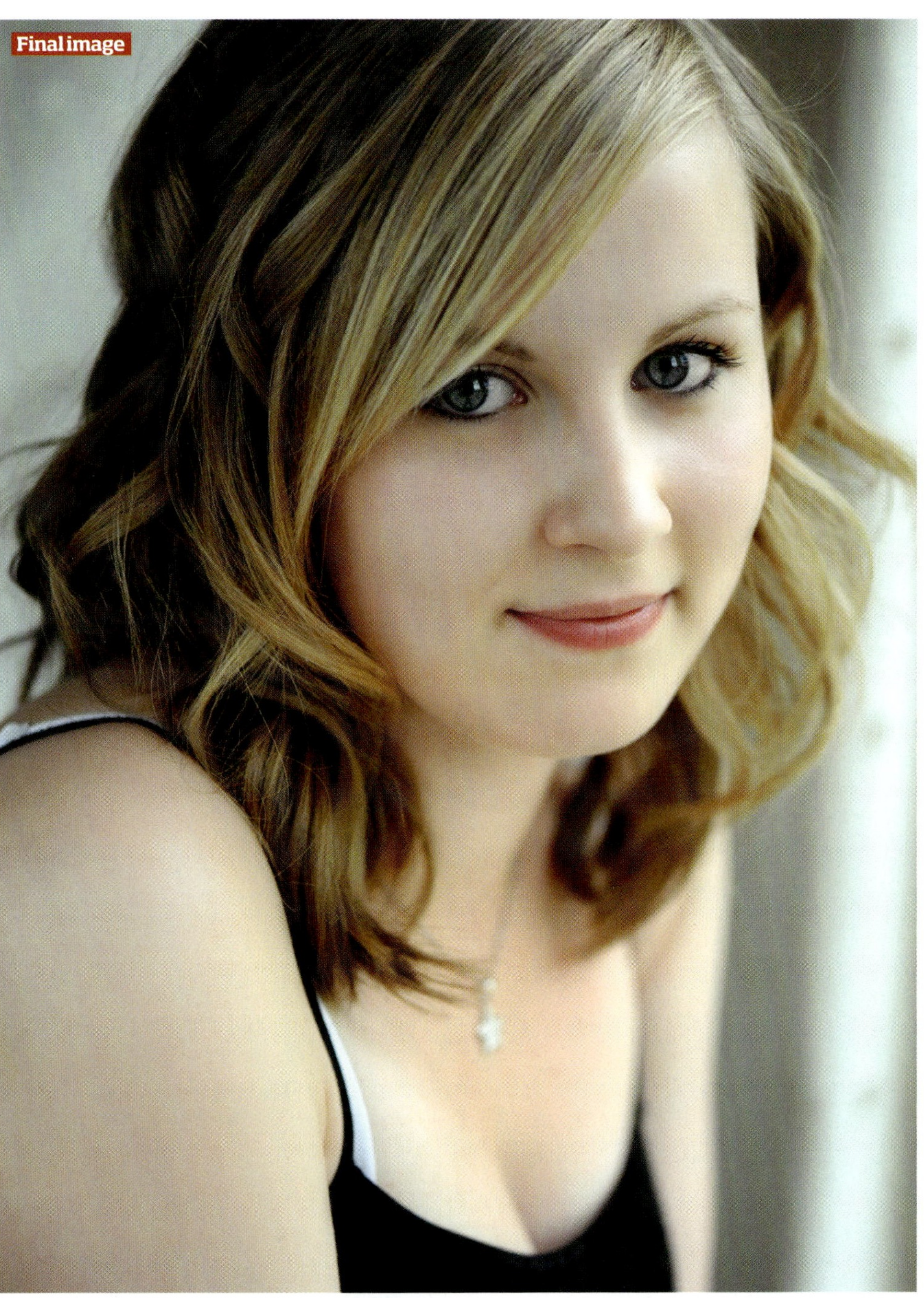

Clone tool & healing brush

As you can see from Step 3, the Clone Stamp Tool is great at copying pixels from one part of the image and pasting them on to another. But what is the Healing Brush Tool and what situation is right for each tool? The Healing Brush Tool also allows you to fix blemishes, but this time the tool takes clean pixels from around the area you're attempting to fix and pastes them over the problem, trying to match the texture, lighting and shading for a more natural look. So, if you're just trying to erase something from your image, try the Clone Tool, but, if you are working on something more detailed, the Healing Brush is best.

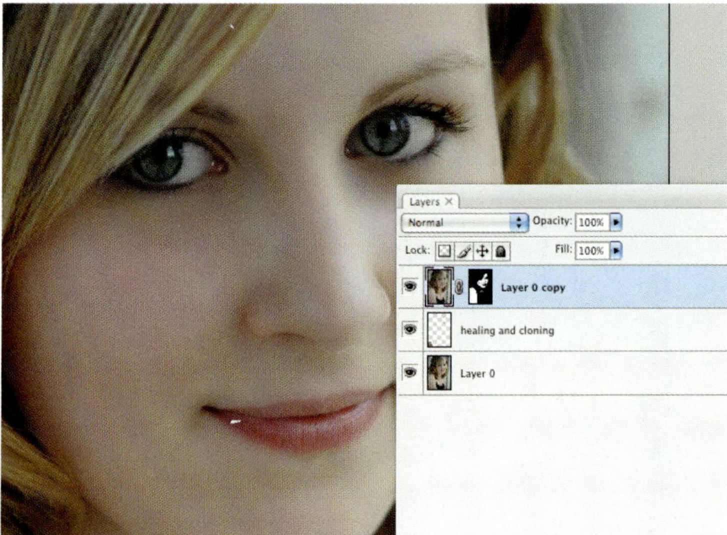

6 If you are using the full version of Photoshop, a much more elegant solution is to add a layer mask (*Layer>Add Layer Mask>Hide All*), which will hide the blurred layer. You can then paint the blur back on to the skin by clicking the mask icon in the Layers palette and using Photoshop's Paint Brush Tool to apply white paint. To remove blur, switch to black paint.

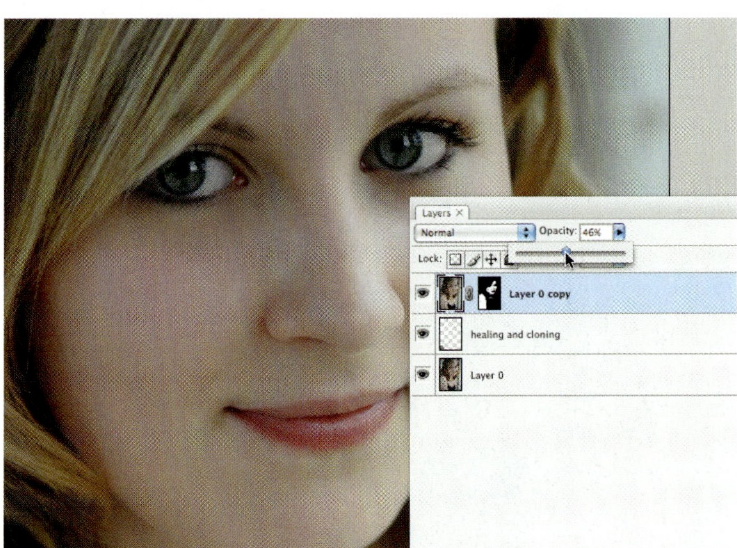

7 Whichever method you choose, you will end up with an over-the-top result. Throttle this back by decreasing the opacity of the blurred layer, which will let some of the original shine through. How much to adjust this control depends on the picture you are working on, so feel free to experiment. It's important to give you subject's skin some texture or it will look very odd.

Boost contrast with blending modes

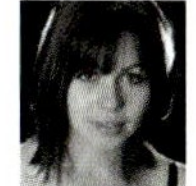

CAROLINE WILKINSON: Manipulating contrast and colour saturation is what Adobe Photoshop excels at, but these two properties are often interlinked. Boost an image's contrast and you'll notice the colours may look oversaturated too. While adjusting the Levels or Curves is the most common way to change contrast and the Hue/Saturation tool for adjusting colour, using blending modes in a multi-layered image can be quicker and give you more creative flexibility.

Put simply, blending modes determine how a top layer interacts, or 'blends' with the layer underneath. There are 25 blending modes to pick from, each having a different effect, but there is also a group dedicated to changing contrast, including Soft Light, Hard Light, Linear Light, Hard Mix and, one of the most used, Overlay. Each one handles light and dark differently – so it's worth experimenting – and it's worth noting that you can add them to any layer: a duplicate layer, an adjustment layer, a fill layer or a different image layer.

If you are new to working with multiple layers and blending modes, don't be daunted, this may sound advanced but it's not. In fact, this tutorial could be the encouragement you need to start using layers in all of your Photoshop and Elements editing. Let's see how it's done.

Get ready!

TIME REQUIRED
TEN MINUTES

EQUIPMENT NEEDED
ADOBE PHOTOSHOP OR ELEMENTS

Finding Layer Blend Modes

While you can go to ***Layer>Layer Style>Blending Options*** and find the Blend Mode drop-down menu under General Blending, along with many other advanced options that will look very confusing to you at this stage, there's a much quicker way. All the blend modes can be found on a drop-down list in the top-left corner of the Layers palette, which by default will have Normal blend mode selected.

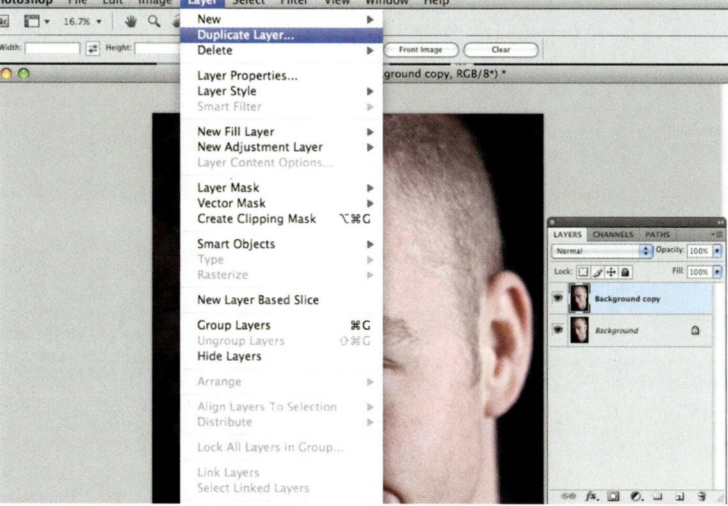

1 You need at least two layers for this technique to work, as a blend mode determines how a top layer interacts with the layer underneath it. So, to begin with, I duplicate the Background Layer, by clicking the layer and choosing ***Layer>Duplicate Layer*** or ***Ctrl+J***.

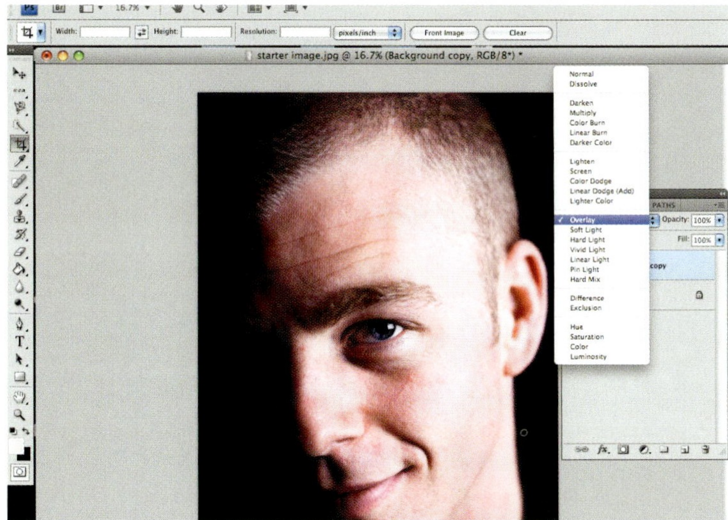

2 I want to boost the contrast, so I run through the list of blend modes and finally opt for Overlay, as it darkens the blacks and lightens the highlights. If the effect is too strong, try reducing the top layer's opacity. By boosting the contrast, however, I've oversaturated the face, making it red.

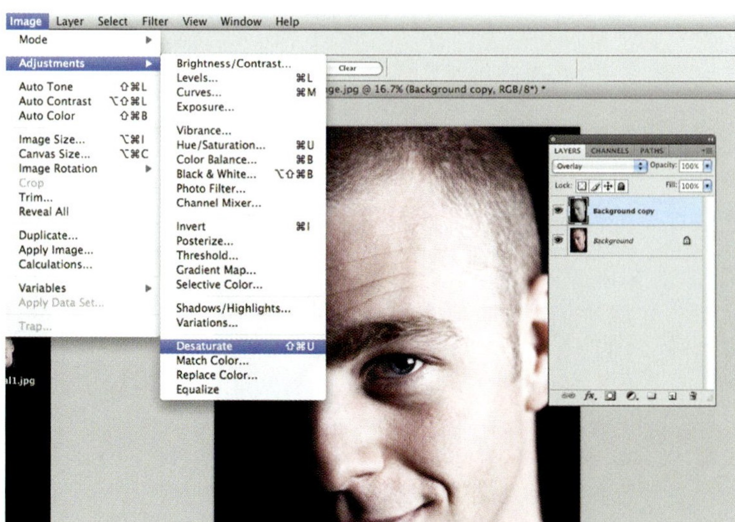

3 I need to separate the contrast and saturation, so sticking with Overlay and at opacity 100%, I take the colour out of the top layer using the command ***Image>Adjustments>Desaturate***. It's given me the boost in contrast I want and muted the colours. I like it!

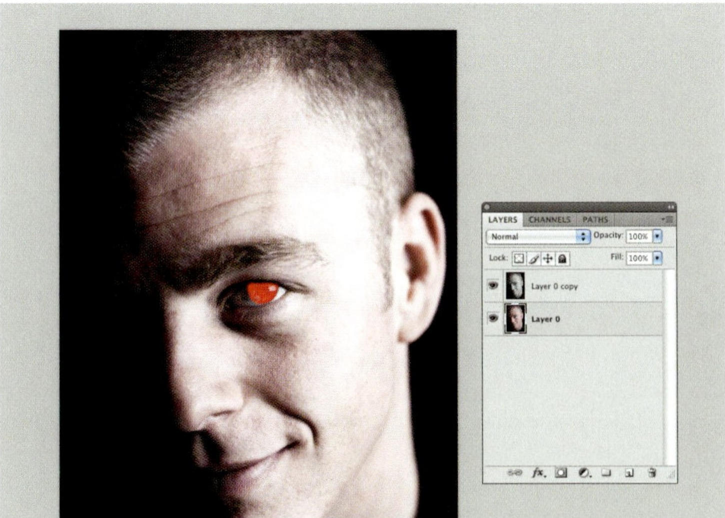

4 By desaturing the shot, I've lost the colour in the eye. To give it back its impact, I have used a Quick Mask and small brush to select the eye on the Background Layer. Click the Quick Mask icon again to reveal marching ants. I then boost the colour ***(Image>Adjustments>Hue/Saturation)***.

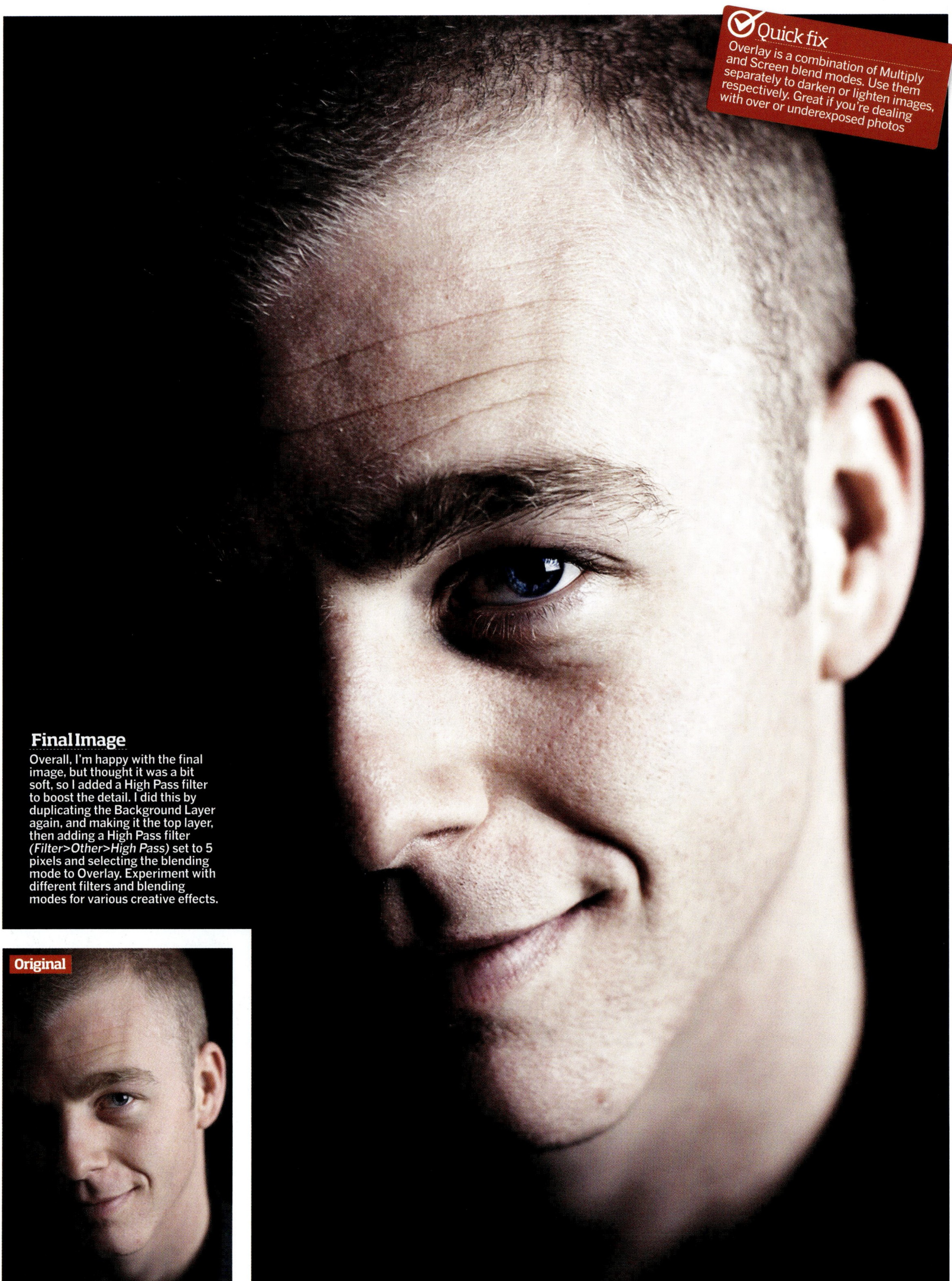

Quick fix
Overlay is a combination of Multiply and Screen blend modes. Use them separately to darken or lighten images, respectively. Great if you're dealing with over or underexposed photos

Final Image
Overall, I'm happy with the final image, but thought it was a bit soft, so I added a High Pass filter to boost the detail. I did this by duplicating the Background Layer again, and making it the top layer, then adding a High Pass filter *(Filter>Other>High Pass)* set to 5 pixels and selecting the blending mode to Overlay. Experiment with different filters and blending modes for various creative effects.

Original

Give your favourite portrait a 1950's style makeover!

Caroline Wilkinson: When someone says Andy Warhol, probably one of the first images to pop into their head is a colourful montage of Marilyn Monroe or a Campbell's soup can. Warhol is one of the most recognised artists of the 1950's pop art movement and we're still replicating his style 60 years later, with a lot more ease since the introduction of Photoshop. When it comes to picking an image for a Photoshopped pop-art image, it's best to choose a shot with good contrast because you'll be, in effect, using the shadows as a black outline for your colours. Without good shadow detail to define the face, your subject may look like they're without a nose or mouth. If you're unsure, check the image by turning it black & white and then clicking *Image>Adjustment>Threshold* to play with the slider to see if enough detail is retained. You should also try to pick an image with a background that contrasts with the subject to make it easier to extract with the Magic Wand Tool. Some shots work better than others, but it's a case of trial and error. So what are you waiting for, give your shots a new lease of life with this graphic Photoshop technique.

Get ready!

TIME REQUIRED
15 MINUTES

EQUIPMENT NEEDED
ADOBE PHOTOSHOP CS4

Be a wand wizard!

If you struggle selecting the whole background, increase or decrease the Tolerance level of your wand slightly and hold ***Shift*** while making multiple selections.

1 **Open the image and drag the Background Layer onto the new layer icon to duplicate the layer. Now add a new coloured layer between the two layers by clicking *Layer> New Layer*, then *Edit>Fill Layer* and pick a colour. Drag this layer between the two and click the top layer.**

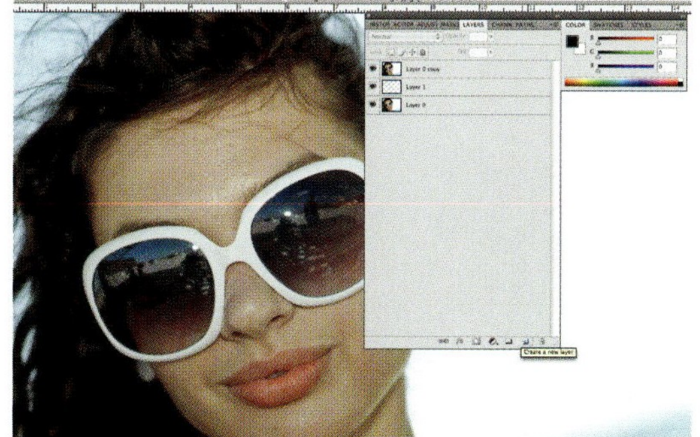

2 **Use the Magic Wand Tool to select the background and hit delete to show the coloured background behind. Go to *Select> Deselect*, then *Image> Adjustments> Desaturate* and *Image> Adjustments> Threshold*, adjusting the slider to retain facial details.**

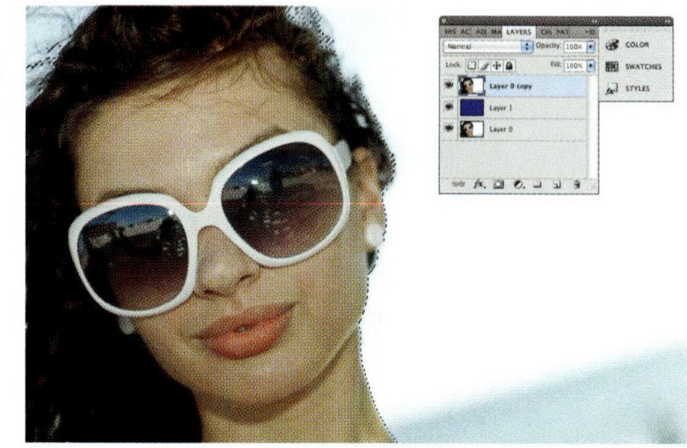

3 **Add a touch of blur by going to *Filter>Blur> Gaussian Blur* and setting the slider to 1px. Drag the top layer onto the New Layer icon to duplicate. Select the Paint Bucket Tool and hit *X* to select a white foreground and click the face. (X changes the foreground colour from black to white).**

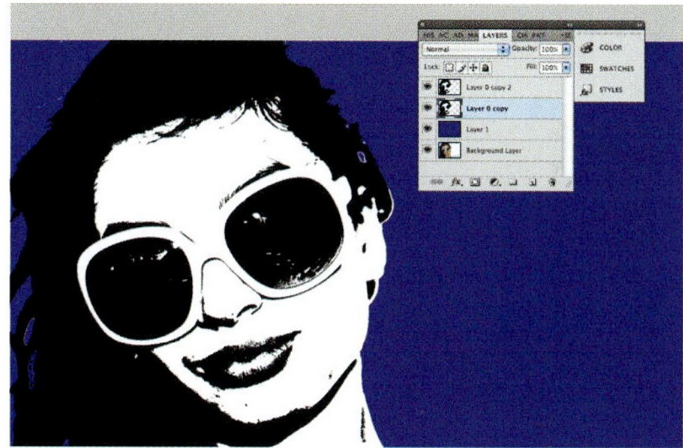

4 **Select the top layer's blending mode to Multiply. Click the second layer and create a Solid adjustment layer (the split circle icon on the Layers palette). Choose a colour to use as a skin tone, then select the Paint Bucket Tool, hit *X*, and fill the layer with black to mask the colour.**

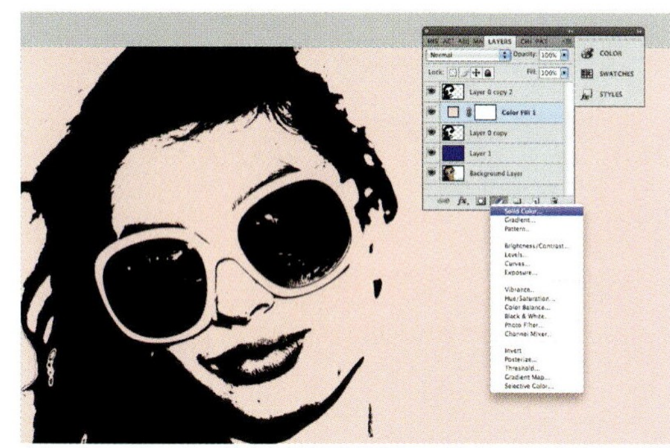

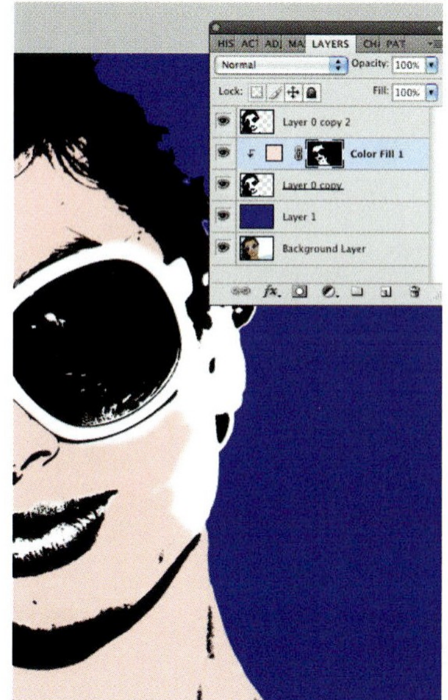

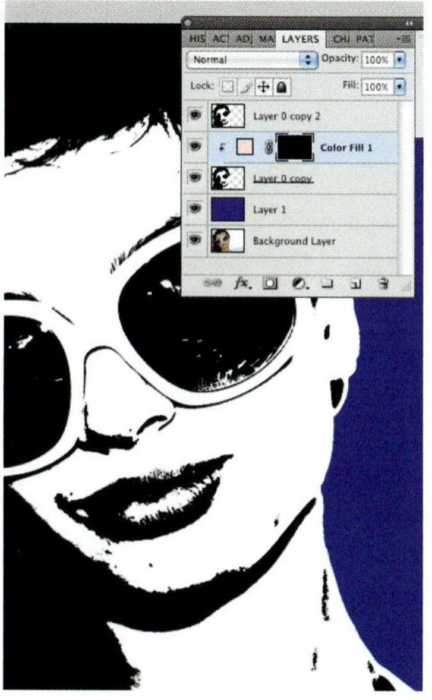

5 **Hold *Alt* and click between the second and third layer. Now select the Brush Tool and hit *X* to choose a white foreground colour and paint over the skin area. Create another Solid colour adjustment layer, choose a second colour, clip the layer below and repeat for each colour.**

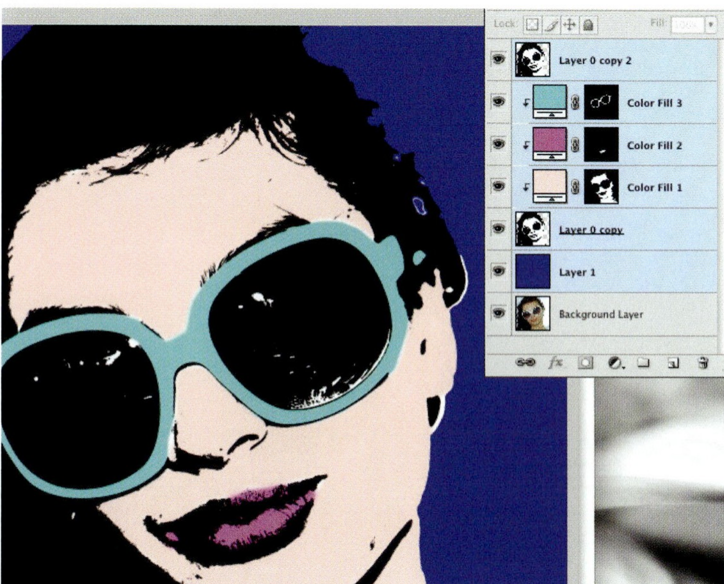

6 **Select the Crop Tool and hold down *Shift* while dragging from top left to bottom right to create a square image. Move the square until you're happy with the crop. Double click to complete. Select all layers except the Background Layer by holding Shift and clicking on each layer.**

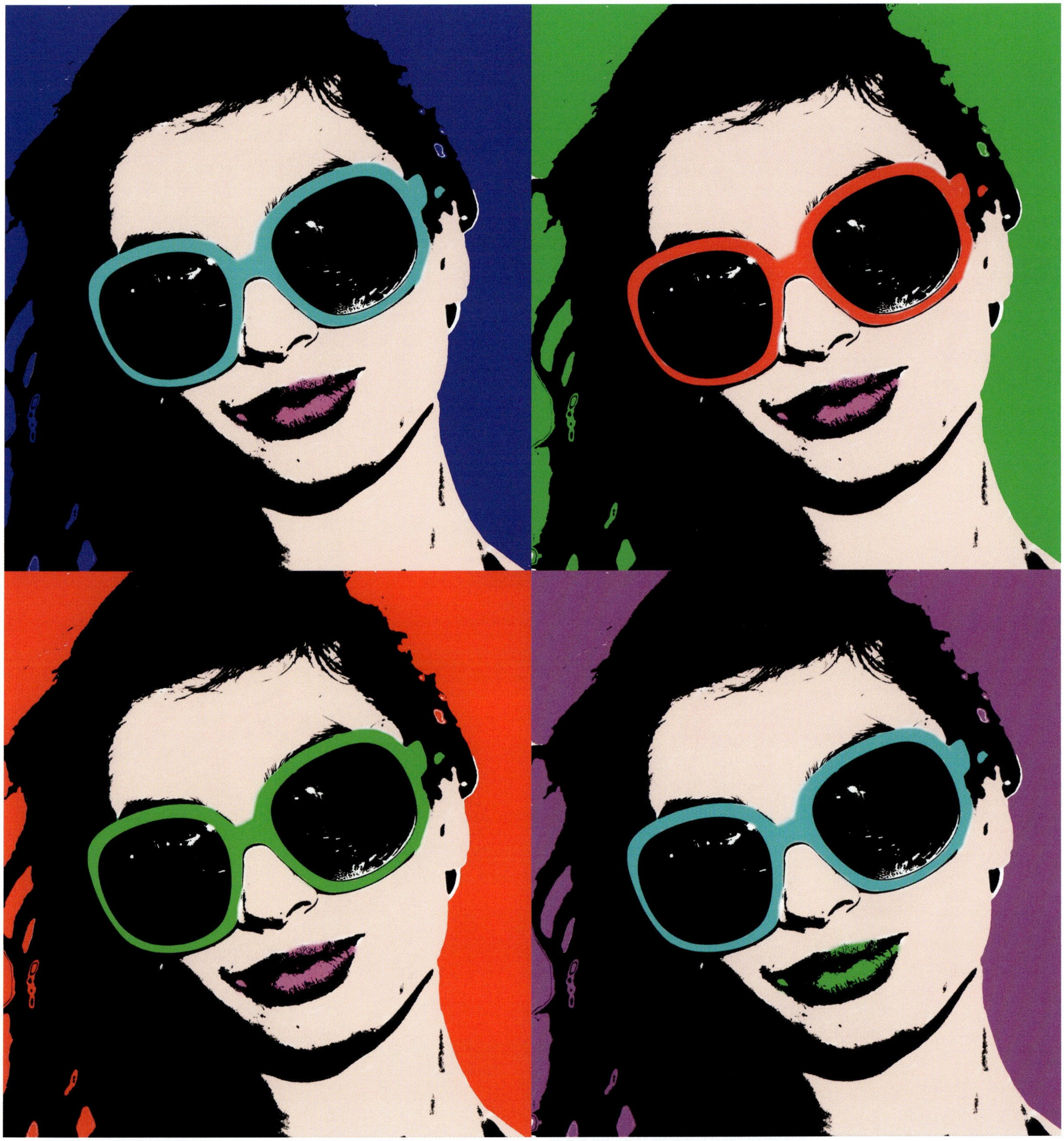

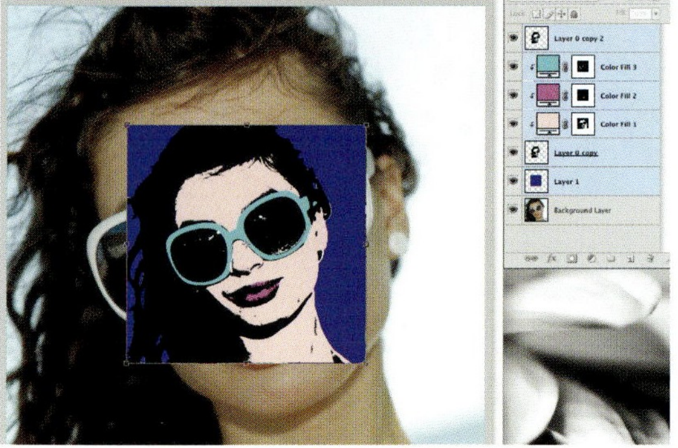

7 Hit *Cmd+T* to enter Free Transform. In the options at the top, change the percentages to 50% for width and height, and move the image to the top left of the picture. Select the Move Tool, hold *Alt*, drag the shot to the top right, making a copy of the image. Repeat three times and position the boxes on the page.

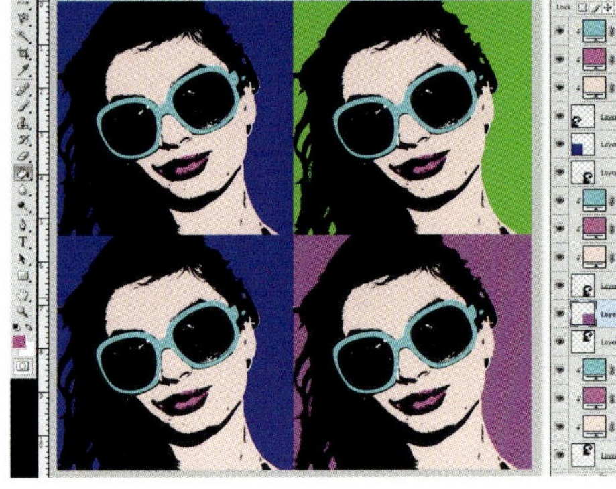

8 To change the background colours, scroll down the Layers palette to select the right layer, then choose a colour and use the Paint Bucket Tool on the square. For other features you want to change the colour of, double click on the corresponding layer's coloured box to bring up the colour picker.

Turn your little angel into a devil

STEWART BYWATER: A technique that I've wanted to try for quite a while is to take a photograph where the subject's shadow appears to be different from the subject that has cast it. I've seen it done a number of times, and often wondered how it was executed. There are several ways in which it could be done, most involving very clever lighting techniques and an understanding of scale and trajectory. This seemed somewhat over-complicated, so I tried to think of a simpler way of doing it. In the end, I decided to shoot two exposures using a white paper studio backdrop, with one light placed in front of it and one light behind. For the 'shadow' exposure I placed the subject behind the paper, as it was thin enough to let his shadow show through, yet thick enough so that it would not be completely transparent. For the portrait image, I placed him in front of the paper and later merge the two pictures in Photoshop. However, it's worth pointing out that if you had two people of roughly the same build and height, casting a similar silhouette, you could get the result with a single shot.

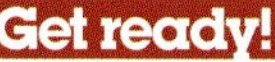

Get ready!

TIME REQUIRED
60 MINUTES

EQUIPMENT NEEDED
CANON EOS 10D WITH 17-40MM LENS, TWO INTERFIT STUDIOFLASH HEADS POCKETWIZARDS, LASTOLITE WHITE STUDIO BACKGROUND PAPER ROLL

ALSO USED
DEVIL PROPS & WINDMILL

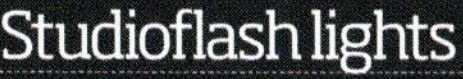

Studioflash lights

While this technique could be achieved without studioflash, it does make it a lot easier. The main reason for this is you can adjust each light's power to find the perfect balance between the foreground subject and the back light. The studio lights can also be moved into various positions until you get the best results, which is particularly useful for situations where subjects, such as children, struggle to stay still. Two Interfit heads were use, the front light had a softbox attached, the back lack was fitted with a spill.

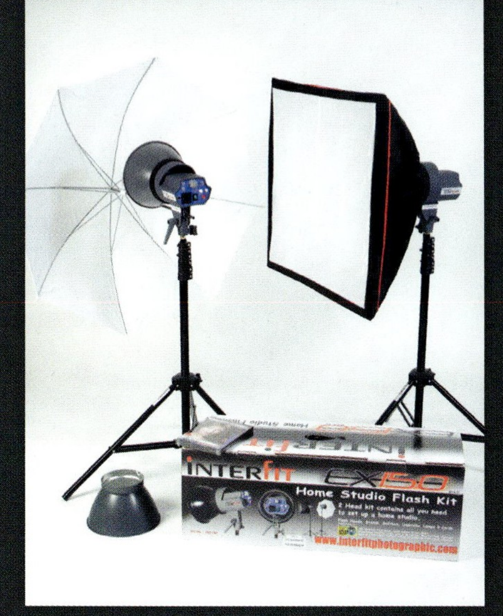

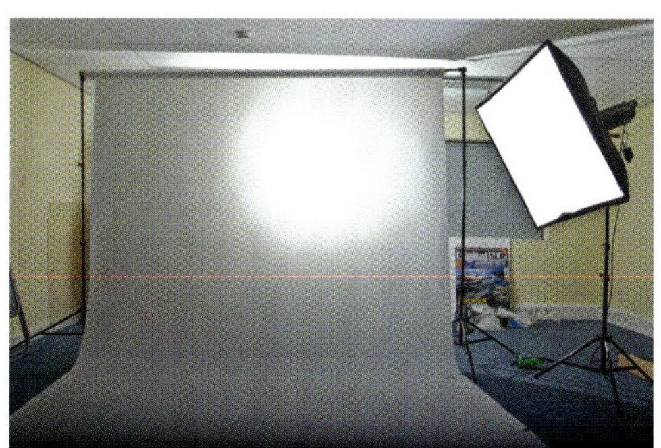

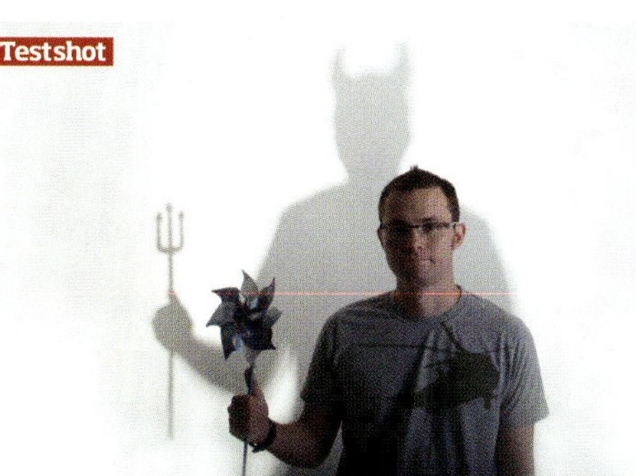

SETTING UP: Small children can get bored very quickly if they're just standing around waiting, so I decided to practise this technique before my subject arrived. I placed one studio light behind the white paper background, pointing roughly at where I wanted the 'devil' shadow to appear. I then set a stool between the two for the subject to stand on. I placed a second studioflash head – this time with a softbox attached – off to the side where I wanted the 'angel' to stand. I then asked two colleagues to stand in place and took a series of test shots until I was happy with my exposure. The backlight was on full power, while the light at the front, fitted with a softbox, was set to around 1/3 power. Next, I switched my DSLR to manual exposure mode, setting the shutter to its maximum flash sync speed of 1/60sec and an aperture of f/22.

1 **Once my subject had arrived, I showed him my test shots, so that he would understand what we were trying to achieve. I then got him to stand in position, and asked his father to stand in the 'devil' position behind the screen. This would help me with my composition, and also make the 'angel' easier to cut out in Photoshop later. I then took some shots of the 'angel' from various heights and reviewed them on my camera.**

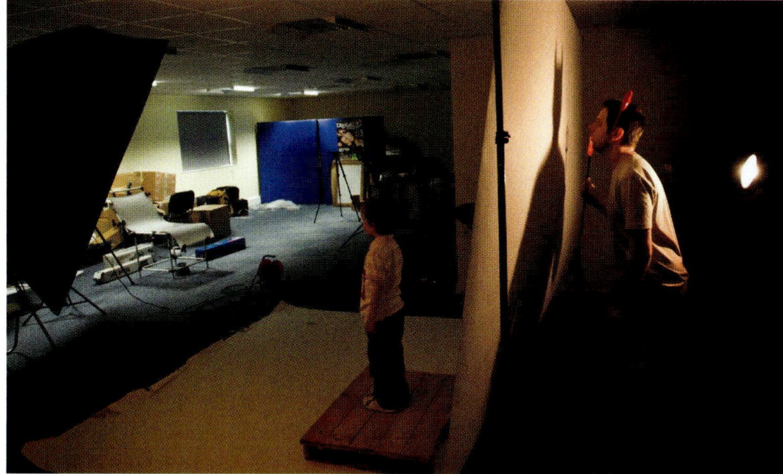

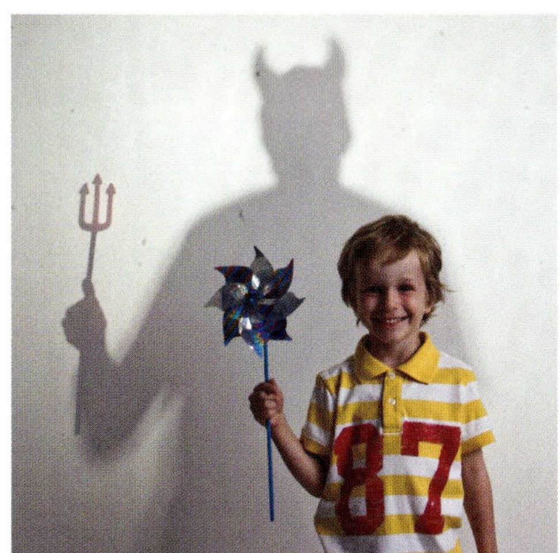

2 **Having captured a good shot of the child smiling, I asked him to put on the devil horns and hold the trident, and to stand on the chair behind the paper background. His mother was also there to make sure he didn't fall or injure himself. I checked the first shot on my camera's LCD screen, and made sure that everything was exactly right, such as the angle of the windmill/trident and the position of his hands. I then took the 'devil' shot.**

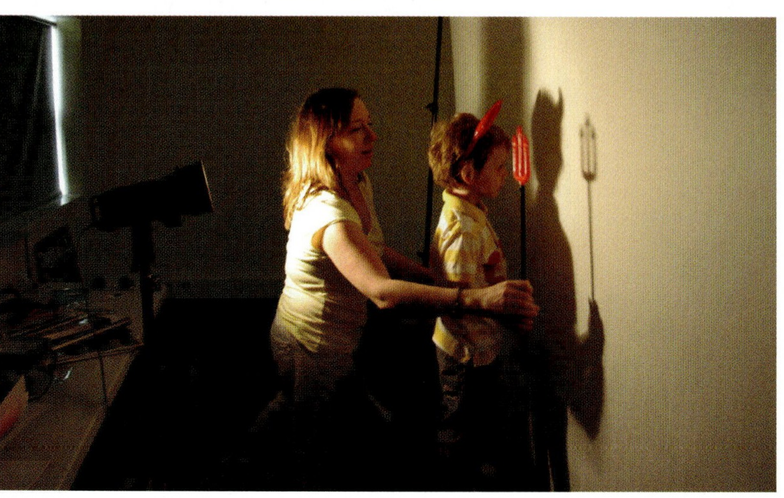

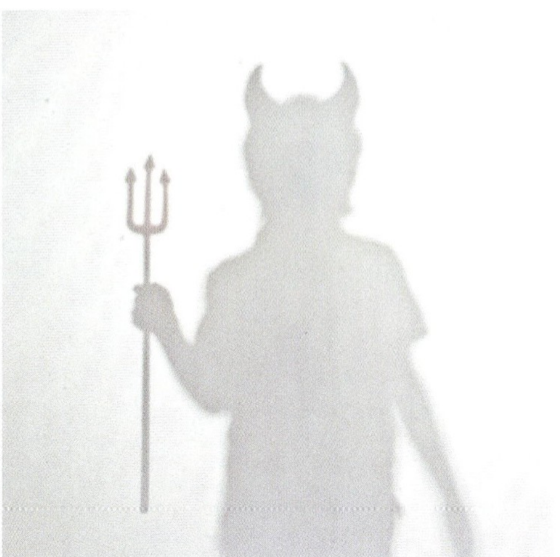

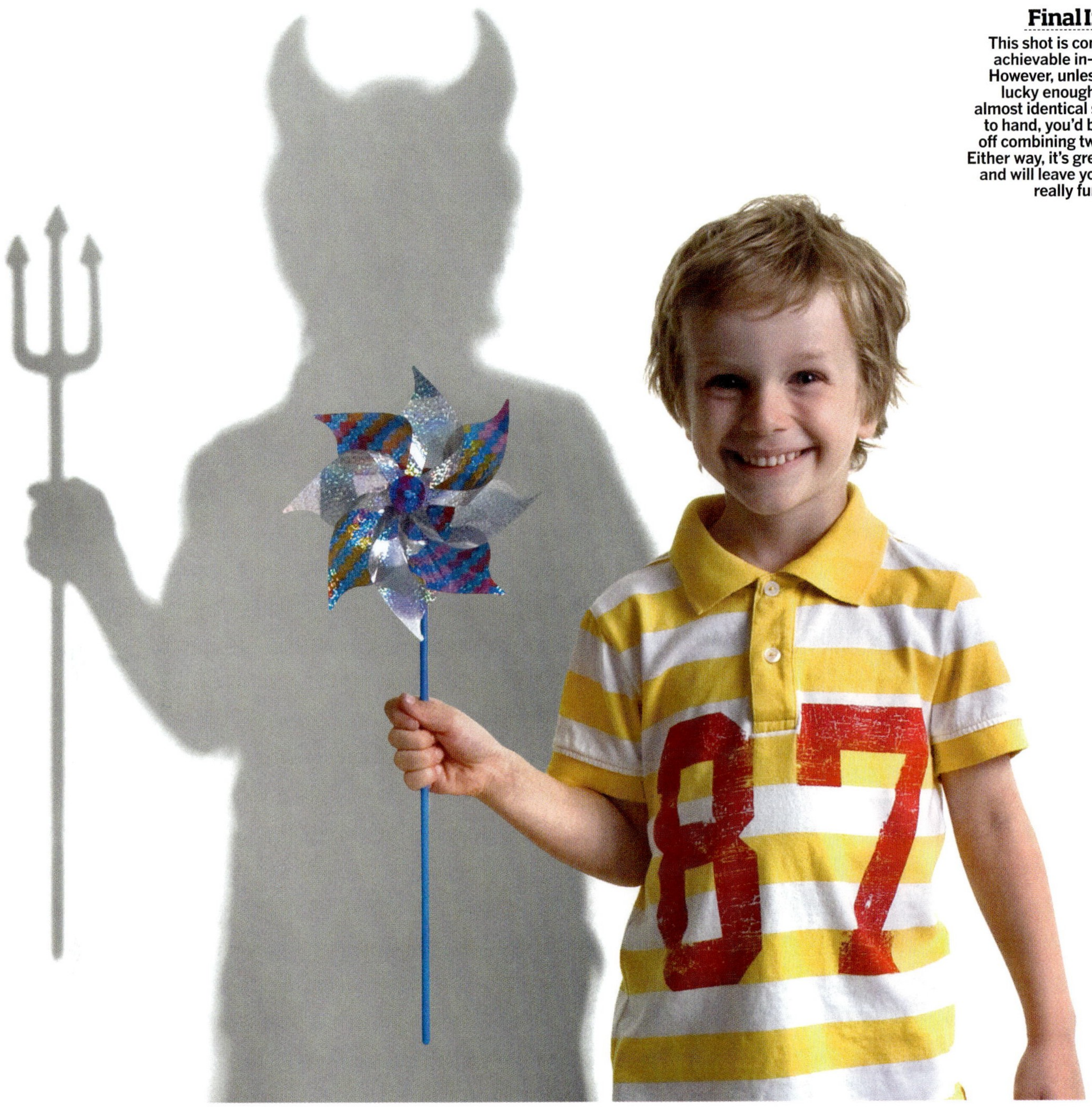

Final Image

This shot is completely achievable in-camera. However, unless you're lucky enough to have almost identical subjects to hand, you'd be better off combining two shots. Either way, it's great to try and will leave you with a really fun image.

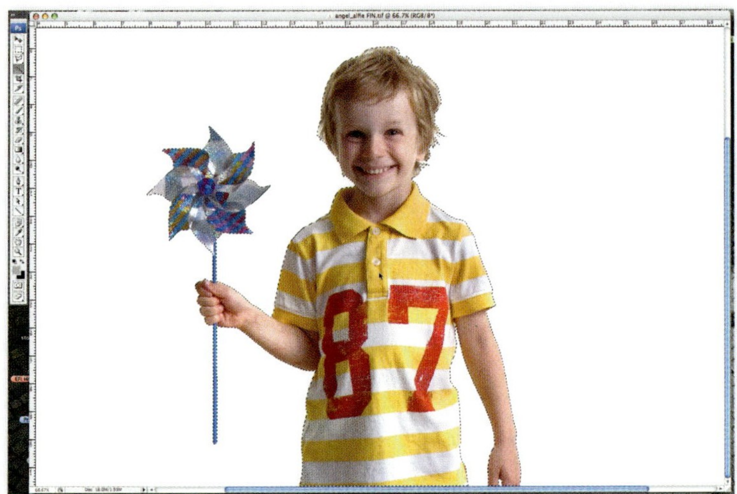

3 Once I had the necessary images, I transferred them to my computer. After spending a short time selecting two ideal frames – one of the shadow, the other of the subject – I opened them both up in Photoshop. I then used *Image>Adjustments>Levels* (Ctrl+L) and moved the white slider to the left until the background was almost pure white. Then, using the *Magic Wand Tool*, I set the Tolerance to 10 pixels and clicked on the white background to make a selection. I then use *Select>Inverse* to select the subject.

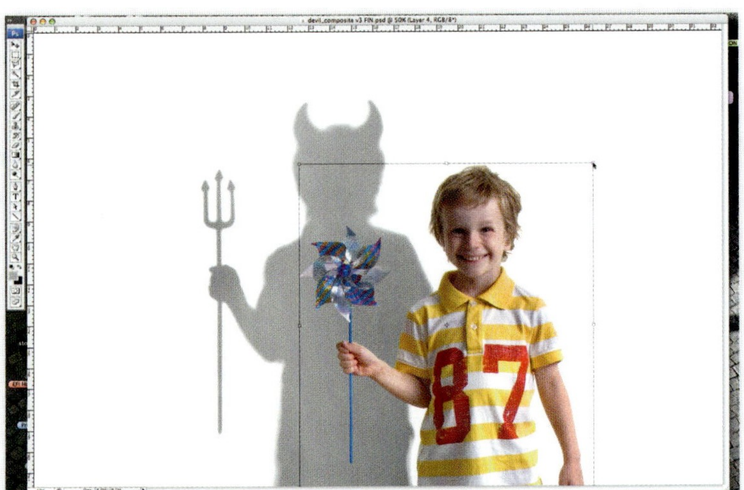

4 Using *Edit>Copy* (Ctrl+C) I made a copy of the subject selection and closed the file, then moved on to the shadow image. I used *Levels* here as I did on the other image to achieve a clear white background then, using *Edit>Paste* (Ctrl+V), I placed the copied selection onto the shadow shot. I can move the subject by holding the *Ctrl* key and by moving the mouse or using *Edit>Free Transform* (Ctrl+T), I resize the subject slightly by dragging any of the corner points while holding the *Shift* key to ensure scaling remains proportional.

Add an artistic edge to portraits

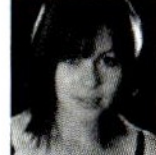

CAROLINE WILKINSON: When shooting a portrait there is a lot we can do to control key elements such as poses, lighting and composition. But there are also many instances when you can't control it all. For example, this bridal portrait had great lighting coming from the window but the backdrop was cluttered and distracting – ruining the photograph. Often, you can add blur in Photoshop to recreate a shallow depth-of-field, softening the imposing background. But in this case, it's not enough and for this picture to be a success the backdrop needs to be simplified. Using a coloured layer to mask the background is an effective way of transforming most images that have great light but a messy backdrop. If you have images with a similar problem, then give this technique a try!

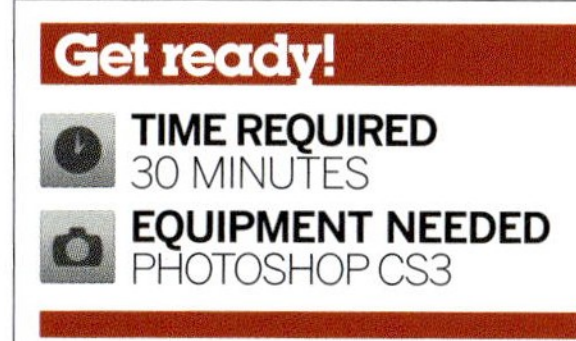

Get ready!

TIME REQUIRED
30 MINUTES

EQUIPMENT NEEDED
PHOTOSHOP CS3

Brushes & layers!

this technique requires you to create a new 'black' layer and use the Paint Brush Tool to remove the colour and reveal the image underneath. A fair amount of trial and error is needed to get an even result, but one way is to keep a soft medium-sized, very low-opacity brush moving and gradually strip away the colour. If you do make a mistake, change the brush Mode to Darken and go over the areas where the opacity is too thin.

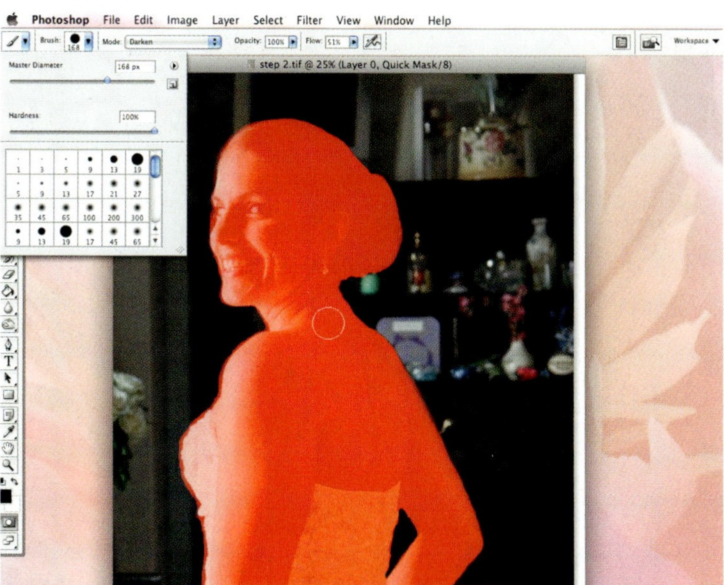

1 I tried to blur the background by masking off the bride and applying the maximum lens blur to the background by using *Filter>Blur>Lens Blur* and setting the Radius to 100%. I wanted a simple image that focused on the bride and lighting; this technique didn't do that.

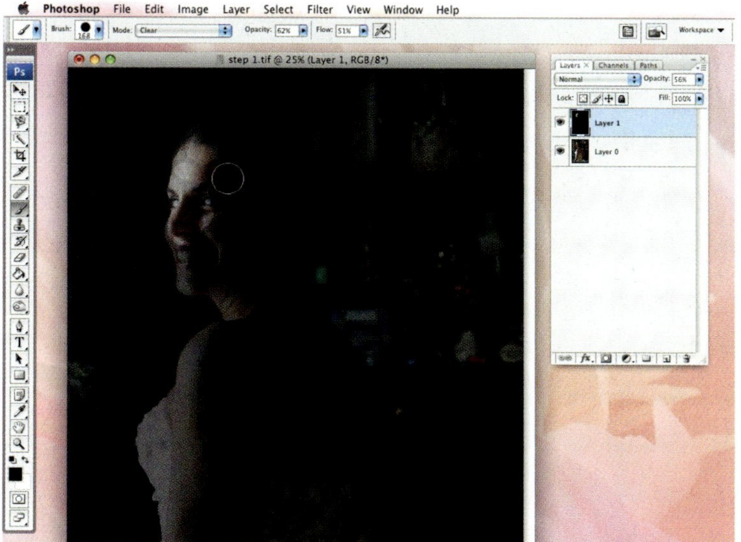

2 I made a second layer (*Layer>New>Layer*) and, with the Paint Bucket Tool, coloured it black. I brought the opacity of the layer down to 56% so as to see the image underneath and, using the Clear brush mode and opacity of 62%, started to erase areas I wanted to reveal.

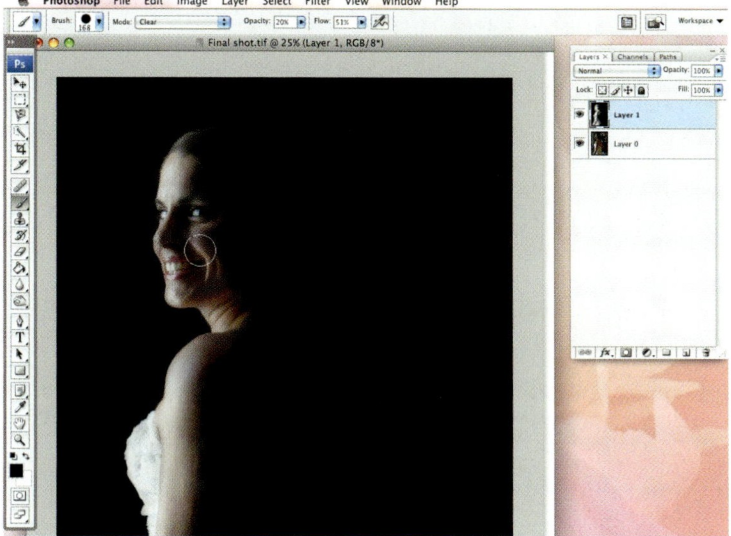

3 It's worth playing around with the different brush modes, sizes and opacities to get the desired effect. I found that 62% was too harsh to get a smooth finish and I got a better result with the layer's opacity at 100% and by varying the brush opacity between 9 and 17%.

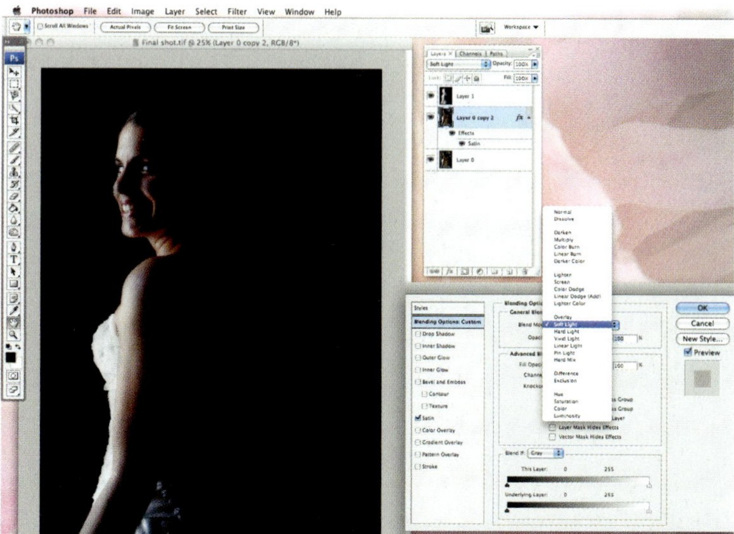

4 Once I was happy with the detail I'd brought forward, I felt that the graduation between the bride's profile and the black fill layer needed to be smoother, so I played with the different blending options (*Layer>Layer Style*). The Satin blend gave me the smoothest finish.

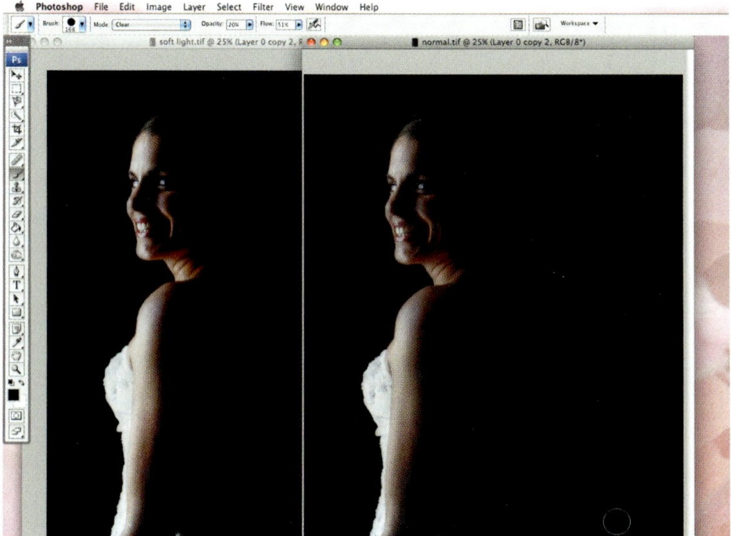

5 Each Blend Option has a range of Blend Modes to experiment with. I was tempted to use Soft Light as it boosted the bride's glow and contrast, but in the end I opted for the Normal setting as it offered a less stark result with more natural skin tones, which suited my image better.

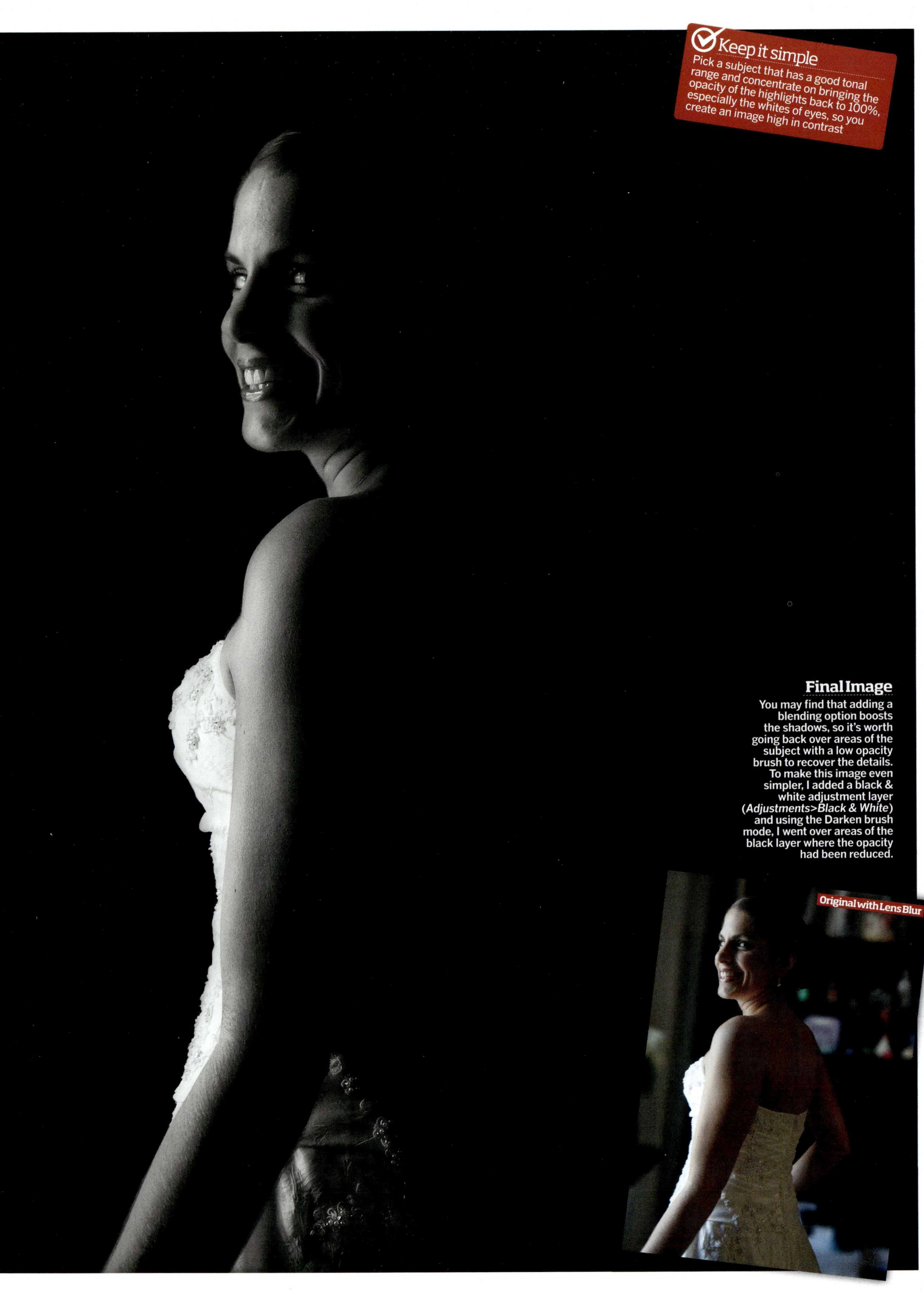

Keep it simple

Pick a subject that has a good tonal range and concentrate on bringing the opacity of the highlights back to 100%, especially the whites of eyes, so you create an image high in contrast

Final Image

You may find that adding a blending option boosts the shadows, so it's worth going back over areas of the subject with a low opacity brush to recover the details. To make this image even simpler, I added a black & white adjustment layer (*Adjustments>Black & White*) and using the Darken brush mode, I went over areas of the black layer where the opacity had been reduced.

Original with Lens Blur

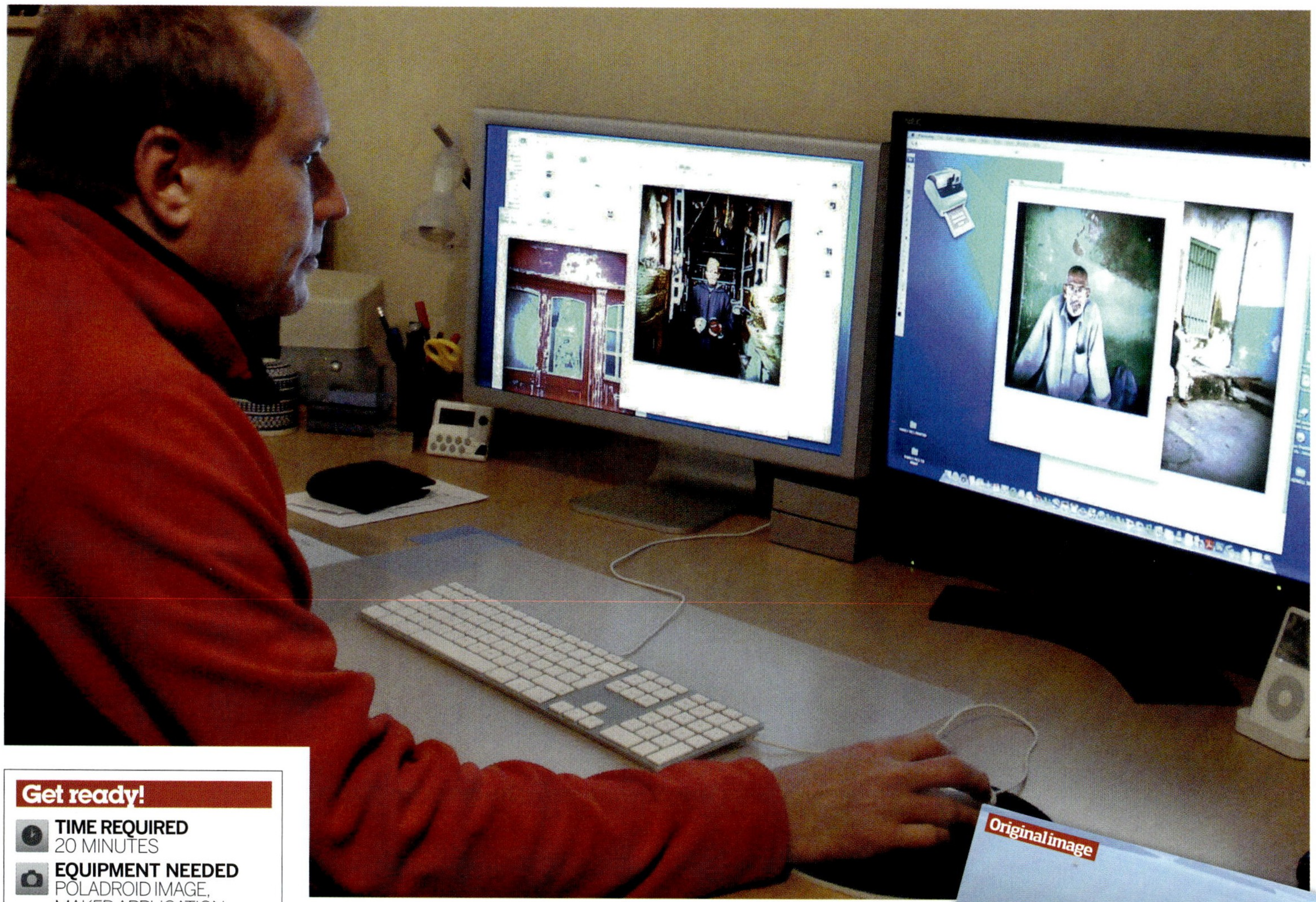

Get ready!

TIME REQUIRED
20 MINUTES

EQUIPMENT NEEDED
POLADROID IMAGE, MAKER APPLICATION, APPLE MAC COMPUTER

ALSO USED
DIGITAL IMAGES

Create your own Polaroids

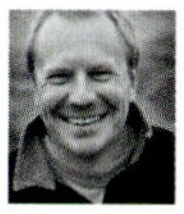

LEE FROST: Polaroid instant photos are legendary. Everyone's heard of them and, if you grew up in the '70s, as I did, you'll remember the characteristic 'click-whirrr' of the camera in action, and then everyone crowding around the newly-ejected print to watch the image magically appear before their eyes. I still use Polaroid cameras today – vintage SX-70s picked-up for peanuts on eBay. It's not the fact that I can see the results immediately that attracts me (digital SLRs are far more capable), but the distinctive look that Polaroid prints have – the slightly weird colours, the softness of the image, the shady corners and wonderful cross-hatched white border. Fortunately, you no longer need a Polaroid camera or Polaroid film to create this look, because a free download from www.poladroid.net will recreate it for you. Here's how...

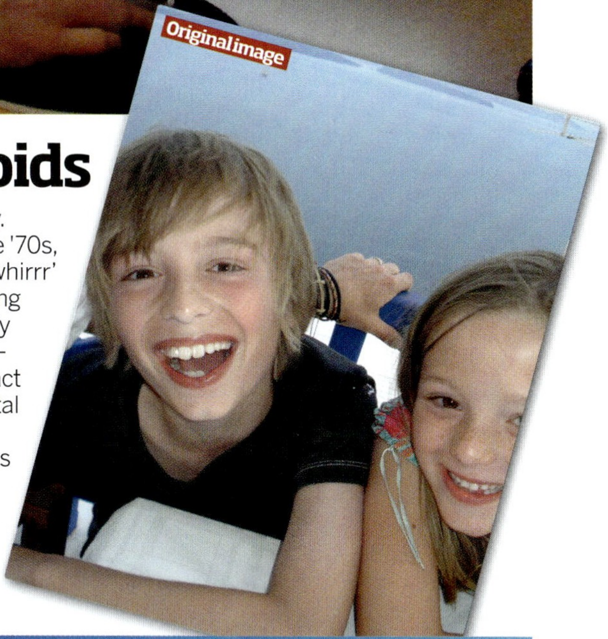

Original image

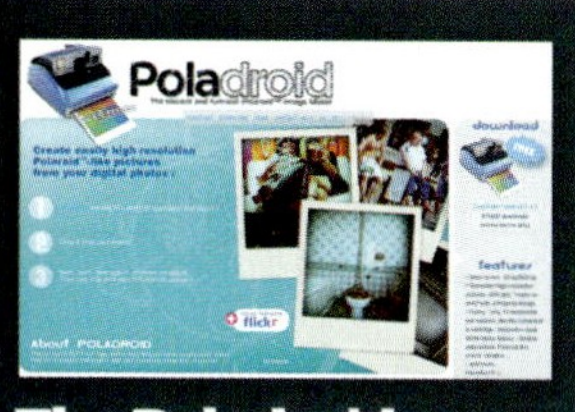

The Poladroid image maker

The only thing you need to create fantastic and convincing Polaroid-like images is the free application available to download from www.poladroid.net. Anyone can do it, as it's compatible with Mac and PC computers. The drag-and-drop application converts any digital image, in JPEG format, into a 400dpi print-ready file, complete with Polaroid-style border and the characteristics of a Polaroid instant image. It is possible to create a Photoshop action yourself that does the same conversion, but you really need to know what you're doing to produce convincing results – and why bother when this freebie will do the job for you!

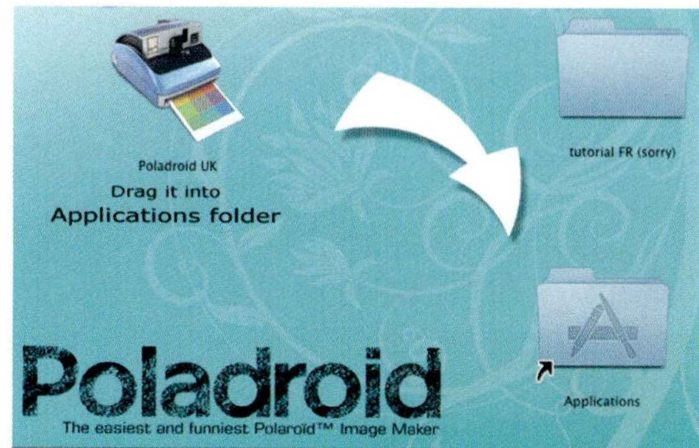

1 Download the Poladroid software to your PC or Mac from www.poladroid.net. There's nothing to pay, no membership or commitment required – just click the Download icon, wait a couple of minutes for the download to finish, and then install it. My steps were performed on a Mac.

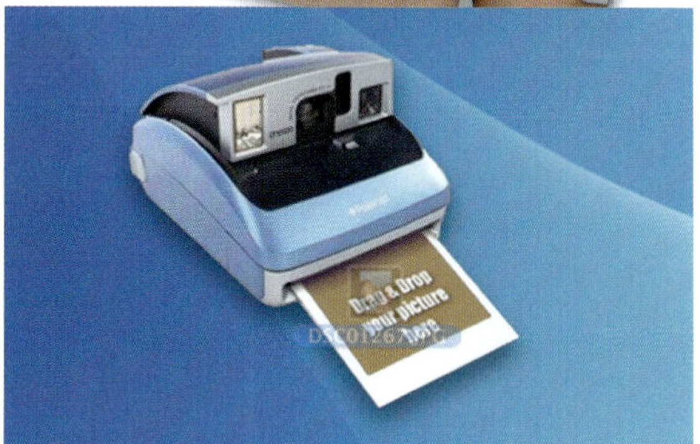

2 Double-click the Poladroid icon to launch the application. A Polaroid camera will appear on your desktop and you should move it to a convenient spot. All you need to do now is drag and drop a JPEG file onto the camera and the software will do all the work for you.

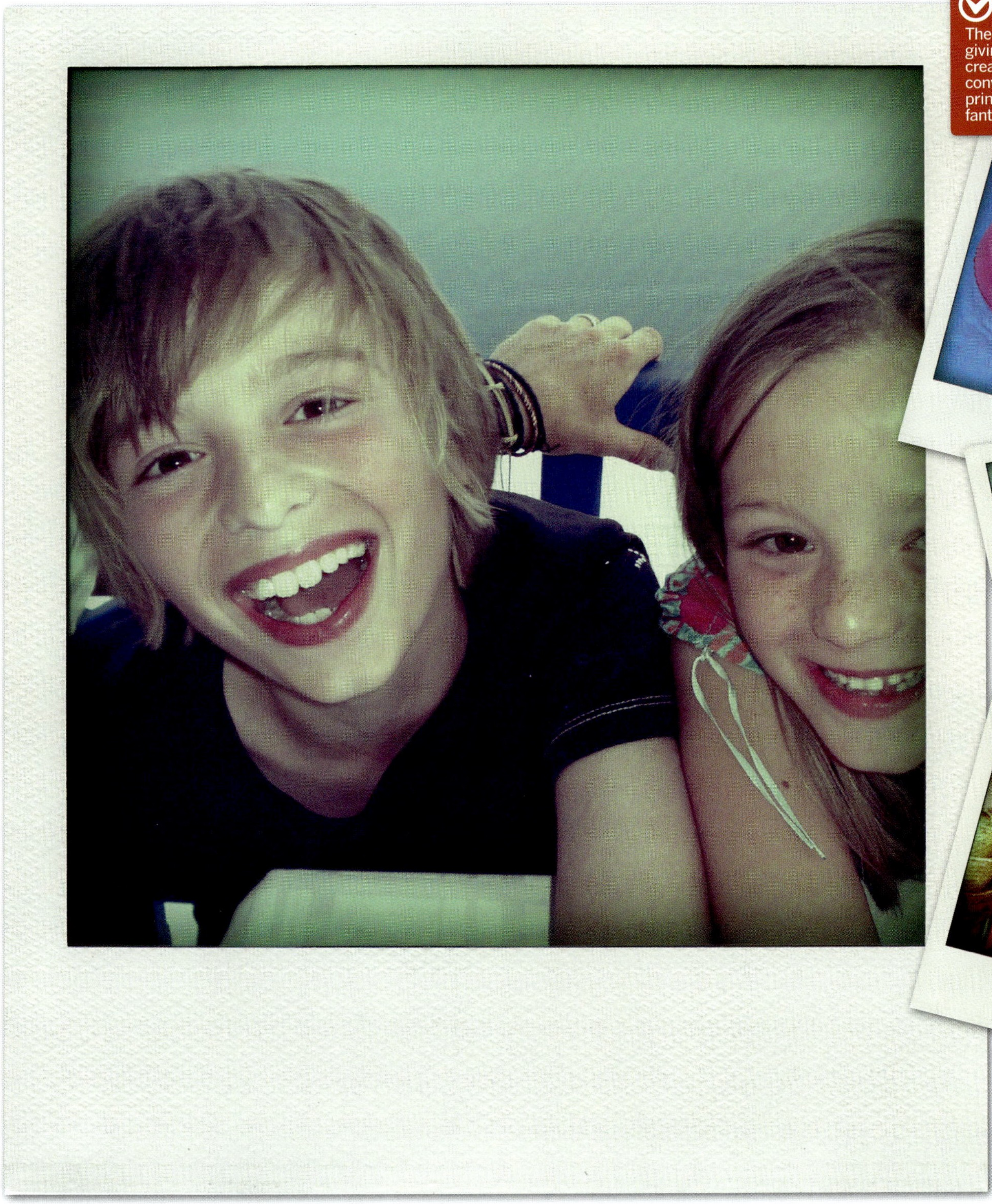

Family favourites

The Poladroid software is ideal for giving your family snaps a more creative look, so why not begin by converting a selection and then print and frame them or create a fantastic photo book?

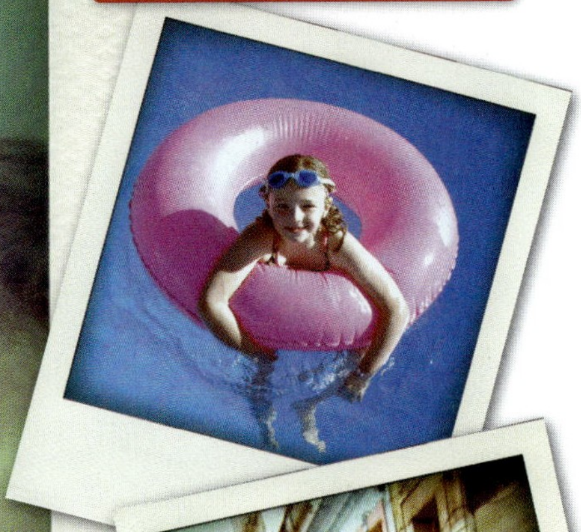

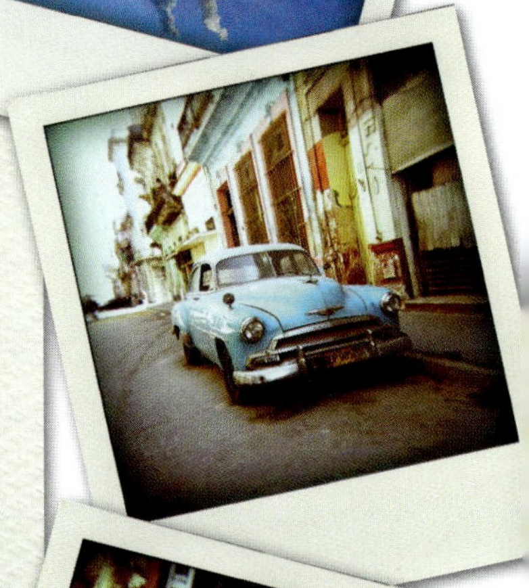

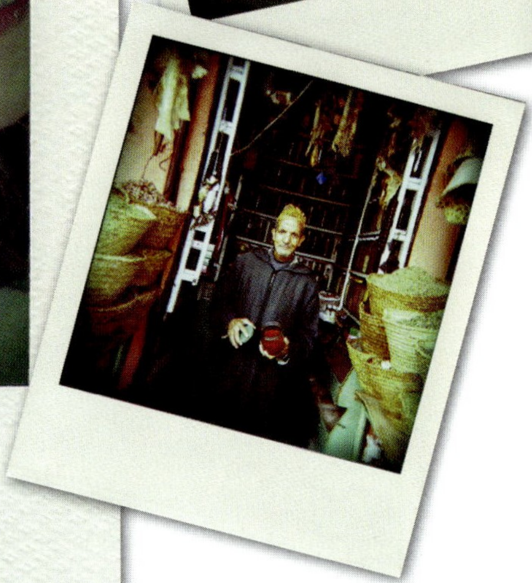

Final Polaroid

Your final image has been given the complete Polaroid experience, with the white cross-hatched border and authentic colouring!

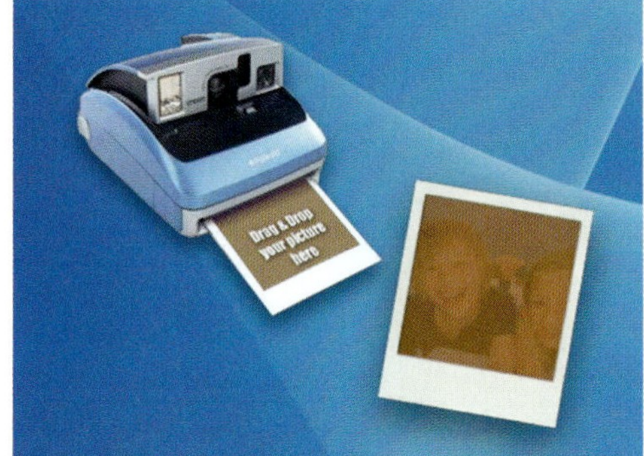

3 First you hear the 'Click, whirrr' of a Polaroid camera, then a small Polaroid print is ejected onto your desktop. What's really clever is that, in true Polaroid fashion, you have to wait for the image on the screen to transpire before you!

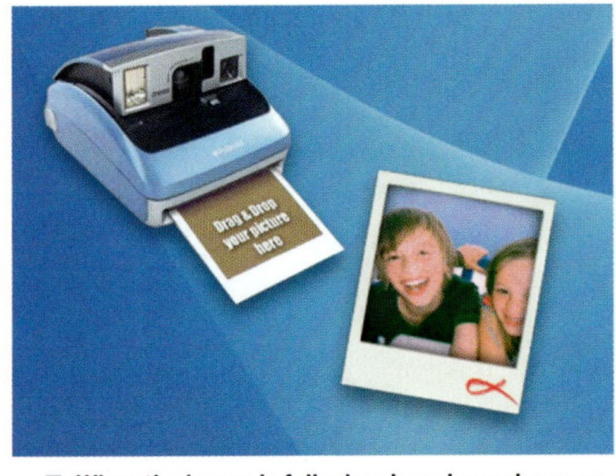

4 When the image is fully developed, a red crayon mark appears on the print to indicate it's ready. A JPEG icon will also appear on your computer desktop with pola.jpg at the end of its name. Double-click this to see your image.

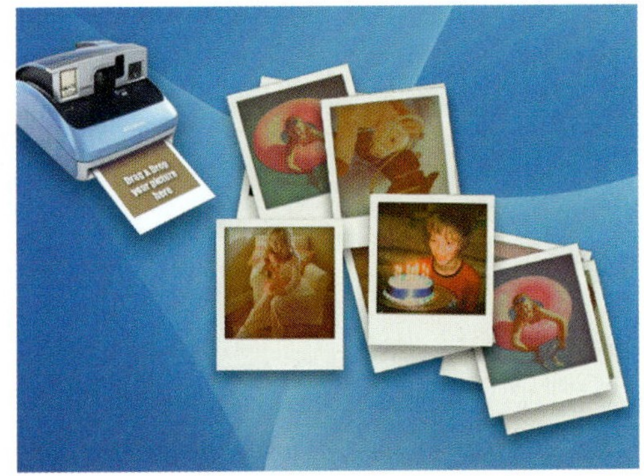

5 You can create up to ten Poladroid images, then you have to quit the software and re-open it. This is because Polaroid film cartridges contain ten shots, so the software is mimicking how you would use a real Polaroid camera!

Black & white in portraits

There are several factors that you need to consider when you shoot images that you plan to convert to monochrome

THE STRENGTH OF a monochromatic picture is determined by its raw components: form, composition and tonal range all have to be at their strongest. As well as geometry, there has to be a good balance of tones throughout the picture so that the eye is not forced to linger on areas that are too black or white heavy and encourage it to move around the whole image. It's amazing how many brilliant colour images fail when they are turned into monochrome and how many images that don't work in colour can come to life as a black & white conversion!

The whole concept of black & white is so different to colour that you have to pre-visualise the scene, and this isn't an easy thing to do. For example, if you have a subject wearing a blue coat and they stand against green foliage, the tones will end up being very similar in black & white due to the limited tonal separation, and thus you'll lose the depth between foreground and background. In a colour image, you can see the depth because of the disparity between the green and blue, but in mono that same image will look flat and two-dimensional. It's the distinction between the relative lightness and darkness of tones that becomes so important in monochrome pictures. You have to think about tonality that much more. There is a monochromatic filter on the market that can help. You put it to your eye and hold it up to a scene and, while it doesn't remove the colour in its entirety, it does reduce it somewhat. It's a definite aid for evaluating a scene's monochromatic potential in terms of tonal range and geometry.

To capture your best black & white pictures, you need to get used to thinking in a colourless world and pick your model and background appropriately. For example, if your location has green foliage you would be better off choosing a model with blonde rather than brown hair. Blonde hair will look that much lighter in monochrome and provide better separation from this sort of background. If you have to work with a specific model, you might think about moving them across to a different background if things don't look tonally distinct, or perhaps change their clothes if background choice is limited.

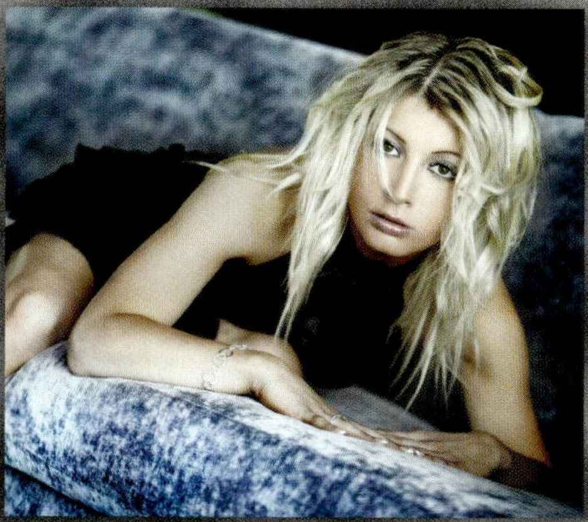

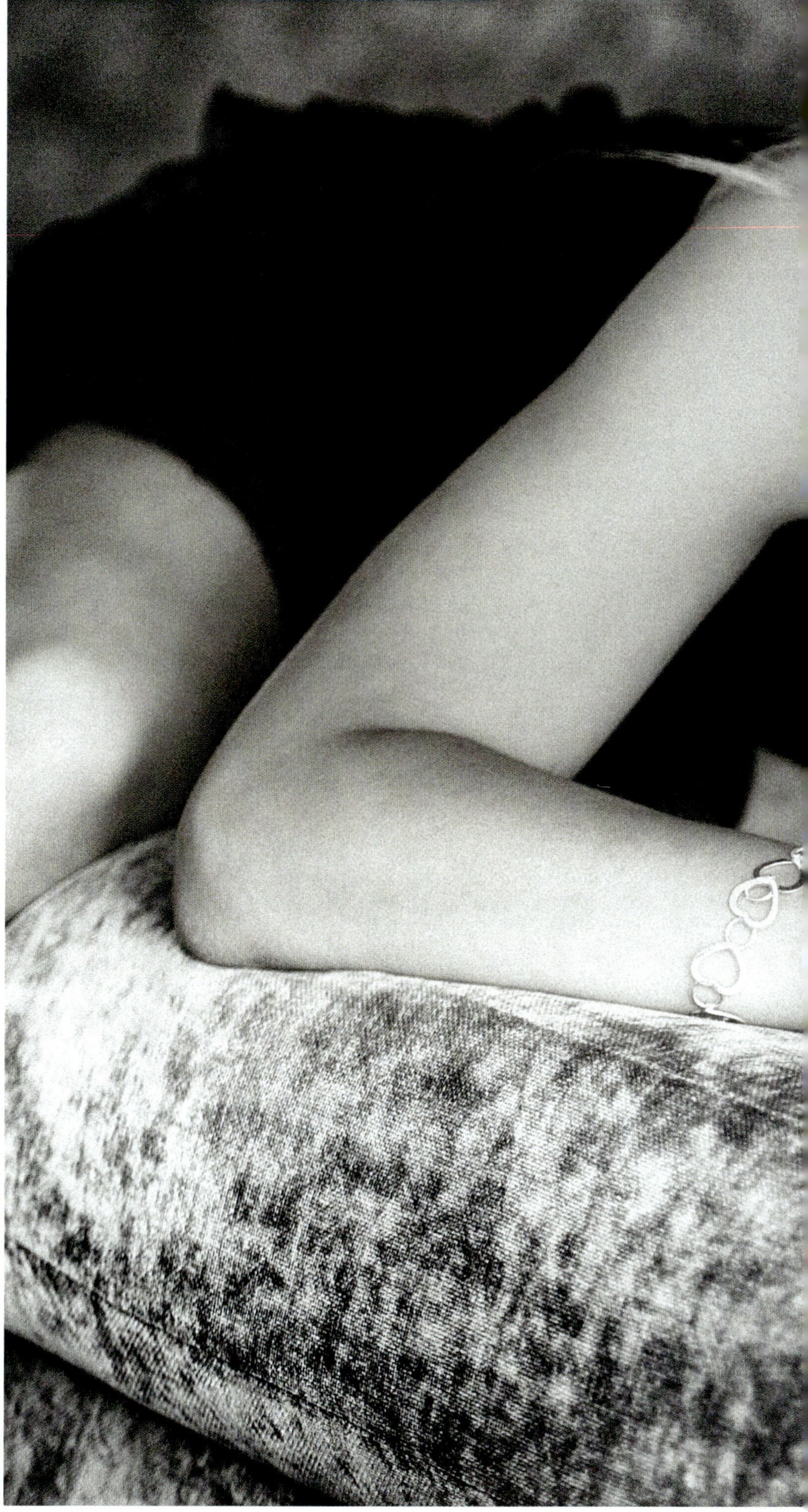

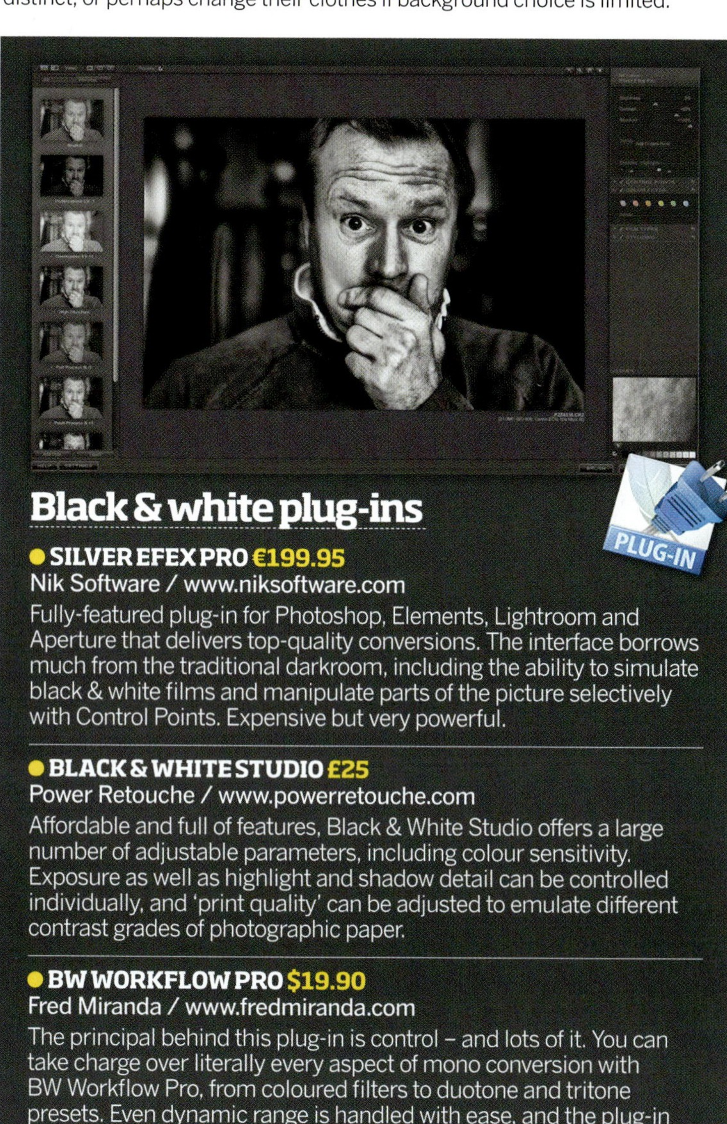

Black & white plug-ins

PLUG-IN

- **SILVER EFEX PRO €199.95**
Nik Software / www.niksoftware.com
Fully-featured plug-in for Photoshop, Elements, Lightroom and Aperture that delivers top-quality conversions. The interface borrows much from the traditional darkroom, including the ability to simulate black & white films and manipulate parts of the picture selectively with Control Points. Expensive but very powerful.

- **BLACK & WHITE STUDIO £25**
Power Retouche / www.powerretouche.com
Affordable and full of features, Black & White Studio offers a large number of adjustable parameters, including colour sensitivity. Exposure as well as highlight and shadow detail can be controlled individually, and 'print quality' can be adjusted to emulate different contrast grades of photographic paper.

- **BW WORKFLOW PRO $19.90**
Fred Miranda / www.fredmiranda.com
The principal behind this plug-in is control – and lots of it. You can take charge over literally every aspect of mono conversion with BW Workflow Pro, from coloured filters to duotone and tritone presets. Even dynamic range is handled with ease, and the plug-in can simulate black & white infrared photography too.

Mono magic
While this colour image is striking, as a black & white, its composition and tonal range has made it even more dynamic and visually pleasing.

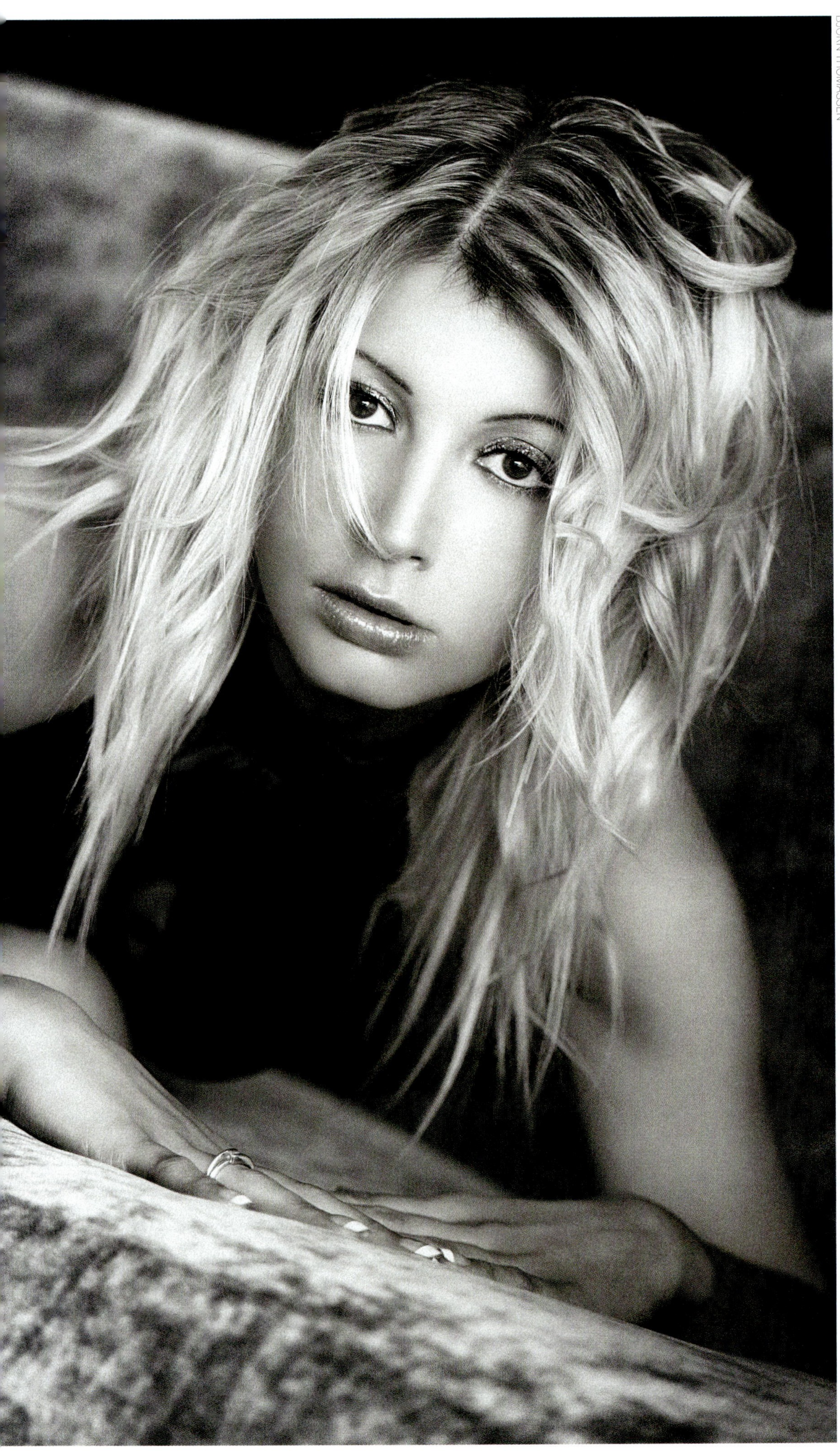

BJORN THOMASSEN

THE TOP TEN WAYS OF CONVERTING TO MONOCHROME

There is more than one way to convert a photograph to black & white. Some are easy, others more involved. Some allow no control at all, others give more than you could ever want. Here are ten Photoshop techniques to get you started – if you know of any more, please do let us know!

1) *Grayscale mode* Switching from RGB to Grayscale mode (***Image>Mode>Grayscale***) dumps all colour information.

2) *Desaturate* In the ***Image>Adjustments*** menu, select Desaturate to drain the colour from your image in one click.

3) *Convert to B&W* The Black & White command, found in the ***Image>Adjustments*** menu is a more controllable way to turn to mono. You can add it as an adjustment layer too.

4) *Channel Mixer* Choose ***Image>Adjustments>Channel Mixer***. Tick the monochrome box and now you can play with colour sensitivities with the red, green and blue sliders.

5) *Just one channel* Looking at just one channel will give you a black & white view. Choose the one that gives the best result from the Channels palette (***Windows>Channels***)

6) *Gradient Map* Often discovered by mistake as it's the next command down from Channel Mixer in the ***Image>Adjustments*** menu, the Gradient Map can be used to send an image to pure black & white

7) *Hue/Saturation* A Hue/Saturation adjustment layer with the saturation slider moved all the way down to the left will remove colour from your image. And it's non-destructive too.

8) *LAB Colour* In LAB colour mode (***Image>Mode>LAB***) choose either A or B from the Channels palette. Both will give you a mono result.

9) *Raw files* The latest version of Adobe Camera Raw works with monochrome images. Click the HSL tab and you'll be presented with colour sensitivity sliders so you can mimic the effect of using coloured optical filters.

10) *Duotone* Not strictly mono, but we wanted to include it here anyway. Duotone images use black, white and an extra colour for a subtle tint. With a Grayscale image choose ***Image>Mode>Duotone*** and experiment or try one of the built-in presets.

Give it a boost with b&w

THIS STEP-BY-STEP will show you how to convert your portraits into mono with ease. With black & white portraiture you can choose to go one of two ways. You can keep an image smooth and simple – an approach that works well for women and children – or you can push for grain, contrast and a much harsher treatment that works well for pictures of men. Here the latter approach is used. The original picture was shot with nothing more than a Canon EOS 350D and a 50mm f/1.8 standard lens. Only natural light was used with the subject, Andy, standing in the shade of a nearby building to shield him from direct sunlight. A large aperture gave provided a shallow depth-of-field that has held his eye in focus, while the rest of his features fall naturally out of focus.

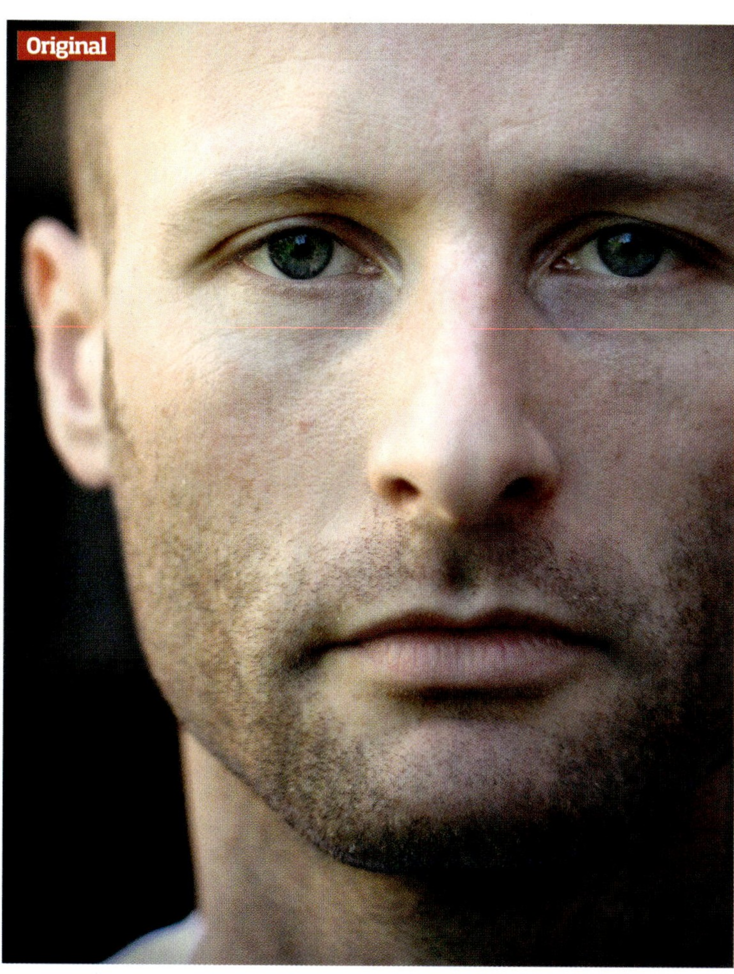

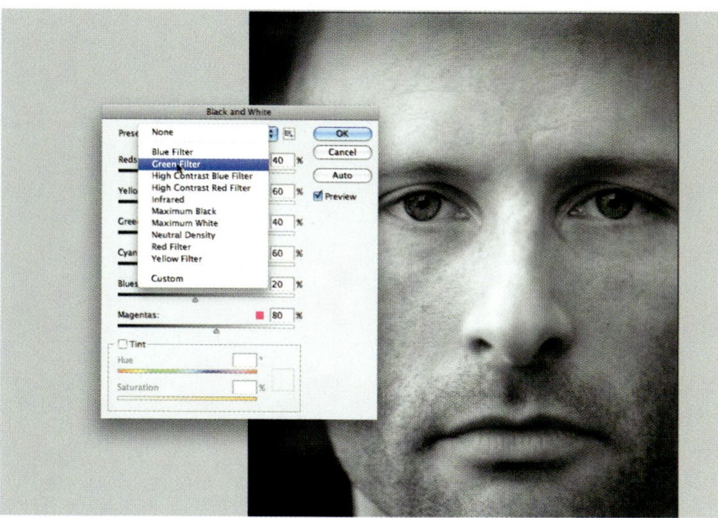

Step 1 The conversion itself is non-destructive as a Black & White adjustment layer (***Layers>New Adjustment Layer>Black & White***) is used, so the original image remains untouched. Here the red tones are darkened a bit, which will emphasise the texture in Andy's skin. If you are trying to de-emphasise texture then do the opposite.

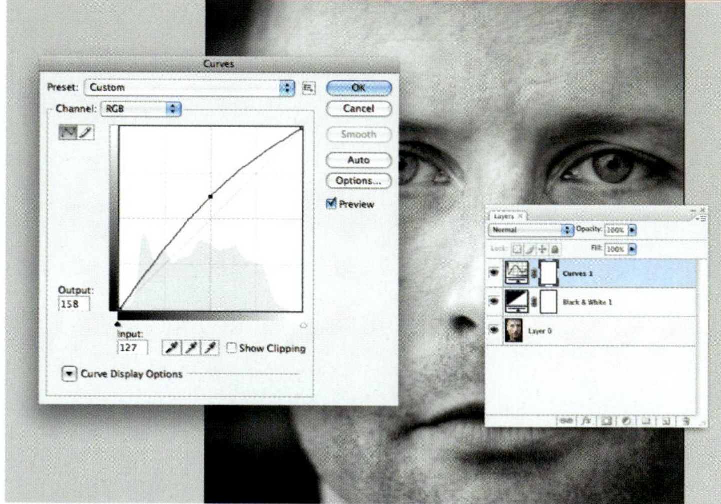

Step 2 Darkening the red tones means the brightness of the whole picture needs to be boosted. We do this using a Curves adjustment layer, though it could easily be done with Levels too. Again this is non-destructive so you can come back and tweak both the Curves and Black & White adjustment layers later to get the right look and feel.

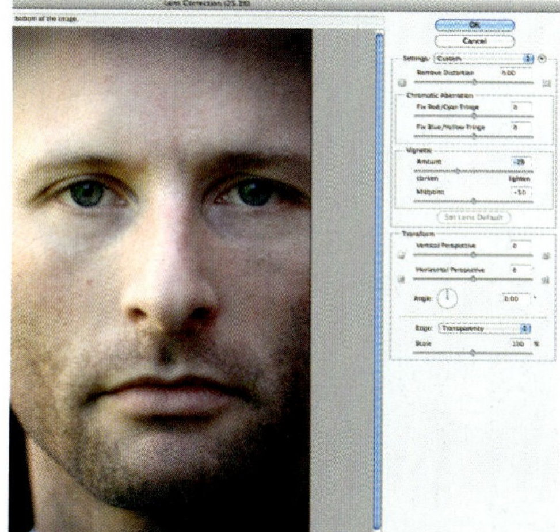

Step 3 To add a bit of light fall-off at the edges of the image and to help focus on the eyes, use the Lens Correction filter (***Filter>Distort>Lens Correction***). Now adjust the Vignette slider to the left to darken the edges of the frame just a little. Click *OK* to confirm the effect.

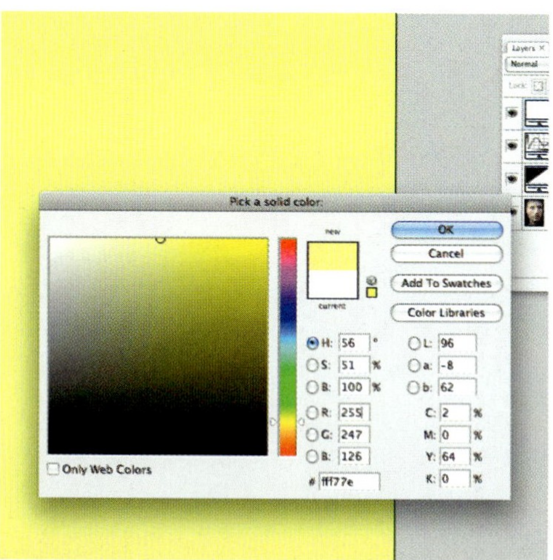

Step 4 Next up is to add a coloured tint – a gentle, warm coloured wash reminiscent of coffee staining. To do this non-destructively too, insert a solid colour layer (***Layer>New Fill Layer>Solid Color***), then choose a colour (light ones work best) and change the blending mode to Color.

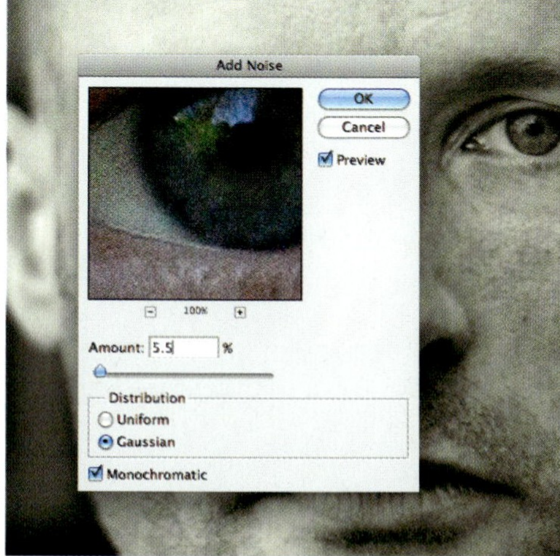

Step 5 We want to add some grain, but it's a good idea to sharpen first, so that you don't sharpen the grain too, which can look awful. Click ***Filters>Sharpen>Smart Sharpen*** to sharpen the image. Grain is added by selecting ***Filters> Noise>Add Noise.*** Set an initial amount of 4%, which should do the trick.

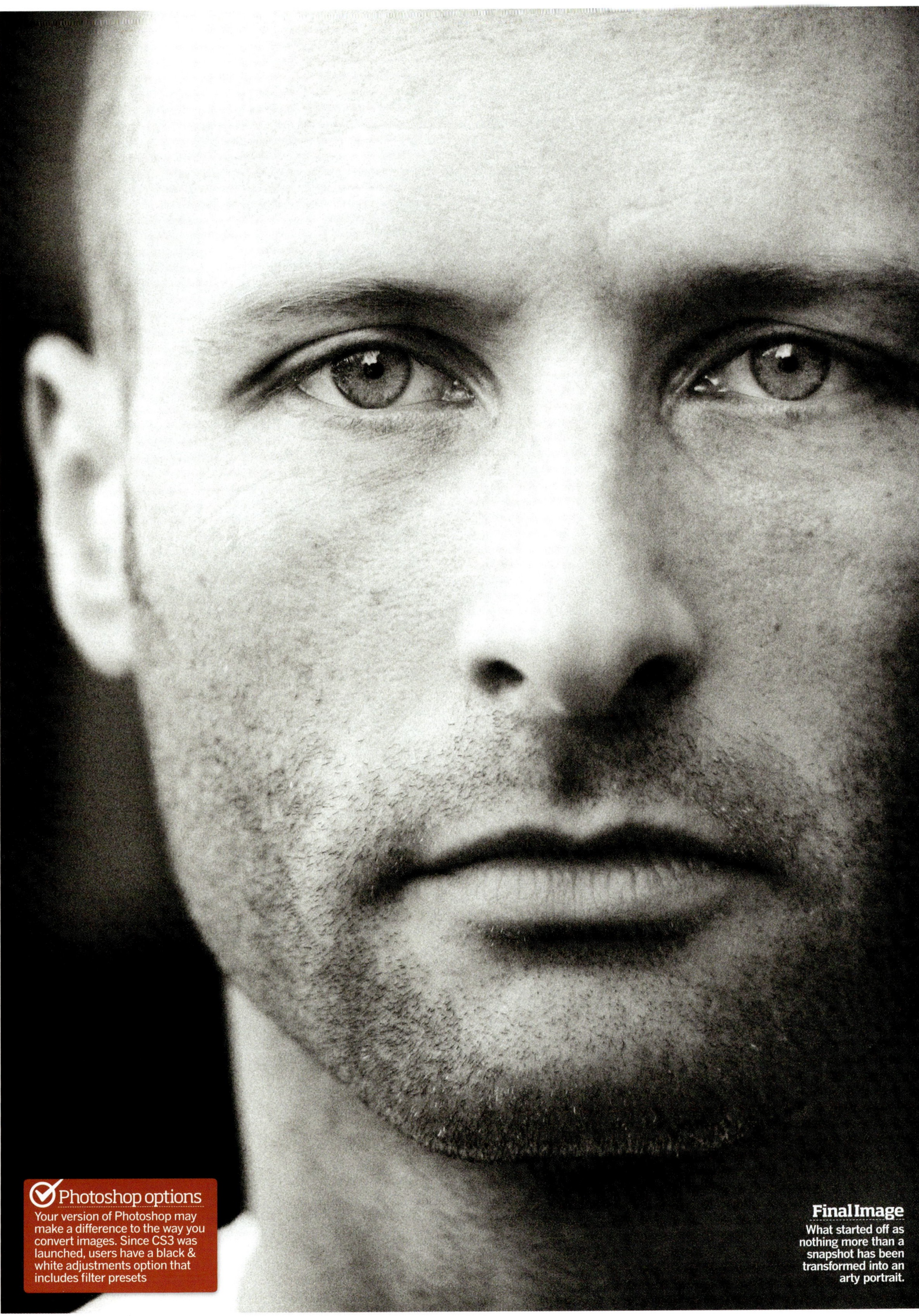

Photoshop options
Your version of Photoshop may make a difference to the way you convert images. Since CS3 was launched, users have a black & white adjustments option that includes filter presets

Final Image
What started off as nothing more than a snapshot has been transformed into an arty portrait.

Add a touch of tone

Bring mood to mono by toning images with a tint of colour. Here are just a few ways of adding colour using Photoshop

ADDING APPROPRIATE TONES to a black & white image can imbue pictures with subtle moods. Photoshop offers many variations in colour and more control over toning than traditional chemical treatments. Adding a monochromatic (single) colour can not only make an image more aesthetically pleasing but alter the feel too. Blue will give an image a cool finish and is ideally suited to wintery scenes, while sepia provides warmth and an effect reminiscent of photos from yesteryear. For more complicated toning, and to combine an extensive colour palette, Photoshop also offers duotone, tritone and quadtone effects that allows a photographer to blend two or more colours.

Method One: **Hue/Saturation**

This is a fairly straightforward way of adding colour. Open the Hue/Saturation dialogue box (**Image>Adjustments>Hue/Saturation**). The quickest way is **Cmd/Cntrl + U**. The first thing to do is tick the Colorize and Preview boxes. Now alter the Hue slider, which creates a range of colours to choose from. You can alter the intensity of the colour by increasing or decreasing the Saturation slider. Leave the Lightness slider alone. You can Colorize a colour photo but the results are not as smooth as converting to Grayscale and back to RGB.

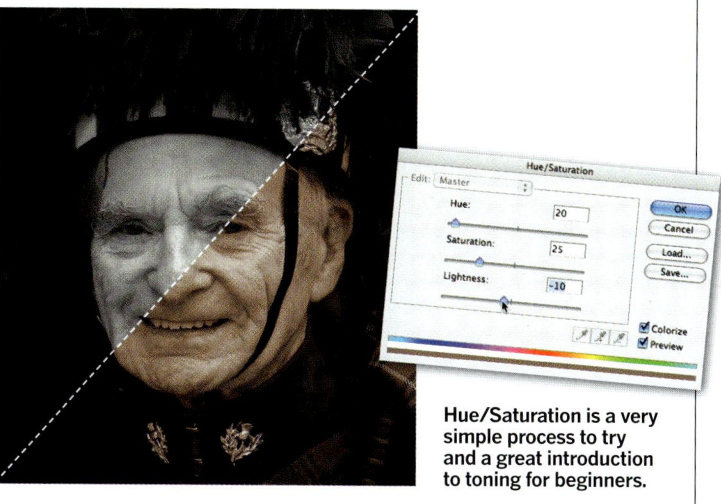

Hue/Saturation is a very simple process to try and a great introduction to toning for beginners.

Method Two: **Photo Filter**

Another easy way to alter the colour is using **Image>Adjustments>Photo Filter**, which is available in Adobe Elements and Photoshop CS. Again convert to grayscale then back to RGB. This is a group of colours that mimic certain camera filters. Choose a colour from the Filter drop-down menu or click the Colour box to bring up the Colour Picker where you can create your very own colour. Tick Preserve Luminosity or the image will go rather flat and lifeless. The Density slider allows you to create a subtle or heavy colour effect.

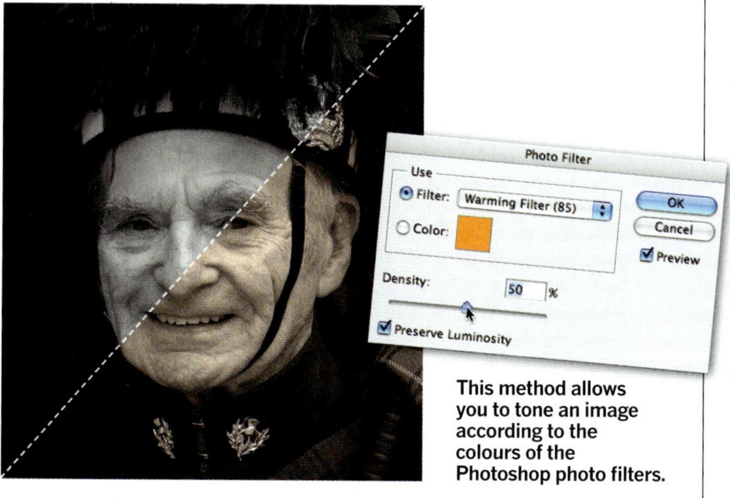

This method allows you to tone an image according to the colours of the Photoshop photo filters.

Method Three: **Duotones**

Traditionally, many monochrome images have been printed reprographically (CMYK) as duotones using two or more colours to 'beef up' the contrast and tonal range. Normally you would choose black for the shadows and one other colour, usually grey, for mid-tones and highlights. But for a more dramatic toning effect, try substituting the grey for a colour or add several colours to the mix.

This toning process gives photographers the option of adding extra colours to their image, making tritone (three colours) or even quadtone (four colours) pictures. Keeping it simple though usually gives the best results. While this is the most involved of the four techniques covered here, it is relatively straightforward and we'd recommend you give it a try to see for yourself how easy it is to create some nice effects.

First of all change the image to Grayscale (**Image>Mode>Grayscale)** followed by **Image>Mode>Duotone**. A dialogue box opens with black as the default Ink 1. Select the Type drop-down menu to select Duo/Tri/Quadtone. Double-click the white box in Ink 2 and the Custom Colors box appears. Choose a general colour by using the colour slider and click a specific colour from the boxes on the left. You can double-click the Curves dialogue box on the right of Ink 1 to alter the contrast and brightness of each colour. This technique works well when printed on inkjet printers, which also use CMYK inks.

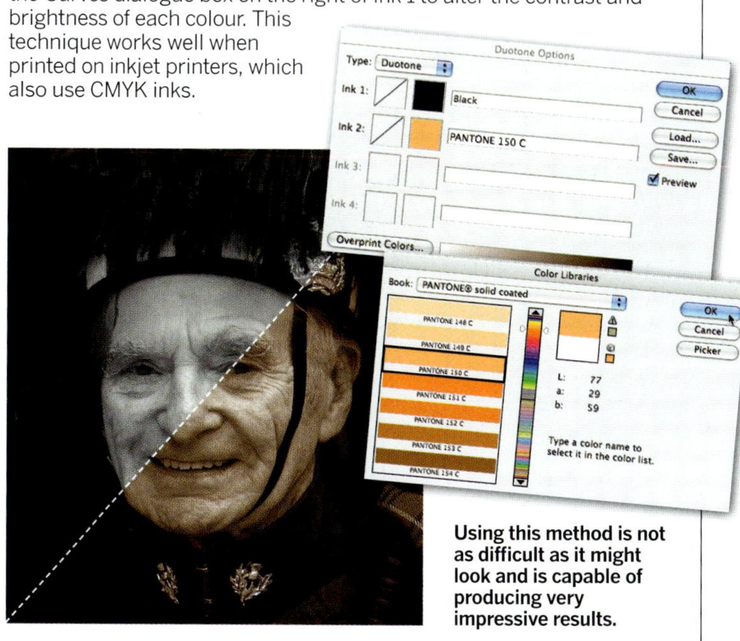

Using this method is not as difficult as it might look and is capable of producing very impressive results.

Method Four: **Gradient Map**

This technique is perhaps a little gimmicky but if you like 1970's psychedelic effects, then you might want to give it a try! Go to **Image>Adjust>Gradient Map** and click on the graduated box (not the arrow) to reveal the dialogue box. Click on a colour and use the sliders to play around with the effect. It gives a dramatic pseudo-solarised effect, which may occasionally be useful. You can explore this tool further by creating your own colour gradients, choose colours similar to duotones for a split-toned effect.

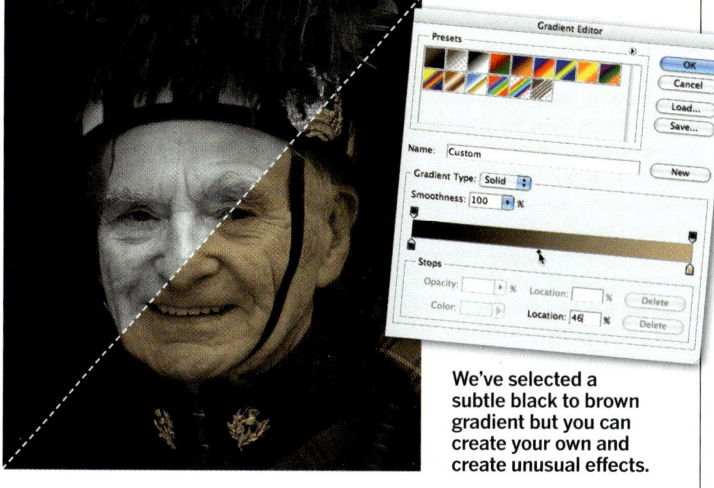

We've selected a subtle black to brown gradient but you can create your own and create unusual effects.

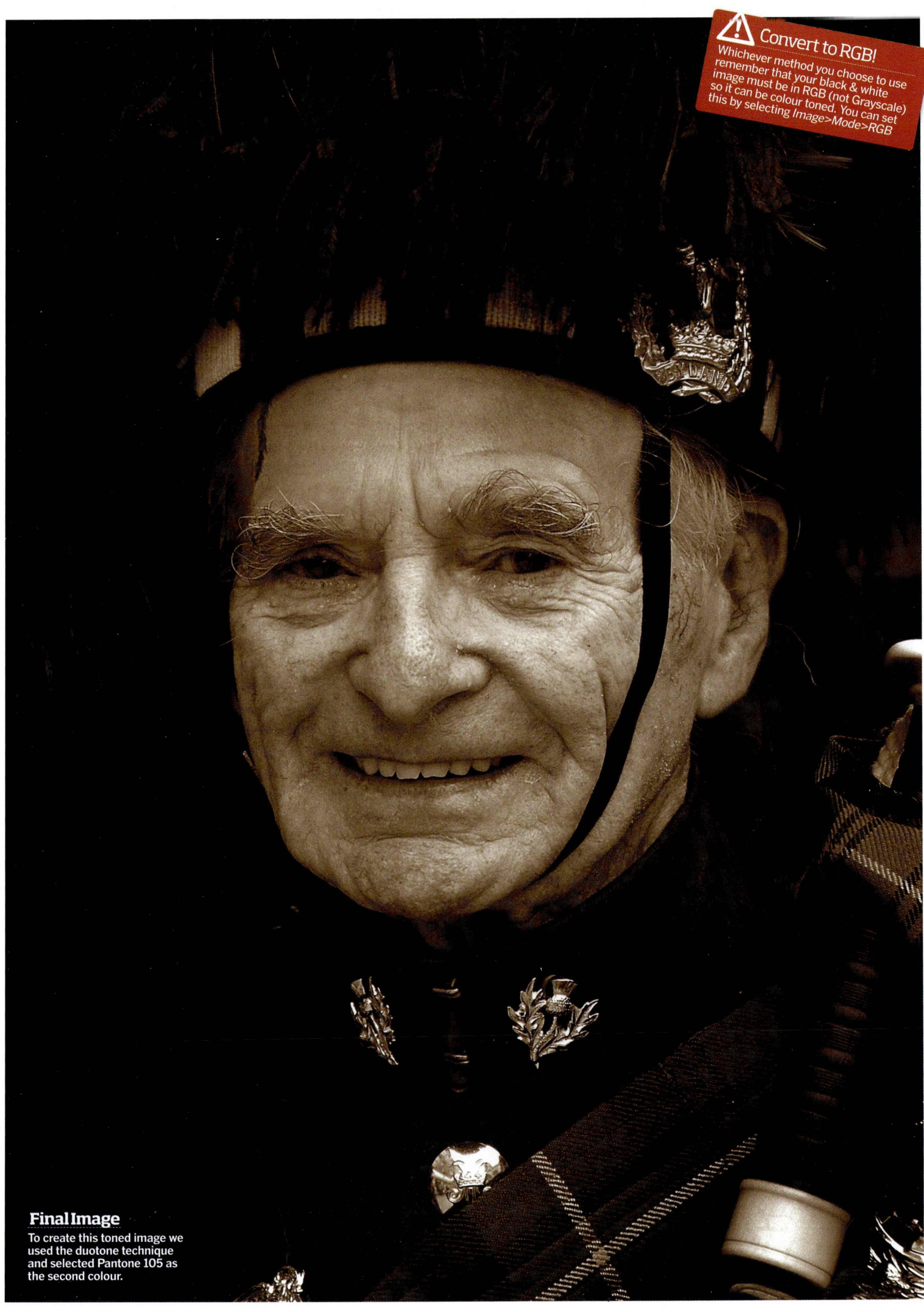

Convert to RGB!

Whichever method you choose to use remember that your black & white image must be in RGB (not Grayscale) so it can be colour toned. You can set this by selecting *Image>Mode>RGB*

Final Image

To create this toned image we used the duotone technique and selected Pantone 105 as the second colour.

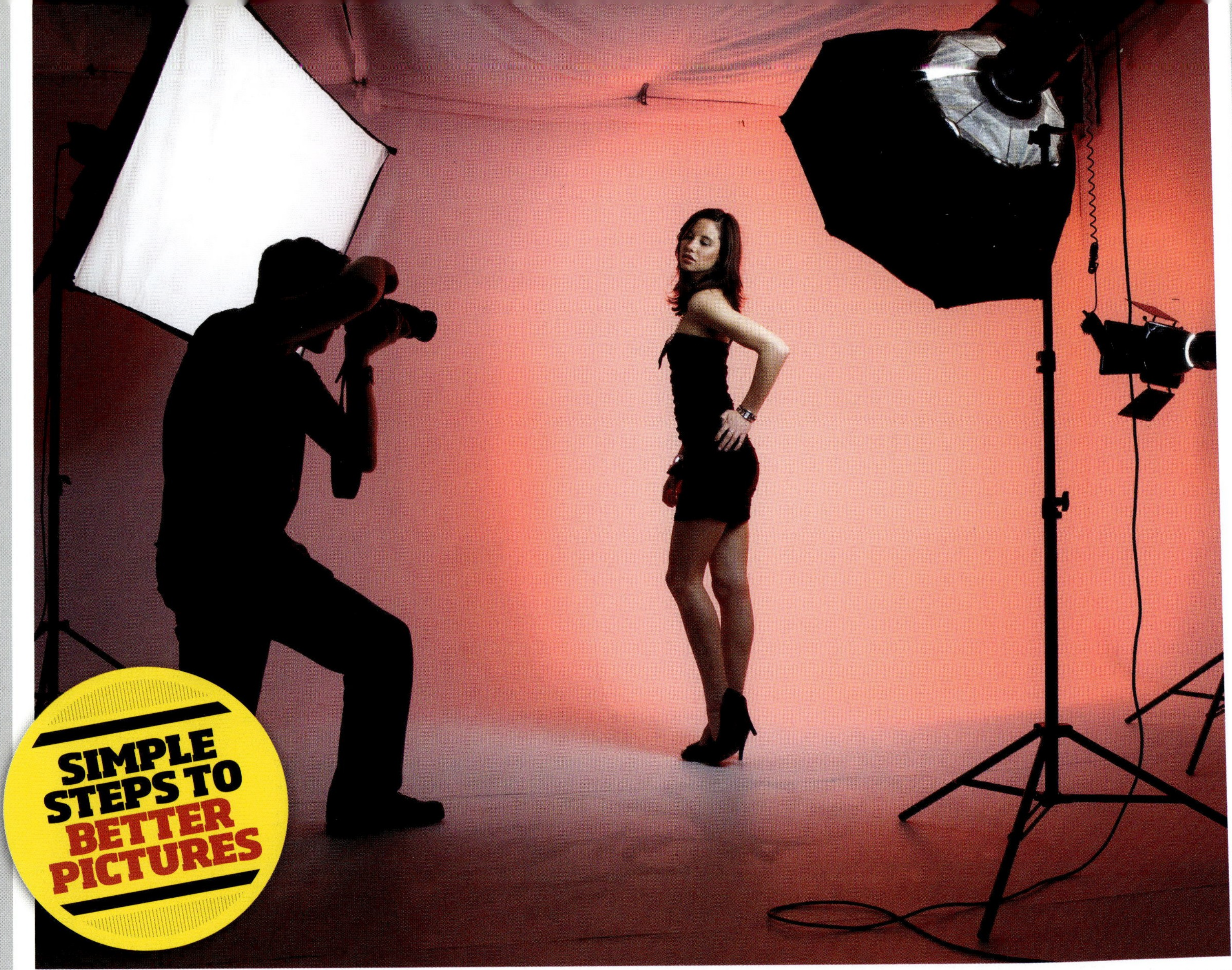

SIMPLE STEPS TO BETTER PICTURES

PORTRAIT GEAR

EXPERT ADVICE TO HELP YOU CHOOSE AND USE THE BEST KIT FOR SHOOTING PORTRAITS

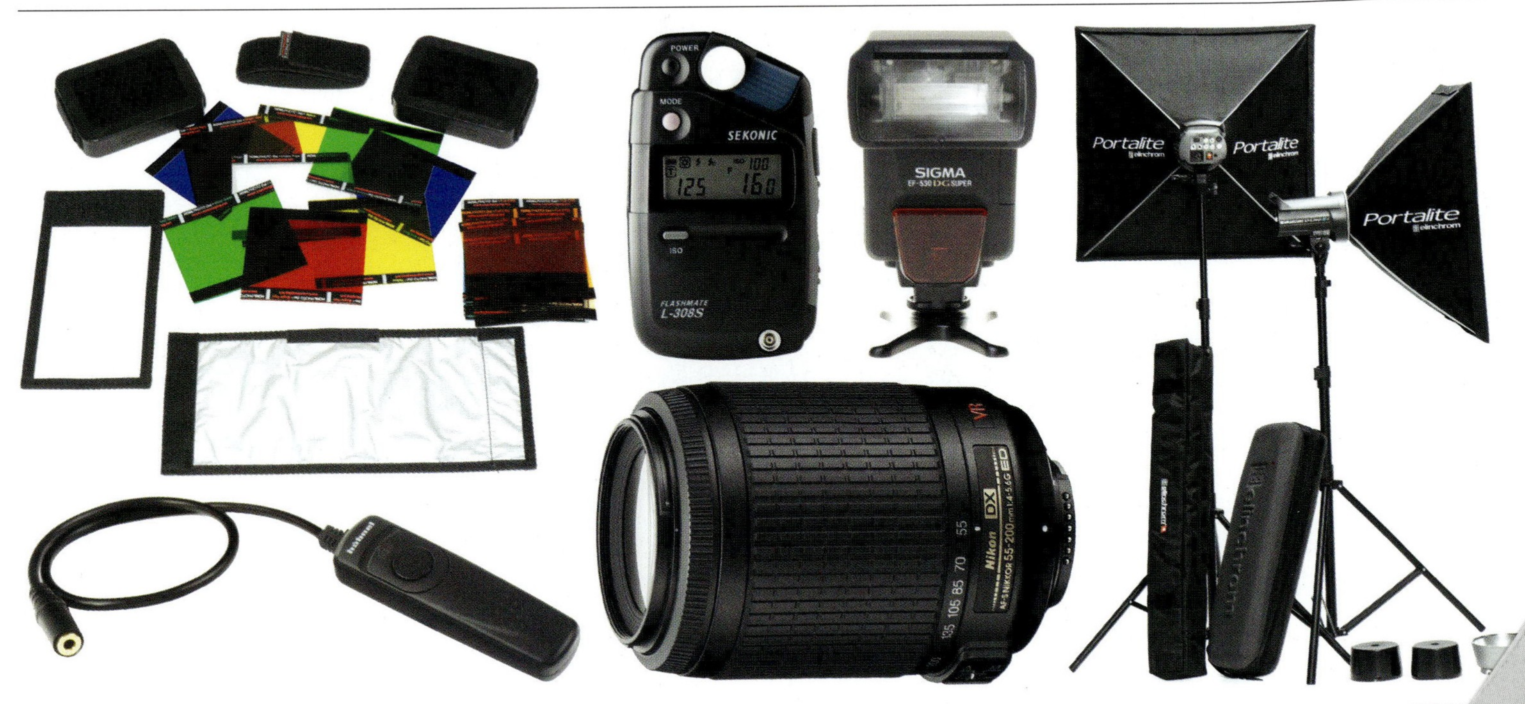

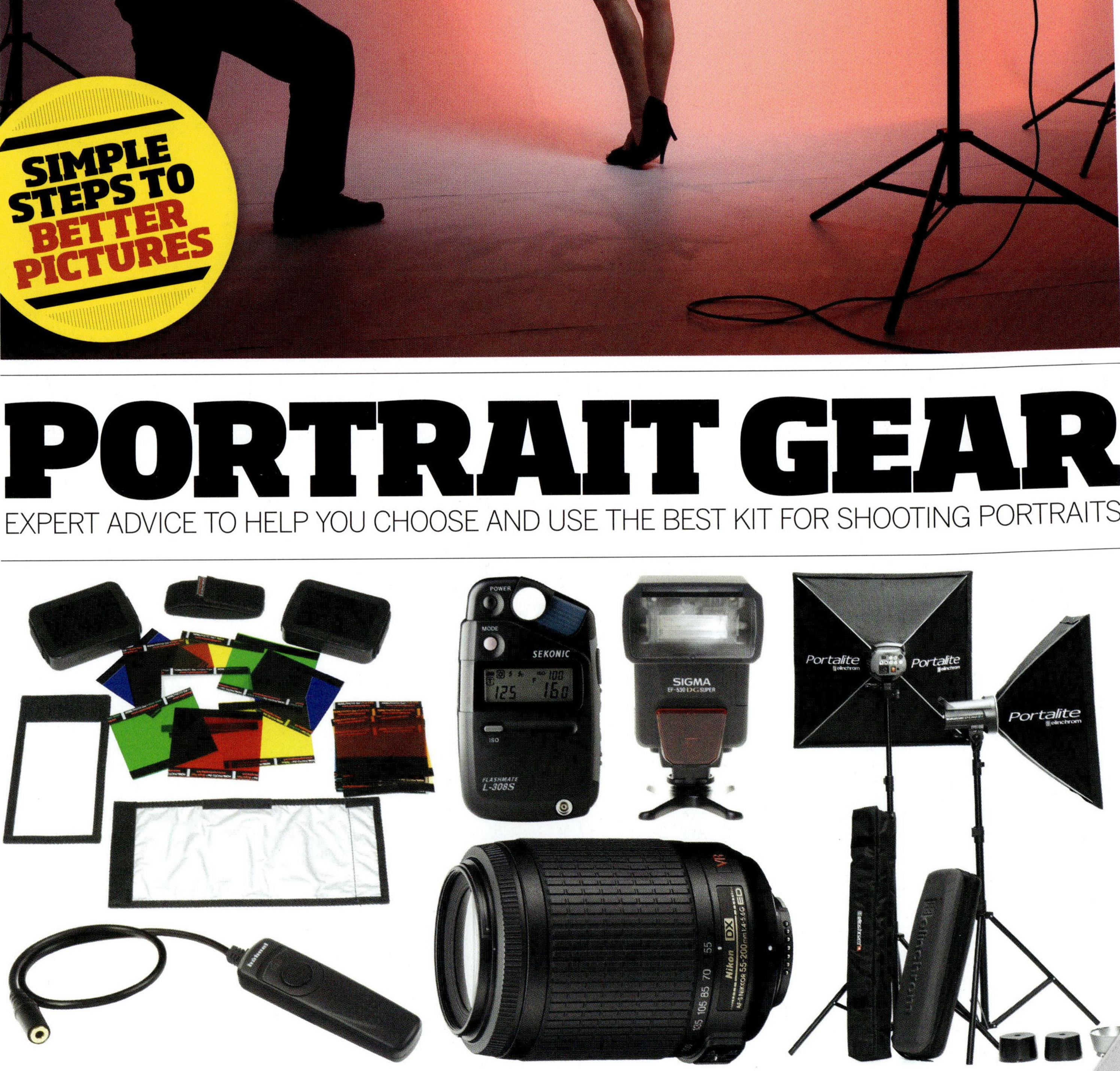

The best lenses for portraits

The standard kit zoom supplied with your DSLR is a good general purpose lens that is suitable for taking portraits, but we'd recommend you consider one of these two types of optics for better quality results

The 'standard' 50mm f/1.8

In the days of 35mm film SLRs, you'd invariably find a 50mm f/1.8 prime lens attached to the front of virtually every SLR. It was the first lens that virtually everyone with an SLR used and remained popular until the late eighties. It was around this time that standard zooms started to appear. With variable focal lengths ranging from wide-angle to short-telephoto, the 28-70mm (and similar) lens represented a step forward in terms of flexibility and sadly it led to the demise of the 50mm as the standard lens of choice. However, its popularity has recently seen a resurgence for a number of reasons.

The first is that it's a very inexpensive lens to get hold of. With 50mm lenses from the likes of Canon, Nikon and Sony costing just over £100 new, and used versions available for a little over half that, they're an affordable choice for most of us. To add further credence to the value-for-money argument, consider this fact. The lens of choice for many portrait pros has long been the 85mm telephoto, which for an f/1.8 version will set you back around £300. If your DSLR uses an APS-C sensor, as most do, a 50mm that costs you £100 equates to a 75mm f/1.8 (or 80mm f/1.8 if you use Canon) – but with an effective saving of around £200!

Also, if you don't mind buying a used manual focus lens, you can pick one up for around £25. So for the price of a decent memory card, you can get a high-quality piece of glass that may be a few decades old and lack AF, but won't leave you wanting in the optical department. So, there's no denying a 50mm lens is affordable, but what else does it offer? Well, the biggest selling point must surely be its maximum aperture of f/1.8. Having a lens with such a fast maximum aperture offers stacks of potential. With your average 18-55mm having a maximum aperture of f/3.5-5.6, the 50mm is two to three stops faster, giving a brighter viewfinder image and allowing you to shoot handheld in low light, while using lower ISO ratings than you would normally get away with.

The main benefit of the wide maximum aperture is the extremely shallow depth-of-field when you shoot wide open, which helps isolate the main subject from its surroundings. This single feature provides significant creative opportunities, especially in the field of portraiture. The 50mm also scores better than virtually any lens in the size and weight department. Weighing around 150 grams and measuring about 5cm in length, it's the perfect optic to keep with you, especially when you're travelling and storage is at a premium.

The final benefit is possibly the most important – image quality. As with the majority of prime lenses, the optical quality from the humble 50mm lens is arguably better than all but the high-end zooms and in terms of sharpness, is far superior to a standard zoom. In terms of sharpness, distortion, light fall-off and contrast and even when used wide open, you'll have little to complain about. So, there you have it, a small, lightweight and highly affordable lens with a super-fast aperture and razor-sharp optics. Is it not time you bought one?

Current AF 50mm f/1.8 lenses

You'll find that brands with full-frame DSLRs in their range have retained 50mm lenses in their line-up. If you're on a budget, avoid the faster f/1.4 and f/1.2 variants aimed at pros, as they're larger and cost far more. The Canon and Nikon lenses have been around for years, so look for mint-condition used lenses!

CANON EF 50mm f/1.8II

Guide Price: £130
Street Price: £110
Dimensions (WxL): 68.2x41mm
Weight: 130g
The MkII lens is virtually identical to the original – both are well worth buying.

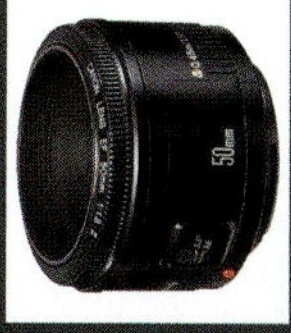

NIKON 50mm f/1.8D

Guide Price: £130
Street Price: £100
Dimensions (WxL): 63x39mm
Weight: 160g
Small, light and very sharp. Look for the 'D' tag to avoid buying an older series lens.

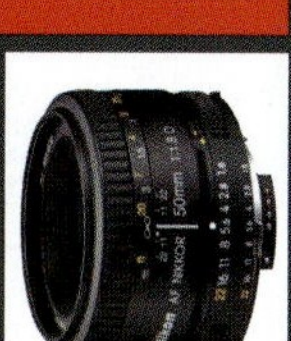

SONY DT 50mm f/1.8 SAM

Guide Price: £160
Street Price: £130
Dimensions (WxL): 70x45mm
Weight: 170g
A great lens but not so easy to find. Remember, Minolta Dynax lenses fit too!

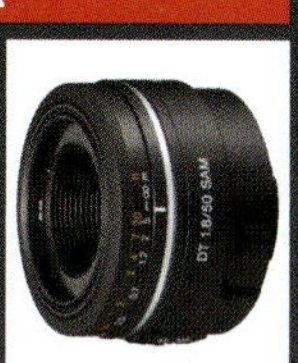

What's the big deal about the 50mm's f/1.8 aperture?

You have to experience a lens as fast as the 50mm to really understand and appreciate its benefits but, trust us, once you've tried you'll be hooked. The 50mm's f/1.8 aperture enables you to throw the background completely out of focus and isolate the main subject from its setting. This set of images shows the changes in depth-of-field at various apertures from f/1.8 to f/22.

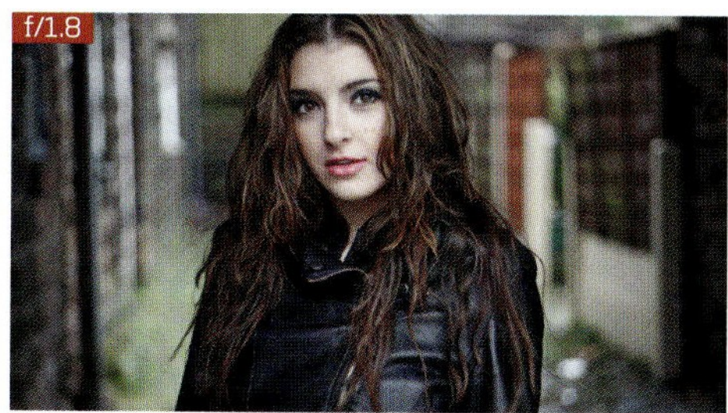
f/1.8

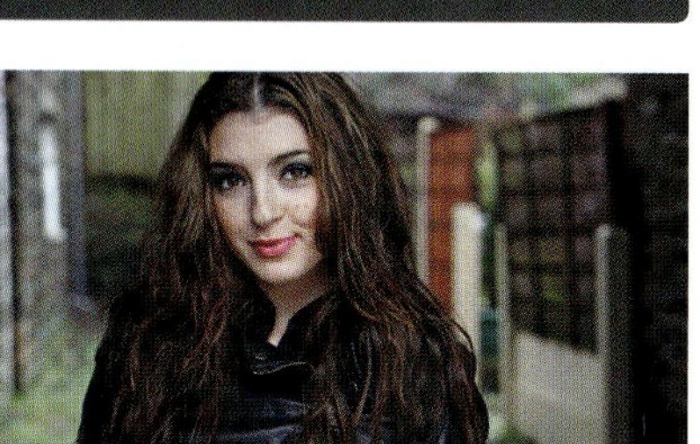
f/3.2

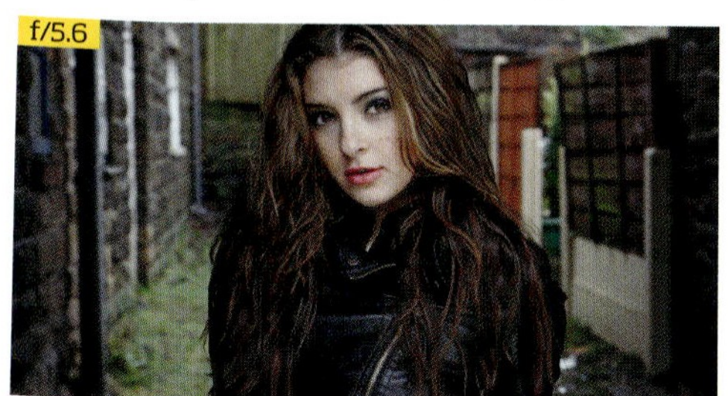
f/5.6

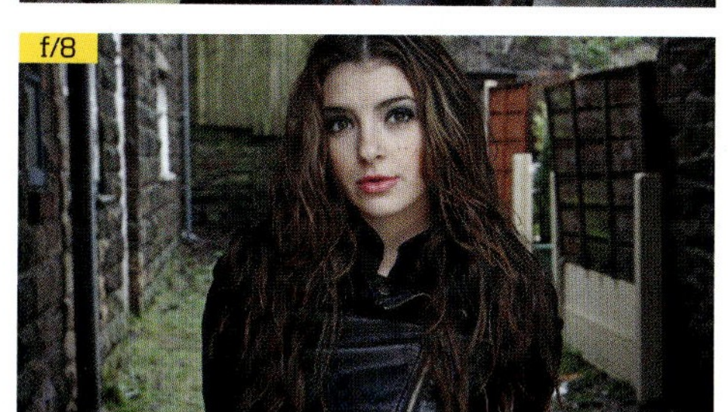
f/8

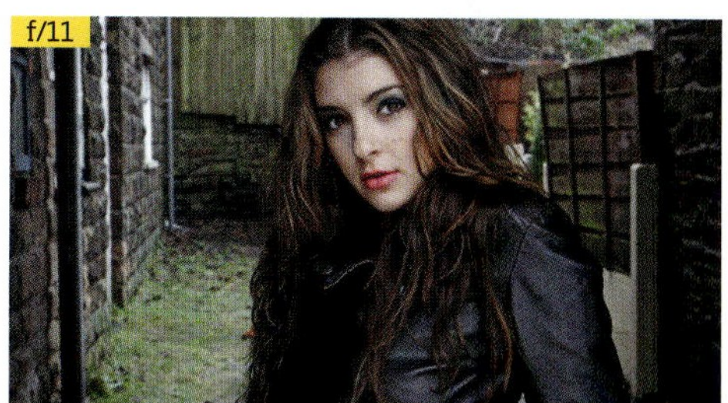
f/11

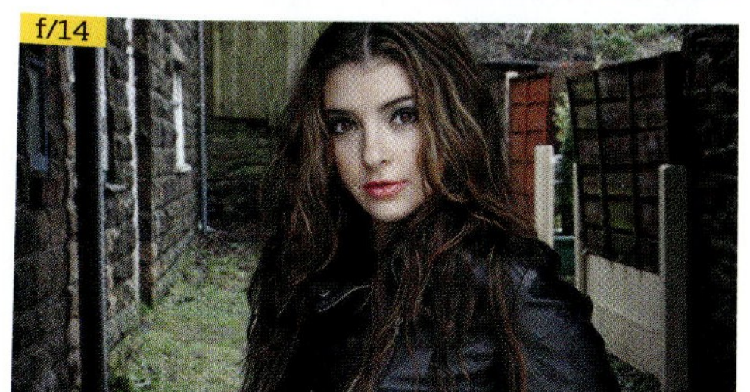
f/14

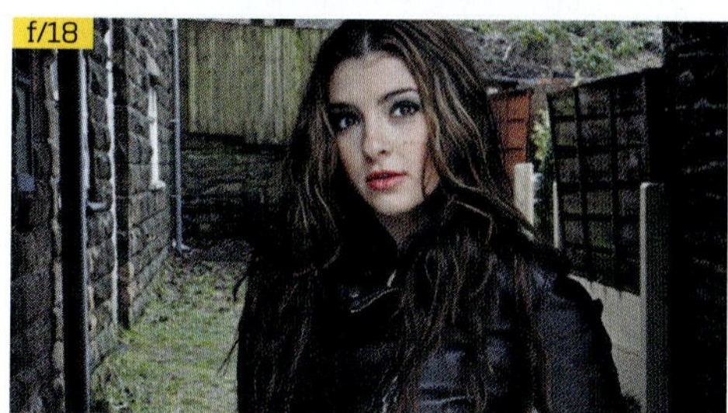
f/18

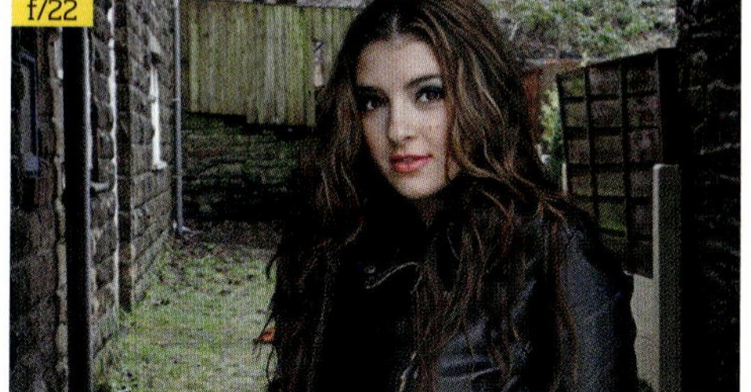
f/22

Telephoto zooms

IN THE LATTER YEARS of the film era, the 70-300mm was the most popular choice of telezoom due to the versatility of its focal lengths. For most digital SLR users, the 55-200mm covers a similar zoom range, thanks to the 1.5x effective increase in focal length associated with the smaller sensor size. That's great news, as a 55-200mm lens is smaller and lighter than a 70-300mm lens and its also far more affordable.

The 55-200mm zoom is suitable for a wide variety of subjects. At its widest end, it's perfect for general portraiture, while zooming to the telephoto end is ideal if your subject is further away or you are shooting candids. There is a wide number of 55-200mm zooms available and all produce a decent performance, although we've featured the Nikon and Tamron zooms as they offer particularly good value for money. Most 55-200mm lenses are budget zooms, offering good enough quality for general purpose photography, but if you're intending to produce large prints, you should look at upgrading to a mid-range zoom with a faster maximum aperture and better optics. We've included Canon's 70-200mm f/4L USM as its one of the best in its class. You may find stores try selling you a 70-300mm, which effectively behaves as a 105-450mm. While a great choice for digital SLRs with a full-frame sensor, we'd not recommend the 70-300mm for use with cameras using the APS-C sensor due to problems associated with the increased focal length, such as camera shake and its restrictive angle-of-view at close range.

Canon EF 70-200mm f/4L USM

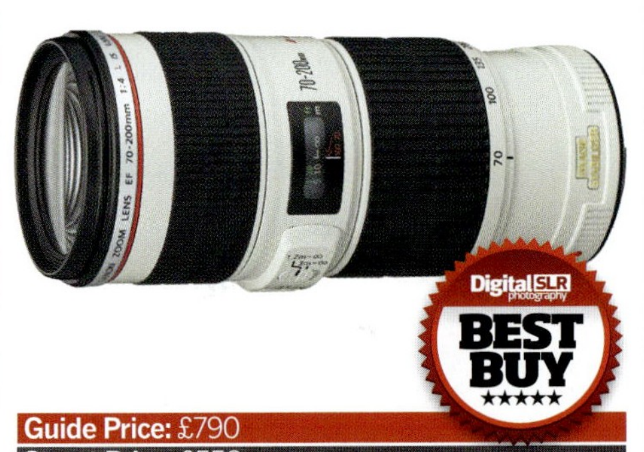

Guide Price: £790
Street Price: £550

www.canon.co.uk

Lens optics: 16 elements in 13 groups
Lens mount: Metal
Maximum aperture: f/4
Minimum aperture: f/32
Minimum focus: 1.2m
Filter thread: 67mm
Weight: 705g
Supplied accessories: None
Dimensions: 76x172mm
Compatibility: All Canon EOS models

Canon has a number of budget zooms and also a couple of pro-spec f/2.8 options. This is one of two mid-range f/4 lenses (the other offers an image stabiliser) and arguably the best value of Canon's four 70-200mm zooms. It boasts an f/4 maximum aperture throughout its range and these faster optics result in it being a longer and heavier zoom than budget alternatives. However, this drawback is soon forgotten once you use it – the autofocus is whisper-quiet and very accurate, while the image quality is far superior to cheaper zooms, with less distortion, far more detail and better contrast. Unless you're a pro requiring the f/2.8 maximum aperture, this lens (or the more expensive IS version) is good enough for all your needs. Well worth checking out.

Verdict

It costs far more than budget zooms but optical quality is far superior and worth the extra.

Handling	★★★★★
Features	★★★★★
Autofocus	★★★★★
Image quality	★★★★★
Value for money	★★★★☆
OVERALL	★★★★★

Nikon AF-S VR DX 55-200mm f/4-5.6G ED

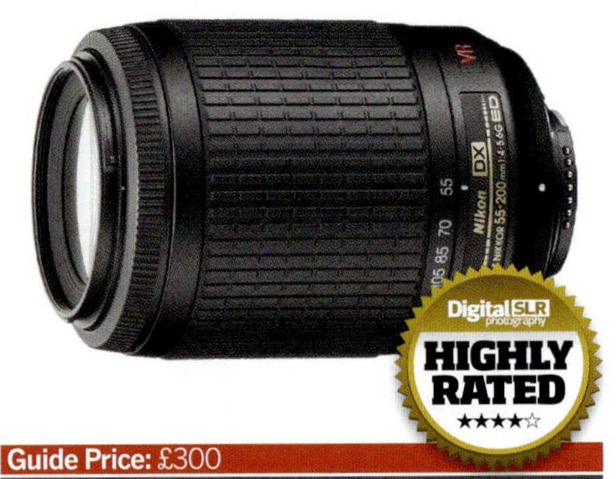

Guide Price: £300
Street Price: £190

www.nikon.co.uk

Lens Optics: 15 elements in 11 groups
Lens mount: Plastic
Maximum aperture: f/4-5.6
Minimum aperture: f/22-32
Minimum focus: 1.1m
Filter thread: 52mm
Weight: 335g
Supplied accessories: Case and hood
Dimensions: 73x99.5mm
Compatibility: APS-C

This version sits alongside the original Nikon DX 55-200mm G ED Nikkor lens but boasts a VR (Vibration Reduction) facility. The result is a slight increase in the size and weight but more importantly improved performance in low light and at the telephoto end due to shake being minimised. The Nikon boasts a very wide zoom ring but the slim manual focus ring at the end of the barrel could do with more width. The autofocus is quick, quiet and responsive even in low light and is one of the better lenses in terms of sharpness. As with other zooms of this type, images at the wide to mid-focal lengths are better than at 200mm. At maximum aperture sharpness is fair, and improves significantly as soon as the lens is stopped down, proving best at f/8-13.

Verdict

A great telezoom thanks to decent all-round performance and the VR facility.

Handling	★★★★☆
Features	★★★★☆
Autofocus	★★★★☆
Image quality	★★★★☆
Value for money	★★★★☆
OVERALL	★★★★☆

Tamron AF 55-200mm f/4-5.6 LD Di II

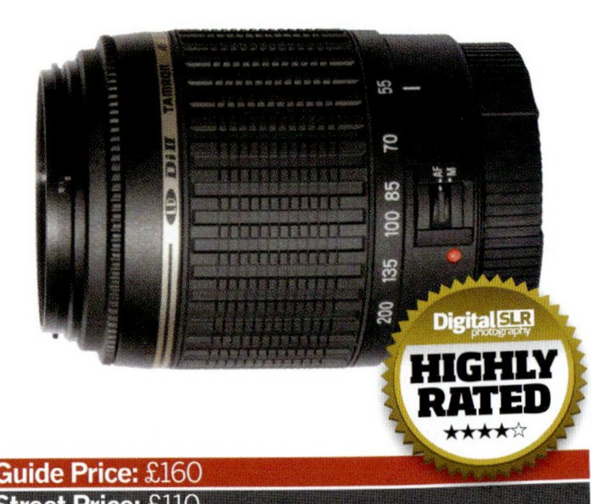

Guide Price: £160
Street Price: £110

www.intro2020.co.uk

Lens Optics: 13 elements in nine groups
Lens mount: Plastic
Maximum aperture: f/4-5.6
Minimum aperture: f/32
Minimum focus: 0.95m
Filter thread: 52mm
Weight: 300g
Supplied accessories: Hood
Dimensions: 71.6x83mm
Compatibility: APS-C

This zoom has proven extremely popular thanks to a combination of low price, decent build quality and good all-round performance. The wide zoom ring is very easy to grip and has a nice action, but as with the Nikon, the manual focusing ring is thin and not the easiest to use. The autofocus turns in a good performance – it's not the quickest or quietest but it is accurate and performs better than expected in low light. As with most 55-200mm zooms, it performs best at the shorter end but quality through the range is good, especially once the aperture is stopped down, with f/8-11 giving the sharpest results. Please note this lens is designed for use with APS-C sensors only and isn't compatible with larger sensor sizes. It is available in Canon, Nikon and Sony fittings.

Verdict

A budget zoom lens that turns in a better performance than you expect for the price.

Handling	★★★★☆
Features	★★★★☆
Autofocus	★★★½☆
Image quality	★★★★☆
Value for money	★★★★½
OVERALL	★★★★☆

Studioflash for enthusiasts

If you're serious about studioflash, you need a kit to match your passion. A more advanced set of lights will meet your needs for extra features, power and performance, giving you the tools to get better results. These three outfits from leading brands offer excellent value, a great range of features and first-class performance

Elinchrom D-Lite 4 IT Studio 2 Go kit

Guide Price: £669
Street Price: £559*
www.theflashcentre.com
Sophisticated budget studioflash

Elinchrom are one of the top brands in studioflash and have long been recognised for delivering high quality, reliable products. However, in the past, the prices of the Swiss firm's outfits meant they were usually reserved for enthusiasts and professionals. That changed with the launch of its D-Lite system in 2006, a budget kit that brought the quality of Elinchrom to the masses. It has proved to be a best-seller and four years on, Elinchrom hope its updated outfits enjoy similar success.

These new models aren't just a simple redesign and the odd feature addition either, they offer real improvements over the original set, which itself was excellent. The 'IT' in the name stands for Intelligent Triggering and hints at the biggest changes to the heads. The inclusion of an intelligent, programmable slave cell enables it to synchronise with 'strobist' Speedlite systems (in other words the heads won't fire due a flashgun's pre-flash). Also, and in our view more importantly, there's a built-in Skyport receiver. This allows the heads to be triggered wirelessly, (in other words without the need of a sync lead) using a hotshoe-mounted Skyport Eco transmitter, which is supplied as part of the kit. The Skyport system is a radio trigger with four frequencies (just on the off-chance someone nearby has one, you can set a different frequency so you don't keep setting each other's lights off! It allows for fast flash syncs up to 1/250sec, as well as a standard setting of 1/160sec).

The heads are available in 200 and 400-Watt versions (D-Lite 2 IT & D-Lite 4 IT respectively) and if possible, we recommend you buy the 400-Watt heads as the extra power is very useful.

Elinchrom has taken on board comments from users of its original D-Lite system and have improved its design and construction, with a more robust handle, which houses a spare fuse, and an improved stand fitting that is significantly stronger than its predecessor.

The heads feature a cooling fan that switches on when the internal temperature becomes too high, and has a visual safety indicator should the fan be blocked or stop working.

With beginners in mind, it's no surprise to find it's a very easy set of lights to use. Fitting accessories via Elinchrom's tried-and-tested bayonet mount is fast and easy. Should you wish to add to the generous options supplied with the kit, you'll find there is an extensive number of suitable attachments available.

The D-Lite IT's control panel couldn't be easier to use. An LED shows the current power setting with two large buttons beneath allowing it to be increased or decreased. Other controls allow you to set the modelling light to be on at minimum or full power, off, or proportional to the power setting, which is set in 1/10th increments. There is also a button to switch the audible ready 'beep' on or off. Setting up the D-Lite IT was simple and straightforward to do, taking only a few minutes (preparing the softboxes took the most time). In use, the D-Lite 4 IT worked effortlessly and the Skyport wireless trigger performed perfectly. Recharge times are fast at around one second and the 1/10-stop power adjustments are more than suitable for general studio work.

The D-Lite 4 IT kit has everything you need to get started in studioflash photography and the supplied cases ensure you can easily pack away and protect the kit for storage or for transport from one place to another.

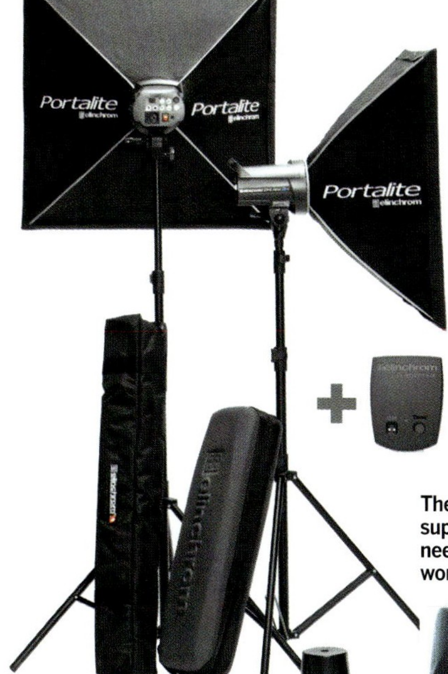

Shot using the D-Lite 4 IT kit

Digital SLR photography BEST BUY ★★★★★

The Elinchrom D-Lite IT kits come supplied with everything an enthusiast needs to take their first steps into the world of studio photography.

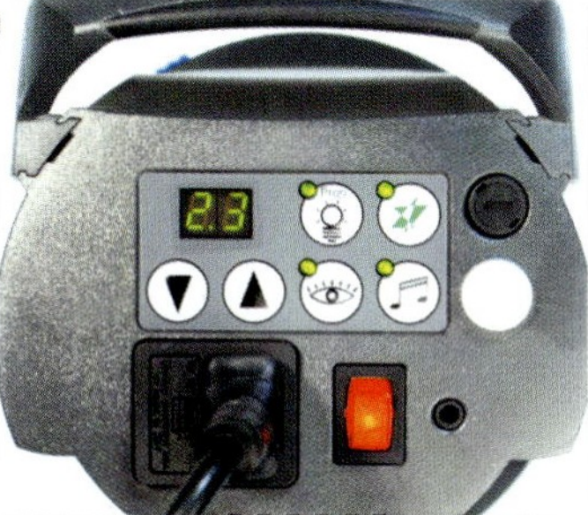

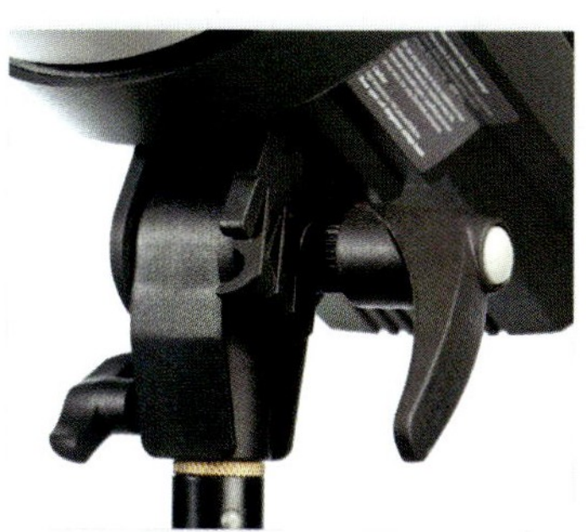

Elinchrom D-Lite kits *

ELINCHROM D-LITE IT 4 STUDIO TO GO TWO HEAD KIT £580
2x D-Lite 4 IT heads;
2x Portalite 66cm softboxes;
1x 16cm reflector;
2x ClipLock stands;
1x Skyport Eco transmitter;
carry cases and cables

ELINCHROM D-LITE IT 2 STUDIO TO GO TWO HEAD KIT £510
2x D-Lite 2 IT heads;
2x Portalite 66cm softboxes;
1x 16cm reflector;
2x ClipLock stands;
1x Skyport Eco transmitter;
carry cases and cables

ELINCHROM D-LITE IT 2/4 TWO HEAD UMBRELLA KIT £475
1x D-Lite 2 IT head;
1x D-Lite 4 IT head;
1x silver umbrella;
1x translucent umbrella; 2x 16cm reflectors; 2x ClipLock stands;
1x Skyport Eco transmitter;
carry cases and cables

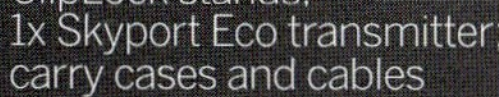

**All quoted prices are taken from www.theflashcentre.com*

Verdict

The Elinchrom D-Lite 4 IT outfit offers a level of reliability, range of features, performance and access to lighting attachments that is hard to match. Whichever outfit you decide to go for, it comes highly recommended.

Build	★★★★½
Features	★★★★★
Performance	★★★★½
Value for Money	★★★★★
OVERALL	**★★★★★**

Elinchrom BXRi 500/500 twin-head kit

Guide Price: £1,028
Street Price: £950
www.theflashcentre.com
Compact studioflash outfit

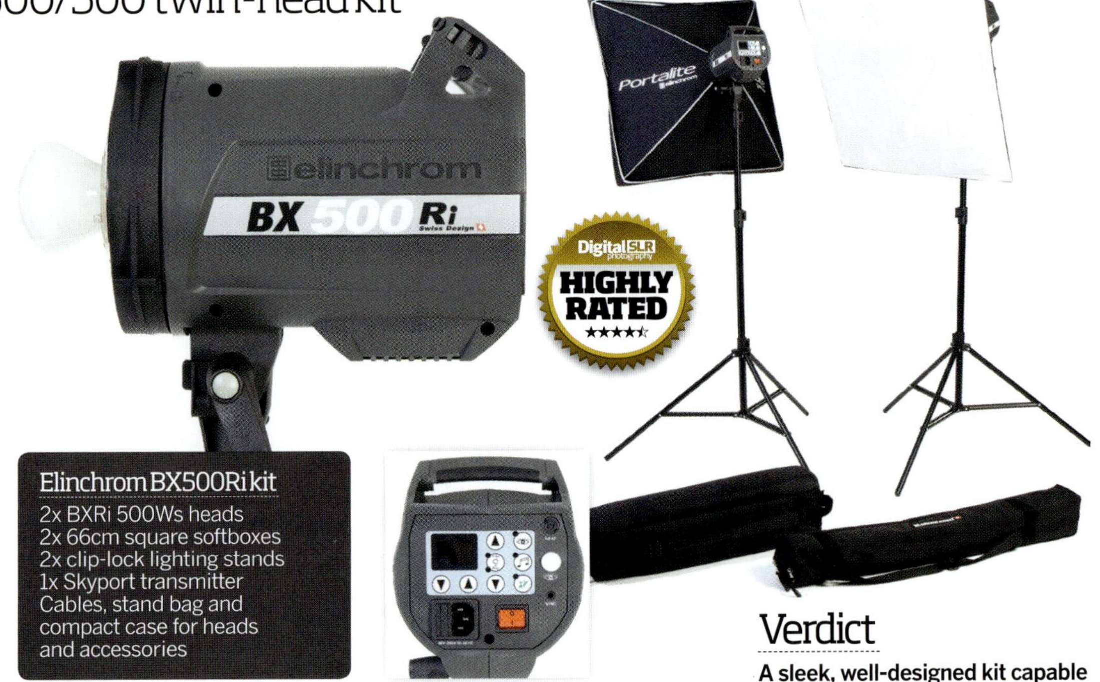

Elinchrom BX500Ri kit
2x BXRi 500Ws heads
2x 66cm square softboxes
2x clip-lock lighting stands
1x Skyport transmitter
Cables, stand bag and compact case for heads and accessories

This recent addition to the Elinchrom range combines some of the winning features of its D-Lite budget outfits, with the benefits of the BX range, resulting in a simple but powerful lighting system. The lights come in a choice of 250-Watt and 500-Watt heads, but with a difference in price of just £115 between the twin 250-Watt kit and the twin 500-Watt kit, it's worth opting for the more powerful option.

The lights have a full digital back panel that includes the power display – a five-stop range from 1/16 to full-power – modelling lamp controls, and various flash settings from audible recharge confirmation to pre-flash detection. Multiple button presses can also be used to program additional functions from Intelligent Photo-cell learning mode to EL Skyport controls using the radio trigger system included in the kit. The modelling light can be controlled independently of the flash power, as well as proportionately, via its own set of power buttons.

Like the budget D-Lite kit, the BXRi500 outfit is very compact, and comes in a stylish carry case that looks too small for a full lighting set, and a second small stand bag, making the kit very portable. Even when in use, the kit takes up very little room. The heads themselves are stubby and the supplied softboxes are relatively small in size too. The smaller softboxes, however, create a more high-contrast image and require a greater distance for full-length shots. Results are slightly on the warm side but still very good, and the lights kick out more power than Interfit's Stellar 600. Thanks to the short flash duration, they're also good for freezing motion. The BXRi range competes with the Bowens Gemini, with just £57 between it and the standard Gemini 500R kit.

Verdict

A sleek, well-designed kit capable of delivering a huge amount of power and very advanced control.

Build	★★★★★
Features	★★★★☆
Performance	★★★★★
Value for Money	★★★★☆

OVERALL ★★★★☆

Bowens Gemini 500/500R twin-head kit

Guide Price: £980
Street Price: £900
www.bowens.co.uk
High-quality studioflash system

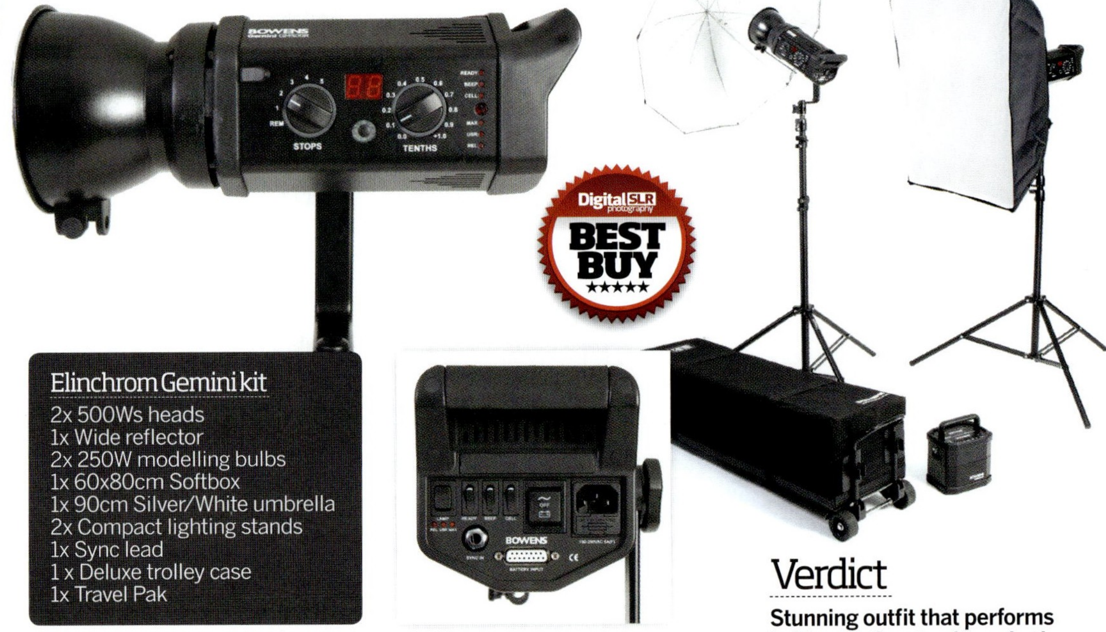

Elinchrom Gemini kit
2x 500Ws heads
1x Wide reflector
2x 250W modelling bulbs
1x 60x80cm Softbox
1x 90cm Silver/White umbrella
2x Compact lighting stands
1x Sync lead
1 x Deluxe trolley case
1x Travel Pak

These are the latest in the Gemini range, and a revamp will see the new Gemini R replacing the Esprit, Esprit DX, Esprit Gemini digital, and Esprit 750 Pro. Bowens' claim that this is 'the world's most advanced monolight' is certainly a bold one, so has it got what it takes? So far there are only 250-Watt and 500-Watt versions but they are both mains and Travel Pak compatible, and feature a twin dial control and a digital display, which shows power information as well as other info from the user set-up mode. These modes include pre-exposure flashes, soft start and lamp-saver options for the modelling bulb, allowing it to dim when left inactive for a set amount of time. The kit includes more sturdy stands than the Gemini 400 kit, and a 60x80cm softbox in addition to a spill kill and silver/white umbrella. An optional remote (RC3) controls functions, and the optional radio trigger is compatible with Pulsar, Litelink and Pocket Wizard devices.

On the side of the head, one dial controls the power in stops, while the second in tenths of stops. On the back panel are the model lamp controls, cell and ready functions, battery and power inputs. Flash duration is a slower 1/900sec on this model but this is plenty for portrait photography. This kit is also available with the Travel Pak for outdoor use for an extra £300, (more than worth it for the serious snapper). The whole kit fits into a large reinforced case, on a trolley for easy transport. This kit just oozes quality and professionalism. The results are very natural – slightly warmer than the 400s but not as warm as the Elinchrom BXRi's – and benefit not only from the extra power, but also from the softbox. If you can afford to, opt for the Travel Pak version for added versatility.

Verdict

Stunning outfit that performs brilliantly. Great value, whether or not you choose the Travel Pak.

Build	★★★★★
Features	★★★★★
Performance	★★★★★
Value for Money	★★★★☆

OVERALL  ★★★★★

Reflectors and diffusers

Reflectors and diffusers provide an inexpensive and versatile means of controlling daylight and studioflash. There is a wide variety available from small handhelds to huge panels measuring metres across. Here we highlight a few of our favourites

Useful contacts

- **California Sunbounce** www.theflashcentre.com
- **Calumet** www.calumetphoto.co.uk
- **Elemental** www.studio-flash.com
- **Interfit** www.interfitphotographic.com
- **Lastolite** www.lastolite.com

Collapsible reflectors

These are the most affordable types of reflector and are suitable for a variety of uses in all forms of lighting. They're available in many sizes. from 30cm to over a metre in diameter, but we'd recommend 80cm or 107cm as a good size to start with. They're available in various colour finishes but begin with the silver and white version as these will be the two most useful colours, proving suitable to use in most lighting conditions, giving a clean, neutral effect. The gold and sunfire options add warmth to skin tones but can be overpowering so take care. Most collapsible reflectors are round but there are rectangular versions too. Lastolite is the market leader and offers an extensive range, so check out their website.

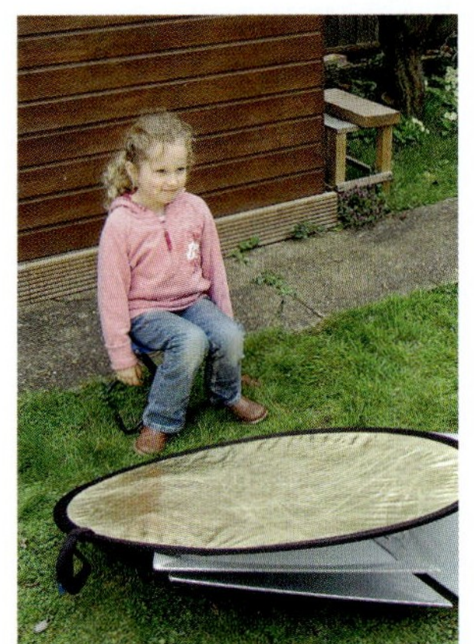

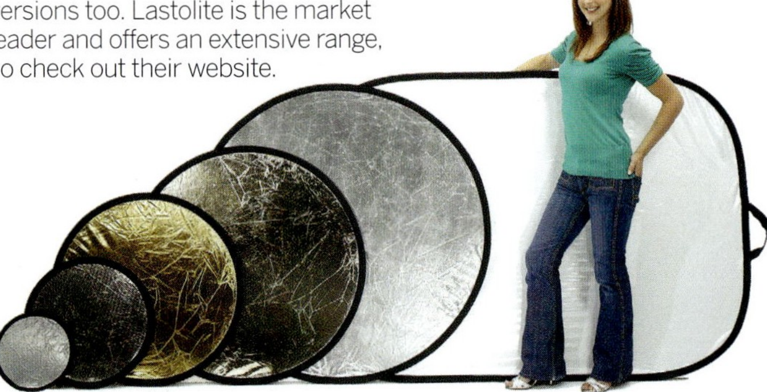

5-in-1 kits

These are the best option as a first lighting aid as they offer lots of versatility at a low price, making them excellent value. The kit comes in its own bag, which holds a collapsible translucent reflector and a multi-colour reversible sleeve. The translucent panel can be used as a diffuser or as a very soft white reflector, but in truth you'll most likely have it covered by the sleeve, which zips over the panel to offer black, silver, white and gold reflector panels. 5-in-1 kits are generally supplied in 56cm, 81cm and 107cm sizes with prices from around £25 for the smallest to £50 for the largest size, which is the one we'd suggest you go for. Your local dealer should stock them, with Elemental, Lastolite, Kenro and Interfit being popular brands.

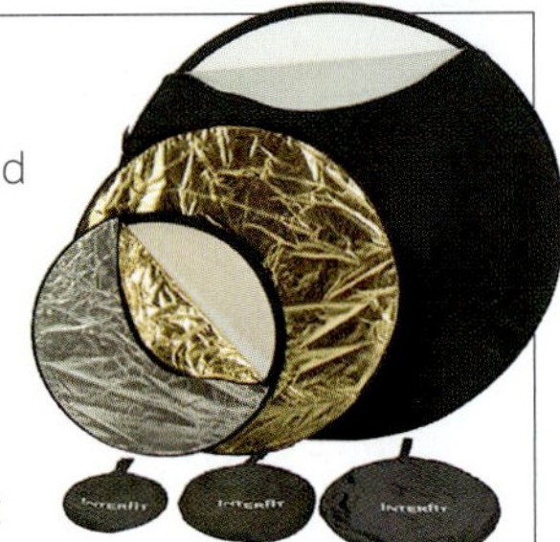

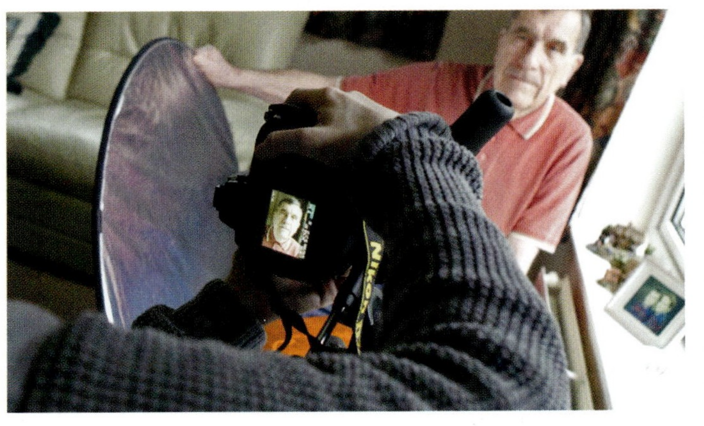

Reflectors with handle

These collapsible reflectors have the added benefit of a moulded handle, which makes it far easier to use if you're working on your own. Also, if you've an assistant, they can hold two reflectors (or a reflector and diffuser) very easily too. Lastolite's TriGrip and Interfit's Easy Grip ranges both offer a good choice and while they're more expensive than a standard collapsible, they're worth paying the premium for.

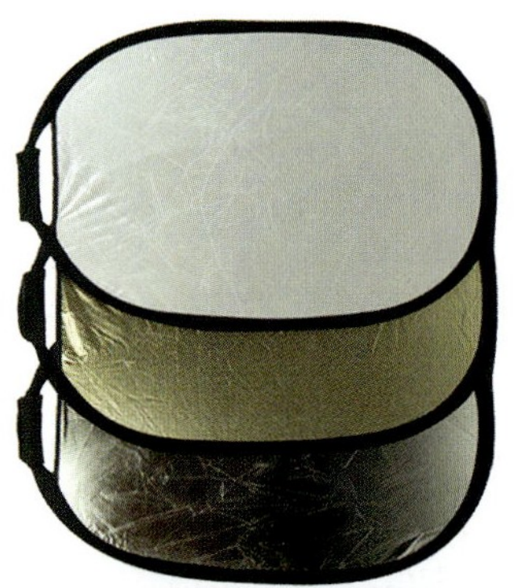

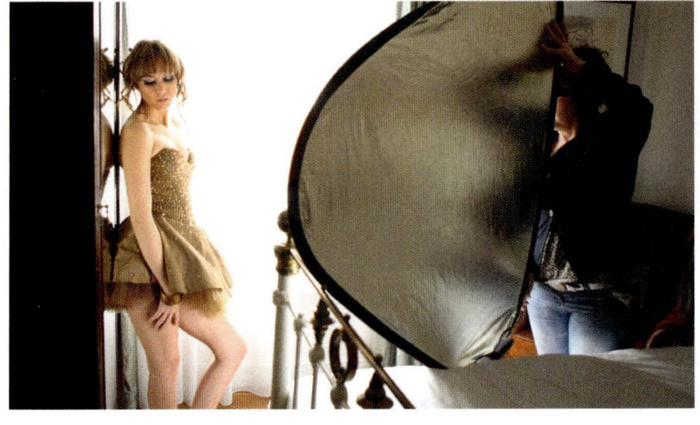

Framed aids

If you're really serious about portrait photography, consider investing in a framed lighting aid, which is essentially a collapsible aluminium frame onto which reflector and diffuser panels are attached. They're sturdy and incredibly versatile but relatively expensive, so only opt for these if you plan to do lots of portraits. While suitable for use in the studio, it's mainly outdoor photographers wishing to control daylight who use it. Lastolite and California Sunbounce are the leading brands, offering frames in various sizes that can hold a variety of reflector and diffuser options.

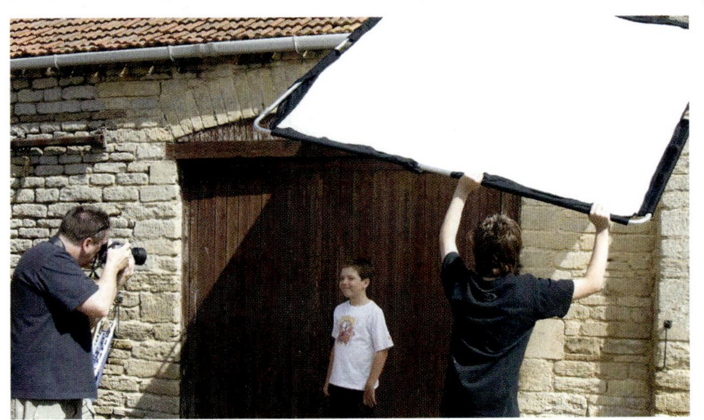

General portrait accessories

While not essential, the products covered on these pages will prove extremely useful if you plan to take your portrait photography further. We've selected our favourite accessories, all providing great value for money

Sekonic Flashmate L-308S

Guide Price: £165
Street Price: £140
www.johnsons-photopia.co.uk
Ambient and flash handheld meter

Most photographers are happy with the performance of their camera's metering system, so why would anyone consider splashing out more than a hundred pounds on a handheld meter when it could be spent on a lens, tripod or another useful accessory? Well, in truth, the argument for owning a handheld meter isn't anywhere near as strong as in the days of film, but there are still some valid reasons. For starters, it can be used to measure flash readings (cordless or via a flash sync lead) as well as ambient light, so it's as useful in the studio as it is outdoors. Another benefit is that, by sliding the white dome over the sensor, it can take incident light readings (light falling on the subject), which are more accurate than reflected readings (light bouncing off the subject) – the system used by all cameras. You can set it to meter in 1/3, 1/2 or full-stop increments, to match how your DSLR works and taking a reading couldn't be easier. Choose the mode (ambient or flash), set the ISO to match your DSLR and then place the meter in front of your subject, facing the camera and press the measuring button. If measuring ambient light, you specify the shutter speed and the meter selects the corresponding aperture. This isn't ideal if you're working in aperture-priority as you need to use the up and down buttons to get to the aperture you want to use and then read off what is the correct shutter speed. The wide LCD on the front has large digits making it easier to read, although there's no backlit function to illuminate it in low light. Out in the field, and in the studio, Sekonic to be extremely accurate and consistent. But with DSLRs offering instant review and histograms, it's no surprise that its appeal is limited. However, if you regularly mix ambient and flash light, you'll find it extremely useful.

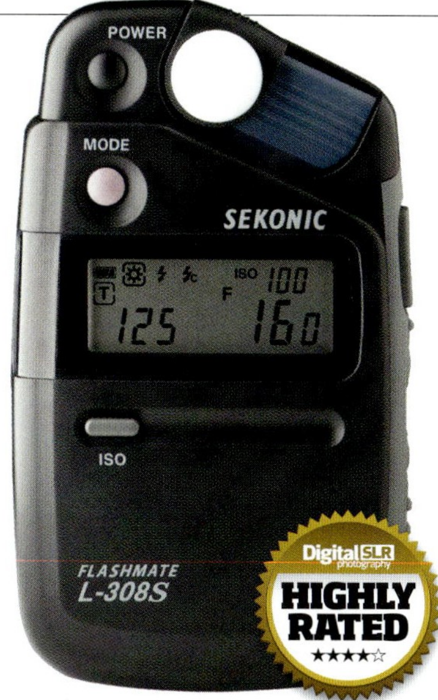

Whether you really need one or not depends on how happy you are with the exposures delivered by your camera and if you plan to regularly shoot flash as well as ambient exposures. If you are considering a light meter, this one is worth a look.

Specifications

Measuring methods: Incident and reflected
Measuring modes: Ambient and flash (corded & cordless)
ISO: 3-8000
Shutter speeds (ambient): 60 seconds to 1/8000sec
Shutter speeds (flash): One second to 1/500sec
Apertures: f/0.5 to f/90.9
EV range: 0 to EV19.9
Power Source: 1x AA battery
Size (WHD): 63x110x22mm
Weight: 95g (including battery)
Supplied accessories: Soft case, strap and Lumidisc

Verdict

Compact, light and a very versatile meter that is the ideal low-cost option for studio and outdoor work.

Build	★★★★☆
Features	★★★★☆
Performance	★★★★☆
Value for Money	★★★★☆
OVERALL	★★★★☆

Nissin Speedlite Di622

Guide Price: £174
Street Price: £100
www.kenro.co.uk
Budget flashgun with lots of features

The Nissin Di622 has excellent build quality for a flash unit that costs around £100, it's as good as models costing twice its price. This flashgun also has some rewarding features that set it apart from many other flashguns at this price range. These include second-curtain sync, slave flash and a standby mode that kicks in after two minutes of non-use to save your battery power. It also includes a flash stand and a diffuser for coverage as wide as 16mm and a fill-in reflector. There is no LCD panel on the rear, instead a series of LEDs indicate power and a single button handles the modes. The Nissin is available for Canon and Nikon DSLRs and considering the features and the reasonable price, offers a decent cut-price option.

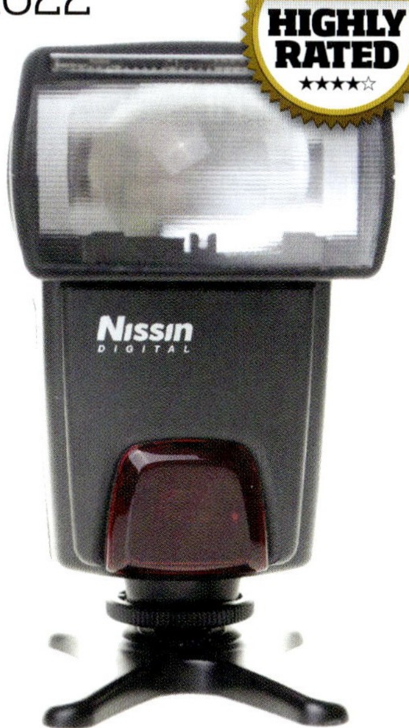

Main specifications

Guide Number: 45-62 (ISO 200)
Flash coverage: 16-70mm (24-105mm)
Recycling time: four - six seconds
Bounce facility: Yes (0 to 90°)
Swivel facility: Yes (0 to 270°)
TTL: Yes; **AF assist beam:** Yes
Strobe flash: No; **Wireless:** Yes

Verdict

Well worth the current £100 street price tag. Decent build, features and performance.

Build quality	★★★★☆
Features	★★★☆☆
Performance	★★★☆☆
Value for Money	★★★★☆
OVERALL	★★★★☆

Sigma EF-530 DG Super

Guide Price: £255
Street Price: £200
www.sigma-imaging-uk.com
Highly-sophisticated flashgun

Sigma not only make great value lenses, it also boasts a couple of excellent flashguns, with this being its top model. This model is available in Canon, Nikon, Pentax, Sigma and Sony versions and is packed with stacks of features. In fact, it will take you quite a while to read the EF-530's instruction manual to get to grips with them all! One interesting feature is the High Speed Sync, which allows you to fire the unit at shutter speeds above your camera's usual flash sync speed. The unit can also be used as a master or a slave unit and offers a wide-angle flash diffuser panel. The Sigma is also easy to use with the buttons spaced out and a bright and clear LCD monitor. An excellent flash and well worth considering.

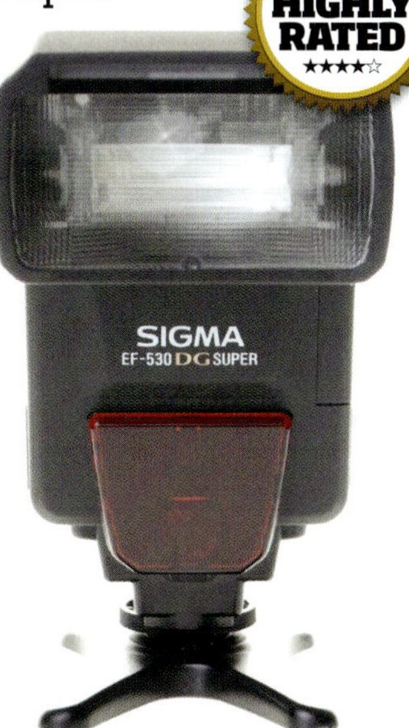

Main specifications

Guide Number: 28-53 (ISO 100)
Flash coverage: 16-70mm (24-105mm)
Recycling time: four - six seconds
Bounce facility: Yes (0-90°)
Swivel facility: Yes (0-270°)
TTL: Yes; **AF assist beam:** Yes
Strobe flash: Yes; **Wireless:** Yes

Verdict

The Sigma offers a decent alternative to more expensive marque flashguns.

Build quality	★★★☆☆
Features	★★★★☆
Performance	★★★★☆
Value for Money	★★★★☆

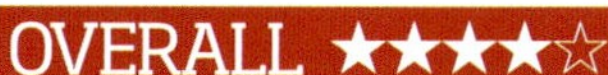

OVERALL	★★★★☆

Lastolite 1108 background support

Guide Price: £160
Street Price: £150
www.lastolite.com
Portable studio background support

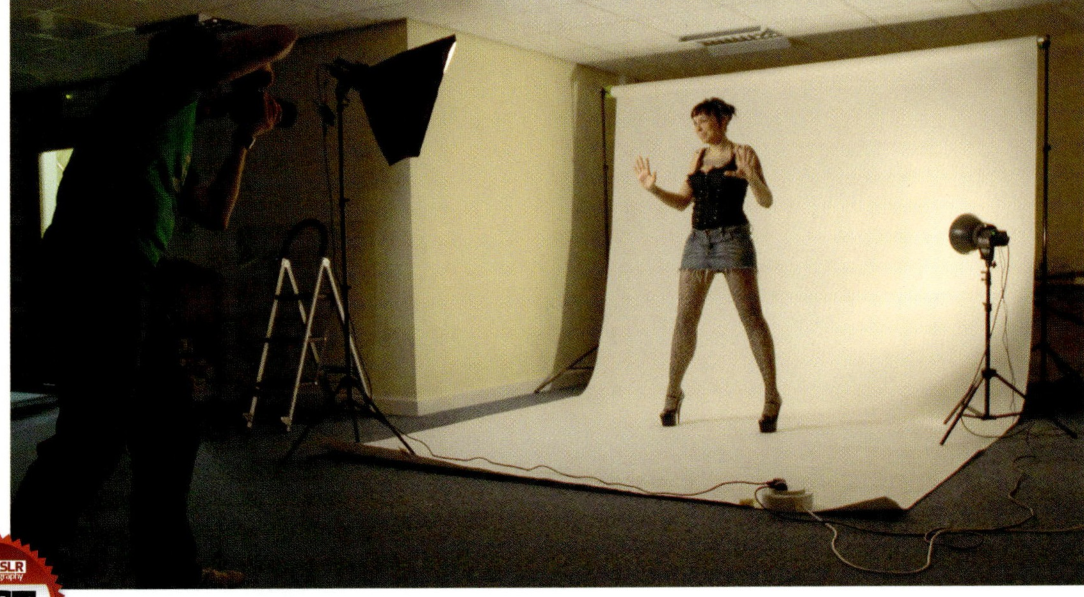

Unless you're working in a custom-built studio, you'll need some form of backdrop for your photography. The most common are either paper rolls or material. The Lastolite background support system is designed to accommodate either of these, and the heavy duty 1150 version can also support the superwhite vinyl backdrops. The kit includes two sturdy lighting stands and a telescopic cross bar to suit different widths of roll or a curtain of up to 3m (1108 model) or 6m (1150 model), the 1150 also uses a third support stand. The system can be constructed in minutes and when not in use, can be easily packed away into a small carry bag. This makes it ideal for those photographers wanting to create a temporary studio set up, or those on the move. However, it is sturdy enough to use on a more permanent basis. Having used this kit in our *Digital SLR Photography* studio for several months, we couldn't recommend it enough. Not only is it hard-wearing enough to cope with regular changing of backdrops, and a flurry of models, it comes at a very affordable price too. If you're looking to set up a small studio in your home or garage, then this Lastolite set-up is definitely one to add to your shortlist and represents great value.

Digital SLR Photography BEST BUY ★★★★★

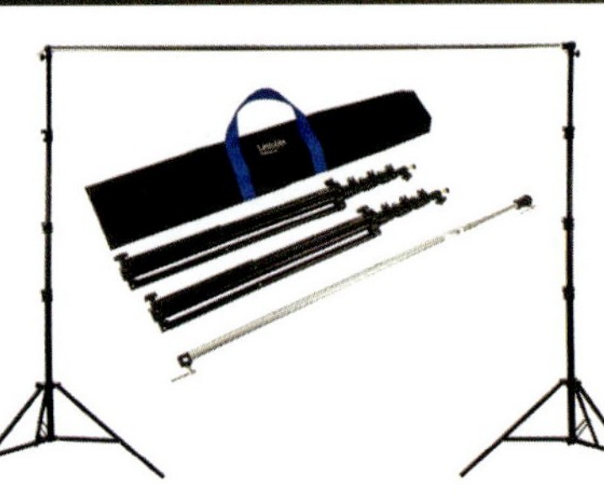

Verdict

A simple, affordable solution whether in the studio or home.

Build	★★★★☆
Features	★★★★☆
Performance	★★★★½
Value for Money	★★★★★
OVERALL	★★★★★

Hama Remote Control 5348

Guide Price: £35
Street Price: £30
www.hama.co.uk

Similar in specification to Nikon's MC-30, the Hama is half the price. It's small, the plastic shell is light at 34g, while its 80cm cord is a good length. The pimpled button has a two-stage action and by sliding it forward it locks into place, with a red strip acting as a visual indicator. It's a no-frills remote that does its job well. It's very affordable compared to marque brands, but faces stiff competition from the Hähnel and Seculine remotes.

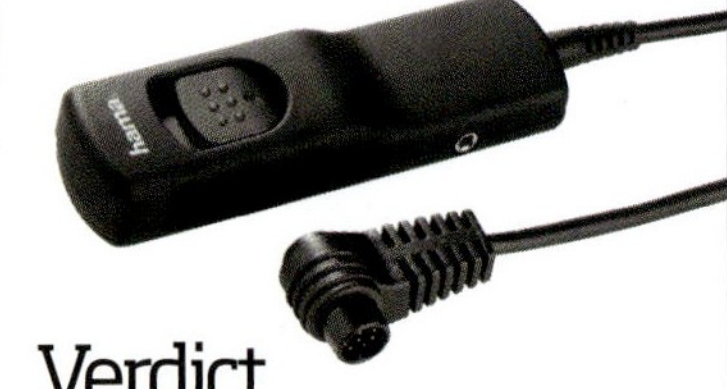

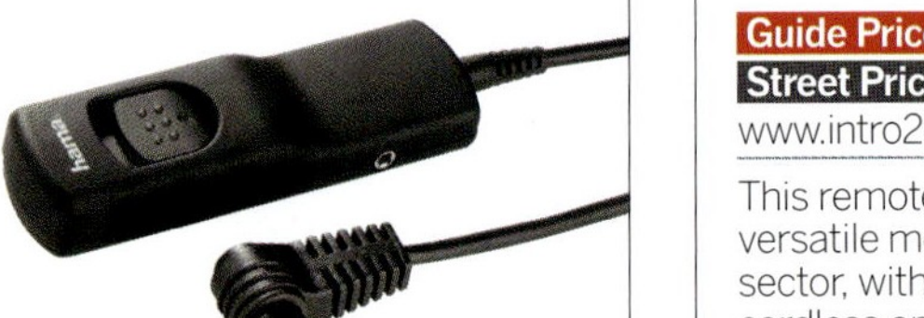

Verdict

A reliable, low-cost option.

Build quality	★★★☆☆
Performance	★★★★☆
Value for Money	★★★☆☆
OVERALL	★★★★☆

Hähnel Remote Shutter Release

Guide Price: £25
Street Price: £20
www.hahnel.ie

The Hähnel is larger than the Hama, but this makes it easier to handle, and while its nearly double the weight at around 60g, it's still incredibly lightweight. The two-stage button has a far more positive action and the sliding lock facility is better. The 80cm cord is a useful length but the inclusion of the extension lead is a real bonus. Best of all are the pair of interchangeable connections that allow it to be used with a variety of cameras. A brilliant budget buy.

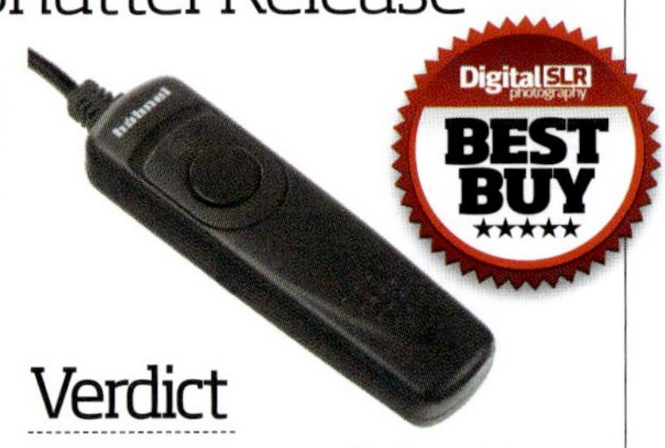

Digital SLR Photography BEST BUY ★★★★★

Verdict

Perfect choice as a first remote.

Build quality	★★★★☆
Performance	★★★★★
Value for Money	★★★★☆
OVERALL	★★★★★

Seculine Twin-1 R4 Nikon

Guide Price: £50
Street Price: £40
www.intro2020.co.uk

This remote is one of the most versatile models in the budget sector, with both corded and cordless operation to suit your Nikon DSLR. The kit is based around the £35 UT set-up of a wireless transmitter and 50cm cord, but with the addition of a small bulbous receiver that will attach to Nikon DSLRs with the ten-pin socket. If your camera has a built-in infrared receiver, you only need to use the transmitter, if it has the ten-pin socket on the front, such as the D300s, then you can either attach the lead or the receiver. We tested the Seculine with a D300s and found it worked well with both the cord and cordless option. The infrared transmitter proved very effective – at close range it triggered the shutter when used behind or in front of the camera while longer distances required clear line of sight between transmitter and receiver. A small button on the receiver allows it to be set to Bulb, which proved a little fiddly to use, but other than that, it's a well made outfit that's very well priced too. A neat touch is the flashlight mode, which allows you to use the transmitter's small white LED as a torch, useful when shooting in low light! If you use a compatible Nikon DSLR, it's certainly worth checking out.

Digital SLR Photography BEST BUY ★★★★★

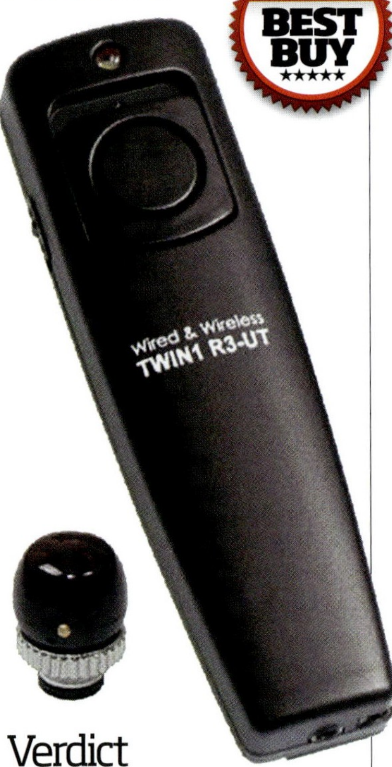

Verdict

A versatile remote with lots of features at an attractive price.

Build quality	★★★★★
Performance	★★★★★
Value for Money	★★★★☆
OVERALL	★★★★★

Flash accessories for portraits

There are a wide variety of lighting accessories available for your flashgun, which while not essential for general snaps, can make a difference when you're trying to be more creative with your photography. We highlight a selection of the best diffusers, softboxes and kits for your flashgun

WHILE SOME photographers prefer to only use available light, a true master is able to sculpt light from many sources, with one of the most common being the good old flashgun. Flashes are fantastic for supplementing light so you can get a suitable exposure, but they can also be used to override the ambient light and become more creative with your shots. While a direct, naked flash is sufficient for some situations, many photographers frown on this basic approach to flash photography as the light is rarely flattering and control is limited. So for professional results you need to start looking at adding some complementary accessories to your flash outfit, which will modify the flash to suit your picture and flash effect.

Before picking from the plethora of accessories available, you need to understand the difference between hard and soft light and know the flash effect you want to achieve. In basic terms, hard light produces strong shadows with sharp edges and high contrast, while one that casts weak shadows, with no definite edge, is described as soft light. You also need to decide if want the light to be dispersed and natural-looking or harsher and more selective. The following selection covers every type of accessory that your flashgun could ever need!

Stofen Omni-bounce

Guide Price: £17 | **Street Price:** £11

www.newprouk.co.uk

Some flashguns come supplied with a clip-on diffuser, but if yours doesn't, buy a Stofen. They are devilishly effective in softening the light from your flashgun, with many snappers leaving them attached for all their on-camera flash shooting. They're available for almost every flashgun. Well worth the modest outlay.

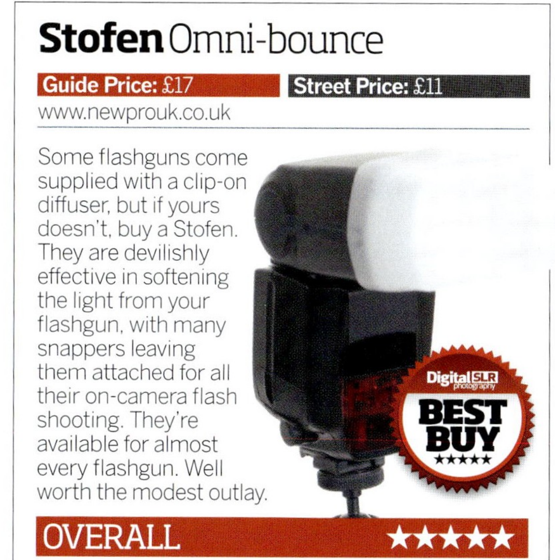

OVERALL ★★★★★

Hama Uni Flash Diffuser

Guide Price: £20 | **Street Price:** £16

www.hama.co.uk

A basic flash diffuser that has been made to fit most flashguns on the market. It can be secured to the flashgun with its own Velcro strap, making it suitable for use in the field. The price is a little high but it's worth keeping one in your camera bag, should you have to use a flashgun unit you're not familiar with.

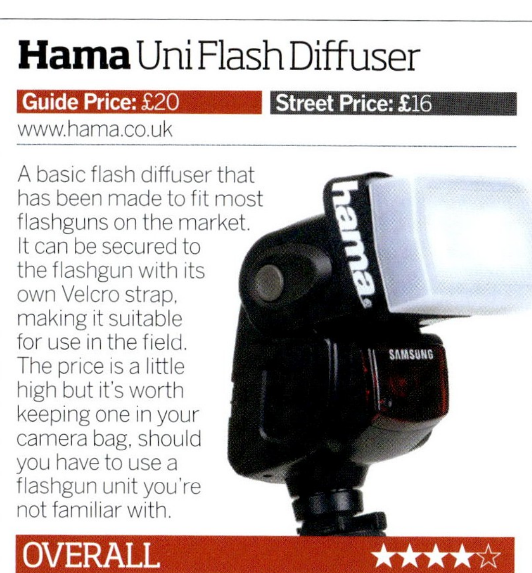

OVERALL ★★★★☆

Lumiquest Softbox III

Guide Price: £45 | **Street Price:** £40

www.newprouk.co.uk

The largest of the Lumiquest range, the Softbox III produces an extremely soft light that is no easy feat when you take the size and portability of it into account. One of the reasons for the great light is that the centre of the front panel is thicker than the edges, which reduces the possibility of a hot spot caused by the head of the flashgun.

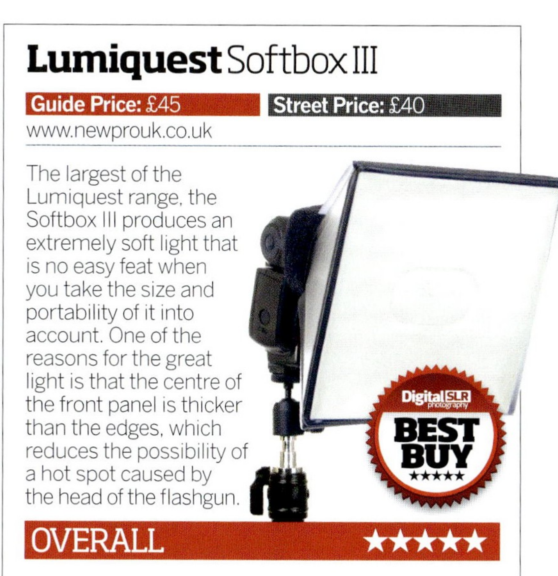

OVERALL ★★★★★

Lastolite Ezybox kit (38cm)

Guide Price: £170 | **Street Price:** £160

www.johnsons-photopia.co.uk

While many of the other products have a slight 'DIY' appearance to them, the Ezybox oozes quality and build stability like nothing else in this test. While the Ezybox is value for money for pros, its high price may prove too much for most enthusiasts, even though it offers such a good performance.

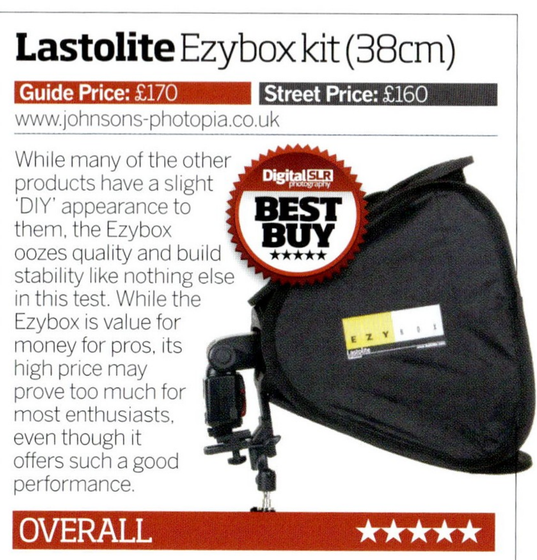

OVERALL ★★★★★

Speedlight Pro Beauty Dish

Guide Price: £67 | **Street Price:** £67

www.speedlightprokit.co.uk

When you see the dish in its pre-assembled state, you'd be forgiven for having low expectations. However, once you put it all together things start to look up and then the results blow you away. The value for money is outstanding, as is the quality of the light it produces. One of the best accessories on the market!

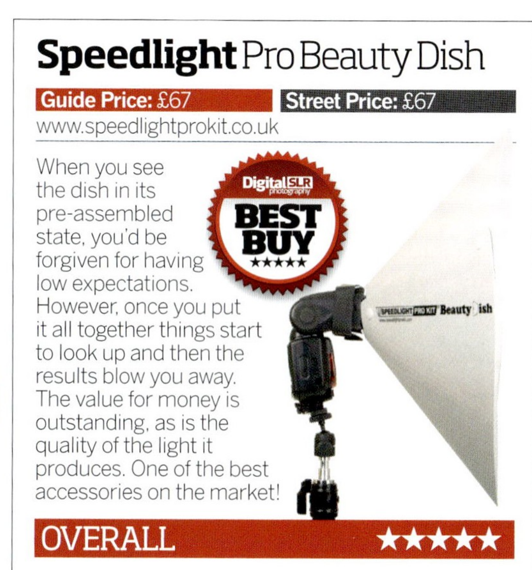

OVERALL ★★★★★

Main types of flash accessories

Most flash modifiers fall into one of the following five categories, although some may also overlap

DIFFUSERS
This is a very general term for anything that softens light and is usually in the form of an opaque or white surface, which is placed in front of the flash. Softboxes and standard diffusion domes are the most common type of flash modifier in this category.

REFLECTORS
Bounced light has plenty of opportunity to spread out and, as a result, often softens the light. Reflectors come in white, silver and gold depending on how you want to alter the light's temperature. Beauty dishes also fall into this category.

COLOUR GELS
These serve one of two purposes – colour correction or colour effects. Colour correction gels are placed over the flash to match the colour of the flash with the temperature of the ambient lighting, such as tungsten or fluorescent. Colour-effect gels change your flash's colour for creative effects.

HONEYCOMB
Also known as grids, the honeycomb provide a smoother transition between shadows and highlights than a naked flash. The light falls off more gradually than other modifiers, in a vignette-like manner, which can bring some impressive lighting effects to your images.

SNOOTS
Designed like a cone, the snoot channels a stream of light that allows you to illuminate certain parts of the scene more selectively for a spotlight effect. They are often used in combination with honeycombs for maximum creative effect.

Honl Flash Kit

Guide Price: £130
Street Price: £110
www.flaghead.co.uk

Contains: Two straps, ¼ Grid, 1/8 Grid, 8in Snoot, 5in Snoot, Gobo bounce card, Colour Correction Kit, Colour Effects Kit

It's not often that a range of products comes along and changes the way that photographers work. But the Honl kit has done just that. The snoots and bounce cards are made from high-grade webbing, which can take the rigours of heavy use. Many of these accessories are available separately but this bundle offers great value for money.

BOUNCE CARD The most obvious use for this card is to use the white side to bounce light off and to soften the light landing on your subject. But it can be used for much more than that. If you get two you then have a simple set of barn doors that allow you to control the spill of the light across your image.

8IN & 5IN SNOOTS The Honl snoots are very versatile pieces of kit, which lend themselves to a number of applications. They can be used closed to direct the light from your flashgun in a very direct, almost spotlit manner, so you can highlight one element in your camera's viewfinder. Alternatively, you can open the snoot, which works in the same manner as a bounce, directing the light up and forward towards your subject.

¼ GRID & 1/8 GRID SPOTS These grids look and feel very robust and attach to your flashgun by combining with the Speed Strap (included in the kit). Once attached the strong Velcro holds incredibly well so you'll have no worries about the grids slipping.

COLOUR CORRECTION GEL & COLOUR EFFECTS KIT Possibly the highlight of the Honl kit, these easy to use gels are fast becoming one of the most popular accessories for flasht. Using the Speed Strap, the gels have Velcro edges and attaching them to the flashgun is easy and hassle-free as you just place the gel over the flash and push on the Velcro until it takes hold. Just like the Honl grids, the gels stay in place securely and cover the whole flashgun.

Digital SLR photography BEST BUY ★★★★★

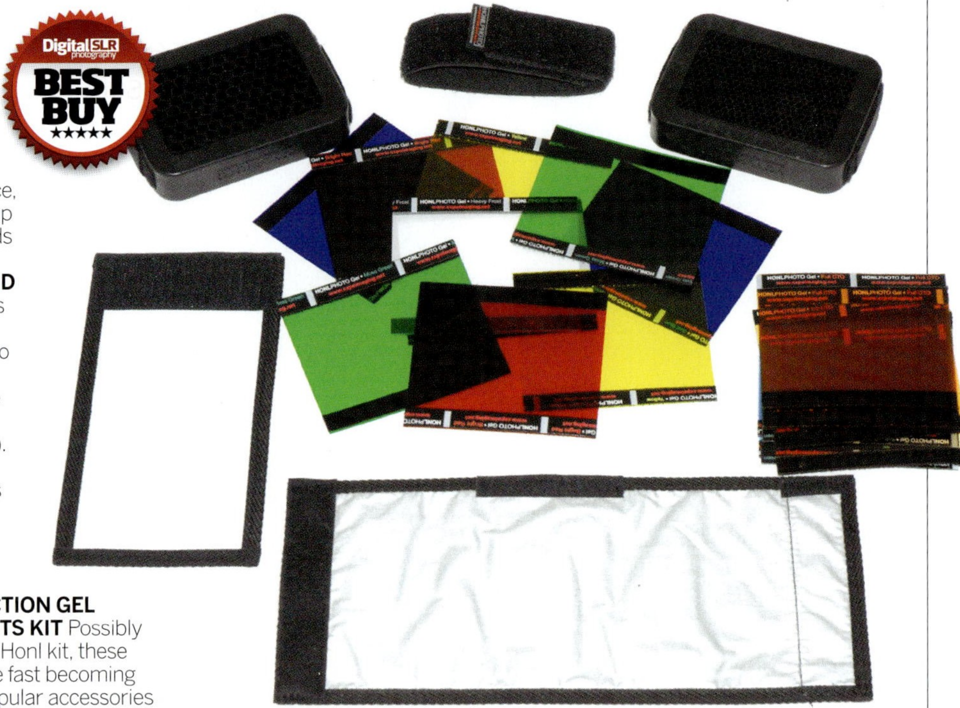

Verdict

The price isn't low but the quality of the kit is superb. The outfit slips easily into just about any camera bag, weighs next to nothing and is really simple to set up.

Build quality	★★★★★
Features	★★★★★
Performance	★★★★★
Value for money	★★★★☆
OVERALL	★★★★★

Interfit Strobies Portrait Flash Kit

Guide Price: £120
Street Price: £100
www.interfitphotographic.com

Contains: Flashgun Mount, Globe, Beauty dish, Softbox, Barn Doors, Snoot and Honeycomb

The Interfit Strobies kit is a scaled down version of larger studio accessories, so while the attachments are fairly sturdy, they aren't very compact or easy to transport, particularly the Globe option that is shaped like a small football. The accessories attach to a mount before they fit to a flashgun, so you'll need a separate mount if you wish to use more than one flashgun at a same time, which is highly likely.

SOFTBOX The softbox is a miniature version of the one you get in studios and is also just as difficult to assemble. We would only recommend this softbox for a home studio as you wouldn't want to put it together more than once. That said, once assembled, the build quality is decent and as long as it isn't given too much abuse, it should give you a good few years of service.

BEAUTY DISH The small beauty dish can be slipped on to the kit's standard mount and, despite its compact size, delivers an even spread of light. Unlike some models, when attached, this lightweight dish won't make your flashgun feel top-heavy.

GLOBE DIFFUSER This is an unusual piece of equipment that attaches to your flashgun via a supplied mount. For the best results, you will have to set your flashgun head to bounce (so it's pointing towards the ceiling) before attaching the diffuser. Once triggered, the dome fills with light and then emits the light in a spherical direction. Be careful when attaching the Globe, as one fall on to a hard surface will most likely crack it into pieces.

BARNDOOR The barndoor has four flaps that allow you to 'cover up' some of the light from your flashgun for more control over its distribution. When using the barndoors open, the light from the flashgun spreads over a wide area and makes an ideal accessory for a background light. The build quality is okay, but don't match the Honl kit.

SNOOT & HONEYCOMB The Snoot and Honeycomb work in combination with each other. With the Snoot fixing to the mount, it can be used on its own to create a spotlight. The Honeycomb grid slides down the barrel of the Snoot and is dense enough to block the light quite well.

Digital SLR photography HIGHLY RATED ★★★★☆

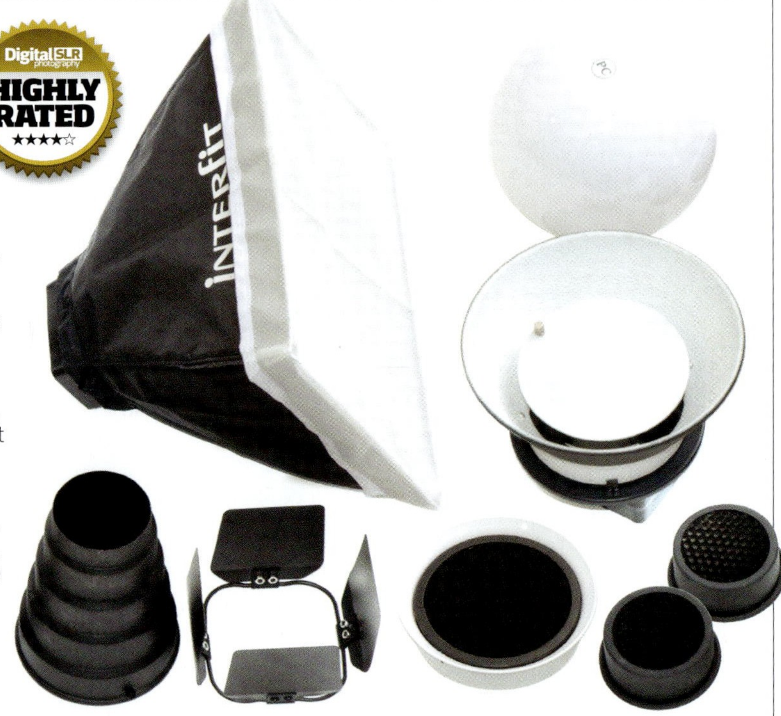

Verdict

This kit has some useful applications and would prove a frugal and rewarding buy for the photographers taking their first steps with flashgun accessories.

Build quality	★★★★☆
Features	★★★★☆
Performance	★★★★☆
Value for money	★★★★☆
OVERALL	★★★★☆

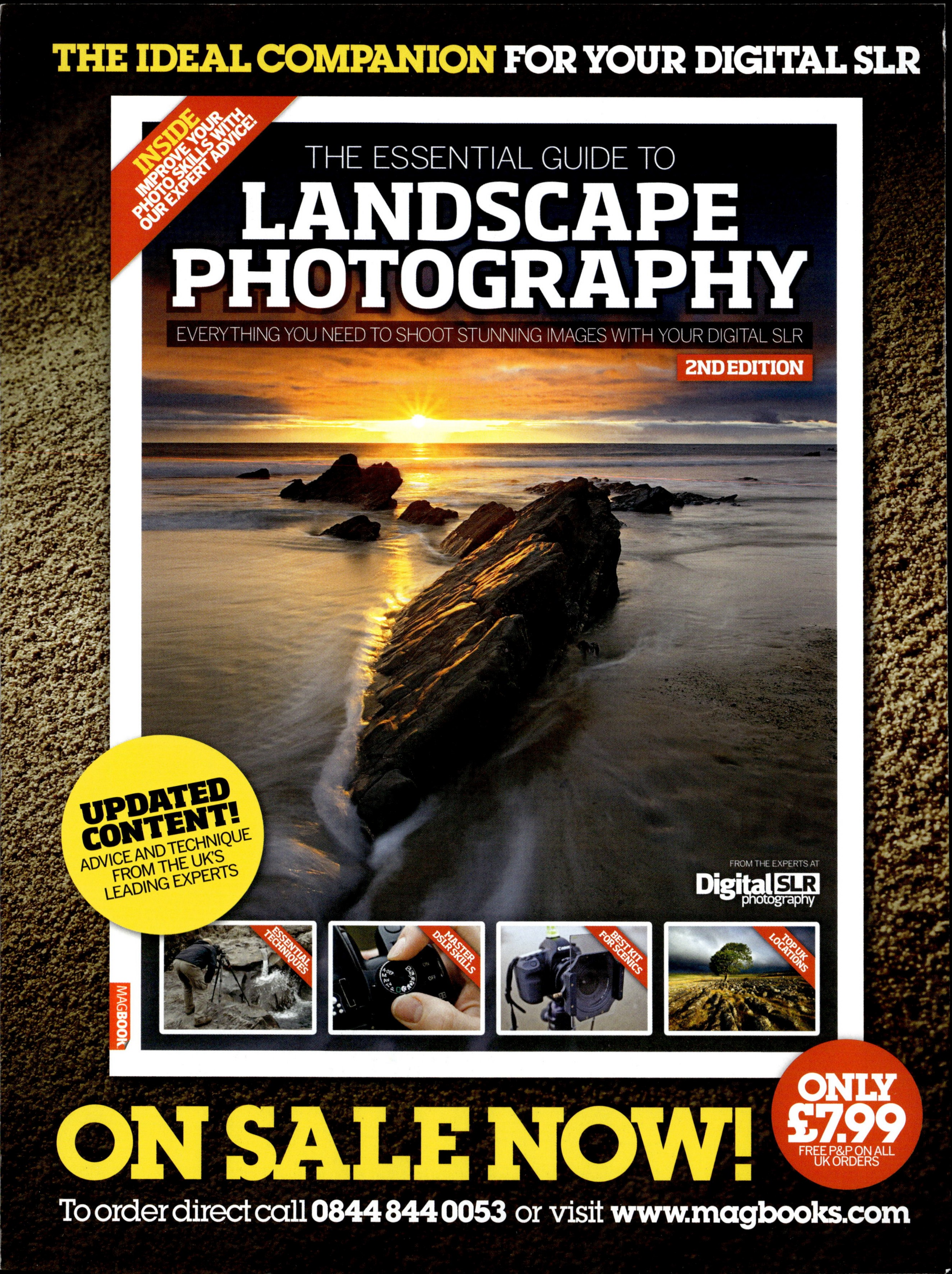

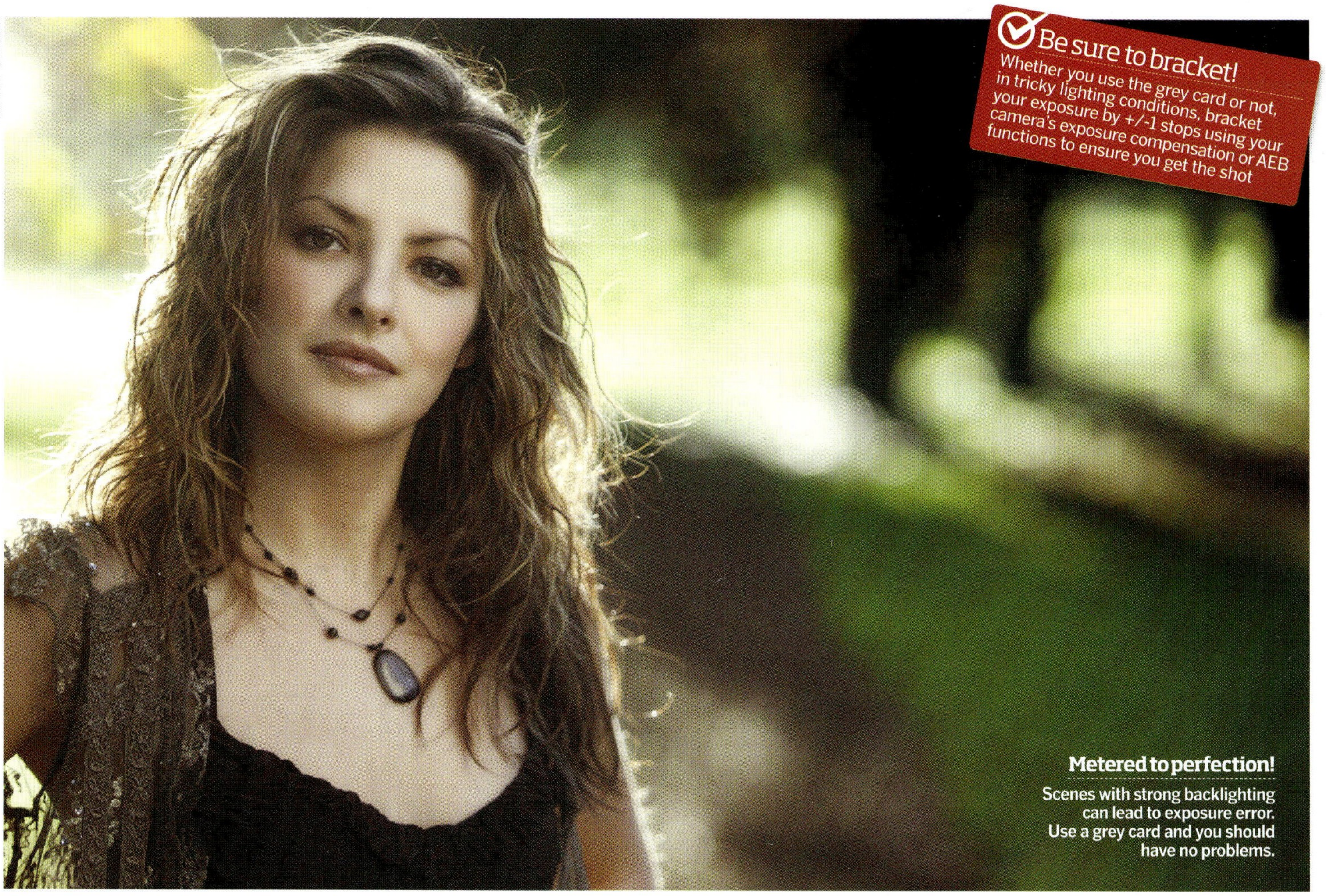

BJORN THOMASSEN

Be sure to bracket!
Whether you use the grey card or not, in tricky lighting conditions, bracket your exposure by +/-1 stops using your camera's exposure compensation or AEB functions to ensure you get the shot

Metered to perfection!
Scenes with strong backlighting can lead to exposure error. Use a grey card and you should have no problems.

How to use your free metering & White Balance cards

The 18% grey card can be used to ensure perfect exposures when shooting in tricky lighting conditions. Both reference cards can also be used to set a custom White Balance, but how you take a reading off the cards depends on your camera (refer to your DSLR's manual). In the meantime, here is a brief explanation to get you started

DIGITAL SLRS USE sophisticated exposure systems with a choice of metering patterns to suit different lighting situations. The systems work on the assumption that the area of the scene being metered is a mid-tone, or 18% grey to be precise; the average if all dark, light and mid-tones were mixed together. It's the basis of all metering patterns and works surprisingly well, but can render incorrect exposures when the overall scene or subject is considerably lighter or darker than 18% grey. For example, very dark areas or subjects can fool the metering system into overexposing the image, while a very light areas can fool the camera into underexposure, as the light meter will take a reading that renders it as a mid-tone.

As a camera is trying to render an image 'grey', it's your job to ensure you compensate to keep the tones true to life. You can do this by either using one of your camera's exposure override facilities, such as exposure compensation, the AE-Lock button or by metering from an area of the scene that has a mid-tone. And that's where our grey card comes in. Using it is very simple as our step-by-step guide below illustrates.

The key thing to remember is that you need to place the grey card in similar lighting to your subject, for instance, don't place it in a shaded area if your subject is bathed in sunlight. Also, make sure that the card fills the metering area – we would recommend you use spot or partial metering as the card won't need to fill the entire image area – but any is suitable. You can either lock the exposure using your camera's AE-Lock facility or note the aperture and shutter speed, then switch to manual mode and dial in these settings. This latter method isn't suitable on days where lighting is variable. The card has AF reference lines to help your camera's autofocus lock on to it. However, you don't necessarily need it to be in focus to work correctly. The grey card (as well as the white card) can also be used to take a custom White Balance reading from too.

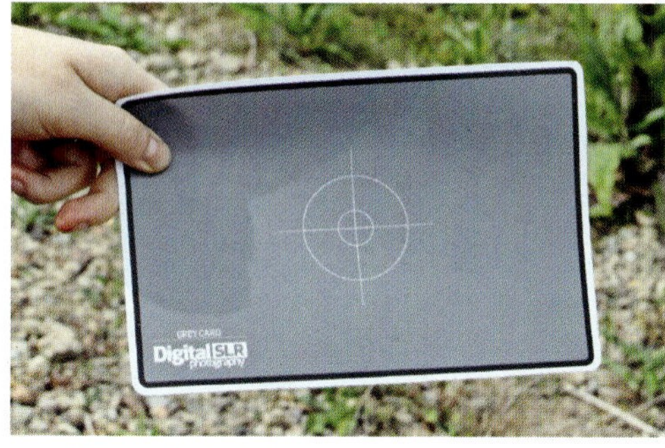

1 GETTING STARTED If you're shooting portraits in difficult lighting conditions, such as backlighting, give your subject the grey card and ask them to hold it angled towards you.

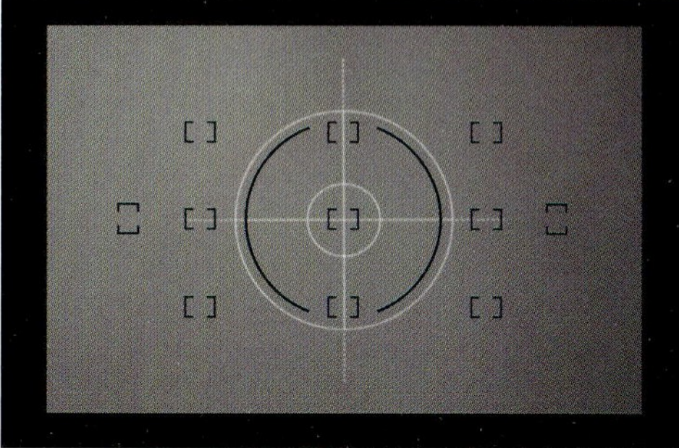

2 TAKE A METER READING Ensure that the entire metering area is filled by the grey card (in this instance we're using spot metering) and lock the exposure with the AE-Lock button.

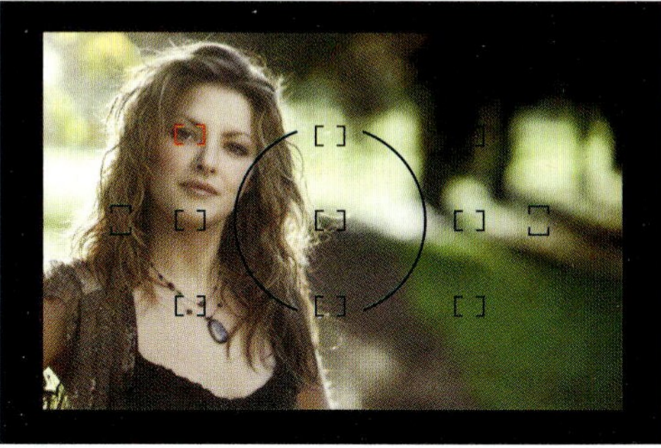

3 COMPOSE & SHOOT With this exposure locked, you can compose your scene and take your shots. When you check it on your LCD monitor, the exposure should be perfect.